FROM THE
DESK OF **Bill O'Reilly**

Killing
Lincoln

Killing Lincoln

THE

SHOCKING ASSASSINATION

THAT CHANGED AMERICA

FOREVER

BILL O'REILLY

and

MARTIN DUGARD

Henry Holt and Company
New York

Henry Holt and Company, LLC
Publishers since 1866
175 Fifth Avenue
New York, New York 10010
www.henryholt.com

Henry Holt® and 🏛® are registered trademarks of Henry Holt and Company, LLC.

Library of Congress Cataloging-in-Publication Data

O'Reilly, Bill.
  Killing Lincoln : the shocking assassination that changed America forever / Bill O'Reilly
and Martin Dugard.—1st ed.
    p.   cm.
  Includes index.
  ISBN 978-0-8050-9307-0
  1. Lincoln, Abraham, 1809–1865—Assassination.   I. Dugard, Martin.   II. Title.
  E457.5.O74 2011
  973.7092—dc22   2011014342

Henry Holt books are available for special promotions and premiums.
For details contact: Director, Special Markets.

Designed by Meryl Sussman Levavi
Maps by Gene Thorp

Printed in the United States of America

43 45 47 49 50 48 46 44

For Makeda Wubneh,
who makes the world a better place

Killing
Lincoln

A NOTE TO READERS

The story you are about to read is true and truly shocking. It has been 150 years since the beginning of the Civil War, the bloodiest war in our nation's history, a conflict so full of horror it is almost impossible to describe. The assassination of President Abraham Lincoln, only days after the end of the war, was a terrible tragedy. Much has been speculated about the events leading up to the murder and immediately afterward, but few people know what *really* happened.

Before historian Martin Dugard and I began writing this book, I *thought* I understood the facts and implications of the assassination. But even though I am a former teacher of history, I had no clue. The ferocious assassination plan itself still has elements that have not been clarified. This is a saga of courage, cowardice, and betrayal. There are layers of proven conspiracy and alleged conspiracy that will disturb you. You will learn much in these pages, and the experience, I believe, will advance your understanding of our country, and how Lincoln's murder changed it forever.

This book is a departure from the

contemporary nonfiction I have written for more than a decade and from the daily news analysis that I do on television. But the lessons you will learn within these pages are relevant to all our lives. For those of us who want to improve the United States and keep it the greatest nation in the world, we must be aware of the true heroes who have made the country great as well as the villains who have besmirched it.

Finally, this book is written as a thriller. But don't let the style fool you. What you are about to read is unsanitized and uncompromising. It is a no spin American story, and I am proud of it.

BILL O'REILLY
April 3, 2011
Long Island, New York

PROLOGUE

———

The man with six weeks to live is anxious.

He furls his brow, as he does countless times each day, and walks out of the Capitol Building, which is nearing completion. He is exhausted, almost numb.

Fifty thousand men and women stand in pouring rain and ankle-deep mud to watch Abraham Lincoln take the oath of office to begin his second term. His new vice president, Andrew Johnson, has just delivered a red-faced, drunken, twenty-minute ramble vilifying the South that has left the crowd squirming, embarrassed by Johnson's inebriation.

So when Lincoln steps up to the podium and delivers an eloquent appeal for reunification, the spiritual message of his second inaugural address is all the more uplifting. "With malice toward none, with charity for all, with firmness in the right as God gives us to see the right, let us strive on to finish the work we are in, to bind up the nation's wounds, to care for him who shall have borne the battle and for his widow and his orphan, to do all which may achieve and cherish a just and lasting peace among ourselves and with all nations," the president intones humbly.

Despite his exhaustion, Lincoln is charismatic. And momentarily energized.

Suddenly, the sun bursts through the clouds as he speaks, its light enveloping the tall and outwardly serene Lincoln. But 120 miles away in the Virginia railroad junction of Petersburg, any thought of serenity is a fantasy. The Confederate army, under the command of General Robert E. Lee, has been pinned inside the city for more than 250 days by Union forces under the command of General Ulysses S. Grant. Though living in trenches and reduced to eating rats and raw bacon, Lee's men will not surrender. Instead, Lee is making plans to slip out of Petersburg and escape south to the Carolinas. If he succeeds, Lincoln's prayer for a reunified United States of America may never be answered. America will continue to be divided into a North and a South, a United States of America and a Confederate States of America.

❦

Lincoln's inaugural speech is a performance worthy of a great dramatic actor. And indeed, one of America's most famous thespians stands just a few feet away as Lincoln raises his right hand. John Wilkes Booth is galvanized by the president's words—though not in the way Lincoln intends.

Booth, twenty-six, raised in Maryland, is an exceptional young man. Blessed with a rakish smile and a debonair gaze, he is handsome, brilliant, witty, charismatic, tender, and able to bed almost any woman he wants—and he has bedded quite a few. It's no wonder that the actor has known success on the Broadway stage.

His fiancée stands at his side, a sensual young woman whose senator father has no idea that his daughter is secretly engaged to a man of Booth's lowly theatrical calling. Lucy Hale and John Wilkes Booth are a beautiful young couple quite used to the adoration of high society and the opposite sex. Yet not even she knows that Booth is a Confederate sympathizer, one who nurses a pathological hatred for Lincoln and the North. Lucy has no idea that her lover has assembled a crack team of conspirators to help him bring down the president. They have guns, financing, and a precise plan. At this point, patience is their watchword.

Standing in the cold Washington drizzle in the shadow of the Capitol dome, Booth feels nothing but hot rage and injustice. The

*John Wilkes Booth: celebrity, Confederate
sympathizer, assassin*

actor is impulsive and prone to the melodramatic. Just before Lincoln's
speech, as the president stepped out onto the East Portico, Booth's
carefully crafted conspiracy was instantly forgotten.

Though he had no gun or knife, Booth lunged at Lincoln. An officer from Washington's Metropolitan Police, a force known to be
heavily infiltrated by Confederate sympathizers, grabbed him hard by
the arm and pulled him back. Booth struggles, which only made Officer John William Westfall grasp him tighter. Like everyone else in
the city, Westfall is well aware that there are plots against Lincoln's
life. Some say it's not a matter of if but when the president will die.
Yet rather than arrest Booth, or even pull him aside for questioning,
Westfall accepted Booth's excuse that he merely stumbled. Arresting
a celebrity like Booth might have caused the policeman problems.

But Booth is definitely not finished. He seethes as he listens to Lincoln's speech. The grace and poetry of the words ignite his rage. The sight of so many black faces beaming up at Lincoln from the crowd makes him want to vomit. No, Booth is most definitely not finished. If anything, his determination to knock Lincoln off his "throne" becomes more intense.

Lincoln isn't finished, either. The president has epic plans for his second term in office. It will take every one of those four years, and maybe longer, to heal the war-torn nation. Healing is Lincoln's one overriding ambition, and he will use every last bit of his trademark determination to see it realized. Nothing must stand in his way.

But evil knows no boundaries. And it is a most powerful evil that is now bearing down on Abraham Lincoln.

Part One

TOTAL WAR

Lincoln with Union troops at Antietam

CHAPTER ONE

The man with fourteen days to live is himself witnessing death. Lincoln (he prefers to go by just his last name. No one calls him "Abe," which he loathes. Few call him "Mr. President." His wife actually calls him "Mr. Lincoln," and his two personal secretaries playfully refer to him as "the Tycoon") paces the upper deck of the steamboat *River Queen*, his face lit now and again by distant artillery. The night air smells of the early spring, damp with a hint of floral fragrance. The *River Queen* is docked at City Point, a bustling Virginia port that was infiltrated by Confederate spies last August. Yet Lincoln strides purposefully back and forth, unprotected and unafraid, as vulnerable as a man can be to sniper fire, the bombardment serving as the perfect distraction from his considerable worries. When will this war ever end?

As one Confederate soldier will put it, "the rolling thunder of the heavy metal" began at nine P.M. Once the big guns destroy the Confederate defenses around Petersburg, the Union army—*Lincoln's army*—will swarm from their positions and race across no-man's-land into the enemy trenches, hell-bent on capturing the city that has eluded them for ten long months.

What happens after that is anyone's guess.

In a best-case scenario, Lincoln's general in chief, Ulysses S. Grant,

Federal supply boats in the harbor of City Point, Virginia, 1865

will trap Confederate general Robert E. Lee and his army inside Petersburg, forcing their surrender. This is a long shot. But if it happens, the four-year-old American Civil War will be over, and the United States will be divided no more. And this is why Abraham Lincoln is watching the battlefield.

But Marse Robert—"master" as rendered in southern parlance—has proven himself a formidable opponent time and again. Lee plans to escape and sprint for the North Carolina border to link up with another large rebel force. Lee boasts that his Army of Northern Virginia can hold out forever in the Blue Ridge Mountains, where his men will conceal themselves among the ridges and thickets. There are even bold whispers among the hardcore Confederates about shedding their gray uniforms for plain civilian clothing as they sink undercover to fight guerrilla-style. The Civil War will then drag on for years, a nightmare that torments the president.

Lincoln knows that many citizens of the North have lost their stomach for this war, with its modern technology like repeating rifles and long-range artillery that have brought about staggering losses of life. Anti-Lincoln protests have become more common than the battles themselves. Lee's escape could guarantee that the northern states rise up and demand that Lincoln fight no more. The Confederates, by default, will win, making the chances of future reunification virtually nonexistent.

Nothing scares Lincoln more. He is so eager to see America healed that he has instructed Grant to offer Lee the most lenient surrender terms possible. There will be no punishment of Confederate soldiers. No confiscation of their horses or personal effects. Just the promise of a hasty return to their families, farms, and stores, where they can once again work in peace.

❧

In his youth on the western frontier, Lincoln was famous for his amazing feats of strength. He once lifted an entire keg of whiskey off the ground, drank from the bung, and then, being a teetotaler, spit the whiskey right back out. An eyewitness swore he saw Lincoln drag a thousand-pound box of stones all by himself. So astonishing was his physique that another man unabashedly described young Abraham Lincoln as "a cross between Venus and Hercules."

But now Lincoln's youth has aged into a landscape of fissures and contours, his forehead and sunken cheeks a road map of despair and brooding. Lincoln's strength, however, is still there, manifested in his passionate belief that the nation must and can be healed. He alone has the power to get it done, if fate will allow him.

Lincoln's top advisers tell him assassination is not the American way, but he knows he's a candidate for martyrdom. His guts churn as he stares out into the night and rehashes and second-guesses his thoughts and actions and plans. Last August, Confederate spies had killed forty-three people at City Point by exploding an ammunition barge. Now, at a rail-thin six foot four, with a bearded chin and a nose only a caricaturist could love, Lincoln's unmistakable silhouette makes him an easy target, should spies once again lurk nearby. But Lincoln is not afraid. He is a man of faith. God will guide him one way or another.

On this night Lincoln calms himself with blunt reality: right now, the most important thing is for Grant to defeat Lee. Surrounded by darkness, alone in the cold, he knows that Grant surrounding Lee and crushing the will of the Confederate army is all that matters.

Lincoln heads to bed long after midnight, once the shelling stops and the night is quiet enough to allow him some peace. He walks belowdecks to his stateroom. He lies down. As so often happens when he stretches out his frame in a normal-sized bed, his feet hang over the end, so he sleeps diagonally.

Lincoln is normally an insomniac on the eve of battle, but he is so tired from the mental strain of what has passed and what is still to come that he falls into a deep dream state. What he sees is so vivid and painful that when he tells his wife and friends about it, ten days later, the description shocks them beyond words.

∽

The dream finally ends as day breaks. Lincoln stretches as he rises from bed, missing his wife back in Washington but also loving the thrill of being so close to the front. He enters a small bathroom, where he stands before a mirror and water basin to shave and wash his hands and face. Lincoln next dons his trademark black suit and scarfs a quick breakfast of hot coffee and a single hard-boiled egg, which he eats while reading a thicket of telegrams from his commanders, including Grant, and from politicians back in Washington.

Then Lincoln walks back up to the top deck of the *River Queen* and stares off into the distance. With a sigh, he recognizes that there is nothing more he can do right now.

It is April 2, 1865. The man with thirteen days left on earth is pacing.

CHAPTER TWO

SUNDAY, APRIL 2, 1865
PETERSBURG, VIRGINIA

There is no North versus South in Petersburg right now. Only Grant versus Lee—and Grant has the upper hand. Lee is the tall, rugged Virginian with the silver beard and regal air. Grant, forty-two, is sixteen years younger, a small, introspective man who possesses a fondness for cigars and a whisperer's way with horses. For eleven long months they have tried to outwit one another. But as this Sunday morning descends further and further into chaos, it becomes almost impossible to remember the rationale that has defined their rivalry for so long.

At the heart of it all is Petersburg, a two-hundred-year-old city with rail lines spoking outward in five directions. The Confederate capital at Richmond lies twenty-three miles north—or, in the military definition, based upon the current location of Lee's army, to the rear.

The standoff began last June, when Grant abruptly abandoned the battlefield at Cold Harbor and wheeled toward Petersburg. In what would go down as one of history's greatest acts of stealth and logistics, Grant withdrew 115,000 men from their breastworks under cover of darkness and marched them south, crossed the James River without a single loss of life, and then pressed due west to Petersburg. The city was unprotected. A brisk Union attack would have taken the city within hours. It never happened.

Robert E. Lee and Ulysses S. Grant

Grant's commanders dawdled. Lee raced in reinforcements. The Confederates dug in around Petersburg just in time, building the trenches and fortifications they would call home through the blazing heat of summer, the cool of autumn, and the snow and bitter freezing rain of the long Virginia winter.

Under normal circumstances, Grant's next move would be to surround the city, cutting off those rail lines. He could then effect a proper siege, his encircled troops denying Lee's army and the inhabitants of Petersburg all access to food, ammunition, and other supplies vital to life itself—or, in more graphic terms, Grant's men would be the hangman's noose choking the life out of Petersburg. Winning the siege would be as simple as cinching the noose tighter and tighter with each passing day, until the rebels died of starvation or surrendered, whichever came first.

∽

But the stalemate at Petersburg is not a proper siege, even though the press is fond of calling it that. Grant has Lee pinned down on three sides but has not surrounded his entire force. The Appomattox River

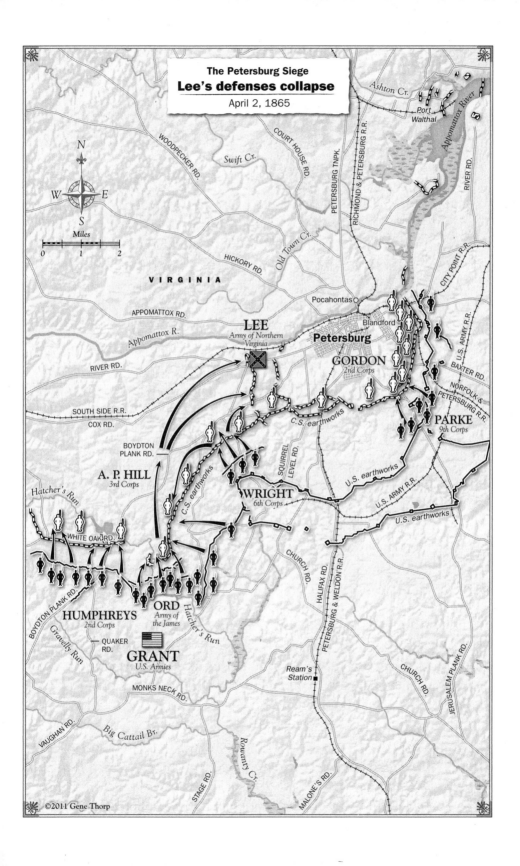

The Petersburg Siege
Lee's defenses collapse
April 2, 1865

©2011 Gene Thorp

makes that impossible. Broad and deep, it flows through the heart of Petersburg. The Confederates control all land north of the river and use it as a natural barrier against Union attack from the rear. This allows resupply trains to chug down from Richmond on a regular basis, keeping the Confederates armed and fed.

In this way there is normalcy, allowing men like Lee to attend church on Sundays, as he would in peacetime. Or a young general like A. P. Hill to live on a nearby estate with his pregnant wife and two small daughters, enjoying parenthood and romance. The men on both sides of the trenches live in squalor and mud, enduring rats and deprivation. But there is order there, too, as they read their newspapers and letters from home and cook their meager breakfast, lunch, and dinner.

The Confederate lines are arranged in a jagged horseshoe, facing south—thirty-seven miles of trenches and fortifications in all. The outer edges of the horseshoe are two miles from the city center, under the commands of A. P. Hill on the Confederate right and John B. Gordon on the left. Both are among Lee's favorite and most courageous generals, so it is natural that he has entrusted Petersburg's defenses to them.

The cold, hard truth, however, is that Robert E. Lee's dwindling army is reduced to just 50,000 men—only 35,000 of them ready to fight. String them out along thirty-seven miles and they are spread very thin indeed. But they are tough. Time and again over the past 293 days, Grant has attacked. And time and again, Lee's men have held fast.

Lee cannot win at Petersburg. He knows this. Grant has almost four times as many soldiers and a thousand more cannon. The steam whistles of approaching trains have grown less and less frequent in the past few months, and Lee's men have begun to starve. Confederate rations were once a pound of meal and a quarter pound of bacon a day, with an occasional tin of peas. Now such a meal would be considered a fantasy. "Starvation, literal starvation, was doing its deadly work. So depleted and poisoned was the blood of many of Lee's men from insufficient and unsound food that a slight wound which would probably not have been reported at the beginning of the war would often cause blood poison, gangrene, and death," one Confederate general will later write.

Many Confederate soldiers slide out of their trenches on moonless nights and sprint over to the Union lines to surrender—anything to fill their aching bellies. Those that remain are at their breaking point. The best Lee can hope for is to escape. For months and months, this has meant one of two options: abandon the city under cover of darkness and pull back toward Richmond or punch a hole in the Union lines and march south. In both cases, the goal is to reach the Carolinas and the waiting Confederate reinforcements.

∽

On the afternoon of April 1, Grant removes the second option. At the decisive Battle of Five Forks, General Phil Sheridan and 45,000 men capture a pivotal crossing, cutting off the main road to North Carolina, handing General George Pickett his second disastrous loss of the war—the first coming at Gettysburg, and the infamous ill-fated charge that bears his name. Five Forks is the most lopsided Union victory of the war. More than 2,900 southern troops are lost.

It is long after dark when word of the great victory reaches Grant. He is sitting before a campfire, smoking one of the cigars he came to cherish long ago in the Mexican War. Without pausing, Grant pushes his advantage. He orders another attack along twelve miles of Confederate line. He hopes this will be the crushing blow, the one that will vanquish Lee and his army once and for all. His soldiers will attack just before dawn, but the artillery barrage will commence immediately. This is the bombardment Lincoln watches from eight miles away in City Point—the president well understanding that the massive barrage will cause devastating casualties and panic in the Confederate ranks.

The infantry opens fire at four A.M., per Grant's orders, with a small diversionary attack to the east of Petersburg—cannon and musket fire mainly, just enough to distract the Confederates.

Forty-five minutes later, as soon there is enough light to see across to the enemy lines, Grant launches hell. Some 100,000 men pour into the Confederate trenches, screaming curses, throwing themselves on the overmatched rebels. The fighting is often hand to hand, and at such close range that the soldiers can clearly see and smell the men they're killing. And, of course, they hear the screams of the dying.

The Union attack is divided into two waves. Just a few hours earlier, Major General John G. Parke was so sure that the assault would fail that he requested permission to call it off. But now Parke obeys orders and leads the bluecoats to the right flank. Major General Horatio Wright, employing a revolutionary wedge-shaped attack column, charges from the left flank. Wright is a West Point–trained engineer and will later have a hand in building the Brooklyn Bridge and completing the Washington Monument. He has spent months scrutinizing the Confederate defenses, searching for the perfect location to smash the rebels. Wright is far beyond ready for this day—and so are his men.

General Wright's army shatters Lee's right flank, spins around to obliterate A. P. Hill's Third Corps, then makes a U-turn and marches on Petersburg—all within two hours. The attack is so well choreographed that many of his soldiers are literally miles in front of the main Union force. The first rays of morning sunshine have not even settled upon the Virginia countryside when, lacking leadership and orders, Wright's army is stymied because no other Union divisions have stepped up to assist him. Wright's army must stop its advance.

⁂

Meanwhile, Lee and his assistants, Generals Pete Longstreet and A. P. Hill, gape at Wright's army from the front porch of Lee's Confederate headquarters. They can see the destruction right in front of them. At first, as Longstreet will later write, "it was hardly light enough to distinguish the blue from the gray." The three of them stand there, Lee with his wrap against the chill, as the sun rises high enough to confirm their worst fears: every soldier they can see wears blue.

A horrified A. P. Hill realizes that his army has been decimated. Lee faces the sobering fact that Union soldiers are just a few short steps from controlling the main road he plans to use for his personal retreat. Lee will be cut off if the bluecoats in the pasture continue their advance. The next logical step will be his own surrender.

Which is why, as he rushes back into the house and dresses quickly, Lee selects his finest gray uniform, a polished pair of riding boots, and then takes the unusual precaution of buckling a gleaming ceremonial sword around his waist—just in case he must offer it to his captors.

It is Sunday, and normally Lee would be riding his great gray gelding, Traveller, into Petersburg for services. Instead, he must accomplish three things immediately: the first is to escape back into the city; the second is to send orders to his generals, telling them to fall back to the city's innermost defenses and hold until the last man or nightfall, whichever comes first. The third is to evacuate Petersburg and retreat back across the Petersburg bridges, wheel left, and race south toward the Carolinas.

There, Lee believes, he can regain the upper hand. The Confederate army is a nimble fighting force, at its best on open ground, able to feint and parry. Once he regains that open ground, Lee can keep Grant's army off balance and gain the offensive.

If any of those three events do not take place, however, he will be forced to surrender—most likely before dusk.

Fortune, however, is smiling on Lee. Those Union soldiers have no idea that Marse Robert himself is right in front of them, for if they did, they would attack without ceasing. Lee is the most wanted man in America. The soldier who captures him will become a legend.

The Union scouts can clearly see the small artillery battery outside Lee's headquarters, the Turnbull house, and assume that it is part of a much larger rebel force hiding out of sight. Too many times, on too many battlefields, soldiers who failed to observe such discretion have been shot through like Swiss cheese. Rather than rush forward, the Union scouts hesitate, looking fearfully at Lee's headquarters.

Seizing the moment, Lee escapes. By nightfall, sword still buckled firmly around his waist, Lee crosses the Appomattox River and then orders his army to do the same.

The final chase has begun.

CHAPTER THREE

MONDAY, APRIL 3, 1865
PETERSBURG, VIRGINIA

L ee's retreat is unruly and time-consuming, despite the sense of urgency. So it is, more than eight hours after Lee ordered his army to pull out of Petersburg, that General U. S. Grant can still see long lines of Confederate troops marching across the Appomattox River to the relative safety of the opposite bank. The bridges are packed. A cannon barrage could kill hundreds instantly, and Grant's batteries are certainly close enough to do the job. All he has to do is give the command. Yes, it would be slaughter, but there is still a war to be won. Killing those enemy soldiers makes perfect tactical sense.

But Grant hesitates.

The war's end is in sight. Killing those husbands and fathers and sons will impede the nation's healing. So now Grant, the man so often labeled a butcher, indulges in a rare act of military compassion and simply lets them go. He will soon come to regret it.

For now, his plan is to capture the Confederates, not to kill them. Grant has already taken plenty of prisoners. Even as he watches these rebels escape, Grant is scheming to find a way to capture even more.

The obvious strategy is to give chase, sending the Union army across the Appomattox in hot pursuit. Lee certainly expects that.

But Grant has something different in mind. He aims to get ahead of Lee and cut him off. He will allow the Confederates their unmolested thirty-six-hour, forty-mile slog down muddy roads to Amelia Court House, where the rebels believe food is waiting. He will let them unpack their rail cars and gulp rations to their hearts' content. And he will even allow them to continue their march to the Carolinas—but only for a while. A few short miles after leaving Amelia Court House, Lee's army will run headlong into a 100,000-man Union roadblock. This time there will be no river to guard Lee's rear. Grant will slip that noose around the Confederate army, then yank on its neck until it can breathe no more.

ℳ

Grant hands a courier the orders. Then he telegraphs President Lincoln at City Point, asking for a meeting. Long columns of rebels still clog the bridges, but the rest of Petersburg is completely empty, its homes shuttered, the civilians having long ago given them over to the soldiers, and soldiers from both sides are now racing across the countryside toward the inevitable but unknown point on the map where they will fight to the death in a last great battle. Abandoned parapets, tents, and cannons add to the eerie landscape. "There was not a soul to be seen, not even an animal in the streets," Grant will later write. "There was absolutely no one there."

The five-foot-eight General Grant, an introspective man whom Abraham Lincoln calls "the quietest little man" he's ever met, has Petersburg completely to himself. He lights a cigar and basks in the still morning air, surrounded by the ruined city that eluded him for 293 miserable days.

He is Lee's exact opposite: dark-haired and sloppy in dress. His friends call him Sam. "He had," noted a friend from West Point, "a total absence of elegance." But like Marse Robert, Grant possesses a savant's aptitude for warfare—indeed, he is capable of little else. When the Civil War began he was a washed-up, barely employed West Point graduate who had been forced out of military service, done in by lonely western outposts and an inability to hold his liquor. It was only through luck and connections that Grant secured a commission in an Illinois regiment. But it was tactical brilliance, courage under fire, and steadfast leadership that saw him rise to the top.

THE REISSUE OF

HARPER'S WEEKLY.

A JOURNAL OF CIVILIZATION.

VOL. VII.—No. 343.] NEW YORK, SATURDAY, JULY 25, 1863. [SINGLE COPIES SIX CENTS.
$2.00 PER YEAR IN ADVANCE.

Entered according to Act of Congress, in the Year 1863, by Harper & Brothers, in the Clerk's Office of the District Court for the Southern District of New York.

MAJOR-GENERAL ULYSSES S. GRANT ("UNCONDITIONAL SURRENDER" GRANT).—FROM A NEW PHOTOGRAPH JUST RECEIVED FROM VICKSBURG.—[SEE PAGE 475.]

General Grant, "Sam" to his friends

The one and only time he met Lee was during the Mexican War. Robert E. Lee was already a highly decorated war hero, while Grant was a lieutenant and company quartermaster. He despised being in charge of supplies, but it taught him invaluable lessons about logistics and the way an army could live off the land through foraging when cut off from its supply column. It was after one such scrounge in the Mexican countryside that the young Grant returned to headquarters in a dirty, unbuttoned uniform. The regal Lee, Virginian gentleman, was appalled when he caught sight of Grant and loudly chastised him for his appearance. It was an embarrassing rebuke, one the thin-skinned, deeply competitive Grant would never forget.

∞

Lee isn't the only Confederate general Grant knows from the Mexican War. James "Pete" Longstreet, now galloping toward Amelia Court House, is a close friend who served as Grant's best man at his wedding. At Monterrey, Grant rode into battle alongside future Confederate president Jefferson Davis. There are scores of others. And while he'd known many at West Point, it was in Mexico that Grant learned how they fought under fire—their strengths, weaknesses, tendencies. As with the nuggets of information he'd learned as a quartermaster, Grant tucked these observations away and then made keen tactical use of them during the Civil War—just as he is doing right now, sitting alone in Petersburg, thinking of how to defeat Robert E. Lee once and for all.

Grant lights another cigar—a habit that will eventually kill him—and continues his wait for Lincoln. He hopes to hear about the battle for Richmond before the president arrives. Capturing Lee's army is of the utmost importance, but both men also believe that a Confederacy without a capital is a doomsday scenario for the rebels. Delivering the news that Richmond has fallen will be a delightful way to kick off their meeting.

The sound of horseshoes on cobblestones echoes down the quiet street. It's Lincoln. Once again the president has courted peril by traveling with just his eleven-year-old son, a lone bodyguard, and a handful of governmental officials. Lincoln knows that, historically, assassination is common during the final days of any war. The victors are jubilant, but the vanquished are furious, more than capable of venting their rage on the man they hold responsible for their defeat.

A single musket shot during that horseback ride from City Point could have ended Lincoln's life. Despite his profound anxieties about all other aspects of the nation's future, Lincoln chooses to shrug off the risk. At the edge of Petersburg he trots past "the houses of negroes," in the words of one Union colonel, "and here and there a squalid family of poor whites"—but no one else. No one, at least, with enough guts to shoot the president. And while the former slaves grin broadly, the whites gaze down with "an air of lazy dislike," disgusted that this tall, bearded man is once again their president.

Stepping down off his horse, Lincoln walks through the main gate of the house Grant has chosen for their meeting. He takes the walkway in long, eager strides, a smile suddenly stretching across his face, his deep fatigue vanishing at the sight of his favorite general. When he shakes Grant's hand in congratulation, it is with great gusto. And Lincoln holds on to Grant for a very long time. The president appears so happy that Grant's aides doubt he's ever had a more carefree moment in his life.

The air is chilly. The two men sit on the veranda, taking no notice of the cold. They have become a team during the war. Or, as Lincoln puts it, "Grant is my man, and I am his." One is tall and the other quite small. One is a storyteller, the other a listener. One is a politician; the other thinks that politics is a sordid form of show business. But both are men of action, and their conversation shows deep mutual respect.

Former slaves begin to fill the yard, drawn back into Petersburg by the news that Lincoln himself is somewhere in the city. They stand quietly in front of the house, watching as the general and the president proceed with their private talk. Lincoln is a hero to the slaves—"Father Abraham"—guiding them to the promised land with the Emancipation Proclamation.

✑

Lincoln and Grant talk for ninety minutes, then shake hands goodbye. Their parting has a bittersweet feel, the two great men perhaps sensing that they are marching toward two vastly different destinies. Grant is off to finish an epic war and subsequently to become president himself. Lincoln is off to heal a nation, a noble goal he will not live to see realized.

Now, as the president looks on, Grant saddles up his charger and gallops off to join his army.

Before leaving himself, Lincoln shakes hands with some people in the crowd gathered in front of the meeting place. He then rides back to City Point, once again exposing himself to possible violence. The way is littered with hundreds of dead soldiers, their unburied bodies swollen by death and sometimes stripped bare by scavengers. Lincoln doesn't look away, absorbing the sober knowledge that these men died because of him. Outrage about Lincoln's pursuit of the war has many calling for his death—even in the North. "Let us also remind Lincoln, that Caesar had his Brutus," one speaker cried at a New York rally. And even in Congress, one senator recently asked the simple question "How much more are we going to take?" before going on to allude to the possibility of Lincoln's murder.

Lincoln endures all this because he must, just as he endures the slow trot through the battlefield. But there is a purpose to all he does, and upon his return to City Point he receives a great reward when he is handed the telegram informing him that Richmond has fallen. Confederate troops have abandoned the city to link up with Lee's forces trying to get to the Carolinas.

"Thank God that I have lived to see this," Lincoln cries. "It seems to me that I have been dreaming a horrid dream for four years, and now the nightmare is gone."

But it's not really gone. President Lincoln has just twelve days to live.

CHAPTER FOUR

As blood flows in Virginia, wine flows in Rhode Island, far removed from the horrors of the Civil War. It is here that John Wilkes Booth has traveled by train for a romantic getaway with his fiancée. Since the Revolutionary War, Newport has been a retreat for high society, known for yachting and mansions and gaiety.

John Wilkes Booth is one of eight children born to his flamboyant actor father, Junius Brutus Booth, a rogue if there ever was one. Booth's father abandoned his first wife and two children in England and fled to America with an eighteen-year-old London girl, who became Booth's mother. Booth was often lost in the confusion of the chaotic household. His father and brother eclipsed him as actors, and his upbringing was hectic, to say the least. Now anger has become a way of life for him. Throughout his journey to Rhode Island he has been barraged by news of the southern demise. Northern newspapers are reporting that Richmond has fallen and that Confederate president Jefferson Davis and his entire cabinet fled the city just hours before Union troops entered. In cities like New York, Boston, and Washington, people are dancing in the streets as the rebel collapse appears to be imminent. It is becoming clear to Booth that he is a man with a destiny—the only man in America who can end the

North's oppression. Something drastic must be done to preserve slavery, the southern way of life, and the Confederacy itself. If Robert E. Lee can't get the job done, then Booth will have to do it for him.

Booth's hatred for Lincoln, and his deep belief in the institution of slavery, coalesced into a silent rage after the Emancipation Proclamation. It was only in August 1864, when a bacterial infection known as erysipelas sidelined him from the stage, that Booth began using his downtime to recruit a gang that would help him kidnap Lincoln. First he contacted his old friends Michael O'Laughlen and Samuel Arnold. They met at Barnum's City Hotel in Baltimore, and after several drinks Booth asked them if they would join his conspiracy. Both men agreed. From there, Booth began adding others, selecting them based on expertise with weapons, physical fitness, and knowledge of southern Maryland's back roads and waterways.

In October, Booth traveled to Montreal, where he met with agents of Jefferson Davis's. The Confederate president had set aside more than $1 million in gold to pay for acts of espionage and intrigue against the Union and housed a portion of the money in Canada. Booth's meeting with Davis's men not only provided funding for his conspiracy, it forged a direct bond between himself and the Confederacy. He returned with a check for $1,500, along with a letter of introduction that would allow him to meet the more prominent southern sympathizers in Maryland, such as Samuel Mudd and John Surratt, who would become key players in his evil plan. Without their help, Booth's chances of successfully smuggling Lincoln out of Washington and into the Deep South would have been nonexistent.

∽

After recovering from his illness, Booth immersed himself deeper into the Confederate movement, traveling with a new circle of friends that considered the kidnapping of Lincoln to be of vital national importance. He met with secret agents and sympathizers in taverns, churches, and hotels throughout the Northeast and down through Maryland, always expanding his web of contacts, making his plans more concise and his chances of success that much greater. What started as an almost abstract hatred of Lincoln has now transformed itself into the actor's life's work.

Yet Booth is such a skilled actor and charismatic liar that no one outside the secessionist movement—not even his fiancée—has known the depth of his rage.

Until today.

Booth's betrothed, Lucy Lambert Hale, is the daughter of John Parker Hale, a staunchly pro-war senator from New Hampshire. She is dark-haired and full-figured, with blue eyes that have ignited a spark in the heart of many a man. Like Booth, she is used to having her way with the opposite sex, attracting beaus with a methodical mix of flattery and teasing. But Lucy is no soft touch. She can quickly turn indifferent and even cruel toward her suitors if the mood strikes her.

Among those enraptured with Miss Hale is a future Supreme Court justice, Oliver Wendell Holmes Jr., now a twenty-four-year-old Union officer. Also John Hay, one of Lincoln's personal secretaries. And, finally, none other than Robert Todd Lincoln, the president's twenty-one-year-old son, also a Union officer. Despite her engagement to Booth, Lucy still keeps in touch with both Hay and young Lincoln, among many others.

Strikingly pretty, Lucy appeals to Booth's vanity. When they are together, heads turn. The couple's initial passion was enough to overcome societal obstacles—at least in their minds. By March 1865 their engagement isn't much of a secret anymore, and they are even seen together at the second inaugural.

But in the past month, with Lucy possibly accompanying her father to Spain, and Booth secretly plotting against the president, their relationship has become strained. They have begun to quarrel. It doesn't help that Booth flies into a jealous rage whenever Lucy so much as looks at another man. One night, in particular, he went mad at the sight of her dancing with Robert Lincoln. Whether or not this has anything to do with his pathological hatred for the president will never be determined.

Booth has told her nothing about the conspiracy or his part in it. She doesn't know that his hiatus from the stage was extended by his maniacal commitment to kidnapping Lincoln. She doesn't know about the secret trips to Montreal and New York to meet with other conspirators, nor about the hidden caches of guns or the buggy that

Booth purchased specifically to ferry the kidnapped president out of Washington, nor about the money transfers that fund his entire operation. She doesn't know that his head is filled with countless crazy scenarios concerning the Lincoln kidnapping. And she surely doesn't realize that her beloved has a passion for New York City prostitutes and a sizzling young Boston teenager named Isabel Sumner, just seventeen years old. Lucy knows none of that. All she knows is that the man she loves is mysterious and passionate and fearless in the bedroom.

ഈ

Perhaps, with all of Booth's subterfuge, it is not surprising that their lovers' getaway to Newport is turning into a fiasco.

Booth checked them into the Aquidneck House hotel, simply signing the register as "J. W. Booth and Lady." He made no attempt whatsoever to pretend they are already married. It's as if the couple is daring the innkeeper to question their propriety. There is no question that Booth is spoiling for a fight. He is sick of what he sees as the gross imbalance between the poverty of the war-torn South and the prosperity of the North. Other than the uniformed soldiers milling about the railway platforms, he saw no evidence, during the train ride from Washington to Newport, via Boston, that the war had touched the North in any way.

After checking into the hotel, he and Lucy walk the waterfront all morning. He wants to tell her about his plans, but the conspiracy is so vast and so deep that he would be a fool to sabotage it with a careless outburst. Instead, he rambles on about the fate of the Confederacy and about Lincoln, the despot. He's shared his pro-southern leanings with Lucy in the past, but never to this extent. He rants endlessly about the fall of Richmond and the injustice of Lincoln having his way. Lucy knows her politics well, and she argues right back, until at some point in their walk along the picturesque harbor, with its sailboats and magnificent seaside homes, it becomes clear that they will never reach a common ground.

Toward evening, they stop their fighting and walk back to the Aquidneck House. Despite John Wilkes Booth's many infidelities, Lucy Hale is the love of his life. She is the only anchor that might keep him from committing a heinous crime, effectively throwing his life away in the process. In her eyes he sees a happy future replete with marriage, children, and increased prosperity as he refocuses on his career. They can travel the world together, mingling with high society wherever they go, thanks to her father's considerable connections. All he has to do is to choose that love over his insane desire to harm the president.

Booth tells the desk clerk that Lucy isn't feeling well and that they will take their evening meal in the bedroom. Upstairs, there is ample time for lovemaking before their food is delivered. But the acts of intimacy that made this trip such an exotic idea have been undone by the news about Richmond. They will never make love again after tonight, and both of them sense it. Rather than spend the night together, Booth and Lucy pack their bags and catch the evening train back to Boston, where she leaves him to be with friends.

Booth is actually relieved. He has made his choice. Now no one stands in his way.

CHAPTER FIVE

Tuesday, April 4, 1865
Amelia Court House, Virginia

As Booth and Lucy depart Newport long before their supper can be delivered, Robert E. Lee's soldiers are marching forty long miles to dine on anything they can find, all the while looking over their shoulders, fearful that Grant and the Union army will catch them from behind.

Lee has an eight-hour head start after leaving Petersburg. He figures that if he can make it to Amelia Court House before Grant catches him, he and his men will be amply fed by the waiting 350,000 rations of smoked meat, bacon, biscuits, coffee, sugar, flour, and tea that are stockpiled there. Then, after that brief stop to fill their bellies, they will resume their march to North Carolina.

And march they must. Even though Jefferson Davis and his cabinet have already fled Richmond and traveled to the Carolinas on the very same rail line that is delivering the food to Lee's forces, there is no chance of the army using the railway as an escape route. There simply isn't enough time to load and transport all of Lee's 30,000 men.

The day-and-a-half trudge to Amelia Court House begins optimistically enough, with Lee's men happy to finally be away from Petersburg and looking forward to their first real meal in months. But forty miles on foot is a long way, and mile by mile the march turns into a death pageant. The line of retreating rebels and supply wagons stretches for twenty miles. The men are in wretched physical condition after months in the trenches. Their feet have lost their calluses and their muscles the firm tone they knew earlier in the war, when the Army of Northern Virginia was constantly on the march. Even worse, each painful step is a reminder that, of the two things vital to an army on the move—food and sleep—they lack one and have no chance of getting the other.

Lee's army is in total disarray. There is no longer military discipline, or any attempt to enforce it. The men swear under their breaths, grumbling and swearing a thousand other oaths about wanting to go home and quit this crazy war. The loose columns of Confederate soldiers resemble a mob of hollow-eyed zombies instead of a highly skilled fighting force. The men "rumbled like persons in a dream," one captain will later write. "It all seemed to me like a troubled vision. I was consumed by fever, and when I attempted to walk I staggered like a drunken man."

The unlucky are barefoot, their leather boots and laces rotted away from the rains and mud of winter. Others wear ankle-high Confederate brogans with holes in the soles and uppers. The only men sporting new boots are those who stripped them off dead Union soldiers. The southerners resent it that everything the Union soldiers wear seems to be newer, better, and in limitless supply. A standing order has been issued for Confederate soldiers not to dress in confiscated woolen Union overcoats, but given a choice between being accidentally shot by a fellow southerner or surviving the bitter nightly chill, the rebels pick warmth every time. A glance up and down the retreat shows the long gray line speckled everywhere with blue.

∽

Bellies rumble. No one sings. No one bawls orders. A Confederate officer later sets the scene: there is "no regular column, no regular pace. When a soldier became weary he fell out, ate his scanty rations—if indeed, he had any to eat—rested, rose, and resumed the march when the inclination dictated. There were not many words spoken. An indescribable sadness weighed upon us."

It is even harder for the troops evacuating Richmond, on their way to link up with Lee at Amelia Court House. Many are not soldiers at all—they are sailors who burned their ships rather than let them fall into Union hands. Marching is new to them. Mere hours into the journey, many have fallen out of the ranks from blisters and exhaustion.

Making matters worse is the very real fear of Union troops launching a surprise attack. "The nervousness," a Confederate major will remember, "resulting from this constant strain of starvation, fatigue and lack of sleep was a dangerous thing, sometimes producing lamentable results." On several occasions bewildered Confederate troops open fire on one another, thinking they're firing at Yankees. In another instance, a massive black stallion lashed to a wooden fence "reared back, pulling the rail out of the fence and dragging it after him full gallop down the road crowded with troops, mowing them down like the scythe of a war chariot."

It's no wonder that men begin to desert. Whenever and wherever the column pauses, men slip into the woods, never to return. The war is clearly over. No sense dying for nothing.

Lee has long craved the freedom of open ground, but now his objective is to retreat and regroup, not to fight. His strategy that his army "must endeavor to harass them if we cannot destroy them" depends upon motivated troops and favorable terrain. These are essential to any chance of Lee snatching victory from the jaws of defeat. But the fight will have to wait until they get food.

To lighten his army's load and move faster, Lee orders that all unnecessary guns and wagons be left behind. The pack animals pulling them are hitched to more essential loads. A few days from now, as bone thin and weary as the soldiers themselves, these animals will be butchered to feed Lee's men.

Everything about the retreat—starvation, poor morale, desertion—speaks of failure. And yet when messengers arrive saying that the Petersburg bridges were blown by his sappers once the last man was across, making it impossible for Grant to follow, Lee is optimistic. Even happy. He has escaped once again. "I have got my army safely out of its breastworks, and in order to follow me the enemy must abandon his lines and can derive no further benefits from his railroads or James River," he notes with relief.

Grant's army is sliding west en masse, racing to block the road, even as Lee feels relief in the morning air. Lee suspects this. But his confidence in his army and in his own generalship is such that he firmly believes he can defeat Grant on open ground.

Everything depends on getting to Amelia Court House. Without food Lee's men cannot march. Without food they cannot fight. Without food, they might as well have surrendered in Petersburg.

Lee's newfound optimism slowly filters down into the ranks. Against all odds, his men regain their confidence as the trenches of Petersburg recede further and further into memory and distance. By the time they reach Amelia Court House, on April 4, after almost two consecutive days on the march, electricity sizzles through the ranks. The men speak of hope and are confident of victory as they wonder where and when they will fight the Yankees once again.

It's just before noon. The long hours in the saddle are hard on the fifty-eight-year-old general. Lee has long struggled with rheumatism and all its crippling agonies. Now it flares anew. Yet he presses on, knowing that any sign of personal weakness will be immediately noticed by his men. As much as any soldier, he looks forward to a good meal and a few hours of sleep. He can see the waiting railroad cars, neatly parked on a siding. He quietly gives the order to unload the food and distribute it in an organized fashion. The last thing Lee wants is for his army to give in to their hunger and rush the train. Composure and propriety are crucial for any effective fighting force.

The train doors are yanked open. Inside, great wooden crates are stacked floor to ceiling. Lee's excited men hurriedly jerk the boxes down onto the ground and pry them open.

Then, horror!

This is what those boxes contain: 200 crates of ammunition, 164 cartons of artillery harnesses, and 96 carts to carry ammunition.

There is no food.

CHAPTER SIX

While John Wilkes Booth is still in Newport, a hungry Robert E. Lee is in Amelia Court House, Ulysses S. Grant is racing to block Lee's path, and Abraham Lincoln stands on the deck of USS *Malvern* as the warship chugs slowly and cautiously up the James River toward Richmond. The channel is choked with burning warships and the floating corpses of dead draft horses. Deadly anti-ship mines known as "torpedoes" bob on the surface, drifting with the current, ready to explode the instant they come into contact with a vessel. If just one torpedo bounces against the *Malvern*'s hull, ship and precious cargo alike will be reduced to fragments of varnished wood and human tissue.

Again Lincoln sets aside his concerns. For the *Malvern* is sailing into Richmond, of all places. The Confederate capital is now in Union hands. The president has waited an eternity for this moment. Lincoln can clearly see that Richmond—or what's left of it—hardly resembles a genteel southern bastion. The sunken ships and torpedoes in the harbor tell only part of the story. Richmond is gone, burned to the ground. And it was not a Union artillery bombardment that did the job, but the people of Richmond themselves.

When it becomes too dangerous for the *Malvern* to go any farther, Lincoln is rowed to shore. "We passed so close to torpedoes that we could have put out our hands and touched them," bodyguard William Crook will later write. His affection for Lincoln is enormous, and of all the bodyguards, Crook fusses most over the president, treating him like a child who must be protected.

It is Crook who is fearful, while Lincoln bursts with amazement and joy that this day has finally come. Finally, he steps from the barge and up onto the landing.

But what Lincoln sees now can only be described as appalling.

Richmond's Confederate leaders have had months to prepare for the city's eventual surrender. They had plenty of time to come up with a logical plan for a handover of power without loss of life. But such was their faith in Marse Robert that the people of Richmond thought that day would never come. When it did, they behaved like fools.

ℬ

Their first reaction was to destroy the one thing that could make the Yankees lose control and vent their rage on the populace: whiskey. Union troops had gone on a drunken rampage after taking Columbia, South Carolina, two months earlier, and had then burned the city to the ground.

Out came the axes. Teams of men roamed through the city, hacking open barrel after barrel of fine sour mash. Thousands of gallons of spirits were poured into the gutters. But the citizens of Richmond were not about to see all that whiskey go to waste. Some got down on their hands and knees and lapped it from the gutter. Others filled their hats and boots. The streetlamps were black, because Richmond's gas lines had been shut off to prevent explosions. Perfectly respectable men and women, in a moment of amazing distress, found a salve for their woes by falling to their knees and quenching their thirst with alcohol flowing in the gutter.

Many took more than just a drink. Everyone from escaped prisoners to indigent laborers and war deserters drank their share. Great drunken mobs soon roamed the city. Just as in Amelia Court House, food was first and foremost on everyone's minds. The city had suffered such scarcity that "starvation balls" had replaced the standard debutante and charity galas. But black market profiteers had filled entire warehouses with staples like flour, coffee, sugar, and delicious smoked meats. And, of course, there were Robert E. Lee's 350,000 missing rations, neatly stacked in a Richmond railway siding instead of being packed on the train that Lee expected in Amelia Court House.

Little did the general know that Confederate looters had stolen all the food.

The worst was still to come. Having destroyed and consumed a potential supply of alcohol for the Union army, Richmond's city fathers now turned their attention to their most profitable commodity: tobacco. The rebel leadership knew that President Lincoln wanted to capture tobacco stores in order to sell them to England, thereby raising much-needed money for the nearly bankrupt U.S. Treasury.

In their panic, the city fathers ignored an obvious problem: lighting tinder-dry bales of tobacco on fire would also burn the great old wooden warehouses in which they were stacked.

Soon, spires of flame illuminated the entire city of Richmond. The warehouse flames spread to other buildings. The rivers of whiskey caught fire and inferno ensued.

The true nature of a firestorm involves not only flame but also wind and heat and crackling and popping and explosion, just like war. Soon residents mistakenly believed the Yankees were laying Richmond to waste with an artillery barrage.

And still things got worse.

The Confederate navy chose this moment to set the entire James River arsenal ablaze, preferring to destroy their ships and ammunition rather than see them fall into Union hands.

But the effect of this impulsive tactical decision was far worse than anything the northerners would have inflicted. Flaming steel particles were launched into the air as more than 100,000 artillery rounds exploded over the next four hours. Everything burned. Even the most respectable citizens were now penniless refugees, their homes smoldering ruins and Confederate money now mere scraps of paper. The dead and dying were everywhere, felled by the random whistling shells. The air smelled of wood smoke, gunpowder, and burning flesh. Hundreds of citizens lost their lives on that terrible night.

❧

Richmond was a proud city and perhaps more distinctly American than even Washington, D.C. It could even be said that the United States of America was born in Richmond, for it was there, in 1775, in Richmond's St. John's Episcopal Church, that Patrick Henry looked out on a congregation that included George Washington and Thomas Jefferson and delivered the famous "Give me liberty or give me death" speech, which fomented American rebellion, the Revolutionary War, and independence itself. As the capital of Virginia since 1780, it was where Jefferson had served as governor; he'd also designed its capitol building. It was in Richmond that Jefferson and James Madison crafted the statute separating church and state that would later inform the First Amendment of the Constitution.

And now it was devastated by its own sons.

Soldiers of the Confederate Army of Northern Virginia sowed land mines in their wake as they abandoned the city. Such was their haste that they forgot to remove the small rows of red flags denoting the narrow but safe path through the minefields, a mistake that saved hundreds of Union lives as soldiers entered the city.

Richmond was still in flames on the morning of April 3 when the Union troops, following those red flags, arrived. Brick facades and chimneys still stood, but wooden frames and roofs had been incinerated. "The barbarous south had consigned it to flames," one Union officer wrote of Richmond. And even after a night of explosions, "the roar of bursting shells was terrific." Smoldering ruins and the sporadic whistle of artillery greeted the Twenty-fourth and Twenty-fifth Corps of the Union army.

The instant the long blue line marched into town, the slaves of Richmond were free. They were stunned to see that the Twenty-fifth contained black soldiers from a new branch of the army known as the USCT—the United States Colored Troops.

Lieutenant Johnston Livingston de Peyster, a member of General Wetzel's staff, galloped his horse straight to the capitol building. "I sprang from my horse," he wrote proudly, and "rushed up to the roof." In his hand was an American flag. Dashing to the flagpole, he hoisted the Stars and Stripes over Richmond. The capital was Confederate no more.

That particular flag was poignant for two reasons. It had thirty-six stars, a new number owing to Nevada's recent admission to the Union. Per tradition, this new flag would not become official until the Fourth of July. It was the flag of the America to come—the postwar America, united and expanding. It was, in other words, the flag of Abraham Lincoln's dreams.

So it is fitting when, eleven short days later, a thirty-six-star flag will be folded into a pillow and placed beneath Abraham Lincoln's head after a gunman puts a bullet in his brain. But for now President Lincoln is alive and well, walking the ruined streets of the conquered Confederate capital.

CHAPTER SEVEN

TUESDAY, APRIL 4, 1865
RICHMOND, VIRGINIA

Abraham Lincoln has never fought in battle. During his short three-month enlistment during the Black Hawk War in 1832, he was, somewhat oddly, both a captain and a private—but never a fighter. He is a politician, and politicians are seldom given the chance to play the role of conquering hero. It could be said that General Grant deserved the honor more than President Lincoln, for it was his strategy and concentrated movements of manpower that brought down the Confederate government. But it is Lincoln's war. It always has been. To Lincoln goes the honor of conquering hero—and the hatred of those who have been conquered.

No one knows this more than the freed slaves of Richmond. They throng to Lincoln's side, so alarming the sailors who rowed him ashore that they form a protective ring around the president, using their bayonets to push the slaves away. The sailors maintain this ring around Lincoln as he marches through the city, even as his admiring entourage grows from mere dozens to hundreds.

The white citizens of Richmond, tight-lipped and hollow-eyed, take it all in. Abraham Lincoln is their enemy no more. As the citizens of Petersburg came to realize yesterday, he is something even more despicable: their president. These people never thought they'd see the day Abraham Lincoln would be strolling down the streets of

Richmond as if it were his home. They make no move, no gesture, no cry, no sound to welcome him. "Every window was crowded with heads," one sailor will remember. "But it was a silent crowd. There was something oppressive in those thousands of watchers without a sound, either of welcome or hatred. I think we would have welcomed a yell of defiance."

Lincoln's extraordinary height means that he towers over the crowd, providing an ideal moment for an outraged southerner to make an attempt on his life.

∽

But no one takes a shot. No drunken, saddened, addled, enraged citizens of Richmond so much as attacks Lincoln with their fists. Instead, Lincoln receives the jubilant welcome of former slaves reveling in their first moments of freedom.

The president keeps walking until he is a mile from the wharf. Soon Lincoln finds himself on the corner of Twelfth and Clay Streets, staring at the former home of Jefferson Davis.

When first built, in 1818, the house was owned by the president of the Bank of Virginia, John Brockenbrough. But Brockenbrough is now long dead. A merchant by the name of Lewis Crenshaw owned the property when war broke out, and he had just added a third floor and redecorated the interior with all the "modern conveniences," including gaslights and a flush toilet, when he was persuaded to sell it, furnished, to Richmond authorities for the generous sum of $43,000— in Confederate dollars, of course.

The authorities, in turn, rented it to the Confederate government, which was in need of an executive mansion. It was August 1861 when Jefferson Davis, his much younger second wife, Varina, and their three young children moved in. Now they have all fled, and Lincoln steps past the sentry boxes, grasps the wrought iron railing, and marches up the steps into the Confederate White House.

He is shown into a small room with floor-to-ceiling windows and crossed cavalry swords over the door. "This was President Davis's office," a housekeeper says respectfully.

Lincoln's eyes roam over the elegant dark wood desk, which Davis had so thoughtfully tidied before running off two days earlier. "Then this must be President Davis's chair," he says with a grin, sinking into its burgundy padding. He crosses his legs and leans back.

That's when the weight of the moment hits him. Lincoln asks for a glass of water, which is promptly delivered by Davis's former butler—a slave—along with a bottle of whiskey.

Where Davis has gone, Lincoln does not know. He has no plans to hunt him down. Reunification, however painful it might be to southerners, is within Lincoln's grasp. There will be no manhunt for the Confederate president, nor a trial for war crimes. As for the people of Richmond, many of whom actively conspired against Lincoln and the United States, Lincoln has ordered that the Union army command the citizenry with a gentle hand. Or, in Lincoln's typically folksy parlance: "Let 'em up easy."

He can afford to relax. Lincoln has Richmond. The Confederacy is doomed. All the president needs now is for Grant to finish the rest of the job, and then he can get to work. Lincoln still has miles to go before he sleeps.

CHAPTER EIGHT

Wednesday, April 5, 1865
Amelia Court House, Virginia
Noon to Midnight

Wave after wave of retreating Confederate soldiers arrive in Amelia Court House throughout the day of April 4. They have marched long and hard, yanked forward on an invisible rope by the promise of a long sleep and a full belly. But it was a lie, a broken promise, and a nightmare, all at once. Without food they have no hope. Like the sailors who quit the march from Richmond because their feet hurt, many Confederate soldiers now find their own way to surrender. Saying they are going into the woods to hunt for dinner, they simply walk away from the war. And they keep on walking until they reach their homes weeks and months later—or lie down to die as they desert, too weak to take another step.

Lee's optimism has been replaced by the heavy pall of defeat. "His face was still calm, as it always was," wrote one enlisted man. "But his carriage was no longer erect, as his soldiers had been used to seeing it. The troubles of these last days had already plowed great furrows in his forehead. His eyes were red as if with weeping, his cheeks sunken and haggard, his face colorless. No one who looked upon him then, as he stood there in full view of the disastrous end, can ever forget the intense agony written on his features."

His hope rests on forage wagons now out scouring the countryside in search of food. He anxiously awaits their return, praying they will be overflowing with grains and smoked meats and leading calves and pigs to be slaughtered.

The wagons come back empty.

The countryside is bare. There are no rations for Lee and his men. The soldiers become frantic, eating anything they can find: cow hooves, tree bark, rancid raw bacon, and hog and cattle feed. Some have taken to secreting packhorses or mules away from the main group, then quietly slaughtering and eating them. Making matters worse, word now reaches Lee that Union cavalry intercepted a column of supply wagons that raced out of Richmond just before the fall. The wagons were burned and the teamsters taken prisoner.

Lee and his army are in the great noose of Grant's making, which is squeezing tighter and tighter with every passing hour.

∽

Lee must move before Grant finds him. His fallback plan is yet another forced march, this one to the city of Danville, where more than a million rations allegedly await. Danville, however, is a hundred miles south. As impossible as it is to think of marching an army that far on empty stomachs, it is Lee's only hope.

Lee could surrender right then and there. But it isn't in his character. He is willing to demand incredible sacrifice to avoid the disgrace of defeat.

A cold rain falls on the morning of April 5. Lee gives the order to move out. It is, in the minds of one Confederate, "the cruelest marching order the commanders had ever given the men in four years of fighting." Units of infantry, cavalry, and artillery begin slogging down the road. Danville is a four-day march—if they have the energy to make it. "It is now," one soldier writes in his diary, "a race of life or death."

They get only seven miles before coming to a dead halt at a Union roadblock outside Jetersville. At first it appears to be no more than a small cavalry force. But a quick look through Lee's field glasses tells him differently. Soldiers are digging trenches and fortifications along the road, building the berms and breastworks that will protect them from rebel bullets, and then fortifying them with fallen trees and fence rails.

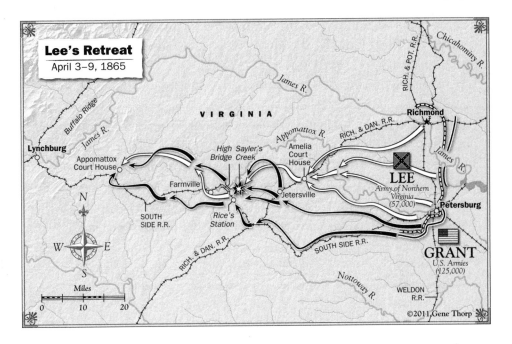

Lee gallops Traveller to the front and assesses the situation. Part of him wants to make a bold statement by charging into the Union works in a last grand suicidal hurrah, but Lee's army has followed him so loyally because of not only his brilliance but also his discretion. Sometimes knowing when *not* to fight is just as important to a general's success as knowing *how* to fight.

And this is not a time to engage.

Lee quickly swings his army west in a grand loop toward the town of Paineville. The men don't travel down one single road but follow a series of parallel arteries connecting the hamlets and burgs of rural Virginia. The countryside is rolling and open in some places, in some forested and in others swampy. Creeks and rivers overflowing their banks from the recent rains drench the troops at every crossing. On any other day, the Army of Northern Virginia might not have minded. But with so many miles to march, soaking shoes and socks will eventually mean the further agony of walking on blistered, frozen feet.

The topography favors an army lying in wait, ready to spring a surprise attack. But they are an army in flight, at the mercy of any force hidden in the woods. And, indeed, Union cavalry repeatedly harass the rear of Lee's exhausted column. The horsemen are not bold or dumb enough to attack Lee's main force, which outnumbers them by thousands. Instead they attack the defenseless supply wagons in a series of lightning-quick charges. On narrow, swampy roads, the Union cavalry burn more than 200 Confederate supply wagons, capture eleven battle flags, and take more than 600 prisoners, spreading confusion and panic.

Sensing disaster, Lee springs to the offensive, ordering cavalry under the command of his nephew Major General Fitzhugh Lee and Major General Thomas Rosser to catch and kill the Union cavalry before they can gallop back to the safety of their Jetersville line. In the running battle that follows, rebel cavalry kill 30 and wound another 150 near the resort town of Amelia Springs. If the Union needs proof that there is still fight in Lee's army, it now has it.

Lee marches his men all day, and then all night. At a time when every fiber of their beings cries out for sleep and food, they press forward over muddy rutted roads, enduring rain and chill and the constant harassment of Union cavalry. The roads are shoulder to shoulder with exhausted men, starving pack animals, and wagons sinking up to their axles in the thick Virginia mud. Dead and dying mules and horses are shoved to the side of the road so as not to slow the march. Dead men litter the ground, too, and are just as quickly tossed to the shoulder—or merely stepped over. There is no time for proper burials. Nothing can slow the march to Danville.

Men drop their bedrolls because they lack the strength to carry them. Many more thrust their guns bayonet-first into the earth and leave them behind. On the rare occasions when the army stops to rest, men simply crumple to the ground and sleep. When it is time to march again, officers move from man to man, shaking them awake and ordering them to their feet. Some men refuse to rise and are left sleeping, soon to become Union prisoners. Others can't rise because they're simply too weak, in the early phases of dying from starvation. These men, too, are left behind. In this way, Lee's army dwindles. The 30,000 who retreated from Petersburg just three days ago have been reduced by half. As the long night march takes a greater toll, even those hardy men stagger like drunks, and some lose the power of speech. And yet, when it comes time to fight, they will find a way to lift their rifle to their shoulder, aim at their target, and squeeze the trigger.

✑

"My shoes are gone," a veteran soldier laments during the march. "My clothes are almost gone. I'm weary, I'm sick, I'm hungry. My family has been killed or scattered, and may be wandering helpless and unprotected. I would die, yes I would die willingly, because I love my country. But if this war is ever over, I'll be damned if I ever love another country."

His is the voice of a South that wants no part of Lincoln and the United States of America—and for whom there can be no country but the Confederacy. Just as the Union officer in Richmond spoke of the "barbarous south," so these soldiers and men like John Wilkes Booth view the North as an evil empire. This is the divisiveness Lincoln will face if he manages to win the war.

Now, in the darkness after midnight, a courier approaches the marching soldiers and hands Lee a captured Union message from Grant to his generals, giving orders to attack at first light.

But at last Lee gets good news, in the form of a report from his commissary general, I. M. St. John: 80,000 rations have been rushed to the town of Farmville, just nineteen miles away. Lee can be there in a day.

He swings his army toward Farmville. It is Lee's final chance to keep the Confederate struggle alive.

CHAPTER NINE

General Sam Grant is also on a midnight ride. The great hooves of his horse beat a tattoo on the bad roads and forest trails of central Virginia. Speed is of the essence. Scouts report that Lee is escaping, marching his men through the night in a bold attempt to reach rations at Farmville. From there it's just a short march to High Bridge, a stone-and-wood structure wide enough to handle an army. Once Lee crosses and burns the bridge behind him, his escape will be complete, and the dreadful war will continue.

Tonight decides everything. Grant is so close to stopping Lee. So very close. Grant digs his spurs into his horse, named Jeff Davis after the Confederate president, in a gesture uncharacteristically vindictive of Grant, who is usually polite and respectful even to his enemies. Grant knows that he must ride hard. Lee must be captured now. And Grant must capture him personally.

As always, his battle plan is simple: Get in front of Lee. Block his path. How many times has he explained this to Generals Sheridan and Meade? Block Lee's path, stop him in his tracks, then attack and crush the Army of Northern Virginia. So how is it that Lee came within spitting distance of the Jetersville roadblock and escaped?

It confounds Grant that his top generals are so terrified of Lee, holding back when they should rush in. The Union soldiers are better armed, better fed, and far more rested than Lee's men. The generals must be relentless, pressing forward without ceasing until the war is won. But they are not.

So it is up to Grant to lead the way.

∽

The culprit, Grant decides, is not General Phil Sheridan. He and the cavalry are more than doing their part, charging far and wide over the Virginia countryside, harassing Lee's wagons and skirmishing with Confederate cavalry. Sheridan is Grant's eyes and ears, sending scouts to track Lee's movements and ensuring that Marse Robert doesn't disappear into the Blue Ridge Mountains. Grant would be lost without Sheridan.

The same cannot be said of General George Meade. His force reached Jetersville at dusk on April 5, after a dreary day of pursuit. But rather than launch an immediate assault on Lee's rear, as Grant ordered, Meade halted for the night, claiming that his men were too tired to fight.

Grant knows there's more to it than that. The problem, in a nutshell, is the unspoken rivalry between infantry and cavalry—between the unglamorous and the swashbuckling. Meade's refusal to fight is his way of pouting about the cavalry divisions sharing the roads with his men, slowing their march. "Behold, the whole of Merritt's division of cavalry filing in from a side road and completely closing the way," one of Meade's aides wrote home. "That's the way it is with those cavalry bucks: they bother and howl about infantry not being up to support them, and they are precisely the people who are always blocking the way . . . they are arrant boasters."

"To hear Sheridan's staff talk, you would suppose ten-thousand mounted carbineers had crushed the entire Rebellion. . . . The plain truth is, they are useful and energetic fellows, but commit the error of thinking they can do everything and that no one else does anything."

So Meade made his point by refusing to attack.

Sheridan was furious. "I wish you were here," he wired Grant. "We can capture the Army of Northern Virginia if enough force be thrown to this point."

Grant reads between the lines. Rather than wait until morning, and the chance that Meade will find another excuse for not fighting, he orders his staff to mount up for the sixteen-mile midnight ride to Jetersville. Never mind that it is a cold, pitch-black night. There is purpose in the journey. They travel carefully, lest they surprise Union troops and be mistakenly shot as southern scouts.

Grant is always one to keep his emotions in check. But as he guides his horse from the village of Nottoway Court House to Jetersville, from the sandy soils west of Petersburg to the quartz and red soil of the Blue Ridge foothills, Grant fears that Lee is on the verge of outfoxing him again.

Grant knows that the Confederates are beatable. His spies captured a note from one of Lee's aides, detailing the poor morale and horrible conditions the Confederates are experiencing. Grant is also aware of the massive desertions. He has heard about the roads littered with rifles and bedrolls, abandoned wagons and broken horses. He knows that an astronomic number of Confederate men have been taken prisoner. But all this means nothing if he cannot get ahead of Lee and block the Confederate escape to the Carolinas. And not just that: he must win what he calls the "life and death struggle for Lee to get south to his provisions."

Once a second-rate fighting force, the Union soldiers have gained remarkable strength since the assault on Petersburg. "Nothing seemed to fatigue them," Grant marvels. "They were ready to move without rations and travel without rest until the end." Unlike Lee's bedraggled force, Grant's men march with a bounce in their step. Bands play. Nobody straggles or falls out of ranks. They walk the unheard-of distance of thirty miles in one day.

☙

Now Grant and the cavalry detail that guards his life walk their horses through a forest to Sheridan's camp. Sentries cry out, ordering them to stop. Grant steps forward to show himself. Within seconds the sentries allow them to pass and usher Grant to Sheridan's headquarters.

Grant speaks briefly with "Little Phil," the short and fiery dynamo who makes no secret that he wants his cavalry "to be there at the death" of the Confederate insurrection. Then the two men saddle up and ride through the darkness to Meade's headquarters in Jetersville. The lanky Pennsylvanian is in bed with what he claims to be a fever. Grant chalks it up to fear and orders Meade to get his army ready to attack.

Meade was a hero of Gettysburg, outwitting Lee on the battle-field despite having a reputation for being timid and temperamental. At forty-nine, the "Old Snapping Turtle" is the oldest and most experienced man in the room. Grant bears him a grudging respect, but respect isn't enough right now. Grant needs a man who will press the attack, day and night, fresh or exhausted, ill or in good health.

Meade is not that man. He never has been. Furthermore, it is not merely a question of heart anymore but of logistics: it is simply impossible for Meade's infantry to outrace Lee to Farmville. Marse Robert had a good head start, and Meade's halt for the night only increased the distance. Grant now thinks of Lee, somewhere out there in the darkness, sitting tall astride Traveller, not letting his men stop their all-night march for any reason. Lee has cavalry, artillery, and infantry at his disposal, should it come to a fight.

It will take a fast and mobile fighting force to beat the rebels. In other words: Sheridan's cavalry.

✐

Grant delivers his orders.

There will be no more waiting, he decrees, proposing a pincer movement, Sheridan in front and Meade from the rear. At first light Meade's infantry will chase and find Lee's army, then harass them and slow their forward movement. Sheridan, meanwhile, will "put himself south of the enemy and follow him to his death." In this way, the Confederate race to North Carolina will stop dead in its tracks. As Sheridan revels in the glory to come, Meade bites his tongue and accepts Grant's decision. He has to.

There is nothing more Sam Grant can do. His midnight ride has produced exactly the results he was hoping for. Promptly at six A.M., the earth shakes with the clip-clop of thousands of hooves as

Sheridan's cavalry trot west in their quest to get in front of Lee. Meade's army, meanwhile, marches north to get behind Lee, the two armies forming Grant's lethal pincers.

Meade's men march past Grant as he sits down at sunrise, lighting a cigar. Grant is confident. Finally, the Black Thursday of the Confederacy has arrived.

CHAPTER TEN

General Robert E. Lee has been up all night yet still looks crisp and composed as he rides, backlit by the rising sun, into Rice's Station. The Army of Northern Virginia, looking for all the world like the most beaten-down fighting force in history, cheers as the beloved general glides past on Traveller. Marse Robert is stately and rugged, six feet tall and afraid of no man. He is almost asleep in the saddle, thanks to the all-night march. But his broad gray hat remains firmly in place as he acknowledges the adulation of his suffering men. Many don't have shoes; those that do can put two fingers through the rotting leather soles. Half of Lee's force has quit the war between Petersburg and this tiny depot, slinking into the woods to search for the slightest morsel of a meal and then not coming back. Those who remain are so crazed from lack of sleep and belly-hollowing hunger that their cheers resemble frantic drunken slurs.

Many are too weak even to shoulder a musket, but Lee knows that somehow they will fight when called to do so. The roads of central Virginia are now littered with the detritus of Lee's retreating army: guns, blankets, broken wagons, artillery limbers, dead horses, and dead men.

It has now been four days since the Confederate army began retreating from Petersburg. The soldiers have endured the betrayal at Amelia Court House, where boxcars full of food had been stolen by Confederate scavengers. Still, Lee's men marched on, nerves frazzled by the threat of Union attack, but never stopping for more than five or ten minutes to sleep in the mud and rain before resuming their march. The general understands their suffering. Still, he orders them to push on.

Now they see that he was right all along. For the Army of Northern Virginia has eluded the army of General Ulysses S. Grant. Better yet, there are rations waiting just a few miles away, in Farmville.

Which is why Lee's crazed soldiers cheer him on this dawn as they march into Rice's Station. Lee is all they believe in right now—not Confederate president Jefferson Davis, not the Army of Northern Virginia, not even terms like "states' rights" or "pro-slavery," which spurred many men to enlist in the Confederate cause. Now those things mean nothing. Only Marse Robert matters.

They would follow him into hell.

∞

Ahead of General Lee is his trusted point man General Pete Longstreet. Behind Lee is the rear guard under the command of General John B. Gordon, the fearless Georgian. In between is a ten-mile-long supply column, supervised by General Richard "Fighting Dick" Anderson and General Richard Ewell, a veteran soldier with just one leg who oversees a scrappy band of bureaucrats, frontline veterans, and landlocked sailors who escaped from Richmond just days earlier.

The tiny hamlet of Rice's Station is a crossroads. One way leads to the Carolinas and safety; the other direction leads back to Petersburg. Longstreet orders cannons pointed down the Petersburg road, to scare off any Union force that might be stalking them. The tired men dig trenches and earthworks to protect themselves from bullets. The woods serve as latrines, the newly dug trenches as beds. Longstreet's mandate is to remain in Rice's Station until Lee's entire army has passed through. Only then will he and his men evacuate.

Incredibly, a bleary-eyed Robert E. Lee is reveling in the moment. The air is fresh, scrubbed clean by the night's rain. Birds are singing to greet this fine spring morning. He knows that Farmville is less than an hour away, with its boxcars filled with smoked meat, cornmeal, and all the makings of a great military feast. Advance scouts have confirmed that the food is actually there this time. Looters have not touched it.

The plan is for Lee's men to fill their empty bellies in Farmville this morning, then march over the great span known as High Bridge, which towers over the Appomattox River, separating central and western Virginia. Lee will order the bridge burned immediately after they cross, preventing the Union from following. The Carolinas will be reached in days.

Lee's escape is so close.

But then grim news arrives. A flying column of Union cavalry galloped through Rice an hour ago. They are now ahead of the Confederates. Longstreet's scouts report that 800 bluecoats on foot and on horseback are headed for High Bridge. Their goal, obviously, is to burn the bridge and close Lee's escape route.

General Lee quietly ponders Longstreet's information. He knows he has no way of stopping this Union advance.

For one of the few times in his adult life, Robert E. Lee is stymied.

∽

Lee hears the thunder of approaching hooves. General Thomas Lafayette Rosser, a gregarious twenty-eight-year-old Texan, gallops his cavalry into Rice's Station. Rosser's classmate at West Point was the equally audacious George Armstrong Custer, now a Union general involved on the other side of this very fight.

Longstreet approaches Rosser and, warning him about the Union plan, screams, "Go after the bridge burners. Capture or destroy the detachment, even if it takes the last man of your command to do it."

Rosser salutes, his face stolid. Only afterward does he grin, then bark the order. His cavalry, enlisted men and officers alike, gallop toward High Bridge. The quiet morning air explodes with noise as hundreds of hooves pound into the narrow dirt road.

When the war first broke out, Thomas Lafayette Rosser was so eager to take up arms for the Confederacy that he dropped out of West Point two weeks before graduation. Starting as a lieutenant, he distinguished himself at more than a dozen key battles, among them Manassas, Bull Run, and Gettysburg. Though wounded several times, Rosser never altered his daring approach to combat. In January 1865, as the Army of Northern Virginia huddled in its Petersburg defenses, Rosser selected 300 of his toughest riders for an impossible mission. They crossed the Allegheny Mountains in the dead of winter, seeking to destroy the Union infantry headquartered in the town of Beverly, West Virginia. Thunderstorms drenched them their second day on the march; then the temperature plummeted below zero, freezing their overcoats stiff. But those hardships actually helped Rosser, making the attack a complete surprise. The daring nighttime raid yielded 800 Union prisoners.

So Longstreet knows that Rosser is the sort of man who will not be afraid of the "kill or be killed" order. Rosser will not let him down.

After Rosser departs, there is nothing to do but wait. As Longstreet directs his men to strengthen their impromptu defenses in Rice's Station, Lee can only wonder how long it will take the rest of his army and its wagon train to catch up. With every passing second, the danger of Grant's scouts finding his army grows. Lee cannot let this happen. He must get over High Bridge by the end of the day.

Overcome with exhaustion, at last the fifty-eight-year-old general instructs his orderly to find someplace for him to nap. It is midmorning. Lee will close his eyes just long enough to feel rejuvenated. Then he will begin perhaps his last campaign. If he doesn't get over High Bridge, Lee knows, he will be defeated.

CHAPTER ELEVEN

THURSDAY, APRIL 6, 1865
FARMVILLE, VIRGINIA
MIDMORNING

The Union force racing to burn High Bridge consists of the Fourth Massachusetts Cavalry, the Fifty-fourth Pennsylvania Infantry, and the 123rd Ohio Infantry. The cavalry comprise 79 soldiers on horseback, who can fight either in the saddle or as dismounted foot soldiers. The two infantry regiments comprise almost 800 fighters who can wage war only on foot.

If the entire Union force were cavalry, the fearless General Rosser and his men would never catch them. A fast-walking soldier, even one on a mission of the utmost military importance, is obviously no match for a cavalry horse.

Colonel Francis Washburn of the Fourth Massachusetts knows this, which is why he orders his cavalry to gallop ahead of the foot soldiers. His men will burn the bridge while the infantry covers the rear.

High Bridge is an engineering marvel, considered by some to be the finest bridge in the world. The architects of the Brooklyn Bridge will steal liberally from its design. And yet High Bridge is situated not in one of the world's great cities but in a quiet, wooded corner of Virginia. Made of stone and felled trees, it stretches a half mile, from the bluff outside Farmville marking the southern shore of the Appomattox River floodplain to the Prince Edward Court House bluff at the opposite end. Twenty 125-foot-tall brick columns support the wooden superstructure. That two great armies, at the most pivotal point in their histories, have descended upon High Bridge at the same time is one of those random acts of fate that so often decide a war.

As Colonel Washburn and his men ride within three miles of High Bridge, they are joined by Union general Theodore Read, who has undertaken a daring mission to warn Washburn that the Confederates are hot on his trail, and that a small force of rebels who have been at High Bridge for months are dug in around the span. Read has full authority to cancel Washburn's mission if he thinks it too risky.

Washburn and Read hold a council of war at a hilltop plantation known as Chatham, roughly halfway between Rice's Station and High Bridge. They can see the bridge in the distance, and the two earthen forts defending it. There are just a few dozen Confederates dug in at the bridge, but they have a clear field of fire. A direct frontal assault would leave Washburn's men badly battered.

Another concern is that the ground between the Chatham plateau and High Bridge is a swampy morass of small creeks, sand, and hills, taking away any advantage of speed—and adding the very real potential of getting caught in a kill zone. Nevertheless, General Read orders Washburn to proceed to the bridge. Read will stay behind, with the infantry, to cover the cavalry's rear. This is a gamble, and both of these brave officers know it—a gamble with their own lives and those of their men.

It is also a gamble that could end the war by sundown.

∽

Washburn leads his cavalry toward High Bridge. He has a reputation for recklessness and impatient courage and shares the commonly held Union belief that the rebels are too demoralized to fight back. He will burn the bridge at any cost.

Washburn's cavalry ride for an hour, taking in the countryside as they prepare for battle. But then, seemingly out of nowhere, they are ambushed by rebel cavalry. It is a scene out of Lexington and Concord, as Confederate sharpshooters take aim. Again and again, and without warning, rebel cavalry charge. Washburn, fearing nothing, gives chase. But it's a clever trap, the rebels drawing the bluecoats in as they link up with the other Confederate force defending the bridge. Suddenly, Confederate artillery rains down on Washburn and his men, putting an instant halt to the Union pursuit. These cannonballs are the slap in the face that Washburn needs, making him realize that the rebels are hardly too demoralized to fight back. He also knows this: Colonel Francis Washburn of the Fourth Massachusetts is right now the one man in America who can end the Civil War this very day. He will go down in history. All he has to do is burn High Bridge.

Washburn is within a quarter mile of the bridge, his force largely intact. But then comes the crackle of gunfire from behind him. Three years of combat experience tells Washburn that he is in deep trouble; Confederate cavalrymen have found his infantry. High Bridge must wait.

The Fourth Massachusetts has been in the saddle since four A.M. It is now almost noon. The men are exhausted, as are their horses. The soldiers gallop their weary animals back across the floodplain, over the Sandy River and on up to the Chatham plateau. Men and horses are breathless from the race and the midday heat, the riders' blue uniforms and gloved hands bathed in sweat. Their stomachs rumble from lack of food, and their lips are chapped from thirst. They expect only a minor battle, because the main Confederate force is still miles away. But that expectation turns out to be brutally wrong.

Some 1,200 Confederate horsemen wait to attack Washburn's cavalry and infantry, which together number just slightly more than 800. Rebel horses and riders hold in a long line, awaiting the inevitable order to charge forth and crush the tiny Union force.

Colonel Washburn remains cool, surveying what could be a hopeless situation. Infantry is no match against the speed and agility of cavalry. His infantry lie on their bellies and peer across at Confederate cavalry. They have had no time to dig trenches or build fortifications, so hugging the ground is their only defense. Washburn is cut off from the rest of Grant's army, with no hope of rescue. How can 79 Union riders possibly hold off 1,200 Confederate horsemen?

∽

Washburn decides that his only hope is to be bold—a quality this Harvard man possesses in abundance.

After conferring with General Read, Washburn orders his cavalry to assemble. They are now on the brow of the hill, just out of rifle range, in columns of four. Washburn addresses the ranks. He barks out his plan, then reminds the infantry to get their butts up off the ground and follow right behind the Union riders to punch a hole through the rebel lines.

On Washburn's command, the Fourth Massachusetts trot their mounts forward. While the Confederates purchased their own horses or brought them from home, the Union horses are government-issue. Each trooper has ridden mile upon mile with the same horse, in the same saddle. As they arrive at this fateful moment, animal and rider alike know each other's moods and movements—the nudge of a knee, the gathering of the haunch muscles, the forward lean to intimate danger or the need for speed—so that they work as one.

Passing the infantry's far right flank, Washburn's cavalry wheels left. The colonel's accent is Brahmin and his tone is fearless. The precision of his cavalry is something that Washburn takes for granted, for they have practiced time and again on the parade ground. And the show of force stuns the enemy. The Confederates see what is coming, even if they don't believe it.

Counting Read and Washburn, there are now 80 Union horsemen. Outnumbered by more than fifteen to one, they shut out all thoughts of this being the last battle of their young lives. They ride hard. Their fate comes down to one simple word: "Charge!"

Washburn screams the command. Spurs dig into horses. Sabers clank as they are withdrawn from their sheaths. Some men fire their Spencer carbines as they gallop within rifle range, clutching the gun in their right hand and the reins in their left. Others wield pistols. Still others prefer the killing blade of a cavalry sword. The audacity of their charge and succeed-at-all-costs desperation ignites panic in the rebel army. The battlefield splits in two as Washburn's men punch through the first wave of the rebel line. The Union charge at Chatham, for a brief instant, is a triumph.

∽

But, stunningly, after the cavalry charges, Washburn's infantry does not move. Not a muscle. Even as the Confederate defenses crumble, and as Washburn organizes his men for the secondary attack that will smash an escape route through the rebel lines, the foot soldiers are still on their bellies, sealing their own doom.

General Rosser senses exactly what's happening. He doesn't waste a second. The Texan yells for his Confederate cavalry to prepare for a counterattack.

The Confederate general James Dearing, just twenty-four years old, leads the way. Both sides race toward each other at top speed before pulling back on the reins in the center of the plain. The fight becomes a brutal test of courage and horsemanship. Men and horses wheel about the battlefield, fighting hand to hand, saddle to saddle. Each man wages his own individual battle with a ferocity only a life-and-death situation can bring. Bullets pierce eyes. Screams and curses fill the air. The grassy plain runs blood-red.

A rifle is too unwieldy in such tight quarters, so men use the butt end rather than the barrel. Pistols and sabers are even more lethal. "I have been many a day in hot fights," the unflappable Rosser will marvel later, "but I never saw anything approaching that at High Bridge."

Rosser's gaze drifts over to the amazing sight of his enemy. Washburn, in the thick of the action, is a frenzied dervish, slaying everything in his path. Men fall and die all around as Washburn rides tall in the saddle, his saber slashing at any man who steps forward to challenge him.

Suddenly, the young Confederate general Dearing shoots the Union general Theodore Read, at point-blank pistol range. Read falls from his saddle to the ground. Seeing this, Colonel Washburn takes his revenge. He engages Dearing in an intense saber duel, brought to a sudden end when a Union soldier fires two bullets into Dearing's chest. His sword falls to the ground, as does he.

Washburn is still sitting tall in the saddle—but not for long. As he turns his head, he is shot through the mouth at point-blank range. The bullet lodges in his lungs. His jaw hangs slack as blood pours from the hole in his face, down onto his sweaty, dusty blue uniform.

The force of the gunshot does not kill Washburn, nor even render him unconscious. It is, however, strong enough to knock him out of the saddle for the first time all day. As the colonel falls, a Confederate flails at his toppling body with a thirty-four-inch saber, burying the blade deep in Washburn's skull. Incredibly, one day later, as a burial detail cleans the battlefield, Washburn will be found alive.

There are many, many casualties.

The Confederates lose 100 men.

The Union loses everyone.

Every single one of the 847 Union soldiers sent to burn High Bridge is either captured or killed. Those who try to fight their way out are slaughtered, one by one. The failure of the Union infantry to obey Washburn's orders to attack sealed their fate.

Rosser leads his weary men back toward Rice's Station, content in the knowledge that he has single-handedly saved the Confederacy.

Lee will now have his escape. Or at least it appears that way.

CHAPTER TWELVE

Thursday, April 6, 1865
On the road to Farmville, Virginia
Afternoon

As the battle for High Bridge commences, Union general George Meade's infantry finally finds the tail end of the Confederate column about ten miles away from the High Bridge fight. A hard rain falls. In the first of what will be many firefights on this day, small bands of Union soldiers begin shooting at the Confederate rear guard. The movement is like a ballet, with skirmishers pushing forward through the trees and craggy ground to engage the rebels. The instant they run out of ammunition, these skirmishers pull back and another group races forward to take their place. And all the while, other infantrymen capture artillery pieces, burn wagons, and force the rebels to turn and fight—and sometimes even dig in, separating them further from Lee's main force.

Confederate general John Gordon's force falls behind first. The ferocious Georgian understands that he is being cut off. In fact, Lee's entire Confederate army is being separated. No longer is it a single force; it has been broken into four separate corps. Under normal conditions, the cavalry would plug these gaps or, at the very least, chase away the Union skirmishers, but the cavalry have their hands full at High Bridge.

Meanwhile, in Rice's Station, Lee rises from his nap and assesses the situation. Hearing the ferocity of the firing from High Bridge, he assumes that the Union force is much bigger than the 800 men who galloped past him a few hours ago. If Lee had any cavalry at his disposal, they would act as his eyes and ears, scouting ahead and returning with the truth. But he doesn't. Lee can only guess at what's happening—and he guesses wrong.

Fearing that the Union general Sheridan has already leapfrogged out in front, Lee holds his entire corps in Rice's Station. At a time when it is crucial to be on the move, Lee chooses to remain in place.

⁂

As Lee waits, Sheridan's three divisions of cavalry are searching high and low for the Army of Northern Virginia. His three commanders are Generals George Armstrong Custer, Thomas Devin, and George Crook. Custer is the youngest and most aggressive, the blond-haired dynamo who roomed with Thomas Rosser at West Point. Custer has a flair for the dramatic. He is the sort of man who rides into battle wearing a flamboyant red kerchief around his neck and accompanied by a brass band.

That kind of display will make George Custer famous. Eleven years later, it will also kill him. As Sheridan holds back to plot strategy, it is Custer who leads the Union cavalry on their search-and-destroy mission against the Confederate column. At midmorning he discovers the heart of the column, perhaps six miles from High Bridge. Custer does not hesitate. His division attacks. But upon meeting resistance, the young general stalls, allowing another cavalry division to attack. In this way, Custer slowly works his way up the Confederate line, riding closer and closer to the very front, toward Sam Grant's objective of getting out in front of Lee.

The pace is cruel. By noon Custer's horses are thirsty and in need of rest. They stop at a small stream. Custer's aide approaches, bringing news that scouts have found a gap in the Confederate line. Now Custer sets aside all thoughts of getting out in front of Lee. He excitedly gives the command to mount up. Without waiting for the other two divisions (a habit that will seal his doom at the Little Bighorn), his cavalry race toward the gap, hoping to drive a permanent wedge between the Confederate divisions.

General George Armstrong Custer

Custer succeeds. By two P.M. Custer's division pours into the small town of Marshall's Crossroads, where they are met by a lone artillery battalion. The Confederate cannons are no match for Custer's horsemen. He captures the small force and sets the rebel guns ablaze. But then another Confederate force counterattacks, pushing Custer out of the town. The Confederates dig in immediately, knowing that more fighting is imminent. The rebels hope to hold on long enough for Lee's main army to reinforce them.

George Custer, however, is not to be denied. He dismounts his men and orders them to assume an infantry posture. Then he scribbles a message to Crook and Devin, requesting help. Within an hour, their divisions are on the scene.

All afternoon, the three Union divisions initiate mounted and dismounted cavalry charges against the dug-in rebels. In the absence of artillery, the bluecoats boldly ride their horses up and over the Confederate breastworks. The Confederates cower in their trenches to avoid being trampled to death. The alternative is to run. Those who do are chased and cut down with sabers.

Even so, the rebels hold fast, repelling each and every charge. The general in charge, "Fighting Dick" Anderson, is a brilliant tactician, placing his limited resources in just the right place to repel the cavalry.

Finally, as daylight turns to evening, Custer assembles his men for one final charge. He orders the regimental band to play, hoping to strike fear in the enemy. Seeing the assembled cavalry, Confederate officers call an immediate retreat. Their goal is to reach Lee at Rice's Station.

Custer and the Union cavalry ride fast and hard into Anderson's lines before they can retreat. By now Sheridan has sent word, saying, "Go right through them. They're demoralized as hell"—an order that the Union cavalry take to heart. Anderson's Confederate corps breaks, the men dropping their weapons and running for their lives.

Of about 3,000 rebels, only 600 escape Custer. But the general is still not satisfied. He orders three Union cavalry divisions to give chase, cutting men down as they run. In a rare act of lenience, those who make it into the woods are allowed to live. Later they will be rounded up as prisoners of war. For now their confinement is the woods itself; those who try to fight their way out are promptly driven back inside.

More than 2,600 Confederates are captured, among them the one-legged General Richard Ewell. As he surrenders to Custer, he knows that a portion of his men are trapped on a grassy hillside a few miles up the road, above a swollen stream known as Sayler's Creek. These men are spoiling for another fight, a battle that will go down as the most barbaric and ferocious of the entire war.

General George Custer has seen much ferocious fighting in his young life, but he has never seen anything like Sayler's Creek.

CHAPTER THIRTEEN

Thursday, April 6, 1865
Sayler's Creek
Late afternoon

In 1865, the Sayler's Creek area of central Virginia is a place of outstanding beauty. Verdant rolling hills compete with virgin forest to present a countryside that is uniquely American, a place where families can grow amid the splendors of nature. But the beauty of the area will soon be defiled by the ugliness of war. Grant's Union army has finally arrived to confront Lee's forces. Lee's men are tired and hungry. Many have fought the north from the beginning, seeing action at Manassas, at Fredericksburg, and at Gettysburg. One group, in particular, the Stonewall Brigade, marched into battle under Stonewall Jackson, who, next to Lee, was the greatest of all southern generals. These same hardened fighters wept tears of grief when Jackson fell from his horse, the victim of friendly fire. Years of battle have reduced the numbers of the Stonewall Brigade from 6,000 soldiers to just a few hundred battle-tested veterans.

These men know the meaning of war. They also know the meaning, if not the precise military definition, of terms like "enfilade" and "field of fire" and "reverse-slope defense," for they can execute them in their sleep. The Stonewall Brigade and the rest of Lee's men, depleted as they are, are practiced experts at warfare.

Lee knows that his fighting force is splintered. Near a bucolic estate called Lockett's Farm, the Jamestown Road crosses over Big Sayler's Creek and Little Sayler's Creek at a place called Double Bridges. There are, as the name implies, two narrow bridges. The wagons must all funnel into a narrow line and cross one at a time. Lee is miles away from his supply train and cannot protect it. His only hope is that the Union army will be too slow in catching up to the wagons.

Grant's army is now in sight. The soldiers' blue uniforms and the glint of their steel bayonets strike fear into the hearts of the teamsters, causing the wagons to attempt to cross Double Bridges two and three at a time. Wheels become tangled. Horses and mules balk in their traces, confused by the noise and smelling the panic. Their pace grows slower and slower, until one of the bridges actually collapses from the weight, and the Confederate advance comes to an abrupt halt.

Within minutes, the Union attacks. Sweeping down from the high ground, General Meade's infantry pounces on the terrified Confederates, who abandon their wagons and race into the woods on foot.

The Confederate infantry waits a few hundred yards ahead of the chaos, watching. They stand shoulder to shoulder, their line of battle almost two miles wide. Thus are 4,000 of Lee's troops poised to meet the Union attack.

Behind them, rebel wagons are burning on the double bridges above Sayler's Creek. To the left of the Confederate force is the Appomattox River. Straight in front of them are thousands of advancing blue-clad Yankees. At first, the Confederate infantry line holds. But under withering artillery fire the men begin to fall back.

It is a mile-long retreat over open ground that offers almost no cover. The rebel infantry topple the wagons that have made it across the double bridges, using them as an impromptu breastworks, hiding behind a spoked wheel or a tilted axle. The sun cannot set quickly enough for these men. With 10,000 Union troops almost on top of them, darkness is the rebels' only hope.

∽

Night does not come soon enough, and the fight begins. Almost immediately, the Confederates take incredible losses. Artillery and bullets level any man who dares to stand still. Many soldiers quit the war right then and there, convinced that this endless wave of blue is unbeatable. They see the wagons afire, and hear the explosions of the ammunition inside, and know in an instant that of the three things a soldier needs to survive in wartime—bullets, sleep, and food—they have none.

Others, however, are more game. They abandon the cover of the wagons and begin to splash across Sayler's Creek. They are rewarded.

Just as the North surges forward, hope arrives. It comes in the form of Robert E. Lee, who has spent the afternoon on horseback, trying to find his own army. He sits astride Traveller, looking down from a nearby ridgeline. "The disaster which had overtaken the army was in full view," one of his officers will later write. "Teamsters with their teams and dangling traces, retreating infantry without guns, many without hats, a harmless mob, with massive columns of the enemy moving orderly on."

This "harmless mob," Lee realizes, is his own Army of Northern Virginia.

"My God," says a horrified Lee, staring down at the columns of smoke and tongues of flames and stacks of bodies—so many that the ground along both branches of Sayler's Creek is a carpet of gray and blue. "Has the army been dissolved?"

✑

Two miles south of Lee's viewpoint, and a half mile north of where General Custer still has a Confederate force pinned down, perhaps the most ferocious battle ever seen on American soil is unfolding.

"At three o'clock in the afternoon," one Confederate soldier will remember, "we reached Sayler's Creek, a small creek that at the time had overflowed its banks from the continuous rains of the past few days, giving the appearance of a small river. We halted a few minutes then waded across this stream and took our positions on the rising ground one hundred yards beyond."

The hill is grassy, but the site of the Confederate stand is toward the back of the rise, under the cover of broom sedge and pine shrubs. Now the rebels hold the high ground. Any force attacking Lee's army of almost 4,000 will have to expose themselves to fire while wading the four-foot-deep morass of Sayler's Creek. If they get across safely, they will then have to fight their way uphill to the rebel positions.

"We threw ourselves prone upon the ground. Our battle line was long drawn out, exceedingly thin. Here we rested awaiting the attack, as the enemy had been following closely behind us," a Confederate major will later chronicle.

At five-thirty, the Union artillery opens fire on the grassy hill, lobbing shells at the Confederate positions from just four hundred yards away. The rebels have no artillery of their own and cannot fire back. The screams of the wounded are soon drowned out by the whistle and explosion of shells. All the Confederates can do is hug the ground and pray as the Union gunners take "their artillery practice without let or hindrance."

The shelling lasts twenty minutes. Under cover of that heavy fire, long blue lines of Union infantry wade the creek, separated into two battle lines, and slowly march up the hill. The Confederates are devastated by the precision artillery, but do not retreat. Instead, they lie flat on the ground, muskets pointed at the stream of blue uniforms picking their way up the grassy slope. A Confederate major steps boldly in front of the line and walks the entire length, exposing himself to fire as he reminds the rebels that no one is allowed to shoot until ordered to do so. He later recalls the instruction: "That when I said 'ready' they must all rise, kneeling on the right knee; that when I said 'aim' they must all aim about the knees of the advancing line; and that when I said 'fire' they must all fire together."

⁓

Everything, as one officer notes, is as "still as the grave." The advancing line of blue moves forward in a giant scrum, slowly ascending the hill. Some of the men wave white handkerchiefs, mocking the Confederates, jeering that they should surrender. But the rebels say nothing, letting the Union soldiers believe that the South is already beaten. The bluecoats refrain from charging, preferring to plod, letting the notion of surrender sink in, for the rebels surely know there is no way they can get off this hill alive.

"Ready!" comes the cry from the Confederate lines. They are low on ammunition and may get only a shot or two. Even then, reloading a musket takes time. Better to make each shot count.

"The men rose, all together, like a piece of mechanism, kneeling on their right knees and their faces set with an expression that meant—everything," a Confederate officer will write.

On the cry of "Aim!" a line of horizontal musket barrels points directly at the blue wall. Then: "Fire!"

"I have never seen such an effect, physical and moral, produced by the utterance of one word," marvels the Confederate major. "The enemy seemed to have been totally unprepared for it."

The entire front row of Union soldiers falls in bloody chaos. The second line turns and runs down the hill.

This is Grant's vaunted army, a force better rested, better fed, and better equipped than the half-dressed Confederates. And yet the blue-coats flee in terror, their white handkerchiefs littering the ground. It is a triumph, and in that instant the Confederate force is overcome by righteous indignation. The memory of that hard overnight march in the rain, the starvation, the delirious craziness born of exhaustion—all of it blends into a single moment of fury. The rebels leap to their feet and chase after the bluecoats. Down the hill they run, caps flying off, curses streaming from their mouths. Dead men are everywhere, on both sides, and the Confederates have to hop and jump over bodies. But the rebels never stop running.

The Union soldiers finally gather themselves. They stop, turn, and fire. Knowing they are outgunned, the Confederates retreat back to their positions, only to be surrounded as the Union force quickly counterattacks the hill.

And this time the bluecoats aren't plodding. Union soldiers sprint up the hill, overrunning the Confederate positions. Out of ammunition, and heavily outnumbered, the Army of Northern Virginia still refuses to surrender. The fighting becomes hand to hand. Soldiers claw at each other, swinging fists, kicking. "The battle degenerated into a butchery and a confused melee of personal conflicts. I saw numbers of men kill each other with bayonets and the butts of muskets, and even bite each other's throats and ears and noses, rolling on the ground like wild beasts," one Confederate officer will write. "I had cautioned my men against wearing Yankee overcoats, especially in battle, but had not been able to enforce the order perfectly—and almost at my side I saw a young fellow of one of my companies jam the muzzle of his musket against the back of the head of his most intimate friend, clad in a Yankee overcoat, and blow his brains out."

Although the battle is little remembered in history, witnesses will swear they have never seen more suffering, or a fight as desperate, as during the final moments of Sayler's Creek.

◇

And still it grows more vicious. None other than General George Armstrong Custer, who has been killing Confederates since breakfast, has broken off from his former position and races his cavalry through the pine thickets behind the rebel lines. His horsemen ride into the action behind him, sabers swinging. Custer is impervious to personal injury, his savagery today adding to his growing legend for fearlessness. Custer slashes his sword, showing no mercy. He spurs his men to do the same. Rebel troops on foot are cut to pieces by bullets and steel blades.

The Union artillerymen, not wanting to be left out, pull their guns to the edge of Sayler's Creek and take aim into those stray bands of Confederate soldiers on the fringes of the fighting. Firing rounds of canister and grape—lethal small balls and bits of sharpened metal designed to maim and disfigure—the artillery adds to the chaos. On the ground, bodies missing heads, legs, and arms are sprawled in absurd contortions, a gruesome reminder of what close-quarter combat will yield.

Soon, one by one, the rebels raise their musket butts in the air as a signal of surrender. Union soldiers round up these men, whom they have fought so savagely for the previous hour. Then, shocked by the sunken eyes and gaunt Confederate faces, some of the bluecoats open their rucksacks and share their food.

The last rebels to surrender are the sailors and marines recently converted to infantry. Surrounded in a grove of trees, with no hope of escape, they lay down their rifles.

◇

One Confederate corps has managed to escape from the confusion of Sayler's Creek, and now it reaches General Lee at the top of the ridge. Seeing his forces trudging back toward him, Lee grabs a battle flag and holds it aloft. The Confederate Stars and Bars snaps in the wind, the flag's bright red color a compass beacon guiding the weary surviving soldiers to safety. Union forces try to give chase but abandon the effort when the darkness makes it impossible to tell whether they are shooting at friend or foe.

A day that started so well for the Confederates at Rice's Station, then saw triumph at High Bridge, is now finished. In the morning, Lee will continue his escape, but without 13 battle flags, 300 wagons, 70 ambulances, and almost 8,000 men, either killed or taken prisoner. Ten of Lee's top officers are either dead or captured. Among the captured is his eldest son, Custis Lee.

The Union army, on the other hand, suffers 1,200 casualties. So fierce is the fighting, and so courageous the actions of the fighters, that 56 Union soldiers will receive the Congressional Medal of Honor for their actions on the field that day.

Night falls, and so ends what will come to be known as the Black Thursday of the Confederacy. Half of Lee's army is gone. Except for General Longstreet, his remaining generals think the situation is hopeless. Lee continues to improvise, still looking for a way to save his army and get to the Carolinas. Yet even he is devastated. "A few more Sayler's Creeks and it will all be over," sighs Marse Robert.

But Lee cannot bring himself to utter the one word he dreads most: "surrender."

CHAPTER FOURTEEN

Lincoln is desperate for news from the front. The time away from Washington was meant to be a working vacation, and it has clearly revived the president. The "incredible sadness" he has carried for so long is gone, replaced by "serene joy." Mary Lincoln has joined her husband at City Point, bringing with her a small complement of guests from Washington. The mood in the nation's capital has turned festive since the fall of Richmond. Mary and her guests plan to visit Richmond in the morning, as if the burned-out husk of a city has become a tourist attraction. Lincoln will stay behind on the riverboat and tend to the war. Still, he is glad for the company. He tells jokes and makes small talk, all the while wondering when the next telegram from General Grant will arrive.

Early on the morning of April 7, just hours after Sayler's Creek, Lincoln receives the news for which he's been waiting. Grant's telegram states that Sheridan has ridden over the battlefield, counting Confederate dead and captured, particularly the many top Confederate generals now in Union custody. "If the thing is pressed," Grant quotes Sheridan as saying, "I think Lee will surrender."

Lincoln telegraphs his heartfelt reply: "Let the thing be pressed."

CHAPTER FIFTEEN

———

Palm Sunday, April 9, 1865
Appomattox Court House

The end has come. General Robert E. Lee rides forth from the Confederate lines, into the no-man's-land separating his dwindling force from the vast Union forces. The Army of Northern Virginia is cornered in a sedate little village called Appomattox Court House—Lee's 8,000 men surrounded on three sides by Grant's 60,000. After escaping Sayler's Creek the rebels reached Farmville, only to be attacked again and forced to flee before they could finish eating their rations. They raced across High Bridge, only to find that mortar wouldn't burn. The Union army crossed right behind them. Grant was then able to get ahead and block Lee's path to the Carolinas.

Lee's final great hope for a breakout came the previous night. He had entrusted his toughest general, John Gordon from Georgia, with punching a hole in the Union lines. The attack began at five P.M. Three hours later, after Gordon encountered wave after never-ending wave of blue-clad soldiers—too many for his men to beat down—he sent word back to Lee that he had "fought my corps to a frazzle."

In other words: Gordon could not break through.

Lee's proud shoulders slumped as he received the news. "There is nothing left for me to do but go and see General Grant," he said aloud. Lee was surrounded by his staff but was talking to himself. The man who had succeeded his entire life, excelling at everything and failing at nothing, was beaten. "I would rather die a thousand deaths," he said.

∽

Dressed in an impeccable formal gray uniform, polished black boots, and clean red sash, Lee now rides forth. A spectacular ceremonial sword is buckled around his waist. He expects to meet Grant once he crosses over into the Union lines, there to surrender his sword and be taken prisoner.

But before Grant's soldiers march him off to the penitentiary, Lee plans to argue on behalf of his men, seeking the best possible terms of surrender for the Army of Northern Virginia. He has written to Grant repeatedly on this subject. Grant's evasive replies have given little evidence as to which way he leans on the issue.

Lee and a small group of aides ride to a spot between the Union and Confederate lines. They halt their horses in the middle of the country lane and wait for Grant to meet them.

And they wait. And they wait some more. All the while it becomes more obvious that the Union forces are not just enjoying a quiet Sunday morning—cleaning rifles, filling cartridge cases, putting out the breakfast fires. No, they are preparing for battle. Lee can see it in the way the gun crews have unlimbered the cannons and howitzers and are now sighting them toward his lines. The big guns—those M1857 Napoleons—can drop a twelve-pound projectile on top of a man's head from a mile away, and those howitzers can lob an eighteen-pound shell nearly as far. Looking at the Union lines, Lee sees dozens of these guns, capable of inflicting catastrophic damage.

If this is a display of force by Grant to hasten Lee's surrender, it is working.

But Grant does not show himself. In fact, he is miles away, suffering from a severe migraine headache. Lee sits astride Traveller, painfully vulnerable to a sniper's bullet despite his flag of truce. After about two hours with no response, Lee sees a Union soldier riding out. The soldier informs Lee that the attack will be launched in a few moments. For his own safety, Lee must return to the Confederate lines.

∽

The boom of artillery breaks the morning quiet. Lee jots a quick note intended for Grant and hands it to an orderly, who gallops toward the Union lines under a white flag. He also requests that the attack be postponed until Grant can be located.

With the irrefutable logic of a man conditioned to follow orders, the Union colonel in charge tells Lee's courier that he does not have the authority to halt the attack. It will go forward as planned.

As the courier gallops back to Lee, Union skirmishers march to the front and prepare to probe the Confederate lines for vulnerability.

Lee writes another letter to Grant, asking for "a suspension of the hostilities pending the adjustment of the terms of the surrender of this army."

Even as fighting threatens to break out all around him, Lee is unruffled. He sits astride Traveller, whose flanks are flecked with mud, waiting for permission to surrender. But when the first wave of skirmishers is just a hundred yards away, Lee has no choice but to find safety. With a reluctant tug on Traveller's reins, he turns back toward his men.

~

Moments later he is stopped. A Union courier tells Lee that his letter has not found Grant, but it has found General George Meade, whom Lee knew long before the war. Meade has ordered a sixty-minute truce, hoping that Grant can be located in the meantime.

Lee turns Traveller once again. He rides back toward the front and dismounts. It's been four hours since he first sought the surrender meeting. The sun is now directly overhead. Lee sits on a pile of fence rails, in the meager shade of an apple tree bearing the first buds of spring. There, he writes yet another letter to Grant, hoping to impress upon the Union general the seriousness of his intentions. This, too, is sent off under a white flag through the Union lines. Finally, at twelve-fifteen, a lone Union officer and his Confederate escort arrive to see Lee. The officer, a colonel named Babcock, delivers a letter into Lee's hands:

GENERAL R. E. LEE
COMMANDING C.S. ARMIES:
Your note of this date is of but this moment (11:50 a.m.) received. In consequence of my having passed from the

Richmond and Lynchburg road to the Farmville and Richmond road, I am at this writing about four miles west of
Walker's church, and will push forward to the front for
the purpose of meeting you. Notice sent on this road
where you wish the interview to take place will meet me.

Very respectfully, your obedient servant

U. S. Grant

Lieutenant-General

With a mixture of sadness and relief, Lee and his three aides ride
past the Union lines. These troops do not cheer him, as the Army of
Northern Virginia is in the habit of doing. Instead, the Sunday afternoon is preternaturally quiet after so many days and years of war.
There is no thunder of artillery or jingle of a cavalry limber. Just
those miles-long lines of men in blue, staring up at Lee as he rides
past, dressed so impeccably and riding so tall and straight-backed in
the saddle. Not even his eyes give away his mourning, nor the
dilemma that he has endured since Sayler's Creek, when it became
clear that his army was no longer able to acquit itself.

Per Grant's letter, Lee sends his aide Colonel Charles Marshall up
the road to find a meeting place. Marshall settles on a simple home.
By a great twist of fate, the house belongs to a grocer named Wilmer
McLean, who moved to Appomattox Court House to escape the war.
A cannonball had landed in his fireplace during the first Battle of Bull
Run, at the very start of the conflict. Fleeing to a quieter corner of
Virginia was his way of protecting his family from harm.

But the Civil War once again finds Wilmer McLean. He and his
family are asked to leave the house. Soon, Lee marches up the front
steps and takes a seat in the parlor. Again, he waits.

∽

At one-thirty, after a half hour, Lee hears a large group of horsemen
galloping up to the house. Moments later, General U. S. Grant walks
into the parlor. He wears a private's uniform; it is missing a button. He
has affixed shoulder boards bearing the three stars of a lieutenant general, but otherwise there is nothing elegant about the Union leader. He
has been wearing the same clothes since Wednesday night, and they

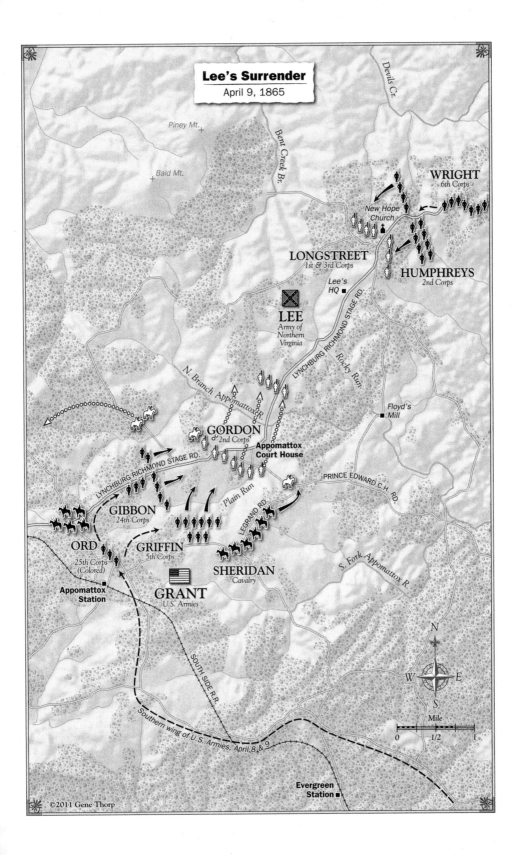

Lee's Surrender
April 9, 1865

Piney Mt.

Bald Mt.

Devils Cr.

Bent Creek Br.

WRIGHT
6th Corps

New Hope
Church

LONGSTREET
1st & 3rd Corps

Lee's
HQ

HUMPHREYS
2nd Corps

LEE
Army of
Northern
Virginia

LYNCHBURG RICHMOND STAGE RD.

Rocky Run

Floyd's
Mill

N. Branch Appomattox R.

GORDON
2nd Corps

Appomattox
Court House

PRINCE EDWARD C.H. RD.

LYNCHBURG RICHMOND STAGE RD.

Plain Run

GIBBON
24th Corps

LEGRAND RD.

S. Fork Appomattox R.

ORD
25th Corps
(Colored)

GRIFFIN
5th Corps

SHERIDAN
Cavalry

Appomattox
Station

GRANT
U.S. Armies

SOUTH SIDE R.R.

Southern wing of U.S. Armies, April 8 & 9

N
W   E
S

Mile
0   1/2   1

Evergreen
Station

©2011 Gene Thorp

are now further spattered by mud from his thirty-five-mile ride this morning. "Grant," Colonel Amos Webster, a member of the Union general's staff, will later remember, "covered with mud in an old faded uniform, looked like a fly on a shoulder of beef."

Removing his yellow cloth riding gloves, Grant steps forward and shakes Lee's hand.

Almost twenty years earlier, during the Mexican War, he was a mere lieutenant when Lee was a major soon to be promoted to colonel. Grant well recalled how Lee had scolded him because of his slovenly appearance. While not a vindictive man, U. S. Grant does not suffer slights easily. He has an encyclopedic memory. Lee has only a minor recollection of meeting Grant prior to this moment in Wilmer McLean's parlor, but Grant remembers every single word. So while Lee sits before him, proud but fallen, resplendent in his spotless uniform, Grant looks and smells like a soldier who could not care less about appearance or ceremony.

⨯⨯

As the moment of surrender nears, however, Grant starts to feel a bit embarrassed by the prospect of asking one of history's great generals to give up his army and has second thoughts about his dress. "General Lee was dressed in a full uniform which was entirely new," he will later write in his memoirs, "and was wearing a sword of considerable value, very likely the sword that had been presented by the State of Virginia. At all events, it was an entirely different sword than the one that would ordinarily be worn in the field. In my rough traveling suit, the uniform of private with the straps of a lieutenant general, I must have contrasted very strangely with a man so handsomely dressed, six feet high and of faultless form. But this was not a matter that I thought of until afterwards."

As Grant's generals and staff—among them Custer and Sheridan—file into the room and stand to one side, Lee's aides gather behind their leader.

Grant and Lee sit at a small wooden table. An area rug covers the floor beneath them. The room's balance of power is tilted heavily toward the Union—Grant and his twelve to Lee and his two. Lee's men are staff officers, neatly dressed and strangers to the battlefield.

Grant's men, on the other hand, include staff and top generals, men who have spent the last week on horseback, harassing Lee's army. They are dressed for battle, swords clanking and spurs jangling, the heels of their cavalry boots echoing on the wooden floor. They can barely suppress smirks betraying their good fortune, for not only destroying Lee's army but to be present at the moment of Marse Robert's greatest humiliation. Sheridan, in particular, has great reason to be here. He believes that Lee's request for a cease-fire and these negotiations are yet another clever attempt to help his army escape. A shipment of rations is waiting for Lee and his army at the local railway depot, and Sheridan is convinced that Lee means to use the food to get him one step closer to the Carolinas.

What Sheridan and General Custer know, but Lee does not, is that Union cavalry has already captured that station. The food is in Union hands. Even if Lee is lying, and somehow manages to escape, his army will never make it the final hundred miles to freedom on empty stomachs.

"I met you once before, General Lee," Grant starts. His voice is calm, as if this moment is just a random occasion for small talk. "We were serving in Mexico, when you came over from General Scott's headquarters to visit Garland's brigade, to which I belonged. I have always remembered your appearance, and I think I should have recognized you anywhere."

"Yes. I know I met you on that occasion," Lee answers in the same casual tone as Grant, letting the reference sit between them, though certainly not apologizing. His face, in Grant's estimation, is "impassable." "I have often thought of it and tried to recollect how you looked, but I have never been able to recall a single feature," Lee says.

The generals speak of Mexico, recalling long-ago names like Churubusco and Veracruz. Grant finds the conversation so pleasant that he momentarily forgets the reason for their meeting. Lee is the one to take the initiative.

"I suppose, General Grant, that the object of our present meeting is fully understood," he says. "I asked to see you to ascertain upon what terms you would receive the surrender of my army."

Grant calls for his order book, a thin volume of yellow paper with carbon sheets. He lights a cigar and stares at a page, composing the sequence of words that will most amicably end the war. A cloud of smoke hovers around his head. Lee does not smoke, and he watches as Grant, after waving a distracted hand in the air to shoo the cigar smoke away, writes out his terms in pen.

When he is finished, Grant hands the book over to Lee.

Marse Robert digests the words in silence. The terms are remarkable in their lenience. Lee will not even have to surrender his sword. The gist is simple: Put down your guns and go home. Let's rebuild the nation together. This was President Lincoln's vision, to which Grant subscribed.

As if to underscore this point, members of Grant's staff tentatively ask Robert E. Lee for permission to go behind Confederate lines. They have old friends over there, friends they have seen only

Appomattox Court House, 1865: victorious Union soldiers in front of the courthouse

through the lens of a spyglass, across some great width of battlefield, these last four years.

Lee grants permission.

There is little else to say. Lee is humiliated but also grateful that his enemies have granted such favorable terms. He will be able to return to his army with some good news. Grant and Lee rise simultaneously and shake hands. After years of battle, hardship, strategizing, and sleeping in one impromptu lodging after another, the two great warriors and the thousands of men in their armies can now go home.

∽

As Lee rides back to his lines, the Army of Northern Virginia spontaneously gathers on both sides of the road. Lee fights back tears as his men call out to him. His dissolved army will soon turn over their guns and battle flags. This is their last chance to show their great love and respect for their leader. "Men," he calls out to them, "we have fought this war together and I have done the best I can for you."

Each group cheers as Lee rides past, only to give in to their sorrow and break down in sobs, "all along the route to his quarters."

Meanwhile, the reconciliation is beginning. Confederate and Union officers are renewing old friendships. "They went over, had a pleasant time with their old friends, and brought some of them back with them when they returned," Grant will write twenty years later, recalling that the McLean household became their de facto meeting place that night. The men swapped stories of their lives and remembrances of battles won and lost. "Here the officers of both armies came in great numbers, and seemed to enjoy the meeting as much as though they had been friends separated for a long time while fighting under the same flag.

"For the time being it looked very much as if all thought of the war had escaped their minds."

But the war is not so easily forgotten by others. Unbeknownst to all those men who risked their lives to fight those great battles—men who deservedly savor the peace—plans are being hatched throughout the South to seek revenge for the Union victory.

Part Two

THE IDES
OF DEATH

Lincoln's most famous profile

CHAPTER SIXTEEN

It seems like the entire town is drunk. Lee's Confederate army has surrendered. In the Union capital whiskey is chugged straight out of the bottle, church bells toll, pistols are fired into the air, fireworks explode, newsboys hawk final editions chock-full of details from Appomattox, brass bands play, church hymns are sung, thirty-five U.S. flags are hoisted, and army howitzers launch an astonishing five-hundred-gun salute, which shatters windows for miles around the city.

The war is done! After four long years, and more than 600,000 dead altogether, euphoria now floats through the air like an opiate.

Complete strangers clasp one another's hands like long-lost friends. They rub shoulders in taverns, restaurants, cathouses, and the impromptu glow of blazing streetside bonfires. Revelers march from one place to the next, passing the flask, aimless and amazed. Sooner or later it becomes obvious that their passion needs a purpose—or, at the very least, a focus. The human mass snakes toward the White House, handheld torches lighting the way. The people of Washington, D.C., overcome by news of the war's end, hope to glimpse their president on this historic night. Perhaps, if they are very lucky, he will give one of the speeches for which he has become so famous.

The nation's capital is not yet the cosmopolitan city it will become. The streets are mostly dirt and mud. It is not uncommon for traffic to stop as farmers drive cattle to market. Open spaces have been military staging areas during the war, with the camp followers and soldiers' businesses such a designation implies. The Tiber Creek and its adjacent canal are open sewers, a breeding ground for typhus, cholera, and dysentery. The vile stench is made worse by the Central Market's butchers, fond of heaving freshly cleaved carcasses into the rancid waters each morning. This might not be a problem, were it not for the Tiber being located a stone's throw from the Capitol Building, that beautiful unfinished idea that towers above the city like an allegory for the nation itself.

∽

To Lincoln, the Capitol is the most important structure in Washington. During the war, even when resources were limited and manpower was desperately needed on the battlefields, he refused to halt construction. Its signature element, the dome, was fitted into place just over a year ago. Inside, scaffolding still climbs up the curved walls of the unfinished rotunda. Workmen mingle with the Union soldiers who have used the Capitol as a barracks, sleeping on the sandstone floors and waking each morning to the aroma of baking bread, thanks to the cadre of bakers in the basement turning out sixty thousand loaves each day for shipment to distant battlefields.

The Capitol was an obvious artillery target during the war, so the gas lamps atop the dome remained unlit for the duration. Now they blaze. The Capitol glows above the frenzied crowds like some great torch of freedom, a wondrous reminder that Lincoln's common refrain of "the Union must go on" has, indeed, come to pass.

So it is fitting that on the night the Capitol dome is lit, the crowd of more than two thousand staggers to an unruly halt on the grass outside the White House's front door, waiting for Lincoln to show himself from the windows of the second-floor residence. When Lincoln doesn't appear right away, they cry out for him. At first it's just a few random shouts. Then a consensus. Soon they roar as one: "Lincoln," the people cry. "Speech."

The crowd is crazy to touch President Lincoln, to see him, to hear his voice. They continue calling out to him, the chant getting louder until the sound is deafening.

But Lincoln is in no mood to speak. The president sends a messenger out to the people, letting them know he is not up to it tonight. That only makes the crowd cheer louder. Lincoln tries to mollify them by going to a window, pulling back a curtain, and waving. Upon seeing the president, the crowd explodes. Men hoist their caps and umbrellas and women wave their handkerchiefs.

Still, Lincoln does not give a speech.

✍

The crowd doesn't leave. He goes to the window a second time, hoping his appearance will send them on their way. To his utter amazement, twelve-year-old Tad Lincoln is now down on the grass with all those people, running through the crowd with a captured rebel battle flag. The people laugh good-naturedly at the stunned look on Lincoln's face, then cheer him as he steps alone from the front door of the White House to retrieve his young boy. It will be impossible for him to escape without saying a word or two. Lincoln has no protection as he wades into the crowd to get Tad.

The president returns inside the White House, even as the folks remain in the front yard.

Lincoln, at heart, is a showman. He reappears at the second-floor window, smiling and holding up a hand in acknowledgment. "I am very greatly rejoiced to find that an occasion has occurred so pleasurable that the people cannot restrain themselves," he jokes, knowing that the crowd will respond by cheering even louder.

They do.

The president is tired, having hardly been able to sleep, due to a series of dreadful nightmares and anxiety over the struggles still to come. He sees the bonfires and the lanterns, and basks in the ovation, feeling the fatigue slip away. He hears the hurrahs, along with again the single loud cry in unison of "Speech."

Lincoln sighs inwardly. He has waited so long for this moment, and yet he must hold back. These words cannot be delivered impulsively. Nor can he hope to be bathed in applause after they are spoken.

The people need to hear the truth, even though that's not what they want to hear. The crowd wants retribution, not reconciliation; they want grand and eloquent words. Inspirational words. Fortifying words. Even boastful words. They will tell their children's children about the night after the war was won, the night they heard the great Abraham Lincoln frame the victory in the most beautiful and poetic way possible.

They wish, in other words, to witness history.

Lincoln would like to indulge them. But the sentiments are half-formed and the words not yet written. Instead of telling the crowd what's on his mind—how the thrill about the war's end that filled his heart just yesterday is being replaced by weariness at the prospect of the hard work to come—Lincoln smiles that easy grin for which he is so well known. If you want to hear a speech, Lincoln yells to the crowd, please come back tomorrow night.

There is no malice in his tone, no undercurrent of sarcasm born of the many years of public ridicule. The veteran politician works his audience with professional ease. His unamplified voice carries powerfully through the chill night air.

Spying the Navy Yard brass band taking shelter under the White House eaves, he calls out a request: "I always thought that 'Dixie' was one of the best tunes I ever heard. Our adversaries over the way, I know, have attempted to appropriate it. But I insist that yesterday we fairly captured it.

"It is now our property," he informs the crowd, then directs the band to "favor us with a performance."

As the musicians strike up the Confederate anthem, and the crowd sings and claps to that old familiar rhythm, Lincoln slips back into the White House and starts writing the last speech he will ever give.

CHAPTER SEVENTEEN

Monday, April 10, 1865
Washington, D.C.
Night

John Wilkes Booth picks up his gun.

One mile down Pennsylvania Avenue, so close he can almost hear the beloved strains of "Dixie" being belted out so heretically by a Yankee band, the twenty-six-year-old actor stands alone in a pistol range. The smell of gunpowder mixes with the fragrant pomade of his mustache. His feet are set slightly wider than shoulder width, his lean athletic torso is turned at a right angle to the bull's-eye, and his right arm is extended in a line perfectly parallel with the floor. In his fist he cradles the sort of pint-sized pistol favored by ladies and cardsharps.

He fires.

Booth scrutinizes the target. Satisfied, he reloads his single-shot .44-caliber Deringer. His mood is a mixture of rage and despondence. Things have gone to hell since Lee surrendered. Richmond is gone, and with it the Confederate leadership. The "secesh" community—those southern secessionist sympathizers living a secret life in the nation's capital—is in disarray. There's no one to offer guidance to Booth and the other secret agents of the Confederacy.

At this point, there are at least four Confederate groups conspiring to harm the president. Two are plotting a kidnapping, one is planning to smuggle dress shirts infected with yellow fever into his dresser drawers, and another intends to blow up the White House.

Booth is part of a kidnapping conspiracy. He prefers the term "capture." Kidnapping is a crime, but capturing an enemy during a time of war is morally correct. The Confederate government has strict rules governing its agents' behavior. If Booth does indeed get the chance, he is allowed to capture the president, truss him like a pig, subject him to a torrent of verbal and mental harassment, and even punch him in the mouth, should the opportunity present itself. The one thing he is not allowed to do is engage in "black flag warfare."

Or in a word: murder.

⁓

Booth wonders if the restriction against black flag warfare still applies. And, if not, what he should do about it. That's why he's at the range. He has a major decision to make. Shooting helps him think.

Booth fires again. The split-second bang fills him with power, drowning out the celebrations and focusing his mind. Again, he tamps in a ball and a percussion cap.

There is a darkness to Booth's personality, born of the entitlement that comes with celebrity. He is a boaster and a liar, fond of embellishing stories to make himself sound daring and adventurous. He is cruel and mercurial. He is a bully, eager to punish those who don't agree with his points of view. Outside of his love for his mother, Booth is capable of doing anything to satisfy his own urges.

Booth is also a white supremacist. His most closely guarded secret is that he has temporarily given up the profession of acting to fight for the pro-slavery movement. The abolition movement, in Booth's mind, is the real cause of the Civil War, a serpent that must be crushed. Enslavement of blacks is part of the natural order, Booth believes, and central to the South's economy. Blacks, he maintains, are third-class citizens who should spend their lives working for the white man. Not only does this life fulfill them, but they are begging for correction when they step out of line. "I have been through the whole south and have marked the happiness of master and man," Booth writes. "I have seen the black man whipped. But only when he deserved much more than he received."

As a teenager, Booth was traumatized when runaway slaves killed a schoolmate's father. He is willing to swear an oath that this sort of violence will happen on a much larger scale if the South loses the war. Newly freed slaves will slaughter southern white men, rape their women and daughters, and instigate a bloodbath unlike any other in recorded history.

The only way to prevent that is to reinstate slavery by winning the Civil War.

⌐∽⌐

It crushes Booth to think that the South has lost. He shuts the idea out of his mind. Lee's surrender, Booth believes, was a gross error in judgment. Even the great Marse Robert is allowed an occasional lapse.

Booth takes solace in the 146,000 Confederate troops spread out from North Carolina to Texas that have refused to lay down their weapons. So long as those men are willing to fight, the Confederacy—and slavery—will live on.

And now, Booth will give them another reason to fight.

⌐∽⌐

That he was born just south of the Mason-Dixon Line and nearly a northerner means nothing. Booth nurtures a deep hatred for his father and the nation's father figure, Abraham Lincoln. Booth was jealous of his father, an accomplished actor who never acknowledged his young son's talent. Booth's paternal loathing has now been transferred to the president; it flared to full burn when Lincoln issued the Emancipation Proclamation.

Booth could have enlisted in the war. But soldiering, even for the Confederate cause, is far too mundane for his flamboyant personality. He cares little about battles won or lost, or battlefields hundreds of miles from the fancy hotels he calls home. Booth is fighting the Civil War on his terms, using his talents, choreographing the action like a great director. The grand finale will be a moment straight from the stage, some stunning dramatic conclusion when antagonist and protagonist meet face-to-face, settling their differences once and for all. The antagonist, of course, will win.

That antagonist will be Booth.

And what could be more dramatic than kidnapping Lincoln?

The plan is for Booth to gag and bind him, then smuggle him out of Washington, D.C., into the hands of Confederate forces. The president of the United States will rot in a rat-infested dungeon until slavery has been reinstated. Booth will sit before him and deliver a furious monologue, accusing Lincoln of stupidity and self-importance. It doesn't matter that Lincoln won't be able to talk back; Booth has no interest in anything the president has to say.

Lincoln keeps a summer residence three miles outside Washington, at a place called the Soldiers' Home. Seeking respite from the Washington humidity or just to get away from the office seekers and politicos permeating the White House year-round, the president escapes there alone on horseback most evenings. From George Washington onward, presidents of the United States have usually been comfortable traveling with an entourage. But Lincoln, who enjoys his solitude, has no patience for that.

The president thinks his getaways are secret, but men like Booth and the members of the Confederate Secret Service are always watching. Booth's original mission, as defined by his southern handlers, was to capture Lincoln while he rode on the lonely country road to the Soldiers' Home.

Booth tried and failed twice. Now he has a new plan, one that preys on Lincoln's fondness for the theater. He will grab him in mid-performance, from the presidential box at a Washington playhouse.

The scheme, however, is so crazy, so downright impossible that none of his co-conspirators will go along with it.

∽

One of them has even backed out completely and taken the train home. It is as if Booth has rehearsed and rehearsed for a major performance, only to have the production canceled moments before the curtain rises. He has poured thousands of dollars into the plan. Some of that money has come from his own pocket; most has been supplied by the Confederacy. And now the scheme will never come to pass.

Booth fires at the bull's-eye.

The Deringer is less than six inches long, made of brass, with a two-inch barrel. It launches a single large-caliber ball instead of a bullet and is accurate only at close range. For this reason it is often called a "gentleman's pistol"—small and easily concealed in a pocket or boot, the Deringer is ideal for ending an argument or extracting oneself from a dangerous predicament but wholly unsuited for the battlefield. Booth has purchased other weapons for his various plots, including the cache of revolvers and long-bladed daggers now hidden in his hotel room. But the Deringer with the chocolate-colored wooden grip is his personal favorite. It is not lost on him that the pistol's primary traits—elegance, stealth, and the potential to produce mayhem—match those of its owner.

Booth is almost out of ammunition. He loads his gun for one last shot, still plotting his next course of action.

He is absolutely certain he can kidnap Lincoln.

But as Booth himself would utter while performing Hamlet, there's the rub.

If the war is over, then kidnapping Lincoln is pointless.

Yet Lincoln is still the enemy. He always will be.

So if Booth is no longer a kidnapper, then how will he wage war? This is the question that has bothered him all night.

Booth fires his last shot, slides the Deringer into his pocket, and storms out the door, only to once again find the streets full of inebriated revelers. Outraged, he steps into a tavern and knocks back a drink. John Wilkes Booth thinks hard about what comes next. "Our cause being almost lost, something decisive and great must be done," he tells himself.

Until now, Booth has taken orders from Confederate president Jefferson Davis, currently in hiding. It was Davis who, nearly a year ago, sent two agents to Montreal with a fund of $1 million in gold. That money funded various plots against Lincoln. But Davis is done, fleeing to North Carolina in a train filled with looted Confederate gold, most likely never to return. Booth alone must decide for himself what is wrong and what is right.

From this moment forward he will live and breathe and scheme in accordance with his brand-new identity, and his new mission. The time has come for black flag warfare.

CHAPTER EIGHTEEN

Booth's Washington residence is the National Hotel, on the corner of Pennsylvania Avenue and Sixth. Just around the corner is James Pumphrey's stable, where he often rents a horse. The actor feels perfectly at home at Pumphrey's, for the owner is also known to be a Confederate sympathizer. Now, well past eight, and with no streetlights beyond the city limits, the night is far too dark for a ride into the country. But a half-drunk Booth needs to get on a horse now—right now—and gallop through Washington, D.C., reassuring himself that he has a way out of the city after putting a bullet in Abraham Lincoln.

I am the man who will end Abraham Lincoln's life. That thought motivates Booth as he walks. He returns to the idea over and over again. He is thrilled by the notion, not bothered in the least by his ability to make the mental jump from the passive violence of kidnapping to cold-blooded murder. *I will kill the president of the United States.*

Booth ruminates without remorse. Of course, killing a man is immoral. Even Booth knows that.

This is wartime. Killing the enemy is no more illegal than capturing him.

The actor thinks of Lincoln's second inaugural and how he stood so close to Lincoln on that day. *I could have shot him then, if I had wished.*

Booth regrets the lost opportunity, then sets it aside. There will be another chance—and this time he will stand even closer, so close he can't miss. So close he will see the life drain from Lincoln's eyes.

It occurs to him that no American president has ever been assassinated. *I will be the first man to ever kill a president.* He is now even more dazzled by his own violent plan.

∽

The United States is just three months shy of being eighty-nine years old. There are thirty-six states in the Union, thanks to Nevada's recent admission. Lincoln is the sixteenth president. Two have passed away from illness while in office. None of them, as Booth well knows, has died by someone else's hand. If successful in his assassination attempt, the actor will achieve the lasting recognition he has always craved.

For a nation founded by rebellion and torn open by a civil war, the citizens of the United States have been remarkably nonviolent when confronted with politicians they despise. Only one American president was the target of an assassin. And that was Andrew Jackson, the man whose politics sowed the seeds of Confederate rebellion thirty years earlier.

Jackson was leaving a funeral in the Capitol Building on January 30, 1835, when a British expatriate fired at him twice. Unfortunately for the mentally unbalanced Richard Lawrence, who believed himself to be the king of England, both his pistols misfired. The bullets never left the chamber. Congressman Davy Crockett wrestled Lawrence to the ground and disarmed him, even as Jackson beat the would-be assassin with his cane.

Jackson was also the first and only American president to suffer bodily harm at the hands of a citizen, when a sailor discharged from the navy for embezzlement punched Jackson at a public ceremony in 1833. Robert Randolph fled the scene. Jackson, ever the warrior, refused to press charges.

These are the only acts of presidential insurrection in the nation's entire history. The American people are unique in that their considerable political passion is expressed at the ballot box, not through violence directed at their leaders, whom they can vote out of office. If judged only by this yardstick, the Democratic experiment undertaken by Americans four score and nine years ago seems to be working.

Maybe this is why Lincoln rides his horse alone through Washington or stands fearlessly on the top deck of a ship in a combat zone. The president tries to convince himself that assassination is not part of the American character, saying, "I can't believe that anyone has shot, or will deliberately shoot at me with the purpose of killing me."

A wider look at human history suggests otherwise. Tribal societies murdered their leaders long before the Egyptian pharaoh Tutankhamen was slain by his advisers in 1324 B.C. Stabbing and beating were the earliest methods of assassination. The Moabite king Eglon was disemboweled in his chambers, his girth so vast that the killer lost the knife in the folds of his fat. Over time, well-known historical figures such as Philip II of Macedon (the father of Alexander the Great) and perhaps even Alexander himself were assassinated. And politically motivated killing was not limited to Europe or the Middle East— records show that assassination had long been practiced in India, Africa, and China.

And then, of course, there was Julius Caesar, the victim of the most famous assassination in history. The Roman ruler was stabbed twenty-three times by members of the Roman Senate. Of the two stab wounds to his chest, one was the blow that killed him. The killing took place during a lunar cycle known as the ides, fulfilling a prophecy by a local soothsayer.

⁂

The truth is that Lincoln, despite what he says, secretly believes he will die in office. He is by far the most despised and reviled president in American history. His closest friend and security adviser, the barrel-chested Ward Hill Lamon, preaches regularly to Lincoln about the need for improved security measures. More tangibly, there is a packet nestled in a small cubby of Lincoln's upright desk. It is marked, quite simply, "Assassination." Inside are more than eighty death threats. Every morning, sitting in his office to conduct affairs of state, Lincoln's eyes cannot help but see those letters. "God damn your god damned old hellfire god damned soul to hell," reads one letter. "God damn you and your god damned family's god damned hellfired god damned soul to hell."

"The first one or two made me a little uncomfortable," Lincoln has admitted to an artist who came to paint his portrait, "but they have ceased to give me any apprehension.

"I know I am in danger, but I am not going to worry over little things like these."

Rather than dwell on death, Lincoln prefers to live life on his own terms. "If I am killed I can die but once," he is fond of saying, "but to live in constant dread is to die over and over again."

While the war still raged he told the writer Harriet Beecher Stowe, "Whichever way the war ends, I have the impression that I shall not last long after it is over."

∽

A small number of assassins are delusional or impulsive killers, but on the whole, the successful assassin stalks his target, planning every detail of the crime. This means knowing the victim's habits, schedule, nuances, and security detail. Only then can the two most complex and dangerous tasks be successfully executed.

The first involves the shooting—and in 1865 it must be a shooting, because there is little likelihood of getting close enough to stab a major political figure. The assassin must figure out the when and where (a large crowd is ideal); determine how to get in and out of the building or ceremony; and choose the perfect weapon.

Second is the escape. A successful assassin is a murderer. A perfect assassination, however, means getting away from the scene of the murder without being caught. This is even more of a long shot than the crime itself. Plenty of men in those large crowds will want to play the hero. They will tackle and subdue the assailant without fear for their own lives. And even if an assassin eludes those crowds, he must escape the city in which it takes place, and then the country, until arriving at some foreign location of true refuge.

As Booth strolls to Pumphrey's, he carries a map in his coat pocket showing the location of General Joe Johnston and his Confederate holdouts, who are hiding in North Carolina. Booth knows the map by heart. He can pinpoint the precise route Johnston must take to evade the Federal troops and reignite the war. To Booth, the map is much more than a detailed depiction of contours and boundaries. It is also a glimmer of hope, reminding him that the noble cause is alive and well, and why he must do what he must do.

His mind wanders to his buggy, of all things. Booth bought it to transport Lincoln after the kidnapping. Now it serves no purpose. Booth makes a mental note to put the buggy up for sale. But in an instant, his thoughts revert back to President Lincoln, who now has only five days to live.

CHAPTER NINETEEN

MONDAY, APRIL 10, 1865
WASHINGTON, D.C.
NIGHT

Booth turns onto C Street and then out of the cold, wet night into James Pumphrey's stable. His clothes are damp. He smells of drink and tobacco. A quick glance around the stalls shows that most of the horses are already rented out for the evening. Pumphrey may be a Confederate sympathizer and a full-fledged member of the secessionist movement, but he has no qualms about making an honest buck off this night of Union celebration.

Pumphrey is an acquaintance of twenty-year-old John Surratt, the courier instrumental in ensuring that Booth's operation is fully funded by the Confederacy. Surratt travels frequently between Canada, the South, New York City, and Washington, brokering deals for everything from guns to medicine. Like Booth, the young man is furious that the Confederacy has lost.

∞

John Surratt is often hard to locate, but when Booth needs details about his whereabouts or simply wants to get a message to him, the task is as simple as walking to Sixth and H Streets, where his mother keeps a boardinghouse. Mary Surratt is an attractive widow in her

Mary Surratt

early forties whose husband died from drink, forcing her to move to Washington from the Maryland countryside to make a living. Like her son, Mary is an active Confederate sympathizer who has been involved with spying and smuggling weapons.

She also runs a pro-Confederate tavern in the Maryland town of Surrattsville, where she and her late husband once owned a tobacco farm. The Maryland countryside is untouched by war and not occupied by Union troops.

Washington, D.C., with its Federal employees and Union loyalties, is a city whose citizens are all too prone to report any conversation that suggests pro-Confederate leanings, making it a dangerous place for people like Mary Surratt and John Wilkes Booth. Her boardinghouse and Pumphrey's stable are two of the few places they can speak their minds. For Booth, a man who deeply enjoys doing just that, such locations are safe havens.

It would seem natural that Booth tell the others about his new plan. They might have insights into the best possible means of escape: roads under construction or in need of repair, overcrowded streets, bridges still under wartime guard—for the only way out of Washington, D.C., is on a boat or over a bridge.

The first exit is via the Georgetown Aqueduct, a mile and a half northwest of the White House. The second is Long Bridge, three blocks south of the White House. The third is Benning's Bridge, on the east side of town. And the last one is the Navy Yard Bridge, on Eleventh Street.

But Booth has already made up his mind: the Navy Yard Bridge. The other three lead into Virginia, with its plethora of roadblocks and Union soldiers. But the Navy Yard Bridge will take him into the quiet backcountry of Maryland, home to smugglers and back roads. Friends like Mary Surratt and Dr. Samuel Mudd can offer their homes as way stations for a man on the run, storing weapons for him and providing a place to sleep and eat before getting back on the road. The only drawback is that sentries man the bridge and no traffic is allowed in or out of Washington after ten P.M.

Booth wants to see those sentries for himself. Tonight. Which is why he's come for a horse. He doesn't tell Pumphrey, just to be on the safe side. In the end it doesn't matter: Booth's favorite horse has already been rented.

Not the least bit discouraged, Booth walks up to Ford's Theatre on Tenth Street. This converted Baptist church is Booth's touchstone. After it was burned to the ground in 1862, owner John Ford rebuilt it as a "magnificent thespian temple," replacing the pews with seats and transforming the deacons' stalls into private boxes. Upon completion, Ford's became the most state-of-the-art theater in D.C.

Booth performed one night at Ford's in mid-March, but his theater appearances are few and far between these days. (If asked, he explains that he is taking a hiatus to dabble in the oil business.) He still, however, has his mail sent to Ford's, and his buggy is parked in a space behind the theater that was specially created for him by a carpenter and sceneshifter named Ned Spangler. Booth uses Spangler often for such favors and odd jobs. Thirty-nine and described by friends as "a very good, efficient drudge," the hard-drinking Spangler often sleeps in either the theater or a nearby stable. Despite the late hour, Booth knows he will find him at Ford's.

Inside the theater, rehearsals are under way for a one-night-only performance of the farce *Our American Cousin*. Like most actors, Booth knows it well.

Booth finds Spangler backstage, befuddled, as usual. He asks the stagehand to clean up his carriage and find a buyer. Spangler is devastated—a great many hours of work have gone into modifying the theater's storage space so that the carriage will fit. It's a waste for Booth to sell the carriage, and Spangler tells him so.

"I have no further use for it," Booth replies. "And anyway, I'll soon be leaving town." Booth will not say where he's going, leaving Spangler even more befuddled.

∽

The word "assassin" comes from "Hashshashin," the name of a group of hit men who worked for Persian kings between the eighth and the fourteenth centuries. One of their jobs was to execute the Knights Templar, a legendary band of Christian warriors known for their cunning and ferocity in battle. Legend says that the reward for a successful execution was being able to visit a lush royal garden filled with milk, honey, hashish, and concubines.

None of those things await John Wilkes Booth. He is everything an effective assassin should be: methodical, passionate, determined, and an excellent strategist and planner. He is prone to depression, as many assassins are, but his ability to turn angst into rage makes him even more dangerous. He expects no reward for killing Lincoln, though infamy would be nice.

CHAPTER TWENTY

Lee's surrender at Appomattox is just two days old, but events are moving so quickly that it might as well be two months.

The citizens of Washington have spent today sleeping off their celebratory hangover. Now, as evening falls, they again spill out into the streets and sip a drink or two. Just like that, the party starts all over. As it grows and becomes more rowdy, every guzzle and utterance has a hum, an anticipation: Abraham Lincoln is speaking tonight. Love him or hate him, the president of the United States is making a personal appearance at the White House, and everyone wants to see it.

And then, once again, the crowd is on the march. The spring air is thick with a warm mist as the sea of humanity parades down Pennsylvania Avenue. Thousands upon thousands are on their way to hear Lincoln speak, trampling the White House lawn and standing up to their ankles in the mud of once-manicured daffodil beds, pushing and straining against one another, climbing into trees, and even pressing up against the great building itself. All are desperate to be as close to Lincoln as possible. But hungover, dehydrated, and sullen, this is not the lighthearted crowd of the night before. It is something akin to a lynch mob, thirsty for Lincoln's words, and yet ready to pass judgment on them.

And this is what the mob wants to hear: the South must be punished.

These men and women of the North, who have endured the loss of their sons, brothers, and husbands, want vengeance. They want the Confederate leaders and generals hanged, they want the South to pay war reparations, and they want Lincoln's speech to be full of the same self-righteous indignation they feel so powerfully in their hearts.

∽

Booth leans against a tall tree, using it as a buffer against the crowd. He is close enough that Lincoln will be a mere pistol shot away. With him are two co-conspirators. David Herold is a former pharmacy clerk who was born and raised in Washington, D.C. Like Booth, he possesses matinee-idol good looks. But he is more educated and rugged. Herold's degree comes from Georgetown, and he is fond of spending his leisure time with a rifle in his hand, hunting animals. It was John Surratt who introduced the two, four months earlier. Since then, Herold has been an impassioned and committed member of Booth's team.

The second co-conspirator is Lewis Powell—who also goes by the name Lewis Payne—a twenty-year-old who served as a Confederate soldier and spy before joining Booth's cause. Like Herold, he has fallen under Booth's spell.

The actor hasn't told either man that the plan has changed from kidnapping to assassination. That can wait. He brought them along to hear the speech, hoping that some phrase or anticipated course of action will fill them with rage. Then, and only then, will Booth let them in on his new plan.

Soon Lincoln stands before an open second-story window, a scroll of paper in one hand. The president is wearing the same black garb he usually wears but no hat. He is somber. His speech is now written, and he is ready to give it.

Unseen by the crowd, Mary Lincoln shows her husband her support by standing next to him. She has invited Clara Harris, her dear friend and the daughter of a New York senator, to stand with her and witness this historical moment.

Outside, the mere sight of Lincoln elicits a prolonged ovation. The applause rolls on and on and on, continuing even as Lincoln tries to speak.

The crowd cannot possibly know the tremendous weight pressing down on Lincoln's shoulders. Looking out into the audience, he prepares to tell them about the daunting task ahead and how the ability to trust the southern states to peacefully rejoin the Union will be as great a challenge to the nation as the war itself. Lincoln clearly sees the faces of the crowd, with their spontaneous smiles and unabashed joy, and prepares to deliver a speech that is anything but warmhearted. It is, in fact, a heavy, ponderous, de facto State of the Union address, specifically designed to undercut the revelry and prepare America for years of more pain and struggle.

∽

The president begins gently. "We meet this evening not in sorrow, but in gladness of heart," Lincoln says. He thanks General Grant and the army for their struggle, and promises to have a national day of celebration very soon, with a great parade through Washington.

Lincoln is one of the best speakers in America, if not the world. He can read the mood of a crowd and adjust the cadence and rhythm of his voice for maximum effect, coaxing whatever emotion or response is needed to hold the audience in the palm of his hand. Lincoln's voice is clear, his pronunciation distinct. He understands the power of words and emphasizes certain phrases to make a lasting impression. The Gettysburg Address is perhaps the best example of Lincoln's oratorical genius.

But tonight there is no theatricality. No tricks. Just cold, hard facts, delivered in a somber and even depressing monotone. The speech is so long and so unexciting that people in the audience begin shifting their feet and then lowering their heads and slipping away into the night, off to search for a real celebration. Booth stays, of course. He doesn't want to miss a single word. He listens as Lincoln talks of extending suffrage to literate blacks and those who fought for the Union.

Booth seethes at the outrageous notion that slaves be considered equal citizens of the United States, able to own property, vote, run for elected office, and maybe even marry white women. Suffrage, as preposterous as it sounds, means a black man might someday become president of the United States. Booth cannot let this ever happen.

"That means nigger citizenship," he hisses, pointing to the navy revolver on Powell's hip. Fourteen inches long, with a pistol sight and a .36-caliber round, the Colt has more than enough pop to kill Lincoln from such close range. "Shoot him now," Booth commands Powell. "Put a bullet in his head right this instant."

Powell is a dangerous young man, with powerful shoulders and a psychotic temper. But he refuses to draw his weapon. He is terrified of offending Booth but even more afraid of this mob, which would surely tear him limb from limb.

Booth sizes up the situation. It would be easy enough to grab Powell's gun and squeeze off a shot or two before the crowd overpowers him. But now is not the time to be impulsive. Booth certainly doesn't tell this to Powell. Instead he lets Powell believe that he has let Booth down. Only when Powell believes that he has really and truly disappointed Booth will he begin thinking of ways to make it up to him. And that's when Booth will tell him about his amazing new plan.

"*I'll* put him through," Booth sneers, planting another seed about assassination in the minds of Powell and Herold. "By God. I'll put him through."

Then Booth spins around and fights his way back out of the crowd. Twenty-four hours ago he was still thinking of ways to kidnap the president. Now he knows just where and how and when he will shoot Abraham Lincoln dead.

The date will be Thursday, April 13.

Or, as it was known back in Julius Caesar's time, the ides.

CHAPTER TWENTY-ONE

—————

Tuesday, April 11, 1865
Washington, D.C.
Night

"It seems strange how much there is in the Bible about dreams," Lincoln says thoughtfully, basking in the afterglow of his speech. It is just after ten P.M. The people of Washington have moved their party elsewhere, and the White House lawn is nearly empty. Lincoln is having tea and cake in the Red Room with Mary, Senator James Harlan, and a few friends. Among them is Ward Hill Lamon, the close friend with the beer-barrel girth. Lamon, the United States marshal for the District of Columbia, has warned Lincoln for more than a year that someone, somewhere will try to kill him. The lawman listens to the president intently, with a veteran policeman's heightened sense of foreboding, sifting and sorting through each word.

Lincoln continues: "There are, I think, some sixteen chapters in the Old Testament and four or five in the New in which dreams are mentioned. . . . If we believe the Bible, we must accept the fact that in the old days, God and his angels came to men in their sleep and made themselves known in dreams."

Mary Lincoln smiles nervously at her husband. His melancholy tone has her fearing the worst. "Why? Do you believe in dreams?"

Yes, Lincoln believes in dreams, in dreams and in nightmares and in their power to haunt a man. Night is a time of terror for Abraham Lincoln. The bodyguards standing watch outside his bedroom hear him moan in his sleep as his worries and anxieties are unleashed by the darkness, when the distractions and the busyness of the day can no longer keep them at bay. Very often he cannot sleep at all. Lincoln collapsed from exhaustion just a month ago. He is pale, thirty-five pounds underweight, and walks with the hunched, painful gait of a man whose shoes are filled with pebbles. One look at the bags under his eyes and even hardened newspapermen write that he needs to conserve his energies—not just to heal the nation but to live out his second term. At fifty-six years old, Abraham Lincoln is spent.

✑

There have been threats against Lincoln's life ever since he was first elected.

Gift baskets laden with fruit were sent to the White House, mostly from addresses in the South. The apples and pears and peaches were very fresh—and very deadly, their insides injected with poison. Lincoln had the good sense to have them all tested before taking a chance and chomping down into a first fatal bite.

Then there was the Baltimore Plot, in 1861, in which a group known as the Knights of the Golden Circle planned to shoot Lincoln as he traveled to Washington for the inauguration. The plot was foiled, thanks to brilliant detective work by Pinkerton agents. In a strange twist, many newspapers mocked Lincoln for the way he eluded the assassins by wearing a cheap disguise as he snuck into Washington. His enemies made much of the deception, labeling Lincoln a coward and refusing to believe that such a plot existed in the first place. The president took the cheap shots to heart.

The Baltimore Plot taught Lincoln a powerful message about public perception. He adopted a veneer of unshakable courage from that day forward. Now he would never dream of traveling in disguise. He moves freely throughout Washington, D.C. Since 1862 he has enjoyed military protection beyond the walls of the White House, but it was only late in 1864, as the war wound down and the threats became more real, that Washington's Metropolitan Police assigned a select group of officers armed with .38-caliber pistols to protect Lincoln on a more personal basis. Two remain at his side from eight A.M. to four P.M. Another stays with Lincoln until midnight, when a fourth man takes the graveyard shift, posting himself outside Lincoln's bedroom or following the president through the White House on his insomniac nights.

The bodyguards are paid by the Department of the Interior, and their job description, strangely enough, specifically states that they are to protect the White House from vandals.

Protecting Lincoln is second on their list of priorities.

∽

If he were the sort of man to worry about his personal safety, Lincoln wouldn't allow such easy public access to the White House. There is no fence or gate blocking people from entering the White House at this time. The doorman is instructed to allow citizens to roam the first floor. Friends and strangers alike can congregate inside the building all day long, seeking political favors, stealing scraps of the curtains as keepsakes, or just peering in at the president while he works. Some petitioners even sleep on the floor in the hallways, hoping to gain a moment of Lincoln's time.

Lincoln's bright young secretary John Hay frets constantly about his boss's safety. "The President is so accessible that any villain can feign business, and, while talking with him, draw a razor and cut his throat," Hay worries aloud, "and some minutes might elapse after the murderer's escape before we could discover what had been done." Lincoln, however, reminds Hay that being president of the United States stipulates that he be a man of the people. "It would never do for a President to have guards with drawn sabers at his door, as if he were, or were assuming to be an emperor," he reminds them.

∽

Death is no stranger to Abraham Lincoln, and in that way it is less terrifying. The Lincolns' three-year-old son Edward died of tuberculosis in 1850. In 1862, the Lincolns lost eleven-year-old Willie to a fever. Willie was a spirited child, fond of wrestling with his father and riding his pony on the White House lawn. Mary, who already suffered from a mental disorder that made her prone to severe mood swings, was emotionally destroyed by the loss of her boys. Even as Lincoln was mired in the war and dealing with his own grief, he devoted hours to tending to Mary and the silent downward spiral that seemed to define her daily existence. He indulged her by allowing her to spend lavishly, to the point of putting him deeply in debt, though he is by nature a very simple and frugal man. Also to please Mary, he accompanied her to a night at the theater or to a party when he would much rather conserve his energies by relaxing with a book at the White House. And while this indulgence has worked to some extent, and Mary Lincoln has gotten stronger over time, Lincoln of all people knows that she is one great tragedy away from losing her mind.

Normally, their history precludes Lincoln from talking about death with Mary present. But now, surrounded by friends and empowered by the confessional tone of that night's speech, he can't help himself.

"I had a dream the other night, which has haunted me since," he admits soulfully.

"You frighten me," Mary cries.

Lincoln will not be stopped. Ten days ago, he begins, "I went to bed late."

Ten days ago he was in City Point, each man and woman in the room calculates. It was the night Lincoln stood alone on the top deck of the *River Queen*, watching Grant's big guns blow the Confederate defenders of Petersburg to hell. "I had been waiting for important dispatches from the front. I could not have been long in bed when I fell into a slumber, for I was weary. I soon began to dream."

In addition to being the consummate public speaker, Lincoln is also a master storyteller. No matter how heavy the weight of the world, he invests himself in a story, adjusting the tone and cadence of his voice and curling his lips into a smile as he weaves his tale, until the listener eventually leans in, desperate to hear more.

But now there is pain in his voice and not a hint of a smile. Lincoln isn't telling a story but reliving an agony. "There seemed to be a deathlike stillness about me. Then I heard subdued sobs, as if a number of people were weeping. I thought I left my bed and wandered downstairs. There the silence was broken by the same pitiful sobbing, but the mourners were invisible. I went from room to room. No living person was in sight, but the same mournful sounds of distress met me as I passed along. It was light in all the rooms. Every object was familiar to me. But where were all the people who were grieving as if their hearts would break? I was puzzled and alarmed. What could be the meaning of all this?"

Lincoln is lost in the world of that dream. Yet his audience, uncomfortable as it may feel, is breathless with anticipation. "Determined to find the cause of a state of things so mysterious and shocking, I kept on until I arrived in the East Room, which I entered. There I was met with a sickening surprise. Before me was a catafalque, on which rested a corpse wrapped in funeral vestments. Around it were stationed soldiers who were acting as guards. And there were a throng of people, some gazing mournfully upon the corpse, whose face was covered, others weeping pitifully. 'Who is dead in the White House?' I demanded of one of the soldiers. 'The President,' was the answer. 'He was killed by an assassin.' Then came a loud burst of grief from the crowd."

Mary can't take it anymore. "That is horrid," she wails. "I wish you had not told it."

Lincoln is pulled back to reality, no longer sound asleep on the *River Queen* but sitting with a somewhat shell-shocked gathering of dignitaries in the here and now. Young Clara Harris, in particular, looks traumatized. "Well it was only a dream, Mary," he chides. "Let us say no more about it."

A moment later, seeing the uneasiness in the room, Lincoln adds, "Don't you see how it will all turn out? In this dream it was not me, but some other fellow that was killed."

His words convince no one, especially not Mary.

CHAPTER TWENTY-TWO

WEDNESDAY, APRIL 12, 1865
WASHINGTON, D.C.
MORNING

After a light breakfast and a night of restless sleep, Booth walks the streets of Washington, his mind filled with the disparate strands of an unfinished plan. The more he walks, the more it all comes together.

It is the morning after Lincoln's speech and the third day since Lee's surrender.

Booth frames every action through the prism of the dramatic, a trait that comes from being born and raised in an acting household. As he builds the assassination scheme in his head, layer by layer, everything from the location to its grandiosity is designed to make him the star performer in an epic scripted tale. His will be the biggest assassination plot ever, and his commanding performance will guarantee him an eternity of recognition.

He knows there will be an audience. By the morning after Lincoln's speech Booth has decided to shoot the president inside a theater, the one place in the world where Booth feels most comfortable. Lincoln is known to attend the theater frequently. In fact, he has seen Booth perform—although Lincoln's presence in the house so angered Booth that he delivered a notably poor performance.

So the theater it will be. Booth has performed at several playhouses in Washington. He knows their hallways and passages by heart. A less informed man might worry about being trapped inside a building with a limited number of exits, no windows, and a crowd of witnesses— many of them able-bodied men just back from the war. But not John Wilkes Booth.

His solitary walk takes him past many such soldiers. The army hasn't been disbanded yet, so they remain in uniform. Even someone as athletic as Booth looks far less rugged than these men who have spent so much time in the open air, their bodies lean and hard from hours on the march. If he thought about it, their familiarity with weapons and hand-to-hand combat would terrify Booth, with his choreographed stage fights and peashooter pistol.

But Booth is not scared of these men. In fact, he wants to linger for a moment at center stage. With the stage lights shining down on his handsome features, clutching a dagger with "America, Land of the Free" inscribed on the blade, he plans to spend what will surely be the last seconds of his acting career making a political statement. *"Sic semper tyrannis,"* he will bellow in his most vibrant thespian delivery: Thus always to tyrants.

∽

The dagger is useless as a stage prop. Booth has no specific plans to use it, knowing that if he fires a shot from a few feet away and it misses, there will be no chance to run at Lincoln and stab him. He has borrowed the idea from Shakespeare's *Julius Caesar*, which he performed six months earlier on Broadway with his two actor brothers, both of whom he despises. Booth, ironically, played Marc Antony, a character whose life is spared from a potential assassin.

Those performances provided Booth with his inspiration about the ides. In Roman times it was a day of reckoning.

The ides are tomorrow.

Booth walks faster, energized by the awareness that he hasn't much time.

He must find out whether Lincoln will be attending the theater tomorrow night and, if so, which one. He must find out which play is being performed, so that he can select just the right moment in the show for the execution—a moment with few actors on stage, if possible, so that when he stops to utter his immortal line there won't be a crowd to tackle him. The details of his escape are still fuzzy, but the basic plan is to gallop out of Washington on horseback and disappear into the loving arms of the South, where friends and allies and even complete strangers who have heard of his daring deed will see that he makes it safely to Mexico.

But that's not all.

There are rumors that General Grant will be in town. If he attends the theater with Lincoln, which is a very real possibility, Booth can kill the two most prominent architects of the South's demise within seconds.

And yet Booth wants even more. He has been an agent of the Confederacy for a little less than a year and has had long conversations with the leaders of the Confederate Secret Service and men like John Surratt, discussing what must be done to topple the Union. He has, at his disposal, a small cadre of like-minded men prepared to do his bidding. He personally witnessed the northern crowd's malice toward the South at Lincoln's speech last night. Rather than just kill Lincoln and Grant, he now plans to do nothing less than undertake a top-down destruction of the government of the United States of America.

❦

Vice President Andrew Johnson is an obvious target. He is first in line to the presidency, lives at a nearby hotel, and is completely unguarded. Like all Confederate sympathizers, Booth views the Tennessee politician as a turncoat for siding with Lincoln.

Secretary of State William H. Seward, whose oppressive policies toward the South have long made him a target of Confederate wrath, is on the list as well.

The deaths of Lincoln, Grant, Johnson, and Seward should be more than enough to cause anarchy.

To Lewis Powell, the former Confederate spy who watched Lincoln's speech with Booth, will go the task of killing Secretary Seward, who, at age sixty-three, is currently bedridden, after a near-fatal carriage accident. He was traveling through Washington with his son Frederick and daughter Fanny when the horses bolted. While reaching for the reins to try to stop them, Seward caught the heel of one of

Vice President Andrew Johnson   *Secretary of State William H. Seward*

his new shoes on the carriage step and was hurled from the cab, hitting the street so hard that bystanders thought he'd been killed. Secretary Seward has been confined to his bed for a week with severe injuries and is on an around-the-clock course of pain medication. Seward has trouble speaking; he has no chance of leaping from the bed to elude a surprise attack.

Powell's job should be as simple as sneaking into the Seward home, shooting the sleeping secretary in bed, then galloping away to join Booth for a life of sunshine and easy living in Mexico.

For the job of killing Johnson, Booth selects a simpleton drifter named George Atzerodt, a German carriage repairer with a sallow complexion and a fondness for drink. To him will go the job of assassinating the vice president at the exact same moment Booth is killing Lincoln. Atzerodt, however, still thinks the plan is to kidnap Lincoln. He was brought into the plot for his encyclopedic knowledge of the smuggling routes from Washington, D.C., into the Deep South. Booth suspects that Atzerodt may be unwilling to go along with the new plan. Should that be the case, Booth has a foolproof plan in mind to blackmail Atzerodt into going along.

Booth has seen co-conspirators come and go since last August. Right now he has three: Powell, Atzerodt, and David Herold, the Georgetown graduate who also accompanied Booth on the night of Lincoln's speech. One would imagine that each man would be assigned a murder victim. Logically, Herold's job would be to kill Secretary of War Edwin M. Stanton, the man who trampled the Constitution by helping Lincoln suspend the writ of habeas corpus and did more than any other to treat the South like a bastard child. Stanton is the second-most-powerful man in Washington, but in the end no assassin is trained on him. Instead, Herold will act as the dim-witted Powell's guide, leading his escape out of Washington in the dead of night.

Why was the secretary of war spared?

⟋⟍

The answer may come from a shadowy figure named Lafayette Baker. Early in the war, Baker distinguished himself as a Union spy. Secretary of State William Seward hired him to investigate Confederate communications that were being routed through Maryland. Baker's success in this role saw him promoted to the War Department, where Secretary of War Edwin Stanton gave him full power to create an organization known as the National Detective Police. This precursor to the Secret Service was a counterterrorism unit tasked with seeking out Confederate spy networks in Canada, New York, and Washington.

But Lafayette Baker was a shifty character, with loyalties undefined, except for his love of money and of himself, though not necessarily in that order. Secretary Stanton soon grew weary of him, so Baker returned to New York City. His movements during this time are murky, as befitting a man who thinks himself a spy, but one elaborate theory ties together his activities with those of John Wilkes Booth. This theory suggests that Baker worked as an agent for a Canadian outfit known as the J. J. Chaffey Company. Baker received payments totaling almost $150,000 from that firm, an unheard-of sum at the time. The J. J. Chaffey Company also paid John Wilkes Booth nearly $15,000 between August 24 and October 5, 1864. He was paid in gold, credited to the Bank of Montreal. In the same month the last payment was made to him, Booth traveled to Montreal to collect the

Lafayette C. Baker

money and rendezvous with John Surratt and other members of the Confederate Secret Service to plot the Lincoln issue.

The common thread in the several mysterious payments and missives involving Baker and Booth is the mailing address 178½ Water Street. This location, quite mysteriously, is referenced in several documents surrounding payments between the J. J. Chaffey Company, Baker, and Booth.

To this day, no one has discovered why the J. J. Chaffey Company paid Lafayette Baker and John Wilkes Booth for anything. A few clues exist, including a telegram sent on April 2, 1865, the very same day on which Lincoln stood atop the deck of the *River Queen* to watch the fall of Petersburg. A telegram was sent from 178½ Water Street to a company in Chicago. "J. W. Booth will ship oysters until Saturday 15th," it reads, intimating that Booth, a man who never worked a day in his life in the shipping or the oyster business, was involved in some kind of project that was totally inappropriate for his skills. And yet no one has been able to conclusively determine what the telegram alluded to.

Lafayette Baker freely admitted that he had tapped Secretary of War Stanton's telegraph lines, though he never explained why he did what he did. Baker would have known that if Lincoln were assassinated, ascension to the presidency could eventually fall to Stanton— the man who opposed Lincoln's candidacy in 1860. The United States has had a succession plan in place since 1792, with the vice president replacing the fallen president, as when Zachary Taylor died in office and was succeeded by Millard Fillmore. If a more elaborate assassination plot were hatched, one that killed Vice President Andrew Johnson and Secretary of State William Seward along with President Lincoln, a skilled constitutional scholar like Edwin Stanton could attempt to manipulate the process in his favor—and perhaps even become president. This connection between Baker, Booth, and Stanton continues to intrigue and befuddle scholars. Why was Baker, a spy, paid an exorbitant amount for his services? And why did John Wilkes Booth secure a healthy payment from the same company?

Clues such as this point to Stanton's involvement, but no concrete connection has ever been proven. Circumstantially, he was involved. Secretary Stanton employed Baker, who was in regular contact with Surratt and Booth. Some historians believe that Stanton fired Baker as a cover and that the two remained in close contact.

Or so the elaborate theory goes.

Whether or not that is true, Stanton will be the sole reason that Baker's role in the dramatic events of April 1865 is hardly over.

✍

Booth is satisfied that his plan is simple enough that the synchronized slayings will not tax the mental capacities of his underlings. Now all he needs to do is find Lincoln.

The odds of the Lincolns' remaining in the White House on such an auspicious night of celebration are almost nonexistent. The president and Mrs. Lincoln are known to be fond of the theater and prone to making their public appearances in such a venue. They will be either there or at one of the many parties being held to celebrate the city's Grand Illumination.

If it is to be an Illumination party, Booth will canvass the city's notable residences for signs of a celebration. Once the president is located, the next step will be waiting for a moment when he is unguarded, whereupon Booth can use his celebrity to gain entrance and then shoot him.

If it is to be the theater, the obvious choices are either the Grover or Ford's, both of which are staging lavish productions. Booth must reacquaint himself with their floor plans so that when the moment comes he can act without thinking.

Booth turns the corner onto Pennsylvania Avenue. First stop: Grover's Theater. The assassination will be tomorrow.

CHAPTER TWENTY-THREE

Inside the White House, just a few blocks from where John Wilkes Booth is walking the streets, a beaming Mary Lincoln holds a slim leather-bound copy of *Julius Caesar.* She is in a good mood for a change, and the new book is certainly helping her disposition. The president will be thrilled by her purchase. This is most important to Mary Lincoln. Even in her lowest moods, she craves the attention and affection of her husband.

Lincoln's fondness for all things Shakespeare is well known. While he enjoys lowbrow entertainment, like the comedian Barney Williams, who performs in blackface, he never misses the chance to attend a Shakespearean tragedy. During one two-month span in the winter of 1864, he saw *Richard III, The Merchant of Venice, Hamlet,* and, of course, *Julius Caesar.*

The actor playing all the lead roles was Edwin Booth, John's older brother. In addition to his acting, he did the Lincolns an inadvertent favor by saving the life of their eldest son. When twenty-year-old Union officer Robert Todd Lincoln was shoved from a crowded railway platform into the path of an oncoming train, it was Edwin Booth who snatched him by the coat collar and pulled him back to safety.

Robert never mentioned the incident to his father, but his commanding officer, Ulysses S. Grant, personally wrote a letter of thanks to
the actor. Edwin's brother's reaction to this incident has never been
determined—if he knew at all. This is the second remarkable coincidence linking Robert Todd Lincoln to John Wilkes Booth, the first
being his infatuation with Lucy Hale, Booth's fiancée.

Robert is due back in Washington any day, as is Grant. Lincoln's
spirits will soar at the sight of both men, but in the meantime Mary
cannot wait to see his face light up when she presents him with *Julius
Caesar.*

Lincoln is fond of two books more than any other: the Bible and
Shakespeare's collected works. Like his dog-eared Bible, Lincoln's
volume of Shakespeare has become frayed and worn over the years.
This brand-new copy of *Julius Caesar* will certainly keep the president's mood upbeat, which, in turn, will do wonders for Mary's morale.
Their euphorias and depressions are so closely intertwined that it's
hard to say which one's emotional peaks and valleys influence the
other more.

∽

Lincoln is not at the White House right now. He's taken a walk over to
the War Department, where he sits on a comfortable sofa, hard at
work on the business of healing the nation. His first test is immediate.
The Virginia legislature is about to convene in Richmond. These are
the same elected representatives who once voted to leave the Union.
Now this "rebel legislature" will meet in the giant columned building
designed by Thomas Jefferson, determined to rebuild the shattered
state and return it to its former glory.

On the surface, this is a good thing. Lincoln himself urged the legislature to convene during a visit to Richmond the previous week, saying that "the prominent and influential men of their respective counties
should come together and undo their own work."

Secretary of War Edwin Stanton, the brilliant Ohio lawyer who
is for whatever reason not on Booth's list of targets, and in whose
office Lincoln now sits, is strongly opposed. He tells Lincoln that to
"place such powers in the Virginia legislature would be giving away
the scepter of the conqueror, that it would transfer the result of the

Secretary of War Edwin M. Stanton

victory of our arms to the very legislature which four years before said, 'give us war.'"

Lincoln disagrees. He is reluctant to see the United States Army turned into an occupying force, policing the actions of legislatures throughout the South. But he also realizes that by allowing Virginia's lawmakers to meet without close Federal observation, he is setting a dangerous precedent. There would be nothing to stop other southern states from passing laws that conspire against the Federal government—in effect, keeping the Confederacy's ideals alive.

Stanton and Lincoln were once sworn rivals, two opinionated and charismatic midwesterners who came to Washington with their own personal visions of what the country needed. They are physical opposites—Stanton's stump to Lincoln's beanpole. Stanton didn't vote for Lincoln in 1860, but that didn't stop the president from crossing party lines to name him secretary of war. Lincoln's low wartime popularity was matched only by that of Stanton, who was relentless in his prosecution of any Union officer concealing Confederate sympathies.

"He is the rock on the beach of our national ocean against which the breakers dash and roar, dash and roar without ceasing," Lincoln once said of Stanton. "I do not see how he survives, why he is not crushed and torn to pieces. Without him I should be destroyed."

As General Sam Grant glibly described Stanton: "He was an able constitutional lawyer and jurist, but the Constitution was not an impediment to him while the war lasted."

Stanton, with a graying beard extending halfway down his chest, has the sort of strong-willed personality that terrifies timid souls. The Civil War may be over, but Lincoln has made it clear that the secretary of war will be instrumental in helping the country rebuild. He trusts Stanton's counsel and uses him as a sounding board when tough decisions like this must be made. In many ways, Stanton does not behave as if he is subordinate to Lincoln. He expresses himself without fear of edit or censure, knowing that while Lincoln has strong opinions of his own, he is a good listener who can be swayed by a solid argument.

Now Stanton paces before the couch where Lincoln reclines, compiling his detailed argument against allowing the Virginia legislature to meet. He warns of the laws that might be passed, limiting the freedom of former slaves. He notes that the legislature has proven itself to be untrustworthy. And he reminds Lincoln that during his recent visit to Richmond the president made it clear that the Virginia lawmakers were being given only conditional authority—but that these same untrustworthy men are surely capable of ignoring those limits once they convene.

At last, Stanton explains his idea for temporary military governments in the southern states until order can be restored.

Lincoln doesn't speak until Stanton finishes. Almost every single one of Stanton's opinions runs contrary to Lincoln's. Nonetheless, Lincoln hears Stanton out, then lets his thoughts percolate.

As Stanton looks on, Lincoln slowly rises off the couch and draws himself up to his full, towering height. He walks to the great oak desk near the window, where he silently composes a telegram withdrawing permission for the Virginia legislature to meet. For those representatives who have already traveled to Richmond for the session, he guarantees safe passage home.

Lincoln hands the telegram to Stanton, whose thick beard cannot hide his look of satisfaction after he finishes reading. Calling the wording "exactly right," he hands the telegram to his clerk.

⁓

During the course of the Civil War, Lincoln's use of telegrams—his "t-mail"—made him the first leader in world history to communicate immediately with his generals on the battlefield. He has sent, literally, thousands of these messages through the Department of War. This is his last.

On the walk back to the White House, Lincoln composes another sort of note in his head. It is to Mary, a simple invitation to go for a carriage ride on Friday afternoon. His words are playful and romantic, a reminder of the way things were before the war, and before the death of Willie. Their eldest son, Robert, is due home from the war any day. Surely, the cloud of melancholy that has hovered over the Lincolns is about to lift.

CHAPTER TWENTY-FOUR

The ides. As Booth takes the train to Baltimore, hoping to reenlist a former conspirator for that night's expected executions, General Ulysses S. Grant and his wife, Julia, arrive in Washington at dawn. They have taken an overnight boat from City Point, Virginia. Grant is in no mood to be there. He is eager to push on to New Jersey to see their four children, but Secretary of War Stanton has specifically requested that the general visit the capital and handle a number of war-related issues. Grant's plan is to get in and get out within twenty-four hours, with as little fuss as possible. With him are his aide Colonel Horace Porter and two sergeants to manage the Grants' luggage.

Little does Grant know that an adoring Washington, D.C., is waiting to wrap its arms around him. "As we reached our destination that bright morning in our boat," Julia later exclaimed, "every gun in and near Washington burst forth—and such a salvo!—all the bells rang out merry greetings, and the city was literally swathed in flags and bunting."

If anything, Grant is even more beloved than the president right now. Strangers cheer the Grants' open-air carriage on its way to the Willard Hotel, on the corner of Pennsylvania Avenue and Fourteenth Street. As

Julia Grant

they pull up to the entrance, workers are on the roof, installing the gas jets that will spell out UNION for that evening's Grand Illumination—a mass lighting of every candle, gas lamp, and firework in the city. Thousands upon thousands of people are now streaming into Washington to witness what will be an attempt to turn night into day as yet another celebration of war's end.

Grant, who has seen more than his share of fiery explosions, could not care less about the Illumination. Their journey has been an odyssey, and the Grants are exhausted. Since leaving Lee at Appomattox, Grant has endured two days of train derailments, another day waiting for a steamer in City Point, and then the dawn-to-dusk journey up the Potomac. But standing beside his beloved Julia revives Grant.

They have been a couple for more than twenty years and have endured many a long separation, thanks to the military life. It was

Julia's letters that sustained him during the Mexican War, when he was a homesick young lieutenant. And it was Julia who stood by her husband's side during the 1850s, when he was discharged from the army and failed in a succession of businesses. They are happiest in each other's company. Both are still young—he is not quite forty-three; she is thirty-nine. They have their whole lives in front of them. The sooner they can flee Washington, D.C., and get back to normal life, the better. And right now that means getting to their room, washing up, and letting the general race over to the War Department as quickly as possible.

There's just one problem: the Grants don't have a reservation at the Willard.

∽

Grant has slept so many nights in impromptu battlefield lodgings procured on the fly by his staff that it never crossed his mind to send a telegram asking for a room. What he wants, he tells the flustered desk clerk, is a simple bedroom with an adjacent sitting room. It's understood that Colonel Porter will need a room, too. The sergeants will bunk elsewhere.

The Willard Hotel is overbooked. Yet to allow the famous Ulysses S. Grant to take a room elsewhere would be an unthinkable loss of prestige.

Some way, somehow, rooms are instantly made available. Within minutes, Julia is unpacking their suitcases. Word about their location is already flying around Washington, and bundles of congratulatory telegrams and flowers soon flood the desk and bedroom. Julia will spend the afternoon reading each one, basking in the awareness that the man whose potential she had seen so long before, when he was just a quiet young lieutenant, has ascended from anonymity and disgrace to the level of great historical figure.

Not that General Grant cares. He just wants to get on with his business and get home. Within minutes, he and Porter meet in the lobby before the short walk to the War Department. It's three blocks, just on the other side of the White House.

The two men step out onto Pennsylvania Avenue. At first the trek is easy, just two regular guys in uniform joining the sea of pedestrians, soldiers, and all those tourists pouring into the city for the Illumination. But Grant is hard to miss. Pictures of his bearded, expressionless face have been on the front pages of newspapers for more than a year. Soon the autograph seekers and the well-wishers, startled but elated by his presence, surround him. Porter tries to push them back, protecting his general in peacetime as he did in warfare. But he is just one man against many, and the diminutive Grant is swallowed by the mob. Porter pushes and elbows, grabbing Grant with one arm while shoving people back with the other. It's a benevolent crowd, cheering for Grant even as they strain to touch him. But Porter knows a simple truth: this is a perfect opportunity for a disgruntled southerner to take a shot at Grant, then disappear in an instant.

Just when the situation begins to border on pandemonium, the Metropolitan Police come to their rescue. Grant and Porter are soon on their way again, this time inside a carriage, with a cavalry escort.

An introvert, Grant is pained by the attention and stares. Once inside the War Department, he hurries to formally conclude the logistics of war. Pen in hand and cigar clenched in his teeth, he tells the quartermaster general to stop ordering supplies and suspends the draft and further recruitment. With these orders, he saves the nation $4 million per day.

Though Grant hates public appearances, the city of Washington has planned the Grand Illumination celebration for this very night, specifically so he can be there. The Capitol dome will be lit, the Willard Hotel will illuminate the word UNION, and the governmental buildings are having a competition to see which can be the most brilliantly decorated. Stanton is fussing over the War Department's display, which includes guns and flags as well as lights, while over at the Patent Office some five thousand candles will glow from every window. There will also be a massive fireworks display. And, of course, the bonfires that have blazed all week will still be burning bright. As intensely as Washington celebrated on Monday, Thursday night's Grand Illumination will be even more monumental.

That afternoon, Grant meets with Lincoln at the White House. The last time they met was the day after Petersburg fell, on that veranda in the midst of that shattered city. There, Grant promised Lincoln that he would catch Lee and end the war. Now that Grant has fulfilled that promise, a grateful Lincoln offers his congratulations. He calls for a carriage. The two men ride around the crowded streets of Washington with the top down, shocking the flood of arriving visitors, who can't believe that they are actually laying eyes on President Lincoln and General Grant. The ride is Lincoln's way of giving Grant his moment in the sun after so many months of being second-guessed and labeled a butcher and of deflecting the glory showered upon him onto the man whose genius made it all possible.

It works. The two men are loudly cheered on every street corner.

When it is done, they make plans to meet again that night for the Illumination. They will be the center of attention, these two men who won the Civil War, watched by one and all.

Meanwhile, John Wilkes Booth and his band of assassins tend to their work of sharpening knives and cleaning their pistols, eager for their night of reckoning.

CHAPTER TWENTY-FIVE

The four conspirators squeeze into room 6 at the Herndon House hotel, a few blocks from the White House. Booth, David Herold, Lewis Powell, and George Atzerodt lounge on the chairs and perch on the edge of the bed as Booth talks them through the plan. His recruiting trip to Baltimore was unsuccessful. He is too agitated to sit, so he paces as he thinks out loud. The wooden floor becomes a stage, and his oration a performance that takes him from stage left to stage right, then back to stage left again as he breaks down the plan. The parties outside are neither a distraction nor an offense, but a reminder of why they have gathered. Logically, each man knows that there must be plenty of Confederate sympathizers in Washington, huddled in their homes with jaws clenched as they endure the revelry. But right now the would-be assassins feel that they are the only ones who can right the grievous wrong.

Lewis Powell is the youngest and most experienced of the conspirators. He is a tall, powerfully built, and otherwise very handsome man—save for his face being deformed on one side, thanks to a mule's kick. Unlike the others, Powell has actually killed a man, and may have enjoyed it very much. During the war the Floridian fought in several major battles, was wounded at Gettysburg, successfully escaped from a prisoner-of-war camp, and worked for the Confederate Secret Service. He is a solid horseman and quick with a knife. Thanks to his military training, Powell knows the value of reconnaissance. He prepped for his attack that morning by walking past Secretary of State Seward's home on Madison Place, scoping out the best possible ways in and out of the building. He boldly struck up a conversation with Seward's male nurse, just to make sure the secretary was indeed at home.

The reconnaissance is good news for Booth. He thus knows the location of two of the intended victims. Now it is his job to find Lincoln. An afternoon talking to stage managers had led to the inescapable conclusion that Lincoln is not going to the theater tonight. Booth, it seems, will not have his grand theatrical moment. Much to his dismay, it appears as if shooting Lincoln will be as mundane as putting a bullet into his brain on a crowded street during the Grand Illumination and then running like hell.

∽

It finally dawns on one very drunk George Atzerodt that the plan has shifted from kidnapping to murder. The only reason he joined the conspiracy was that, in addition to running a small carriage-repair business in Port Tobacco, Maryland, he moonlights as a smuggler, ferrying mail, contraband, and people across the broad Potomac into Virginia. It is a hardscrabble and often dangerous existence. Atzerodt's role in the kidnapping was to be an act of commerce, not rebellion. He was to be paid handsomely to smuggle the bound-and-gagged Lincoln into the hands of the Confederates.

But there is no longer a Confederacy, no longer a kidnapping plot, no longer a need for a boat, and certainly no longer a need for a smuggler—at least in Atzerodt's mind. The thirty-year-old German immigrant slurs that he wants out.

Booth calmly springs his blackmail.

Booth cannot do without Atzerodt. His boat and his knowledge of the Potomac's currents are vital to their escape. A massive manhunt will surely begin the instant Lincoln is killed. Federal officials will seal off Washington, D.C., and canvass the Maryland and Virginia countryside, but with Atzerodt's guidance Booth and his men will rush through rural Maryland ahead of the search parties, cross the Potomac, and then follow smugglers' routes south to Mexico.

Booth has rehearsed for this moment. He knows his lines and recites them with great drama.

"Then *we* will do it," Booth says, nodding at Herold and Powell, never taking his eyes off the drunk German. "But what will come of you?"

And then, as if pulling the solution out of thin air: "You had better come along and get your horse."

At the word "horse," Atzerodt's heart skips a beat. He's trapped. Booth long ago suggested that the two men share horses from time to time. The horse a man rides is part of his identity. By sharing Booth's favorite horse—which seemed like such a simple and thoughtful gesture on the actor's part all those weeks ago—Atzerodt is now visibly connected to the assassination plot. Atzerodt has ridden Booth's horse all over Washington and has even helped him sell a few animals; so there will be no shortage of witnesses.

Atzerodt sighs and nods his head. Murder it is. There is no way out for him.

The time has come. The four men stand, aware that they are about to commit the greatest crime in the history of the United States.

⁓

Before opening the door, Booth reminds them that their post-assassination rendezvous point is the road to Nanjemoy, on the Maryland side of the Potomac. Normally the sight of a lone horseman galloping out of Washington, D.C., long after dark would make the sentries guarding the bridges suspicious. But tonight is not a normal night. All those folks who've come into Washington for the Illumination will be making their way back home when it's all done. Booth and his men will easily blend in with the same drunken bleating masses who are now making that wretched noise on the streets outside room 6.

If for some reason they can't do the job tonight, they will remain in Washington and try again tomorrow.

Booth shakes hands with each man. They leave one at a time and go their separate ways.

CHAPTER TWENTY-SIX

There once was a fifth conspirator, the one Booth traveled to Baltimore to corral the day before. Mike O'Laughlen, a former Confederate soldier who grew up across the street from Booth, was one of the first men recruited by him last August. Just a month earlier the two men had lain in wait together for a certain carriage making its way down the lonely country road to the Soldiers' Home, only to find that its occupant was a Supreme Court justice instead of the president.

Hiding in the tall grass along the side of the road, O'Laughlen had weighed the repercussions of actually kidnapping the president of the United States and realized that he would hang by the neck until dead if caught. He was actually relieved that the carriage belonged to Salmon P. Chase instead of Lincoln.

The twenty-four-year-old engraver returned to Baltimore and put the kidnapping plot behind him. He wanted a normal life. When Booth came calling a week later with an even more far-fetched plot to kidnap the president by handcuffing him at the theater and then lowering his body to the stage, O'Laughlen shook his head and told Booth to go away.

But Booth is nothing if not relentless. In Baltimore, he tried to convince O'Laughlen to rejoin the conspiracy. O'Laughlen told the actor he didn't want any part of the killing. Yet the same day he apparently changed his mind, and he traveled to Washington a short time later. O'Laughlen started drinking the minute he arrived, bellying up to the bar at a place called Rullman's until his behavior became erratic. Like Booth, who now prowls Washington in the desperate hope of finding Lincoln, O'Laughlen prowls the bustling thoroughfares, unsure of what to do next.

Meanwhile, General Sam Grant, whose idea of a stellar evening is chain-smoking cigars and sipping whiskey, would be very happy staying in for the evening. But as Julia points out, General and Mrs. Grant have not attended a party together for quite some time. Sitting in their room on this very special night, no matter how luxurious the accommodations, would be a waste. Julia shows her husband invitation after invitation to party after party. She is thrilled to be in the city but also eager to leave as soon as possible to rejoin their four children. Knowing that they have perhaps just this one night in Washington, Grant agrees that they should venture out.

Reluctantly, Grant leaves the hotel. They engage a carriage to take them to the home of Secretary of War Stanton, who is holding a gala celebration for War Department employees. Four brass bands serenade the partygoers from nearby Franklin Square, and a fireworks demonstration will cap the night.

Grant has been a target ever since he took command of Lincoln's army. But even with all the people in the streets he is unafraid. The war is over.

The Grants arrive at Stanton's home. A bodyguard stands at the top of the steps, one of the few the general has encountered in Washington. The Grants are greeted with a loud round of applause as they join the partygoers, but they are soon lost in the sea of other prominent faces. Grant gets a drink and settles in to endure the politicking and glad-handing soon to head his way.

But the Grants have been followed. Mike O'Laughlen, wearing a dark suit, marches up the front steps of Stanton's house and tries to crash the party. The sergeant providing security brushes him off, telling the unwanted guest, "If you wish to see him, step out on the pavement, or the stone where the carriage stops."

O'Laughlen disappears into the night, only to return later asking to see Secretary Stanton. Coincidentally, Stanton and Grant are both standing just a few feet away, watching the fireworks. There is still something of the conspirator in O'Laughlen, a willingness to take risks where others might not. He takes a bold gamble, blends in with the crowd, and slips undetected into the party, despite the security detail. He then goes one better by walking over and standing directly behind Stanton.

But Mike O'Laughlen does nothing to harm the secretary of war. Nor does he bother Grant. The fact is, he doesn't know what Stanton looks like, and as a former Confederate soldier with a deep respect for rank, he is too nervous to speak with Grant.

Observers will later remember the drunk in the dark coat and suggest that his intentions were to kill the general and the secretary. Nothing could be further from the truth: the surprising fact is that O'Laughlen is actually here to warn them about Booth. But even after all those drinks, Mike O'Laughlen still can't summon the courage. He thinks of the repercussions and how if he informs on Booth, his childhood friend will most surely reveal the story about the kidnapping attempt four weeks earlier. That admission would mean the same jail sentence—or even execution—for O'Laughlen as for Booth.

No. Nothing good can come of telling Stanton or Grant a single detail of the plot. Mike O'Laughlen disappears into the night and drinks himself blind.

Meanwhile, a crowd gathers in front of Stanton's home. For all his attempts at avoiding the limelight, word of Grant's location has spread throughout the city. Cries of "Speech!" rock the night air, his admirers thoroughly unaware that Grant is terrified of public speaking.

Stanton comes to the rescue. Never afraid of expressing himself, the secretary throws out a few bon mots to pacify his audience. Grant says nothing, but the combination of a small wave to the crowd and Stanton's spontaneous words are enough to satiate Grant's fans. Soon the sidewalks are bare.

On the other side of town, John Wilkes Booth steps back into the National Hotel, frustrated and tired from hours of walking bar to bar, party to party, searching for Lincoln. The Deringer rests all too heavily in his coat pocket, in its barrel the single unfired round that could have changed the course of history. There has been no news of any other assassinations, so he can only assume that his conspirators have also failed—and he is right. Herold, Atzerodt, and Powell were all unable to conquer their fears long enough to cross the line from fanatic to assassin.

Perhaps tomorrow.

One mile away, in his White House bedroom, Abraham Lincoln slumbers peacefully. A migraine has kept him in for the night.

Hopefully that will not be the case tomorrow evening, for the Lincolns have plans to attend the theater.

Part Three

THE LONG GOOD FRIDAY

The last known photograph of Lincoln,
February 1865

CHAPTER TWENTY-SEVEN

I t is Good Friday morning, the day on which Jesus Christ was cru-
cified, died an agonizing death, and was quickly buried. All of this
after he had been betrayed by Judas and scorned by a public that
had lionized him just days before.

Abraham Lincoln is a religious man but not a churchgoer. He
was born into a Christian home in the wilderness, where established
churches were rare. His father and mother were staunch "hard-shell"
Baptists, and at a young age he attended the Pigeon Creek Baptist
Church. Lincoln's church attendance became sporadic in his adult
life. Nevertheless, he took comfort in reading the Bible on a daily
basis and often used the words of God to make important points in
his public pronouncements. Indeed, his faith has grown because of
the war. But because Lincoln never attached himself to an organized
religion as an adult, his ability to combine the secular and the religious in the way he goes about his life will later have everyone from
atheists to humanists to Calvinists claiming that he is one of theirs.
The truth is, Abraham Lincoln does believe in God and has relied on
Scripture in overcoming all the challenges he has confronted.

Lincoln rises at seven A.M. Outside the White House, the Washington weather is a splendid, sunny fifty degrees. Dogwoods are blooming

along the Potomac and the scent of spring lilacs carries on the morning breeze as the president throws his size 14 feet over the edge of the
bed, slides them into a pair of battered slippers, pulls on an equally
weathered robe, pushes open the rosewood bedroom door, says good
morning to his night watchman, and walks down a second-floor hallway to the White House library. The quiet night at home has been
good for his soul. Lincoln's sleep was restful. All symptoms of his
migraine have disappeared.

Petitioners sleeping in the White House hallway leap to their
feet upon the sight of Lincoln. They have come seeking presidential
favors—a pardon, a job, an appointment. The president is courteous
but evasive at their shouted requests, eager to be alone in the quiet of
the library. That strangers actually sleep on the White House floor
is commonplace at the time. "The multitude, washed or unwashed,
always has free egress and ingress" into the White House, an astonished visitor wrote earlier in Lincoln's presidency.

The White House's open-door policy ends today.

✍

The president's favorite chair is in the exact center of the room. He sits
down and opens his Bible, not because it is Good Friday but because
starting the day with Scripture is a lifelong custom. Glasses balanced
on the end of his prominent nose, he reads a verse, then another, before
setting the Good Book on a side table. He leans back in the chair to
meditate, enjoying the only quiet and solitary moments he will know
this day.

Lincoln traipses down the hall to his office. His desk is mahogany,
with cubbies and shelves. Behind him is the willow-lined Potomac,
seen clearly outside the window.

Secretaries John Nicolay and John Hay have laid the mail on
the desk, having already removed the love letters Lincoln sometimes
receives from young ladies, and the assassination letters more often
sent by older men. Typically, the president gets almost three hundred
letters a day, of which he reads only a half dozen, at most.

Lincoln skims the mail, then jots down a few notes. Each is signed
"A. Lincoln" if it is of a more official nature, or just "Yours truly," as in
the case of his note to William Seward. The secretary of state continues

to recover from his horrible accident, his jaw and shattered skull mending slowly. Now he lies in bed at home, a convenient stone's throw across the street from the White House.

Breakfast is scheduled for eight o'clock. Lincoln finishes his brief business and enters a small room, where he grooms himself. Daily baths and showers are rare, even in the White House. Lincoln is eager to be downstairs, for his son Robert is just back from the war and will be joining him, twelve-year-old Tad, and Mary for breakfast. More importantly, Robert was in the room when Lee surrendered at Appomattox. Though Lincoln heard the story from Grant yesterday, he is keen to hear more about this landmark event. The war's end is one topic he never gets tired of talking about.

Just twenty-one, with a thin mustache and a captain's rank, Robert is still boyish, despite his time at the front. As Lincoln sips coffee and eats the single boiled egg that constitutes his daily breakfast, Robert describes "the stately elegant Lee" and Grant, "the small stooping shabby shy man in the muddy blue uniform, with no sword and no spurs."

When Lincoln asks what it was like to be there, his son is breathless. "Oh, it was great!" the normally articulate Robert exclaims, unable to find a more expressive way to describe being present at one of the seminal moments in American history.

Robert hands Lincoln a portrait of Lee. The president lays it on the table, where it stares up at him. Lincoln tells his son that he truly believes the time of peace has come. He is unfazed by the small but bitter Confederate resistance that remains. His thoughts are far away from the likes of John Wilkes Booth.

∽

Pressing business awaits Lincoln in his office, but he allows breakfast to stretch on for almost an hour. He can permit himself this luxury, with the war finally over. At last he stands, his body stooped, now just an inch or two less than the towering height of his youth. He is relaxed and happy, even though his severe weight loss makes him look like "a skeleton with clothes," in the words of one friend.

Lincoln reminds Mary that they have a date for a carriage ride this afternoon. To Robert, he suggests that the time has come to remove the uniform, return to Harvard, and spend the next three years working on his law degree. "At the end of that time I hope we will be able to tell if you will make a good lawyer or not," he concludes, sounding more serious than he feels. The words are a sign that he is mentally transitioning from the easy part of his day into those long office hours when, even with the war concluded, the weight of the world presses down on his shoulders.

By nine A.M., President Lincoln is sitting at his desk.

Every aspect of Lincoln's early morning has the feel of a man putting his affairs in order: reading the Bible, jotting a few notes, arranging for a last carefree whirl around Washington with his loyal wife, and setting his son on a path that will ensure him a successful future. All of this is done unconsciously, of course, but it is notable.

Even if it is not mentioned on this day in the White House, the potential assassination of the president is a topic of discussion in and around Washington. The chattering class doesn't know when it might occur, but many believe an attempt will come very soon.

"To those familiar with the city of Washington," a member of his cavalry detail will later write, "it was not surprising that Lincoln was assassinated. The surprising thing to them was that it was so long delayed. It is probable that the only man in Washington who, if he thought upon the subject of all, did not think that Mr. Lincoln was in constant and imminent danger, was Mr. Lincoln himself."

But today it is as if Lincoln subconsciously knows what is about to happen.

A mile down Pennsylvania Avenue, the man who *does* know what is about to happen is also setting his affairs in order.

CHAPTER TWENTY-EIGHT

FRIDAY, APRIL 14, 1865
WASHINGTON, D.C.
9:00 A.M.

John Wilkes Booth walks slowly down the hotel corridor, momentarily at a loss for words. He has come to say good-bye to his beloved Lucy. He struggles to think of a way to break off their secret engagement and intimate that he might never see her again. Even though their relationship has been all but dead since Newport, of all the terrible things he must do today, what he is about to do next breaks his heart like no other.

The Hales are living in the National Hotel, on the corner of Pennsylvania and Sixth. Booth lives in the same hotel, room 228. Lucy does charity work for the Sanitation Committee and even rode to the front lines of nearby battlefields to visit the troops. It's well known that her father wishes her to marry someone powerful and well connected. For Lucy to not only slink off to the room of an actor but also agree to marry him would enrage Senator Hale. So while the relationship has slowly become more public, she and Booth have kept their pending nuptials a secret.

It's nine A.M. when Booth knocks on her door. He wears a ring she gave him as a keepsake. Booth has the eccentric habit of kissing the ring absentmindedly when out drinking with friends, and he does so now, as he nervously waits for her to answer. This will be the last time he'll see her for quite a while—perhaps forever. Lucy's father has been appointed ambassador to Spain, and the entire family will accompany him abroad. Booth plans to escape to Mexico after shooting Lincoln and then perhaps sail to Spain for a clandestine visit with Lucy if all goes well.

But how to say good-bye? How to make the next few moments as touching and romantic as any farewell should be, while also not letting her know he's leaving and why?

∽

Their relationship began in 1862. Booth became enchanted after glimpsing her in a crowd and sent Lucy an anonymous Valentine's Day love letter. This was followed shortly afterward by another missive, revealing his identity. If its intended effect was to make twenty-one-year-old Lucy swoon, it worked. Booth was at the height of his fame and good looks, delighting women across the country with his performance as the male lead in a traveling production of *Romeo and Juliet*. One actress even tried to kill herself after he rebuffed her advances.

But Lucy Lambert Hale was not in the habit of throwing herself at men. So while Booth might have had the upper hand at the start, she made him work hard for her affection. The relationship simmered for two years, starting with flirtation and then blossoming into something more. The pair became intimate. When he was on the road, Booth was as faithful as a traveling thespian could be, which is to say that he made love to other women but considered them second to Lucy in his heart.

Booth is not the sort of man to mean it when he says, "I love you." For the most part, women are the objects of his own gratification. But Lucy has long treated men the same way, holding them at arm's length emotionally, basking in their charms, and then discarding them when someone newer and better comes along. In each other, Booth and Lucy met their match.

But they are also opposites in many ways. She comes from a more elite level of society, one that does not consider acting a gentlemanly career. She is an abolitionist, and he is most certainly not. He professes a heartfelt belief in the southern cause, while she is the daughter of a ferociously partisan northern senator. The engagement is doomed.

Booth has not seen Lucy since their ill-fated getaway to Newport. They haven't so much as exchanged letters or passed each other in the hallway, even though they live in the same hotel. He has no idea how she will react to his visit.

A servant answers the door and ushers him inside the suite. Lucy appears a moment later, the unfinished business of their argument hanging between them. They both know that it's over. Nothing more needs to be said, much to Booth's relief. They make small talk, skirting the obvious issue. And then it is time to say good-bye. Before leaving, Booth asks Lucy for a photograph so that he might have something to remember her by.

She steps out of the room and returns with a small portrait of her face in profile. Her hair is pulled back off her forehead and her lips are creased in a Mona Lisa smile. Booth thanks Lucy and gives her a long last look. He then turns and walks out of the Hales' suite, explaining

Lucy Hale in the photograph she gave John Wilkes Booth

breezily that he is off to get a shave, wondering if he will ever make it to Spain to see Lucy again.

As he walks back down the hallway, the sound of the closing door still echoing in the corridor, he admires the picture and slips it into his breast pocket, next to the pictures of four other women who have enjoyed his charms. The life of a narcissist is often cluttered.

The pictures will remain in Booth's pocket for the rest of his short life.

CHAPTER TWENTY-NINE

FRIDAY, APRIL 14, 1865
WASHINGTON, D.C.
10:00 A.M.

Mary Lincoln has tickets for a play—and what a spectacular performance it will be. Grover's Theatre is not only staging a lavish production of *Aladdin, or The Wonderful Lamp* but is adding a grand finale for this night only, during which the cast and audience will rise as one to sing patriotic songs written especially for the occasion. Everyone in Washington is talking about it.

But Mary is torn. Word has come from James Ford, the manager of Ford's Theatre, that he is staging the wildly popular farce *Our American Cousin*. Tonight the legendary actress Laura Keene is celebrating her one thousandth performance in her signature role as Florence Trenchard. This milestone, Ford has politely suggested to Mary, is something not to be missed.

Keene, thirty-eight, is not only one of America's most famous actresses but also very successful as a theater manager. In fact, she is the first woman in America to manage her own high-profile career and purchase a theater. That theater will later be renamed the Winter Garden, and it is still in existence today at a different location in New York City. Offstage, Laura Keene's life is not so tidy—she pretends to be married to her business manager, but in truth she is secretly married to a convicted felon who has run off to Australia. During an

Laura Keene

extended tour of that faraway continent, Keene quarreled mightily with her costar, the equally vain Edwin Booth.

But onstage Laura Keene is a force. The gimlet-eyed actress owes much of that success to *Our American Cousin*. At first she thought very little of the script, which places a country bumpkin in the upper class of British society. But then Keene changed her mind and bought worldwide rights. Debuting seven years earlier at Laura Keene's Theatre on Broadway, it soon became the first blockbuster play in American history. It was performed in Chicago on the same night in May 1860 that Lincoln was confirmed as the Republican nominee for the presidency. Many of the play's screwball terms, like "sockdologizing" and "Dundrearyisms" (named for the befuddled character Lord Dundreary), have become part of the cultural lexicon, and several spin-off plays featuring characters from the show have been written and performed.

Despite all that, ticket sales for this run of the play have been so

FORD'S THEATRE

TENTH STREET, ABOVE E.

SEASON II........WEEK XXXI........NIGHT 191
WHOLE NUMBER OF NIGHTS, 496.

JOHN T. FORD...PROPRIETOR AND MANAGER
(Also of Holliday St. Theatre, Baltimore, and Academy of Music, Phil'a.)
Stage Manager...J. B. WRIGHT
Treasurer..H. CLAY FORD

Friday Evening, April 14th, 1865

THIS EVENING,

The Performance will be honored by the presence of

PRESIDENT LINCOLN

BENEFIT!

—AND—

LAST NIGHT
OF MISS

LAURA KEENE

THE DISTINGUISHED MANAGERESS, AUTHORESS AND ACTRESS,
Supported by

MR. JOHN DYOTT
AND
MR. HARRY HAWK

TOM TAYLOR'S CELEBRATED ECCENTRIC COMEDY

As originally produced in America by Miss Keene, and performed by her upwards of

ONE THOUSAND NIGHTS,
ENTITLED

OUR AMERICAN

COUSIN

FLORENCE TRENCHARD..........MISS LAURA KEENE
(Her Original Character.)
Abel Murcott, Clerk to Attorney..................John Dyott
Asa Trenchard..Harry Hawk
Sir Edward Trenchard..............................T. C. GOURLAY
Lord Dundreary..E. A. EMERSON
Mr. Coyle, Attorney..................................J. MATTHEWS
Lieutenant Vernon, R. N............................W. J. FERGUSON
Captain De Boots......................................C. BYRNES
Binney...G. G. SPEAR
Buddicomb, a Valet...................................J. H. EVANS
John Whicker, a gardener..........................J. L. DeBONAY
Rasper, a groom
Bailiffs..................................G. A. PARKHURST and L. JOHNSON
Mary Trenchard..Miss J. GOURLAY
Mrs. Mountchessington...............................Mrs. H. MUZZY
Augusta..Miss H. TRUEMAN
Georgiana...Miss M. HART
Sharpe...Mrs. J. H. EVANS
Skillet..Miss M. GOURLAY

SATURDAY EVENING, APRIL 15,

BENEFIT of Miss JENNIE GOURLAY

When will be presented BOURCICAULT'S Great Sensational Drama,

THE OCTOROON

Easter Monday, April 17, Engagement of the YOUNG AMERICAN TRAGEDIAN,

EDWIN ADAMS

FOR TWELVE NIGHTS ONLY.

THE PRICES OF ADMISSION:
Orchestra..$1.00
Dress Circle and Parquette.......................................75
Family Circle...25
Private Boxes..$6 and $10

J. R. FORD, Business Manager.

H. Polkinhorn & Son, Printers, D street, near 7th, Washington, D. C.

The playbill for Our American Cousin *from the night the Lincolns were in attendance, April 14, 1865* sluggish that Ford's will be nearly empty. But Mary Lincoln doesn't mind. What matters most to her is that on this most patriotic of evenings, she and the president will celebrate their first visit to the theater since the war's end by enjoying the quintessential American comedy, on a night that features one of America's—if not the world's—most famous actresses.

Aladdin can wait.

∽

With this sudden and impulsive decision to attend one show and not the other, an eerie coincidence will unravel: thanks to the performance that took place in Chicago in 1860, *Our American Cousin* will bracket both the beginning and the end of the Lincoln administration.

Over breakfast a few hours earlier, Mary told the president that she wanted to go to Ford's. Lincoln absentmindedly said he would take care of it.

Now, between appointments, Lincoln summons a messenger. He wants a message delivered to Ford's Theatre, saying that he will be in attendance this evening if the state box is available. General Grant and his wife will be with him, as will Mary.

Abraham Lincoln is the undisputed leader of the world's most ascendant nation, a country spanning three thousand miles and touching two oceans. During the war, he could send men off to die with a single command to his generals. He has freed the slaves. This is a man who has the power to do almost anything he wants. And tonight, if truth be told, he would prefer to see *Aladdin*.

Yet Lincoln would never dream of contradicting Mary's wishes. His life is much easier when she is appeased. A volatile and opinionated woman whose intellect does not match her considerable capacity for rage, Mary Lincoln is short and round, wears her hair parted straight down the middle, and prefers to be called "Madame President," which some believe is pretentious, to say the least. Mary's rants about some person or situation that has angered her can sidetrack Lincoln's day and drain him of precious energy, so he does all he can to make sure nothing upsets her unstable psyche.

But to be fair, Mary Lincoln has also suffered the deaths of two

Mary Todd Lincoln

young sons during her twenty-two-year marriage. Lincoln dotes on her. A compassionate man, he tries more to ease the lingering pain than to merely keep the peace. Mary Lincoln is almost ten years younger than her husband, and they had an on-again, off-again courtship and even broke off their first engagement when Lincoln had cold feet about marrying her. Mary is from an affluent home, which afforded her an education that few American women enjoyed at the time. Lithe in her early twenties, Mary has put on considerable weight. And though she had many suitors as a young woman, few would now consider her to be good-looking. Nevertheless, Lincoln is enamored. The president considers Mary the love of his life. Some historians believe that because Lincoln lost his mother at the age of nine, he was drawn to women with maternal, protective instincts. Mary Lincoln certainly fits that description.

∽

Lincoln is overdue at the War Department. He also has a cabinet meeting scheduled in just over an hour. He hurriedly steps out of the White House and walks over to see Stanton. Mary demands that he wear a shawl, and so he does, not caring in the slightest that the gray garment draped over his shoulders gives him a decidedly nonpresidential appearance.

Lincoln strolls into Stanton's office unannounced, plops down on the couch, and casually mentions that he's going to the theater that night. The words are designed to provoke a reaction—and they do.

Stanton frowns. His network of spies have told him of assassination rumors. Last night, during the Illumination party at his home, Stanton adamantly warned Grant away from going to the theater with the Lincolns. Stanton is no less stern with Lincoln. He thinks the president is a fool for ignoring the assassination rumors and argues that Lincoln is risking his life.

"At least bring a guard with you," Stanton pleads, once it becomes obvious that Lincoln will not be dissuaded. That statement is the best evidence we have that Secretary of War Stanton did not wish Lincoln ill. If, as some conspiracy theorists believe, Stanton wished Lincoln dead, why would he want to provide him with protection?

The president is in a playful mood. "Stanton," Lincoln says, "did you know that Eckert can break a poker over his arm?"

Major Thomas T. Eckert is the general superintendent of the Military Telegraph Corps. He once demonstrated the shoddy nature of the War Department's fireplace irons by breaking the defective metal rods over his left forearm.

"Why do you ask such a question?" Stanton replies, mystified.

"Stanton, I have seen Eckert break five pokers, one after the other, over his arm, and I am thinking that he would be the kind of man who would go with me this evening. May I take him?"

"Major Eckert has a great deal of work to do. He can't be spared."

"Well, I will ask the major himself," Lincoln responds.

But Eckert knows better than to cross Stanton. Despite a barrage of good-natured pleading by the president, Eckert says he cannot attend the theater that evening.

His business with Stanton concluded, Lincoln wraps his shawl tightly around his shoulders and marches back to the White House for his cabinet meeting.

CHAPTER THIRTY

Lincoln's messenger reaches Ford's at 10:30 A.M. "The president of the United States would like to formally request the state box for this evening—if it is available," the note reads.

The state box is available, James Ford immediately responds, barely containing his excitement. He races into the manager's office to share the good news with his brother Harry and then barks the order for the stage carpenter to come see him right this instant.

Ford's may be the city's preeminent stage, but business has been extremely slow this week. The postwar jubilation means that Washington's theatergoers are making merry on the streets, not penned together inside watching a show. In fact, Ford had been anticipating yet another dismal night. *Our American Cousin* is no match for the Grover's *Aladdin*, which has been made all the more spectacular by the postshow victory rally, thus allowing audience members to watch a play *and* make merry. Ford can almost hear the actors' words echoing off empty seats, and the punch lines that will receive a yawn instead of the guffaw a packed and energized theater so often guarantees. But now, with word that the president will be in the audience, the night should be a sellout.

Ford's was originally known as the First Baptist Church of Washington. When the Baptists moved out, in 1861, James's brother John

Ford's Theatre, 1865

purchased the building and turned it into a playhouse. When Ford's Athenaeum was destroyed by fire in 1862, some said it was God's will, because many churchgoers considered the theater to be the devil's playground. But John Ford was undeterred. He not only rebuilt the great brick building; he reshaped it into the nation's most modern theater.

Ford's reopened to rave reviews in August 1863. The building is flanked on either side by taverns—the Greenback Saloon to the left and Taltavul's Star Saloon to the right—so that theatergoers can pop next door for a drink at intermission. The outside of the theater itself features five decorative archways. Patrons enter through the center arch, leading directly into the ticket booth and lobby. The steps leading up from the street are granite. The unpaved streets are often muddy this time of year, so Ford has built a wooden ramp from the street into the lobby. This ensures that ladies won't soil their evening wear when stepping out of their carriages.

Inside, three seating levels face the stage. Gas lamps light the auditorium until the curtain falls, when they are dimmed by a single backstage valve. The chairs are a simple straight-backed cane but, inside his special presidential box, Lincoln prefers to sit in the red horsehair-upholstered rocking chair that Ford's reserves for his personal use.

Boxes on either side of the stage allow the more privileged patrons to look straight down onto the actors. The state box, where the Lincolns and Grants will sit this evening, is almost on the stage itself—so close that if Lincoln were to impulsively rise from his rocking chair and leap down into the actors' midst, the distance traveled would be a mere nine feet.

The state box is actually two side-by-side boxes. When not being used by the president or some other national dignitary, they are available for sale to the general public and simply referred to as boxes 7 and 8. A pine partition divides them.

On nights when the Lincolns are in attendance, the partition is removed. Red, white, and blue bunting is draped over the railing and a portrait of George Washington faces out at the audience, designating that the president of the United States is in the house. Out of respect for the office, none of the other boxes are for sale when the Lincolns occupy the state box.

Now, with the news that this will be such a night, the first thing on James Ford's mind is decorating the state box with the biggest and most spectacular American flag he can find. He remembers that the Treasury Department has such a flag. With governmental offices due to close at noon for the Good Friday observance, there's little time to spare.

By sheer coincidence, John Wilkes Booth marches up those granite front steps at that very moment. Like many actors, he spends so much time on the road that he doesn't have a permanent address. So Ford's Opera House, as the theater is formally known, is his permanent mailing address.

As James Ford reacts to Lincoln's request, an *Our American Cousin* rehearsal is taking place. The sound of dramatic voices wafts through the air. The show has been presented eight previous times at Ford's, but Laura Keene isn't taking any chances with cues or blocking. If this is to be her thousandth and, perhaps, final performance of this warhorse, she will see to it that the cast doesn't flub a single line. This bent toward perfectionism is a Keene hallmark and a prime reason she has enjoyed such a successful career.

Booth's mail is in the manager's office. As he picks up a bundle of letters, stage carpenter James J. Gifford bounds into the room, curious as to why Ford wants to see him. When the theater manager shares the exciting news about the Lincolns, Clifford is ecstatic, but Booth pretends not to hear, instead staring straight down at his mail, acting as if he is studying the return addresses. He grins, though he does not mean to. He calms himself and makes small talk with Ford, then says his good-byes and wanders out into the sunlight. Booth sits on the front step, half-reading his mail and laughing aloud at his sudden good fortune.

Ford walks past, explaining that he is off to purchase bunting—and perhaps a thirty-six-star flag.

☙

Until this moment, Booth has known what he wants to do and the means with which he will do it. But the exact details of the murder have so far eluded him.

Sitting on the front step of Ford's Theatre on this Good Friday morning, he knows that he will kill Lincoln tonight and in this very theater. Booth has performed here often and is more familiar with its hidden backstage tunnels and doors than he is with the streets of Washington. The twofold challenge he now faces is the traditional assassin's plight: find the most efficient path into the state box in order to shoot Abraham Lincoln and then find the perfect escape route from the theater.

The cast and crew at Ford's treat Booth like family. His eccentricities are chalked up to his being a famous actor. The theatrical world is full of a hundred guys just as unpredictable and passionate, so nobody dreams that he has a burning desire to kill the president. So it is, as Booth rises to his feet and wanders back into the theater to plan the attack, that it never crosses anyone's mind to ask what he's doing. It's just John being John.

The seats are all empty. The house lights are up. Onstage, the rehearsal is ending.

John Wilkes Booth prowls Ford's Theatre alone, analyzing, scrutinizing, estimating. His journey takes him up the back stairs to the state box, where he steps inside and looks down at the stage. A music stand provides an unlikely burst of inspiration. He hefts it in his hand, nervous but elated, knowing how he will make use of it tonight. By the time he is done, Booth has come up with an audacious—and brilliant—plan of attack.

On Booth's mind are these questions: Will he commit the perfect crime? And will he go down in history as a great man?

CHAPTER THIRTY-ONE

—————

A hazy sun shines down on Washington's empty streets. The city is so quiet it seems to be asleep. The Good Friday observance means that its citizens are temporarily done celebrating the war's end. They are now in church or at home repenting, leaving the local merchants to lament the momentary loss of the booming business they've enjoyed the past few days.

Hundreds of miles to the south, in Fort Sumter, South Carolina, a massive celebration is about to take place, commemorating the raising of the Stars and Stripes. Major General Robert Anderson stands before forty-five hundred people as the very flag that was lowered there four years earlier, marking the beginning of the war, now climbs the flagpole. A minister offers a prayer of thanksgiving. The Union is reunited.

Back in Washington, General Grant walks to the White House, feeling conflicted. He was supposed to meet with Lincoln at nine A.M., but the president rescheduled for eleven so that Grant can attend the cabinet meeting. Now he feels obligated to attend the theater tonight with the Lincolns. But Julia Grant, who thinks Mary Lincoln is unstable and a gossip, has bluntly refused. When the theater invitation arrived from Mary Lincoln earlier that morning, Julia replied with a firm no, stating that the Grants would be leaving town that afternoon and noting, "We will not, therefore, be here to accompany the President and Mrs. Lincoln to the theatre." She is, in fact, adamant that they catch the afternoon train out of Washington. Going to the theater with Mary Lincoln is out of the question.

General Grant is caught in the middle. Lincoln has become such an ally and dear friend that turning down his invitation seems rude. But displeasing his wife, who has endured many a sacrifice these past years, is equally daunting.

The two soldiers standing guard at the White House gate snap to attention as their general in chief arrives. Grant tosses them a return salute with the casual ease of a man who has done it thousands of times, never breaking stride as he continues on to the front door.

The doorman nods graciously as Grant steps inside, dressed in his soldier's uniform, moving past the police bodyguard currently on duty and a rifle-bearing soldier also in dress uniform. Then it's up the stairs to Lincoln's second-floor office, where another soldier stands guard. Soon Grant is seated in Lincoln's cabinet meeting, somewhat surprised by the loose way in which such matters are conducted. He assumed that Lincoln's entire cabinet would be in attendance, particularly since there are so many pressing matters of state to discuss. But a quick glance around the room shows no sign of Secretary of War Stanton or Secretary of the Interior John P. Usher. Secretary of State William Seward, home recovering from his carriage accident, is represented by his son Frederick. And as Lincoln leans back in his chair along the south window, the half-filled room feels more like a collegiate debating club than a serious political gathering. Lincoln guides the dialogue, which jumps from elation at the war's end to other topics and back, taking no notes as he soaks in the various opinions. His behavior is that of a first among equals rather than the ultimate decision maker.

∽

The meeting is into its second hour as Grant is shown into the room, and his entrance injects a new vitality—just as Lincoln intended. The cabinet, to a man, is effusive in praise of the general and begs to hear details of the Appomattox surrender. Grant sets the scene, describing the quaint McLean farmhouse and the way he and Lee sat together to settle the country's fate. He doesn't go into great detail, and he makes a point of praising Lee. The cabinet members are struck by his modesty but clamor for more.

Lincoln tries to draw him out. "What terms did you make for the common soldiers?" the president asks, already knowing the answer.

"To go back to their homes and families, and they would not be molested, if they did nothing more."

There is a point to Lincoln's inviting Grant to this meeting, as evidenced by this new line of inquiry. Lincoln hopes for a certain pragmatic lenience toward the southern states, rather than a draconian punishment, as his vice president, Andrew Johnson, favors. Lincoln has not seen Johnson since his second inauguration. But Lincoln's lenient plan for the South is not borne solely out of kindness nor with just the simple goal of healing the nation. The South's bustling warm-water ports and agricultural strength will be a powerful supplement to the nation's economy. With the nation mired in more than $2 billion of wartime debt, and with Union soldiers still owed back pay, extra sources of income are vitally needed.

Grant's simple reply has the desired effect. Lincoln beams as the cabinet members nod their heads in agreement.

"And what of the current military situation?"

Grant says that he expects word from Sherman any minute, saying that General Joe Johnston has finally surrendered. This, too, is met with enthusiasm around the table.

Throughout the proceedings, Grant's feeling of unease about that evening's plans lingers. He makes up his mind to tell Lincoln that he will attend the theater. Doing otherwise would be ungracious and disrespectful. Julia will be furious, but eventually she will understand. And then, first thing in the morning, they can be on the train to New Jersey.

꩜

The cabinet meeting drags on. One o'clock rolls past. One-thirty.

A messenger arrives carrying a note for Grant. It's from Julia and she's not happy. Mrs. Grant wants her husband back at the Willard Hotel immediately, so that they can catch the 6:00 P.M. to Burlington, New Jersey.

General Grant's decision has now been made for him. After months and years of men obeying his every order, he bows to an even greater authority than the president of the United States: his wife.

"I am sorry, Mr. President," Grant says when the cabinet meeting ends, just after one-thirty. "It is certain that I will be on this afternoon's train to Burlington. I regret that I cannot attend the theater."

Lincoln tries to change Grant's mind, telling him that the people of Washington will be at Ford's to see him. But the situation is out of the general's hands. Lincoln senses that and says good-bye to his dear friend.

The Grants will make their train. Julia is so eager to leave town that she has chosen the local, which takes thirteen long hours to reach Burlington. The faster option would be the seven-thirty express in the morning, but that would mean a night at the theater with the daft and unbalanced Mary Lincoln. Julia Grant's mind is made up.

What Ulysses S. Grant does not know is that he will be returning to Washington by the same train within twenty-four hours.

CHAPTER THIRTY-TWO

FRIDAY, APRIL 14, 1865
WASHINGTON, D.C.
2:00 P.M.

Two thousand years after the execution of Jesus, there are still many unanswered questions about who was directly responsible for his death and what happened in the aftermath. And so it is, on Good Friday 1865, that a series of bizarre occurrences will take place.

In the hours to come guards will inexplicably leave their posts, bridges that should be closed will miraculously be open, and telegrams alerting the army to begin a manhunt for Lincoln's killer will not be sent—all happenings that have been tied to a murky conspiracy that most likely will never be uncovered. What we do know is that in these hours, John Wilkes Booth is putting the final touches on his murderous plan.

Booth is on an emotional roller coaster, his spirits rising and falling as he ponders the assassination and its consequences, all the while running down his checklist, completing the tasks that must be done for tonight. He is dressed in dashing fashion, with tight black pants, a tailored black coat, and a black hat. With those clothes and his broad black mustache, he couldn't look more like a villain. The only thing he wears that isn't black are his boots—they're tan.

The first stop is Mary Surratt's boardinghouse on H Street. She is walking out the door for a trip into the country to collect on an old debt, but Booth catches her just in time. He hands her a spyglass wrapped in brown paper and tied with a string, telling her to make sure that it doesn't get wet or break. One of Surratt's tenants, Louis Weichmann, is a soldier and government clerk whose job deals with the care and housing of prisoners of war. Weichmann senses that there's something shady about Booth, having listened to his rants and spent enough time around the Surratts to discern the pro-Confederate leanings of the crowd. So he leans in to eavesdrop as Mary and Booth confer by the marble fireplace.

Mary catches him. She calmly orders Weichmann to leave her house at once and pick up a horse and buggy for her journey.

By the time Weichmann returns with the horse and buggy, Booth is gone, walking the five blocks to Herndon House, where Lewis Powell is lying on the bed, staring at the ceiling. He and Booth discuss the evening's plan. The trick in killing Secretary of State Seward, Booth reminds him, isn't the actual murder—Seward is still barely conscious and in great pain after his carriage accident. He is incapable of putting up any resistance.

No, the hard part will be getting in and out of Seward's home. There is at least one male military nurse to protect the secretary, along with Seward's wife and three of his children. In a worst-case scenario, Powell will have to kill them all, Booth says. Powell, mentally impaired since that long-ago mule kick to the head, says he has no problem with mass murder.

Then Booth is on the move again, headed for Pumphrey's stable to arrange for his getaway horse. He prefers a small sorrel, but it's already gone for the day. Instead, Booth rents a compact bay mare with a white star on her forehead. Pumphrey warns Booth that although the mare is just fourteen hands high, she's extremely high-spirited. She mustn't be tied to a post if he leaves her anywhere, because she'll pull away and escape. Better to have someone hold her reins at all times.

The bay tries to bite Booth as the groom cinches the English saddle under her belly and adjusts her stirrups. To demonstrate her high spirits, the groom smacks the mare on the rump. She jumps and kicks, much to Booth's delight.

Booth saddles up. He likes the horse with the black mane and tail, but the stirrups don't feel right. The groom shortens them one notch and Booth is on his way, walking the mare up Sixth Street to Pennsylvania Avenue, where he jabs his spurs into her flanks so she'll run. It's a ludicrous idea. The street is jammed with pedestrians and carriages. Union soldiers, returning from the front, march in loose formation, dog-tired and in no mood for a horseman to romp through their ranks. But today Booth is above the law. He gallops the bay down Pennsylvania, ignoring the angry curses hurled in his mud-splattered wake.

Booth stops at Grover's Theatre, where the marquee announces THE GORGEOUS PLAY OF ALADDIN, OR THE WONDERFUL LAMP. He doesn't have any business there, but theaters are safe refuges no matter what city he's visiting. Booth knows not only the insides of the building but also each nearby bar and restaurant, where he's sure to see a friendly face. On a day like today, when his stomach is churning and he's battling with all his might to stay calm and focused, nothing could be more natural than making his way to a theater, just to experience a few moments of calm reassurance. For the child of actors, raised on greasepaint and footlights, it's like going home.

Against Pumphrey's explicit direction, he ties the mare to a hitching post, then wanders up to Deery's tavern and orders a bottle. Alone at the bar, nursing a brandy and water to the sounds of the clacking of billiard balls from the nearby table, he pauses to reflect on what he is about to do. Getting into the theater should be easy enough. Getting past the bodyguard at the door to the state box, however, might get bloody. And the odds of killing Lincoln and escaping are low. He accepts all that.

But what if nobody knows it's him?

What if the euphoric triumph of shooting Lincoln is followed by the devastating letdown of anonymity—that is, until he reaches some safe refuge where he can shout his accomplishment to the world and then parlay his infamy into some even greater glory. But what if no one believes him? What if John Wilkes Booth shoots the president and makes a clean getaway, only to be ignored when he tells everyone that he's the man who did it?

This cannot be. Booth craves the limelight too much. He needs to make sure he'll get immediate credit for such a bold and dramatic act.

∽

Booth tosses a dollar onto the bar and walks downstairs to the Grover's manager's office. It's empty. Sitting at the desk, Booth removes paper and an envelope from the pigeonholes. He then writes a letter to the editor of the *National Intelligencer* stating, in specific terms, what he is about to do.

He signs his name, then adds those of Powell, Atzerodt, and Herold. They are all members of the same company, in theatrical terms. They deserve some sort of billing—even if they might not want it.

After sealing the envelope, Booth steps outside. He is pleased to see that his feisty bay is still where he left her. A motley and dispirited group of Confederate prisoners is marching down the street as he saddles up. "Great God," he moans, mortified by such a sad sight. "I no longer have a country."

But seeing those downtrodden rebels is yet another reminder of why Booth has embraced violence. Thus fortified, Booth spies fellow actor John Matthews in front of the theater. Booth leans down from his horse to hand him the envelope and gives him specific instructions to mail it the next morning. However, hedging his bets in case things go bad, Booth says he wants the letter back if he finds Matthews before ten tomorrow morning.

It's a petty and spiteful trick, designed to implicate Matthews, who will be onstage in the role of Richard Coyle during *Our American Cousin*. Booth had asked him to be part of the conspiracy and was turned down. The night after his aborted kidnapping attempt on the Soldiers' Home road four weeks earlier, Booth even lounged on Matthews's bed in a small boardinghouse across from Ford's Theatre, trying to cajole the fellow actor to join him.

But Matthews continued to refuse. Now Booth is getting his revenge, implicating Matthews by association.

Matthews, completely unsuspecting, is distracted by an unusual sight. "Look," he says to Booth. "Over there."

Booth is stunned to see General and Mrs. Grant leaving town in an open carriage piled high with luggage. Julia is inside, with another female passenger, while the general sits up top, next to the coachman.

Booth trots after them, just to see for himself. He parades his horse past the carriage, turns around, and guides the bay back toward the Grants at a walk. He stares as the carriage passes, glaring at Sam Grant with such intensity that Julia will later recall quite vividly the crazed man who stared them down. It is only after the assassination that Mrs. Grant will realize who he was.

♋

"I thought he was going to Ford's tonight, with Lincoln," Booth says to a stranger.

"Somebody said he's going to Jersey," the man responds, confirming Booth's worst fears. Glumly, he realizes that one of his two primary targets will not be at Ford's this evening. He wheels the horse around and heads for that theater.

Washington, D.C., is a relatively small city. All the locations

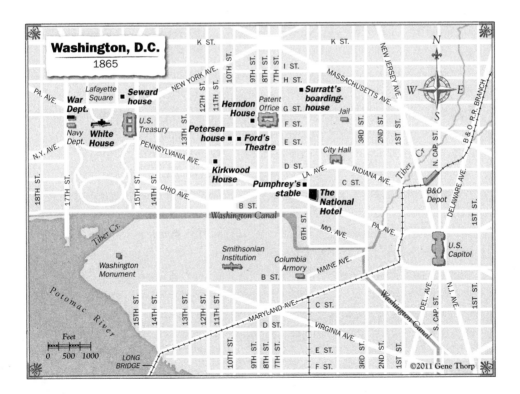

associated with Booth's activities throughout the week are situated close together. Mary Surratt's boardinghouse is just a few blocks from the National Hotel, which is just a few blocks from Kirkwood House, where Vice President Johnson is staying, which is just a few blocks from the White House, which is right across the street from Secretary Seward's home. The National, the White House, and Mary Surratt's boardinghouse constitute the three corners of a broad triangle. Within that triangle are all the other locations. And in the very center is Ford's Theatre, which is right across the alley from Herndon House, where Lewis Powell is now eating an early dinner of cold beef and potatoes before checking out.

The alley is known as Baptist Alley, due to Ford's origins as a house of worship. A maid at Ford's hears the sound of galloping hooves coming from the alley. When she looks outside, she sees a most unusual sight: the famous actor John Wilkes Booth racing a horse north up the alley from E Street, then galloping out the other end on F Street. He does this twice. The maid, Margaret Rozier, watches as Booth dismounts after the second dry run of his escape, not in a million years imagining what she has just witnessed. When he is done, Booth stops at Ford's stage door, where he invites stagehands Jim Maddox and Ned Spangler to join him for a drink next door at Jim Ferguson's Greenback Saloon.

As they come back outside after their drink, Booth mounts the bay and says hello to Jim Ferguson himself. Ferguson has heard about the Lincolns and is making plans to see *Our American Cousin* tonight. "She is a very nice horse," Booth says, noting the way Ferguson admires her. "She can gallop and can almost kick me in the back."

Booth prods her with his spurs and gallops back to the National Hotel, his errands complete. The energy whooshes out of him as the alcohol wears off and the brute realization of what he is about to do hits him hard. His face is so pale that the desk clerk inquires about his health.

Booth says he's fine, orders a cup of tea, and heads upstairs to rest.

CHAPTER THIRTY-THREE

FRIDAY, APRIL 14, 1865
WASHINGTON, D.C.
3:30 P.M.

"Crook," Abraham Lincoln says to his bodyguard, "I believe there are men who want to take my life. And I have no doubt that they will do it."

The two men are walking down Pennsylvania Avenue, on their way back to the War Department for their second meeting of the day. Lincoln wants a short session with Stanton to discuss the fate of a Confederate ringleader who very recently made the mistake of crossing the border from Canada back into the United States. Stanton is in favor of arresting the man, while Lincoln prefers to let him slip away to England on the morning steamer. As soon as Lincoln makes his point, he aims to hurry back to the White House for the carriage ride he promised Mary.

William Crook is fond of the president and deeply unsettled by the comments.

"Why do you think so, Mr. President?"

Crook steps forward as they come upon a group of angry drunks. He puts his body between theirs and Lincoln's, thus clearing the way for the president's safe passage. Crook's actions, while brave, are unnecessary—if the drunks realize that the president of the United States is sharing the same sidewalk, they give no notice.

Lincoln waits until Crook is beside him again, then continues his train of thought. "Other men have been assassinated," Lincoln says.

"I hope you are mistaken, Mr. President."

"I have perfect confidence in those around me. In every one of you men. I know that no one could do it and escape alive," Lincoln says. The two men walk in silence before he finishes his thought: "But if it is to be done, it is impossible to prevent it."

At the War Department, Lincoln once again invites Stanton and telegraph chief Major Thomas Eckert, the man who can break fireplace pokers over his arms, to attend *Our American Cousin* that night. Both men turn him down once again. Lincoln is upset by their rejection, but he doesn't show it outwardly. The only indication comes on the walk back to the White House, when he admits to Crook, "I do not want to go." Lincoln says it like a man facing a death sentence.

∽

Inside the White House, Lincoln is pulled into an unscheduled last-minute meeting that will delay his carriage ride. Lincoln hides his exasperation and dutifully meets with New Hampshire congressman Edward H. Rollins. But as soon as Rollins leaves, yet another petitioner begs a few minutes of Lincoln's time. A weary Lincoln, all too aware that Mary will be most upset if he keeps her waiting much longer, gives former military aide Colonel William Coggeshall the benefit of a few moments.

Finally, Lincoln marches down the stairs and heads for the carriage. He notices a one-armed soldier standing off to one side of the hallway and overhears the young man tell another, "I would almost give my other hand if I could shake that of Lincoln."

Lincoln can't resist. "You shall do that and it shall cost you nothing, boy," he exclaims, smiling broadly as he walks over and grasps the young man's hand. He asks his name, that of his regiment, and in which battle he lost the arm.

Only then does Lincoln say his farewells and step outside. He finds Mary waiting at the carriage. She's in a tentative mood—they've spent so little time alone in the past few months that being together, just the two of them, feels strange. She wonders if Lincoln might be more comfortable if they brought some friends along for the open-air ride.

"I prefer to ride by ourselves today," he insists. Lincoln helps her into the barouche and then is helped up from the gravel driveway to take his seat beside her. The four-wheeled horse-drawn carriage features two facing double seats for passengers and a retractable roof. The driver sits in a box seat up front. Lincoln opts to keep the roof open, then covers their laps with a blanket, even though the temperature is a warm sixty-eight degrees.

The war has been hard on their marriage. Mary is delighted beyond words to see that Lincoln is in a lighthearted mood. She gazes into her husband's eyes and recognizes the man who once courted her.

"Dear Husband," she laughs, "you startle me by your great cheerfulness. I have not seen you so happy since before Willie's death."

"And well I may feel so, Mary. I consider this day, the war has come to a close." The president pauses. "We must both be more cheerful in the future—between the war and the loss of our darling Willie we have been very miserable."

Coachman Francis Burns guides the elegant pair of black horses down G Street. The pace is a quick trot. Behind them ride two cavalry escorts, just for safety. The citizens of Washington are startled to see the Lincolns out on the town. They hear loud laughter from Mary as the barouche passes by and see a grin spread across the president's face. When a group calls out to him as the carriage turns onto New Jersey Avenue, he doffs his trademark stovepipe hat in greeting.

༄

Throughout the war, Lincoln has stayed in the moment, never allowing himself to dream of the future. But now he pours his heart out to Mary, talking about a proposed family trip to Palestine, for he is most curious about the Holy Land. And after he leaves office he wants the family to return to their roots in Illinois, where he will once again hang out his shingle as a country lawyer. The "Lincoln & Herndon" sign has never been taken down, at Lincoln's specific request to his partner.

"Mary," Lincoln says, "we have had a hard time of it since we came to Washington, but the war is over, and with God's blessing we may hope for four years of peace and happiness, and then we will go back to Illinois and pass the rest of our lives in quiet. We have laid by some money, and during this term we will try to save up more."

The carriage makes its way to the Navy Yard, where Lincoln steps on board USS *Montauk*. His intent is just a cursory peek at the storied ironclad, with its massive round turret constituting the deck's superstructure. But soon its crew mobs Lincoln, and he is forced to politely excuse himself so that he can return to Mary. Unbeknownst to Lincoln, the *Montauk* will soon serve another purpose.

Lincoln offers a final salute to the many admirers as coachman Burns turns the carriage back toward the White House. It's getting late, and the Lincolns have to be at the theater.

John Wilkes Booth is expecting them.

CHAPTER THIRTY-FOUR

FRIDAY, APRIL 14, 1865
WASHINGTON, D.C.
7:00 P.M.

William Crook stands guard outside Lincoln's office door. The twenty-six-year-old policeman and presidential bodyguard has had a long day, having arrived at the White House at precisely eight A.M. His replacement was supposed to relieve him three hours ago, but John Parker, as always, is showing himself to be lazy and unaccountable. Crook is deeply attached to Lincoln and frets about his safety. How this drunken slob Parker was designated as the president's bodyguard is a great mystery, but Crook knows that the president does not involve himself in such things.

After their carriage ride, the Lincolns eat dinner with their sons, and then Crook walks the president back to the War Department for a third time, to see if General Sherman has sent a telegraph stating the disposition of his troops in the South. Lincoln has become so addicted to the telegraph's instant news from the front that he still can't let go of the need for just one more bit of information, even though the prospect of another great battle is slim.

Then Crook walks back to the White House with Lincoln, his eyes constantly scanning the crowds for signs that someone means his employer harm. He remembers well the advice of Ward Hill Lamon, the walrus-mustached, self-appointed head of Lincoln's security detail, that Lincoln should not go out at night, under any circumstances. "Especially to the theater," Lamon had added.

But tonight, Lincoln is going to the theater—and it's no secret. The afternoon papers printed news about him attending *Our American Cousin* with General Grant and their wives, almost as if daring every crackpot and schemer with an anti-North agenda to buy a ticket. Indeed, ticket sales have been brisk since the announcement, and—recent outpourings of affection notwithstanding—Lincoln's status as the most hated man in America certainly means that not everyone at Ford's will be there out of admiration for the president.

Lincoln, however, doesn't see it like that. Even though Mary says the carriage ride gave her a headache that has her second-guessing the night out, the president feels obligated to go. He might feel differently if he hadn't missed the Grand Illumination last night. That, plus the fact that the Grants aren't going, makes Lincoln's obligation all the more urgent—he knows his constituents will be deeply disappointed if both of America's two most famous men fail to appear.

And then there's the minor issue of disappointing the Grants' last-minute replacements. Just when it seemed like everyone in Washington was terrified of attending the theater with the Lincolns, Mary found guests, the minor diplomat Major Henry Reed Rathbone and his fiancée (and stepsister) Clara Harris, who watched Lincoln's speech with Mary three nights before. Mary is deeply fond of Clara, the full-figured daughter of Senator Ira Harris of New York. They enjoy an almost mother-daughter relationship. Just as important, Major Rathbone is a strapping young man who saw service during the war; he has the sort of physical presence Lincoln might need in a bodyguard, should such services be required.

The president doesn't know either of them. When he received news that this unlikely couple would be their guests, he was enjoying a quiet dinner with Tad and Robert. Lincoln's response was neither joy nor disappointment but merely a silent nod of acknowledgment.

William Crook is a straightforward cop, not one to search for conspiracies or malcontents where none exist. Yet the bodyguard in him wonders about the tall, athletic Rathbone and whether or not he poses a security risk. What better way to kill the president than shooting him in his own box during the play?

Finally, Crook hears feet thudding up the stairs. Parker ambles down the hallway, patting the bulge in his jacket to show that he is armed. He is a thirty-four-year-old former machinist from Frederick County, Virginia, and the father of three children. Parker served in the Union army for the first three months of the war, then mustered out to rejoin his family and took a job as a policeman in September 1861, becoming one of the first 150 men hired when Washington, D.C., formed its brand-new Metropolitan Police Department.

Throughout his employment, Parker's one distinguishing trait has been an ability to manufacture controversy. He has been disciplined for, among other things, swearing at a grocer, swearing at a supervising officer, insulting a woman who had requested police protection, and being drunk and disorderly in a house of prostitution. At his trial, the madam testified that not only was Parker drunk and disorderly but that he had been living in the whorehouse for five weeks before the incident. Apparently, the authorities chose to ignore that testimony. The trial took place before a police board, rather than in the criminal courts. The board found no wrongdoing by Parker and quickly acquitted him.

⌒

And so Parker continued his questionable behavior. He appeared before the police board just two weeks later for sleeping on duty. Ninety days after that, another police board: this time for using profane language to a private citizen. Both charges were dismissed.

His innocence proven again and again, Parker had no qualms about putting his name into the pool when, late in 1864, the Metropolitan Police Department began providing White House bodyguards. It was prestigious duty and kept him from being drafted back into the army. Mary Lincoln herself wrote the letter exempting him from service. So far, the only blemish on Parker's record while serving the president is a penchant for tardiness, as Crook knows all too well. So when Parker finally appears several hours late for his shift, Crook is upset but not surprised.

Crook briefs Parker on the day's events, then explains that the presidential carriage will be stopping at Fourteenth and H to pick up Major Rathbone and Miss Harris. The presence of two additional passengers means that there will be no room for Parker. "You should leave fifteen minutes ahead of the president," says Crook, pointing out that Parker will have to walk to Ford's Theatre—and that he should arrive before the presidential party in order to provide security the instant they arrive.

As Crook finishes, Lincoln comes to his office door. A handful of last-minute appointments have come up, and he is eager to get them out of the way so he can enjoy the weekend.

"Good night, Mr. President," Crook says.

He and the president have repeated this scene a hundred times, with Lincoln responding in kind.

Only this time it's different.

"Good-*bye*, Crook," Lincoln replies.

All the way home, that subtle difference nags at William Crook.

CHAPTER THIRTY-FIVE

FRIDAY, APRIL 14, 1865
WASHINGTON, D.C.
8:00 P.M.

As Lincoln is bidding farewell to William Crook, Booth is gobbling down a quick dinner in the National Hotel's dining room. Food, sleep, and adrenaline have him feeling sober once more. *Our American Cousin* starts at eight, and his plan will go into action shortly after ten P.M. If all goes well, any residual effects of the afternoon's alcohol will have worn off by then. In fact, Booth is feeling so good that he starts drinking again. What he is about to do is very grave, indeed. Liquid courage will make sure he doesn't get stage fright and miss his cue.

That cue is simple: there is a moment in the third act when the actor Harry Hawk, playing the part of Asa Trenchard, is the only person on stage. He utters a line that never fails to make the audience convulse with laughter. "Don't know the manners of good society, eh?" he says to the character of the busybody, Mrs. Mountchessington, who has insulted him before exiting the stage. "Well, I guess I know enough to turn you inside out, old gal—you sockdologizing old man-trap."

The instant that the punch line hits home and the Ford's audience explodes, Booth will kill Lincoln. If everything goes according to plan, he will already be concealed inside the state box. All he needs to do is pull out his Deringer and fire. Booth will toss the pistol aside after shooting Lincoln, then use his Bowie knife to battle his way out, if cornered.

His plan is to keep moving forward at all times—forward from the back wall of the box, forward to Lincoln's rocking chair, forward up and over the railing and then down onto the stage, forward to the backstage door, forward to Maryland, and then forward all the way to Mexico, exile, and safety.

But Booth will stop for an instant in the midst of all that rapid movement. The actor in him cannot resist the chance to utter one last bold line from center stage. After leaping from the balcony Booth will stand tall and, in his best elocution, announce, *"Sic semper tyrannis"*: Thus always to tyrants.

The Latin phrase is meant to sound smart, the sort of profound parting words that will echo down the corridors of history. He has stolen it, truth be told, from the state of Virginia. It is the commonwealth's motto.

No matter. The words are perfect.

∽

Booth plans to have another last-minute rendezvous with his co-conspirators at eight P.M. He returns to his room and polishes his Deringer, then slips a single ball into the barrel. The gun goes into his pocket. Into his waistband goes the Bowie knife in its sheath. Outside he can hear Washington coming to life once again, with still more of the endless postwar parties, bonfires, and street corner sing-alongs that annoy him no end.

Booth packs a small bag with a makeup pencil, false beard, false mustache, wig, and a plaid muffler. As he is about to leave the hotel on his deadly errand, he realizes that his accomplices might be in need of firearms. So he slips a pair of revolvers into the bag. Their firepower far exceeds the Deringer's.

And yet what Booth leaves behind is just as powerful: among the personal effects that authorities will later find are a broken comb, tobacco, embroidered slippers, and one very telling scrap of paper. On it are written the keys to top-secret coded Confederate messages that link him with Jefferson Davis's office in Richmond and with the million-dollar gold fund in Montreal. Finally, Booth leaves behind a valise filled with damning evidence that implicates John Surratt and, by extension, his mother, Mary.

Booth could have destroyed these items, but such is his malevolence that if he is ever apprehended or killed, he wants everyone else to go down as well. He also wants to show the world that he, Booth, was the mastermind behind killing Abraham Lincoln.

He walks downstairs and slides his key across the front desk. "Are you going to Ford's tonight?" he asks George W. Bunker, the clerk on duty.

"No," comes the reply.

"You ought to go," Booth says with a wink on his way out the door. "There is going to be some splendid acting."

∽

Booth laughs at his own joke as he steps into the night air. Washington is covered in a fine mist, giving the streetlights and the Capitol dome a ghostly appearance. Booth feels like he is viewing the city through frosted glass.

He trots his horse over to Ford's. Once again he examines his escape route, then slides down from the saddle and ties the mare to a hitching post. He steps into a nearby tavern, where he runs into Ford's orchestra director, William Withers Jr., who's having a last quick drink before the eight P.M. curtain. They talk shop, the conversation veering toward mutual friends in the theater. Withers mentions Booth's late father. When Booth suggests that he is the better actor of the two, Withers laughingly shoots back that Booth will never be as talented as his father.

Booth's face hardens, but he manages a thin smile. Focusing his gaze on Withers, he utters the truest sentence he will ever speak: "When I leave the stage I will be the most talked about man in America."

CHAPTER THIRTY-SIX

FRIDAY, APRIL 14, 1865
WASHINGTON, D.C.
8:05 P.M.

"Would you have us be late?" Mary Lincoln chides her husband, standing in his office doorway. Speaker of the House Schuyler Colfax dropped by a half hour ago and was immediately granted a few minutes of Lincoln's time. But those few minutes have stretched into half an hour and, across town, the curtain has already risen on *Our American Cousin*. Making matters worse, the Lincolns still have to stop and pick up their theater guests. They'll be lucky to arrive at Ford's in time for the second act.

It is five minutes after eight. Mary wears a gray dress that shows her ample bosom and a matching bonnet. She is eager to get to the theater but tentative in her approach because Mr. Lincoln's moods have been so unpredictable lately.

Once again, he has lost all track of time. Speaker Colfax stopped in to discuss the possibility of a special session of Congress. Colfax has plans to leave in the morning on a long trip to California but says he will cancel it if Lincoln calls the special session. Lincoln won't hear of it. He tells Colfax to enjoy himself and to enlist the support of the western states in reuniting America.

As he makes to leave, Colfax pauses at the door. He is a true admirer of Lincoln's. Colfax has heard rumors of violence against Lincoln and mentions how afraid he was when Lincoln visited Richmond a week earlier. "Why, if anyone else had been president and gone to Richmond, I would have been alarmed, too," Lincoln chuckles. "But I was not scared about myself a bit."

Lincoln asks Colfax if he has plans for the evening, and, if not, would he be interested in attending *Our American Cousin?* Colfax replies that although he is deeply honored by the invitation, he cannot go.

This marks a half dozen rejections for Lincoln today. First the Grants, then Stanton and Thomas Eckert, then his son Robert just a half hour earlier, and now the Speaker of the House.

Former Massachusetts congressman George Ashmun waits to see Lincoln as Colfax exits. But Mary's pleas finally have an effect. It is time to leave for the theater. Lincoln hastily pulls a card from his jacket pocket and jots a small note inviting Ashmun to return at nine in the morning.

Finally, Lincoln walks downstairs and out onto the front porch, where the presidential carriage awaits.

✍

The roof is now closed, which is a comfort on this misty night. Footman Charles Forbes helps Mary up the steps and into her seat as Lincoln says a few final words to Ashmun and Colfax, who have followed him outside. Suddenly, yet another caller steps out of the night, seeking a few moments of Lincoln's time. The president hears the footsteps on the gravel and the familiar voice of former Illinois congressman Isaac Arnold yelling his name.

Lincoln is about to climb into the carriage, but he waits until Arnold is close enough that they can shake hands. Arnold was a staunch backer of Lincoln's during the war's darkest hours, and the resulting dip in the president's popularity cost him his seat in the House. The least Lincoln can do is acknowledge him. He bends his head to listen as Arnold whispers a quiet petition in his ear.

Lincoln nods but refuses to give an immediate answer. "Excuse me now," he begs. "I am going to the theater. Come see me in the morning."

The Harris residence, at H and Fifteenth Streets, is almost right across the street from the White House, so the Lincolns have little time alone before picking up their guests. But in that short interval Lincoln turns lighthearted and happy, chatting excitedly about the night. Mary is delighted at her husband's sudden jocularity and his ability to seemingly leave the burdens of the White House behind the instant they leave the grounds.

As the carriage threads the seven blocks to the theater, Rathbone, with his muttonchops and broad mustache, sits facing Lincoln, talking about his experiences in the war. Along the way, another impromptu victory parade on Pennsylvania Avenue slows their progress and makes them even later for the show. Once they finally approach Ford's, they can smell and see the tar torches casting their ghostly yellow light on the front of the theater. The carriages of theatergoers line Tenth Street. A crowd of soldiers gathers, there to see Lincoln and Grant. A barker calls out, "This way to Ford's!"

Driver Francis Burns steps down and walks the horses the final few feet to the theater, fearful that the commotion might cause them to bolt. The two cavalry escorts trailing the carriage wheel their horses back to their barracks, knowing that they will return and finish their guard duty once the show ends.

It is eight twenty-five when Lincoln steps through the front door of the theater. A young boy, in a moment he will remember for the rest of his life, shyly offers him a program. The president accepts it with a smile. Now rejoined by bodyguard John Parker, the Lincolns and their guests climb the stairs leading to their box. Onstage, the actors are more than aware that the audience is in a foul mood. Having bought tickets in hopes of seeing Lincoln and Grant, the theatergoers had monitored the state box, only to find that neither was in house.

So when Lincoln finally arrives, there is relief onstage. Laura Keene ad-libs a line that refers to Lincoln, making the audience turn toward the back of the theater in order to witness his appearance. William Withers, the orchestra director who had a drink with John Wilkes Booth less than an hour ago, immediately stops the show's music and instructs the band to perform "Hail to the Chief."

The audience members rise to their feet and cheer, making a noise that Withers can only describe as "breathtaking." Lincoln does not seek out such adulation. Indeed, he has "an almost morbid dread" of causing a scene. But he works the crowd for full effect, allowing Rathbone and Harris to enter the state box first, followed by Mary. Then Lincoln strides forth so the crowd can see him. As patriotic cheering fills the house, he honors his constituents by standing at the edge of the box and bowing twice.

Only when the applause dies down does Lincoln ease into the rocking chair on the left side of the box. A curtain partially shields him from the audience, giving him privacy should he decide to nod off and take a nap. The crowd can see him only if he leans forward and pokes his head over the ledge; otherwise he is entirely invisible to everyone in the theater, except for those in the state box and the actors onstage.

Lincoln takes advantage of the privacy, reaching out for Mary's hand and holding it lovingly. She blushes at such scandalous behavior. "What will Miss Harris make of my hanging on to you so?" she giggles to her husband.

"She will think nothing about it," he replies, squeezing her hand but not letting go.

✑

Behind Lincoln, a single door leads into the state box. On the other side of the door is a narrow unlit hallway. At the end of the hallway is yet another door. This is the only route to and from the state box, and it is John Parker's job to pull up a chair and sit in front of this door, making sure that no one goes in or out.

But on the night of April 14, 1865, as Abraham Lincoln relaxes in his rocking chair and laughs out loud for the first time in months, John Parker gets thirsty. He is bored, and he can't see the play. Taltavul's saloon calls to him. Pushing his chair against the wall, he leaves the door to the state box unguarded and wanders outside. Footman Charles Forbes is taking a nap in the driver's seat of Lincoln's carriage, oblivious to the fog and drizzle.

"How about a little ale?" Parker asks, knowing that Forbes will be an eager drinking buddy. The two walk into Taltavul's and make themselves comfortable. The show won't be over for two more hours—plenty of time to have a couple beers and appear perfectly sober when the Lincolns need them again.

President Abraham Lincoln's only bodyguard, a man with a career-long history of inappropriate and negligent behavior, has left his post for the last time. Incredibly, he will never be punished for this gross dereliction of duty.

CHAPTER THIRTY-SEVEN

FRIDAY, APRIL 14, 1865
WASHINGTON, D.C.
8:45 P.M.

Less than two hours to go.

John Wilkes Booth summarizes the final details with his co-conspirators as the Lincolns settle into their seats. Though Lewis Powell checked out of his hotel room hours earlier, the four men meet outside the Herndon House because of its close proximity to Ford's. With the exception of Atzerodt, each man is on horseback. Though he has been drinking steadily on and off all day, Booth is thinking and acting clearly. None of the co-conspirators has any cause to doubt him.

First, and most important, Booth tells them, the precise time of the president's assassination will be ten-fifteen P.M. Unlike the night before, when the assassination plans had a haphazard quality, tonight's events are timed to the minute. Shows at Ford's usually start promptly. If that's the case, then Harry Hawk will be alone onstage, delivering his punch line, at precisely ten-fifteen.

Second, Booth tells them, the murders of Seward and Johnson must also take place at ten-fifteen. The precision is vital. There can be no advance warning or alarm to the intended targets. The attacks must be a complete surprise. Booth hopes to create the illusion that Washington, D.C., is a hotbed of assassins, resulting in the sort of mass chaos that will make it easier for him and his men to escape. With officials looking everywhere for the killers, on streets filled with bon-fires and spontaneous parades and hordes of drunken revelers, blending in to the bedlam should be as simple as staying calm.

Next comes the list of assignments. The job of murdering of Sec-retary of State Seward will be a two-man affair, with Lewis Powell and David Herold now working together. Powell will be the man who actually walks up to the door, finds a way to enter the house, and commits the crime. The ruse that will get him in the door is a fake bottle of medication, which Powell will claim was sent by Seward's physician.

Herold's role is to assist in the getaway. He knows Washington's back alleys and shortcuts and will guide Powell, who knows little about the city, to safety. During the murder, Herold must wait outside and hold their horses. Once Powell exits the house, the two men will gallop across town by a roundabout method in order to confuse anyone try-ing to give chase. Then they will leave town via the Navy Yard Bridge and rendezvous in the Maryland countryside.

As for George Atzerodt, he will act alone. Killing Vice President Andrew Johnson does not look to be a difficult task. Though Johnson is a vigorous man, he is known to be unguarded and alone most of the time. Atzerodt is to knock on the door of his hotel room and shoot him when he answers. Atzerodt will also escape Washington via the Navy Yard Bridge, then gallop into Maryland to meet up with the others. From there, Atzerodt's familiarity with smugglers' trails will allow him to guide the men into the Deep South.

Once the plans are finalized, Booth will head for Ford's. There he will bide his time, making sure the theater's entries and exits are unguarded, that the secret backstage passageways are clear, and that his horse is ready and waiting.

∽

Booth clears his throat just before they ride off in their different direc-tions. He tells them about the letter he wrote to the *National Intelli-gencer*, implicating all of them in this grand triple assassination. The message is clear: there is no going back. If the men object to Booth outing them, there is no historical record to show it.

Booth looks over his gang. These four unlikely men are about to change the course of history, just as surely as Grant or Lincoln or Lee or any of the hundreds of thousands of men who died during the Civil War. They are now ninety minutes away from becoming the most wanted men in all of the world.

He wishes them good luck, then spurs his horse and trots off to Ford's.

CHAPTER THIRTY-EIGHT

Booth guides his mare into the alley behind Ford's. The night is quiet, save for the peals of laughter coming from inside the theater. He dismounts and shouts for Ned Spangler to come hold his horse. The sceneshifter appears at the back door, visibly distressed about the possibility of missing an all-important stage cue. Booth doesn't care. He demands that Spangler come outside and secure the animal. The last thing Booth needs is for his escape to be thwarted by a runaway mare.

Spangler, completely unaware of the assassination plot, insists that he can't do the job. Booth, ever persuasive, insists. The unshaven, heavy-lidded stagehand weakens but does not capitulate. His employment is contingent on moving the right scenes at the right time. He is willing to do anything for a great actor such as Booth—anything but lose his job. Leaving Booth in the alley, Spangler dashes back into the theater and returns with Joseph Burroughs, a young boy who does odd jobs at Ford's and goes by the nickname "Peanut John." Booth hands Peanut John the reins and demands that he remain at the back door, holding the horse, until he returns. The boy must not leave that spot for any reason.

Peanut John, hoping that Booth will give him a little something for the effort, agrees. He sits on the stone step and shivers in the damp night air, his fist clutched tightly around those reins.

Booth slides into the theater. The sound of the onstage actors speaking their lines fills the darkened backstage area. He speaks in a hush as he removes his riding gloves, making a show of saying hello to the cast and crew, most of whom he knows well. His eyes scrutinize the layout, memorizing the location of every stagehand and prop, not wanting anything to get in the way of his exit.

There is a tunnel beneath the stage, crossing from one side to the other. Booth checks to make sure that nothing clutters the passage. Nobody guesses for an instant that he is checking out escape routes. When he reaches the far side, Booth exits Ford's through yet another backstage door. This one leads to an alley, which funnels down onto Tenth Street.

There's no one there.

In one short dash through Ford's Theatre, Booth has learned that his escape route is not blocked, that nobody is loitering in the alley who could potentially tackle him or otherwise stop him from getting away, and that the cast and crew think it's the most normal thing in the world for him to stroll into and out of the theater.

And, indeed, no one questions why he's there nor finds it even remotely suspicious.

&

Feeling very pleased with himself, Booth pops in Taltavul's for a whiskey. He orders a whole bottle, then sits down at the bar. Incredibly, Lincoln's bodyguard is sipping a large tankard of ale just a few feet away.

Booth smiles as he pours water into his whiskey, then raises the glass in a toast to himself.

What am I about to do? Can I really go through with this?

He pushes the doubts from his head. *We are at war. This is not murder. You will become immortal.*

At ten P.M. Booth double-checks to make sure John Parker is still drinking at the other end of the bar. Then, leaving the nearly full whiskey bottle on the bar, he softly lowers his glass and walks back to Ford's.

CHAPTER THIRTY-NINE

FRIDAY, APRIL 14, 1865
WASHINGTON, D.C.
10:00 P.M.

The third act is under way. Soon the play will be over, and Lincoln can get back to the White House. Meanwhile, the unheated state box has gotten chilly. Abraham Lincoln drops Mary's hand as he rises to put on his overcoat, tailored in a black wool specially for his oversized frame by Brooks Brothers. The silk lining is decorated with an eagle clutching a banner in its beak. The words on the streamer are Lincoln's unspoken manifesto, and every time he slips on the coat he is reminded of his mission. "One country, one destiny," it reads, quite simply.

Sitting back down in the horsehair rocker, Lincoln shifts his gaze from the performers directly below him. He pushes back the privacy curtain, then leans forward over the railing to look down and to the left, at the audience.

Lincoln lets go of the curtain and returns his attention to *Our American Cousin.*

It is seven minutes after ten. At the exact same moment, John Wilkes Booth strolls through the front door of Ford's—heart racing, whiskey on his breath, skin clammy to the touch. He is desperately trying to appear calm and cool. Always a man of manners, Booth takes off his hat and holds it with one hand. When ticket taker John

Buckingham makes a joke of letting him in for free, "courtesy of the house," Booth notices the bulge in Buckingham's lip and asks if he has any extra tobacco. Like so many other minor theater employees, Buckingham is in awe of Booth's celebrity. Not only does he hand over a small plug of tobacco, he also summons the courage to ask if he might introduce Booth to some close friends who happen to be at the show. "Later," Booth promises with a wink.

Buckingham notes the deathly pallor on Booth's face and how incredibly nervous the normally nonchalant actor seems to be. As Booth walks off, Buckingham's fellow Ford's employee Joseph Sessford points out that Booth has been in and out of the theater all day. "Wonder what he's up to?" Sessford mutters to Buckingham. They watch as Booth climbs the staircase to the dress circle, which accesses the hallway to the state box. But neither man thinks Booth's unusual behavior merits closer scrutiny. They watch him disappear up the stairs and then once again return their attention to the front door and to the patrons late in returning from intermission.

∽

At the top of the stairs, Booth enters the dress circle lobby. He is now inside the darkened theater, standing directly behind the seats of the second-level audience. He hums softly to himself to calm his nerves. In hopes of increasing the theater's capacity for this special performance, Ford's management has placed extra chairs in this corridor, and now Booth walks past two Union officers sitting in those seats. They recognize the famous actor and then turn their focus back to the play. They make no move to stop him, because they have no reason to.

Booth approaches the door leading into the state box. It is attended by a White House messenger but not a pistol-packing bodyguard. He sees the chair where John Parker should be sitting and breathes a sigh of relief that the bodyguard is still in the saloon. Handing the messenger one of his calling cards, Booth steps through the doorway without a question.

In the theater below, a young girl who came to the theater hoping to see Lincoln has spent the night staring up at the state box, waiting for him to show his face. Now she is awed by the sight of John Wilkes Booth, the famous and dashing actor, standing in the shadows above her. At the same time, her heart leaps as Lincoln moves his gaze from the stage to the audience, once again poking his head out over the railing. Finally, with the play almost over, she has seen the president! She turns to the man next to her, Taltavul's owner, Jim Ferguson, and grins at her good fortune.

She turns to get another glimpse of Booth, but by then he has already pushed through the door and now stands in the darkened hallway leading into the state box. He is completely alone. If he wants, he can go back out the door and get on with his life as if nothing has happened. The letter boasting of his deed has not yet been sent. Other than the other members of the conspiracy, no one will be the wiser. But if he walks forward down the hallway, then through the rear door of Lincoln's box, his life will change forever.

Booth has a head full of whiskey and a heart full of hate. He thinks of the Confederate cause and Lincoln's promise to give slaves the vote. And then Booth remembers that no one can put a stop to it but him. He is the one man who can, and will, make a difference. There will be no going back.

Earlier that day Booth spied a wooden music stand in the state box. He now jams it into the side of the door leading to the corridor. The music stand has become a dead bolt, and Booth double-checks to make sure it is lodged firmly against the wooden door frame. This seals the door shut from the inside. When he is done, the door might as well be locked, so perfect is his blockade. It's impossible to push open from the other side. No one in the theater can get in to stop him.

Booth then creeps down the hallway. Booth's second act of preparation that afternoon was using a pen knife to carve a very small peephole in the door of the state box. Now he looks through that hole to get a better view of the president.

✍

As Booth already knows, the state box is shaped like a parallelogram. The walls to the left and right of Lincoln slant inward. Booth sees that Clara Harris and Major Rathbone sit along the wall to his far right, at an angle to the stage, and the Lincolns sit along the railing. The Lincolns look out directly onto the stage, while Clara and her beau must turn their heads slightly to the right to see the show—if they look directly forward they will be gazing at Mary and Abraham Lincoln in profile.

But it is not their view of Lincoln that matters. What matters is that Booth, through the peephole, is staring right at the back of Lincoln's head. He can hear the players down below, knowing that in a few short lines Harry Hawk's character Asa Trenchard will be alone, delivering his "sockdologizing old man-trap" line.

That line is Booth's cue—and just ten seconds away.

Booth presses his black hat back down onto his head, then removes the loaded Deringer from his coat pocket and grasps it in his right fist. With his left hand, he slides the long, razor-sharp Bowie knife from its sheath.

Booth takes a deep breath and softly pushes the door open with his knife hand. The box is dimly lit from the footlights down below. He can see only faces. No one knows he's there. He presses his body against the wall, careful to stay in the shadows while awaiting his cue. Abraham Lincoln's head pokes over the top of his rocking chair, just four short feet in front of Booth; then once again he looks down and to the left, at the audience.

"You sockdologizing old man-trap" booms out through the theater. The audience explodes in laughter.

CHAPTER FORTY

─────────

A few blocks away, someone knocks hard on the front door of the "Old Clubhouse," the home of Secretary of State William Seward. The three-story brick house facing Lafayette Park, across the street from the White House, took that name from its day as the headquarters of the elite Washington Club. Tragedy paid a visit to the building in 1859, when a congressman shot his mistress's husband on a nearby lawn. The husband, Philip Barton Key, was a United States attorney and the son of Francis Scott Key, who wrote "The Star-Spangled Banner." Key's body was carried inside the club, where he passed away in a first-floor parlor.

That tragedy, however, will pale in comparison with what will happen in the next ten minutes.

There is another sharp knock, even though it's been only a few seconds since the first one. This time the pounding is more insistent. Secretary Seward does not hear it, for he is sleeping upstairs, his medication causing him to drift between consciousness and unconsciousness. William Bell, a young black servant in a pressed white coat, hurries to the entryway.

"Yes, sir?" he asks, opening the door and seeing an unfamiliar face.

A handsome young man with long, thick hair stares back from the porch. He wears an expensive slouch hat and stands a couple inches over six feet. His jaw is awry on the left, as if it was badly broken and then healed improperly. "I have medicine from Dr. Verdi," he says in an Alabama drawl, holding up a small vial.

"Yes, sir. I'll take it to him," Bell says, reaching for the bottle.

"It has to be delivered personally."

Bell looks at him curiously. Secretary Seward's physician had visited just an hour ago. Before leaving, he'd administered a sedative and insisted that there be no more visitors tonight. "Sir, I can't let you go upstairs. I have strict orders—"

"You're talking to a white man, boy. This medicine is for your master and, by God, you're going to give it to him."

When Bell protests further, Lewis Powell pushes past him, saying, "Out of my way, nigger. I'm going up."

Bell simply doesn't know how to stop the intruder.

✍

Powell starts climbing the steps from the foyer to the living area. Bell is a step behind at all times, pleading forgiveness and politely asking that Powell tread more softly. The sound of the southerner's heavy work boots on the wooden steps echoes through the house. "I'm sorry I talked rough to you," Bell says sheepishly.

"That's all right," Powell sighs, pleased that the hardest part of the plot is behind him. He feared he wouldn't gain access to the Seward home and would botch his part of the plan. The next step is locating Seward's bedroom.

Out front, in the shadow of a tree across the street, David Herold holds their horses, prepared for the escape.

✍

But now the secretary's son Frederick stands at the top of the stairs in a dressing gown, blocking Powell's path. He was in bed with his wife, but the sound of Powell's boots woke him. Young Seward, fresh off a heady day that saw him represent his father at Lincoln's cabinet meeting, demands to know Powell's business.

Politely and deferentially, Powell holds up the medicine vial and swears that Dr. Verdi told him to deliver it to William Seward and William Seward only.

Seward takes one look at Powell and misjudges him as a simpleton. Rather than argue, he walks into his father's bedroom to see if he is awake.

This is the break the assassin is looking for. Now he knows exactly which room belongs to the secretary of state. He grows excited, eager to get the job done as quickly as possible. He can feel the revolver stuffed inside his waistband.

Frederick Seward returns. "He's sleeping. Give it to me."

"I was ordered to give it to the secretary."

"You cannot see Mr. Seward. I am his son and the assistant secretary of state. Go back and tell the doctor that I refused to let you go into the sickroom, because Mr. Seward was sleeping."

"Very well, sir," says Powell, handing Frederick the vial. "I will go."

As Frederick Seward accepts the vial, Powell turns and takes three steps down the stairs. Suddenly he turns. He sprints back up to the landing, drawing a navy revolver. He levels the gun, curses, and pulls the trigger.

But the gun jams. Frederick Seward will later tell police he thought he was a dead man. Frederick cries out in fear and pain, throwing up his arms to defend himself. He has the advantage of standing one step higher than Powell but only for a second. The two men grapple as Powell leaps up onto the landing and then uses the butt of his gun to pistol-whip Frederick. Finally, Frederick Seward is knocked unconscious. His body makes a horrible thud as he collapses to the floor, his skull shattered in two places, gray brain matter trickling out through the gashes, blood streaming down his face.

"Murder, murder, murder!" cries William Bell from the ground floor. He sprints out the front door and into the night, screaming at the top of his lungs.

∾

Across the street, David Herold holds the two getaway horses. Bell's cries are sure to bring soldiers and police to the house within minutes. Suddenly, the long list of reasons why Herold wants to be part of the

Lincoln conspiracy are forgotten. He panics. He ties Powell's horse to a tree, spurs his own mount, and gallops down Fifteenth Street.

Back inside the Seward home, Lewis Powell isn't done. He pounds on Frederick's head without mercy, blood spattering the walls and his own hands and face. The beating is so savage that Powell's pistol literally falls to pieces in his hands. Only then does he stand up straight and begin walking toward the secretary of state's bedroom.

CHAPTER FORTY-ONE

The commotion in the hallway and the sound of a body dropping heavily to the hardwood floor have alerted twenty-year-old Fanny Seward to the intrusion. The daughter of the secretary of state is clad only in a nightdress and has been sitting at the foot of her father's bed, trying to coax him to sleep. Also inside the room is Sergeant George Robinson, sent by the army to watch over Seward. Now Private Robinson pushes his full weight against the door, even as the assassin tries to fight his way in. Soon Lewis Powell forces open the door and slashes at Robinson with his Bowie knife, cutting the soldier's forehead to the bone and almost putting out an eye. As Robinson crumples to the ground, Fanny Seward places herself between Powell and her father. "Please don't kill him," she begs, terrified. "Please, please don't kill him."

Secretary Seward then awakens on the bed. Something about the word "kill" jars him from his slumber.

Powell punches Fanny Seward hard in the face, instantly knocking her unconscious. A split second later he is on the bed, plunging his knife downward into Seward's neck and shoulders.

The room is pitch-black, save for the sliver of light from the open door. Powell's first thrust misses, making a hollow thud as it slams into the headboard. Seward desperately tries to roll away from his attacker and squeeze down into the gap between the mattress and the wall.

He doesn't succeed. Powell kneels over him, stabbing Seward again and again and again. The secretary wears a splint on his broken jaw, which, luckily, deflects the knife away from the jugular vein, but it does little to protect the rest of his skull. The right side of his face is sliced away from the bone and now hangs like a flap. Blood jets from three deep punctures in his neck, drenching his now-useless bandages, his nightdress, and the white bedsheets and spattering all over Powell's torso.

The assassin is almost finished. Powell brings up his knife for one final killer blow. But at that exact moment, Seward's son Augustus enters the room. He is thirty-nine, a decorated graduate of West Point and a career army officer. He has fought in the Mexican War, battled the Apache, and seen action in the Civil War. Never once has he been injured. But now, that changes. Powell leaps at August Seward, stabbing him seven times. In the midst of the attack, Private Robinson staggers to his feet and rejoins the fight. For his trouble, Robinson is stabbed four more times.

∽

Powell is finally exhausted. Lying in front of him are four human beings, all of them still alive. But Powell doesn't know that. He steps over Fanny's limp body and races from the room, still clutching his knife. At that very moment, State Department messenger Emerick Hansell arrives at the Seward home on official business. He sees Powell, covered with blood, running down the steps and turns to flee for his life. But Powell catches him, stabbing the courier just above the fourth vertebrae. Powell is in such a hurry, fortunately, that he pulls the knife back out before it can go any deeper, thus sparing Hansell's life.

"I'm mad! I'm mad!" Powell screams as he runs into the night, hoping to scare off anyone who might try to stop him.

He is, however, anything but mad. Powell is as lucid as he is powerful. He now turns all his focus to the getaway. With adrenaline coursing through his veins, his senses heightened, and his broad shoulders aching from fists rained down upon him in the fight, he hurls the blood-covered knife into the gutter. He then looks right and left into the darkness for David Herold and their getaway horses. Seeing nothing, he listens for a telltale clip-clop of approaching horseshoes.

"Murder! Murder!" William Bell cries from the porch, risking his life by chasing after Powell. Soldiers come running from a nearby sentry box. Powell sees his horse now, tied to the tree where Herold left it. Realizing he has been betrayed, Powell feels his heart sink. He knows that without Herold he will be lost on the streets of Washington. Still, he can't very well just stand around. He needs to get moving. Powell unties the horse and mounts up. He has the good sense to wipe the blood and sweat from his face with a handkerchief. Then, instead of galloping away, he kicks his heels gently into the horse's flanks and trots casually down Fifteenth Street, trailed all the while by William Bell and his shouts of "Murder!" But instead of stopping him, the unsuspecting soldiers ignore the black man and run right past Powell.

After a block and a half, Bell falls behind. He eventually returns to the Seward home, where four gravely injured men and one woman lie. Incredibly, they will all recover. But this horrific night will haunt them for the rest of their lives.

Lewis Powell trots his horse toward the darkness on the edge of town. There he hides in a field and wonders if he will ever find a way out of Washington. Powell's thoughts then turn to President Lincoln and Vice President Johnson. They should be dead by now.

CHAPTER FORTY-TWO

A s John Wilkes Booth tiptoes into the state box and Lewis Powell knocks on William Seward's front door, George Atzerodt, the would-be assassin of Vice President Andrew Johnson, is drinking hard, late for his date with destiny.

If any man in Washington has incurred the wrath of the Confederacy, it is Johnson, the former governor of Tennessee, whom many southerners consider a rank traitor. Johnson's bitter words are seldom compatible with Lincoln's. So it is no surprise that his views on punishing the South stand in stark contrast to Lincoln's lenience. "And what shall be done with the leaders of the rebel host? I know what I would do if I were president. I would arrest them as traitors, I would try them as traitors, and, by the Eternal, I would hang them as traitors," Johnson shouted from the steps of the War Department as recently as Monday night.

Like Johnson, Atzerodt the carriage painter is staying at Kirkwood House, on the corner of Pennsylvania Avenue and Twelfth Street, four blocks from the White House and just one block from Ford's Theatre. He has passed the time aimlessly since his meeting with Booth and the other conspirators, drawing attention to himself through the simple act of trying not to draw attention to himself.

At nine-thirty he visits Naylor's stable on E Street to pick up his horse. The owner knows George Atzerodt and his friend David Herold and does not care for either of them. Nevertheless, when a nervous, sweating Atzerodt asks if he'd like to get a drink, Naylor answers with a quick "Don't mind if I do." He is concerned about Herold, who rented a horse from him earlier that day and is long overdue. Naylor hopes that Atzerodt will disclose his friend's location after a drink or two.

They leave Atzerodt's mare and walk to the bar of the Union Hotel. Atzerodt, whom Naylor suspects has been drinking for some time, orders a stiff whiskey; Naylor chugs a tankard of ale. Atzerodt pays. They return to the stable after just one round, with Naylor none the wiser about Herold's location.

"Your friend is staying out very late with his horse," Naylor finally prods. Atzerodt has just handed him a five-dollar tip for boarding his horse.

"He'll be back after a while," Atzerodt glibly replies as he mounts the mare.

But Atzerodt is too wasted on alcohol to ride a straight line. He almost falls out of the saddle when the mare takes a sudden turn. On a hunch, Naylor decides to follow Atzerodt on foot. The trail, however, is only a block long. Atzerodt dismounts and ties the horse at a hitching post in front of Kirkwood House. Naylor waits across the street, just out of sight. When Atzerodt walks back out a few minutes later and trots the mare over toward Ford's Theatre, Naylor gives up the surveillance and returns to his stable.

∽

Andrew Johnson, meanwhile, is behaving very much like a man waiting to be summoned. He eats an early dinner alone. He turns down a last-minute invitation to attend *Our American Cousin*. His assistant is out for the night, and Johnson has no one to talk with. So he goes up to his room and lies down on his bed, fully clothed, as if some great incident is about to occur and he needs to be ready to spring into action on a moment's notice. Johnson is a boorish man. Largely uneducated, he learned to read and write late in his life. A tailor by trade, he entered politics in his twenties and worked his way up to the Senate. He owes a lot to President Lincoln, who first appointed him the military governor of Tennessee and then chose him to run on the vice presidential ticket after Lincoln asked Hannibal Hamlin of Maine to step down. Hamlin was a hard-core northerner and Lincoln needed a southern presence on the ticket.

Up until this point, Johnson has had no power at all. He is simply a figurehead.

∽

At ten-fifteen George Atzerodt is back inside Kirkwood House, getting thoroughly smashed in the bar. Truth be told, even more than when he tried to bow out a few days earlier, the German-born carriage painter wants no part of murder. A few floors above him, Johnson lies alone in his room. In his lifetime he will suffer the ignominy of impeachment and endure the moniker of "worst president in history." Andrew Johnson will not, however, suffer the far worse fate of death at the hand of an assassin. For that, Johnson can thank the effects of alcohol, as a now very drunk George Atzerodt continues to raise his glass.

CHAPTER FORTY-THREE

John Wilkes Booth takes a bold step out of the shadows, Deringer clutched in his right fist and knife in his left. He extends his arm and aims for the back of Abraham Lincoln's head. No one sees him. No one knows he is there.

Booth squeezes the trigger. Unlike the crazed Richard Lawrence, whose pistols misfired when he attempted to assassinate Andrew Jackson, Booth feels his gun kick. The ball launches down the barrel as the audience guffaws at the play. Abraham Lincoln has chosen this precise moment to lean forward and turn his head to the left for another long look down into the audience. A half second later, he would have been leaning so far forward that the ball would have missed his skull completely. But the president is not so lucky. The man who has worried and fretted and bullied America back from the brink of disaster, holding fast to his faith in the Union at a time when lesser men argued that it should be dissolved, feels a split second snap of pain—and then nothing at all.

"The ball entered through the occipital bone about one inch to the left of the median line and just above the left lateral sinus, which it opened," the autopsy will read. "It then penetrated the dura matter, passed through the left posterior lobe of the cerebrum, entered the left lateral ventricle and lodged in the white matter of the cerebrum just above the anterior portion of the left corpus striatum."

The president's calvarium—or skullcap—will be removed with a saw. A surgeon will probe the exposed brain before slicing into it with a scalpel, using the path of coagulated blood to trace the trajectory of the ball. This will show that the ball entered behind the left ear and traveled diagonally across the brain, coming to rest above the right eye.

Yet the autopsy will be inconclusive. Four different doctors will examine the body. Each will have a different conclusion about what happened once the sphere of Britannia metal poked a neat round hole in Lincoln's skull and then pushed fragments of that bone deep into Lincoln's brain as it traveled precisely seven and a half inches before plowing to a stop in the dense gray matter.

∽

At ten-fifteen on the night of April 14, 1865, President Abraham Lincoln slumps forward in his rocking chair. Mary Lincoln, lost in the play until this very instant, stops laughing. Major Henry Reed Rathbone snaps his head around at the sound of gunfire—a sound he knows all too well from the battlefield. He's had his back to the door, but in an instant he's on his feet, striking a defensive pose.

John Wilkes Booth drops the Deringer and switches the knife to his right hand. Just in time, for Major Rathbone sets aside his own safety and vaults across the small space. Booth raises the knife to shoulder level and brings it down in a hacking motion. Rathbone throws his left arm up in a defensive reflex and instantly feels the knife cut straight down through skin and biceps to the bone.

Booth moves quickly. He steps to the front of the box, ignoring a stricken Mary Lincoln. "Freedom!" he bellows down to the audience, though in all the laughter and the growing confusion as to why the cast has added the sound of gunfire to the scene, his words are barely heard. Harry Hawk stands alone on stage, staring up at the state box with growing concern.

Booth hurls his body over the railing. Up until this point, he has performed every single aspect of the assassination perfectly. But now he misjudges the thickness of the massive United States flag decorating the front of the box. He means to hold on to the railing with one hand as he vaults, throwing his feet up and over the edge, then landing on the stage like a conquering hero.

This sort of leap is actually his specialty. Booth is famous among the theatrical community for his unrehearsed gymnastics, sometimes inserting jumps and drops into Shakespeare plays on a whim. During one memorable performance of *Macbeth*, his fall to the stage was several feet longer than the fall from the state box.

But Booth's right spur gets tangled in the flag's folds. Instead of a gallant two-footed landing on the stage, Booth topples heavily from the state box. He drops to the boards awkwardly, left foot and two hands braced in a bumbling attempt to catch his fall.

The fibula of Booth's lower left leg, a small bone that bears little weight, snaps two inches above the ankle. The fracture is complete, dividing the bone into two neat pieces. If not for the tightness of Booth's boot, which forms an immediate splint, the bone would poke through the skin.

Now Booth lies on the stage in front of a nearly packed house. His leg is broken. He holds a blood-smeared dagger in his right hand. The sound of gunfire has just ricocheted around Ford's. Major Rathbone is bleeding profusely from a severe stab wound. And just above him, slumped forward as if very drunk or very asleep, the president of the United States is unconscious.

∾

Yet still nobody knows what happened. James Ford steps out of the box office and thinks Booth is pulling some crazy stunt to get attention. Observers in the audience have heard the pop and are amazed by the sudden appearance of a famous matinee idol making a cameo on the stage right before their very eyes—perhaps adding some comical whimsy to this very special evening. Harry Hawk still holds center stage, his head turned toward Booth, wondering why in the world he would intrude on the performance.

Time stops for a second—but only one.

Then the assassin takes charge. "Booth dragged himself up on one knee," Hawk will later remember, "and was slashing that long knife around him like one who was crazy. It was then, I am sure, I heard him say, 'The South shall be free!' I recognized Booth as he regained his feet and came toward me, waving his knife. I did not know what he had done or what his purpose might be. I did simply what any man would have done—I ran."

Booth scurries to his feet and limps off the stage, "with a motion," observes one spectator, "like the hopping of a bull frog."

"Stop that man!" Major Rathbone screams from above.

"Won't somebody please stop that man!" Clara Harris echoes.

"What is the matter?" cries a voice from the audience.

"The president has been shot!" she shouts back.

The reverie is shattered, and with it all the joy of Washington's postwar celebration. The theater explodes in confusion. In an instant, the audience is on its feet. It is a scene of utter chaos, "a hell of all hells." Men climb up and over the seats, some fleeing toward the exits while others race to the stage, hoping to climb up into the box and be part of the action. Women faint. Children are trapped in the panic. "Water!" some yell, tending to the collapsed.

A former congressman yells something far more pointed: "Hang the scoundrel!"

Meanwhile, Booth passes within inches of leading lady Laura Keene as he limps off the stage. William Withers, the orchestra leader with whom he had a drink just hours earlier, stands between Booth and the stage door. Withers is paralyzed with fear, but Booth assumes he is intentionally blocking the way and slashes at him, "the sharp blade ripping through the collar of my coat, penetrating my vest and under garments, and inflicting a flesh wound in my neck," Withers will later testify.

Only one man is bold enough to give chase. Set carpenter Jake Ritterspaugh and Booth reach the stage door at the very same time. Booth thrusts the knife blade at him. Ritterspaugh leaps back. And in that instant, Booth is gone, squeezing through the door and hauling himself up into the saddle.

Rather than give Peanut John the shiny nickel the boy had hoped for, Booth kicks him hard and bludgeons him with the butt of his knife.

"He kicked me! He kicked me!" the boy moans, falling to the ground.

At the same instant, yet another spontaneous torchlight parade blocks Booth's getaway on Tenth Street. He swerves into the alley, spurs his horse down the cobblestones dividing two large brick buildings, and then turns onto F Street, completely avoiding the procession.

In an instant, John Wilkes Booth disappears into the night.

ASSASSINATION OF PRESIDENT LINCOLN, FORD'S THEATRE, WASHINGTON, APRIL 14. 1865.

Editorial illustrations depicting the assassination of President Lincoln

CHAPTER FORTY-FOUR

Friday, April 14, 1865
Washington, D.C.
10:20 p.m.

Booth slows the mare to a walk. Word is already spreading through Washington that the president has been shot. The news is shouted, breathlessly exclaimed, passed from citizen to citizen, bonfire to bonfire. People aren't racing away from Ford's, they're racing *to* Ford's, to see for themselves if these wild rumors are true. Victory marches turn into mobs of the curious and scared, determined to fight their way to the theater.

When a drunk shouts into the night, "I'm glad it happened!" a furious mob beats and kicks him unconscious, tearing off his clothes, and hauls his limp body to a lamppost for a lynching. Ironically, he will be rescued by the Union cavalry.

Now another troop of cavalry is summoned to Ford's and plunges recklessly through the throngs assembling outside. Inside, the crowd surges toward the stage, trapping small children in its midst, chanting all the while that Booth must be lynched. Laura Keene has the presence of mind to march to center stage and cry out for calm and sanity, but her words go unheeded. The crush against the stage is made worse as the news explodes into the street in front of Ford's Theatre. Passersby rush inside to see for themselves, some of them hoping that

Booth is still trapped inside but most just wanting a glimpse of the injured president.

Across town at Grover's Theatre, the patriotic celebration is in full swing. A young boy is reciting a poem when a man bursts into the theater and shouts that the president has been shot. As the crowd reacts in horror, a young soldier stands and yells for everyone to sit still. "It's a ruse of the pickpockets," he says, explaining that thieves spread such disinformation to fleece the crowd as people rush for the exit.

The six hundred theatergoers take their seats once again. The boy onstage exits, his poetry reading complete. But he is back just seconds later, struggling to control his voice as he shares the horrific news that President Lincoln has, indeed, been shot. Tad Lincoln, the president's twelve-year-old son, is in the audience with a White House staffer. Stunned, he returns to the White House, where he collapses into the arms of the doorkeeper, shouting, "They've killed Papa dead! They've killed Papa dead."

∽

Soon more bad news begins to spread: Secretary Seward has been assaulted in his bed.

At Rullman's Hotel, on Pennsylvania Avenue, the bartender shouts out the mournful news that Lincoln has been shot. Mike O'Laughlen, the would-be conspirator who stalked the Grants last night, drinks in the corner. He is drunk again but still coherent enough to know in an instant that Booth is the killer—and that he must get out of town before someone implicates him, too.

In front of the Willard Hotel, the stable foreman John Fletcher is still seething that David Herold hasn't return the roan he rented earlier. At that very moment, Herold trots past. "You get off that horse now!" Fletcher cries, springing out into the street and grabbing for the bridle. But Herold spurs the horse and gallops away. Acting quickly, Fletcher sprints back to his stable, saddles a horse, and races after him.

In the midst of all this, a lone rider galloping away from the chaos at Ford's would most certainly attract attention. So Booth guides the mare slowly up and down the streets and alleys of Washington, even as his veins course with adrenaline and euphoria, and pandemonium breaks out all around him. Despite his considerable celebrity, Booth blends in and proceeds unmolested through the streets. It is Friday night, after all, a time when Washington comes to life. There are plenty of men trotting horses through town. It's only when Booth finally nears the end of his three-mile journey to the Navy Yard Bridge that his fears about being caught force him to spur the horse and ride hard to freedom.

It is ten forty-five when Booth pulls back on the reins once again and canters up to the wooden drawbridge by the Navy Yard—almost thirty long minutes since the Deringer did its deadly job. Booth approaches like a man confident that his path will go unblocked. "Where are you going, sir?" cries the military sentry. His name is Silas T. Cobb, and his long and boring shift will be over at midnight. He notices the lather on the horse's flanks, a sign that it's been ridden hard.

"Home. Down in Charles," Booth replies.

"Didn't you know, my friend, that it is against the laws to pass here after nine o'clock?" Cobb is required to challenge anyone entering or exiting Washington, but the truth of the matter is that the war has ended and with it the formal restrictions on crossing the bridge after curfew. He wants no trouble, just to finish his shift in peace and get a good night's sleep.

"No," lies Booth. He explains that he's been waiting for the full moon to rise, so that he might navigate the darkened roads by night. And, indeed, a waning moon is rising at that very moment.

"I will pass you," Cobb sighs. "But I don't know I ought to."

"Hell, I guess there'll be no trouble about that," Booth shoots back. Ignoring the rule that horses be walked across the bridge, he trots the mare into the night.

Booth is barely across the Potomac when David Herold approaches Silas T. Cobb. He gives his name as just "Smith." Once again, after a brief discussion, Cobb lets him pass.

One more rider approaches Cobb that night. He is John Fletcher, the stable foreman who is following David Herold. Fletcher can clearly see Herold on the other side of the bridge, now disappearing into the Maryland night.

"You can cross," Cobb tells him, "but my orders say I can't let anyone back across the bridge until morning."

The Maryland countryside, with its smugglers and spies and illicit operatives, is the last place John Fletcher wants to spend the night. He turns his horse's reins back toward his stable, settling on the hope that Herold and the missing horse will one day make the mistake of riding back into Washington.

In fact, Fletcher will never see the horse again, for it will soon be shot dead, its body left to rot in the backwoods of Maryland—yet another victim of the most spectacular assassination conspiracy in the history of man.

CHAPTER FORTY-FIVE

Lincoln's life is slipping away. Mary Lincoln lays her head to the president's breast as Major Rathbone uses his one good arm to yank the music stand from its notch in the doorway. Booth's knife missed a major artery by just one-third of an inch. Otherwise Rathbone would now be dead.

The major swings open the outer door of the state box. Dozens of unruly theatergoers fill the dress circle and try to fight their way into the state box. "Doctors only!" Rathbone shouts as blood drips down his arm and pools on the floor. The truth is that the major needs medical attention, but all eyes are on Lincoln.

"I'm bleeding to death!" Rathbone shouts as a twenty-three-year-old doctor, Charles Leale, fights his way forward. Dr. Leale came to the theater solely because he wanted to see Lincoln in person. Now he is the first physician to come upon the crime scene. Leale reaches out a hand and lifts Rathbone's chin so that he might look into his eyes and gauge his physical condition. Noting in an instant that Rathbone is quite obviously not bleeding to death, Dr. Leale turns his attention to Lincoln.

"Oh, Doctor," sobs Mary Lincoln as Leale slowly removes her from her husband's body. "Can he recover? Will you take charge of him?"

"I will do what I can," Dr. Leale says calmly. With a nod to the crowd of men who have followed him into the box, the young doctor makes it clear that Mary must be removed. She is ushered to a couch on the other side of the box, next to Clara Harris, who begins stroking her hand.

Leale asks for a lamp and orders that no one else be admitted to the state box except for physicians. Then he stands in front of the rocking chair, facing Lincoln's slumped head. He pushes the body upright, the head lolling back against the rocker. He can feel the slightest breath from Lincoln's nose and mouth, but Leale is reluctant to touch the body without making a preliminary observation. One thing, however, is quite clear: Lincoln is not dead.

Dr. Leale can't find any sign of injury. Onlookers light matches so that he can see better, and the call goes out for a lamp. The front of Lincoln's body shows no sign of physical violence, and the forward slumping indicates that the attack must have come from behind. Yet there's no visible entry wound or exit wound. If Dr. Leale didn't know better, he would swear that Lincoln simply dozed off and will awaken any minute.

"Put him on the floor," the doctor orders. Gently, ever so gently, Lincoln's long torso is lifted by men standing on both sides of the rocking chair and then lowered to the carpet.

∽

Based on Major Rathbone's wounds, and the fact that he didn't hear any gunshot during the performance, Leale deduces that Lincoln was stabbed. He rolls the president on one side and carefully searches for a puncture wound, his fingers slipping along the skin, probing for a telltale oozing of blood. But he feels nothing, and when he pulls his hands away, they're completely clean.

He strips Lincoln to the waist and continues the search, cutting off the president's white shirt with a pocketknife. But his skin is milky white and smooth, with no sign of any harm. Leale lifts Lincoln's eyelids and examines the pupils. Finding clear evidence that the right eye's optic nerve has somehow been cut, he decides to reexamine. Perhaps Lincoln was stabbed in the back of the skull. Head wounds are notorious bleeders, so such a wound is unlikely, but there has to be some explanation.

Dr. Leale, more befuddled by the mystery with each passing moment, runs his hands through Lincoln's hair. This time they come back blood-red.

Alarmed, Leale examines the president's head a second time. Beneath the thick hair, just above and behind the left ear, hides a small blood clot. It's no bigger than the doctor's pinkie, but when he pulls his finger away, the sensation is like a cork being removed from a bottle. Blood flows freely from the wound, and Lincoln's chest suddenly rises and falls as pressure is taken from his brain.

Dr. Leale has been a practicing physician for all of two months, having just graduated from Bellevue Hospital Medical College. He wears an army uniform, as befitting a doctor who currently works in the Wounded Commissioned Officers' Ward at the U.S. Army's General Hospital in nearby Armory Square. The bulk of his medical education took place during the Civil War, so despite his short time as a practicing physician, he has seen more gunshot wounds than most doctors see in a lifetime. Yet he encountered those wounds in hospitals far removed from the battlefield, when the patients were in advanced stages of recovery. He has never performed the sort of critical life-saving procedures that take place immediately after an injury.

But now Dr. Leale somehow knows just what to do—and he does it well.

∽

Working quickly, Leale straddles Lincoln's chest and begins resuscitating the president, hoping to improve the flow of oxygen to the brain. He shoves two fingers down Lincoln's throat and presses down on the back of the tongue, just in case food or drink is clogged in the esophagus. As he does so, two other doctors who were in the audience arrive on the scene. Though far more experienced, army surgeon Dr. Charles Sabin Taft and Dr. Albert King defer to Dr. Leale. When he asks them to stimulate the blood flow by manipulating Lincoln's arms in an up-and-down, back-and-forth manner, they instantly kneel down and each take an arm. Leale, meanwhile, presses hard on Lincoln's torso, trying to stimulate his heart.

Then, as Leale will one day tell an audience celebrating the one hundredth anniversary of Lincoln's birth, he performs an act of great and urgent intimacy: "I leaned forcibly forward directly over his body, thorax to thorax, face to face, and several times drew in a long breath, then forcibly breathed directly into his mouth and nostrils, which expanded the lungs and improved his respirations."

Dr. Leale lies atop Lincoln, his lips locked with Lincoln's, offering what looks to be a lover's kiss. The theater below is a madhouse. Men in the box around him look on, recognizing that Leale is performing a medical procedure, but struck by the awkward pose nonetheless.

Dr. Leale doesn't care. Every bit of his energy is poured into accomplishing the impossible task of saving Lincoln. Finally, he knows in his heart that the procedure has worked. He will later recall, "After waiting a moment, I placed my ear over his thorax and found the action of the heart improving. I arose to the erect kneeling posture, then watched for a short time and saw that the president could continue independent breathing and that instant death would not occur. I then announced my diagnosis and prognosis."

But Dr. Leale does not utter the hopeful words the onlookers wish to hear. They have seen the president breathe on his own. They know that his heart is functioning. Clearly, they think the president might survive.

Only Dr. Leale has seen the dull look in Lincoln's pupils, a sure sign that his brain is no longer functioning. "His wound is mortal," Leale announces softly. "It is impossible for him to recover."

⁂

A soldier vomits. Men remove their caps. Mary Lincoln sits just a few feet away but is in too much shock to comprehend what's been said. Someone hands Dr. Leale a dram of brandy and water, which he slowly dribbles into Lincoln's mouth. The president's prominent Adam's apple bobs as he swallows.

The pandemonium in the theater, meanwhile, has not diminished. The frenzy and shouting are deafening. No one in the state box speaks as Dr. Leale works on Lincoln, but its list of occupants has grown larger and more absurd. With John Parker, Lincoln's bodyguard, still strangely missing, no one is blocking access to the little room. To one side, on the couch, the distraught Mary Lincoln is being comforted by Clara Harris. Major Rathbone drips blood on the carpet, trying to stanch the flow by holding tight to the injured arm. There are three doctors, a half dozen soldiers, and a small army of theater patrons who have battled their way into the box. And then, almost absurdly, the actress Laura Keene forces her way into their midst and kneels at Lincoln's side. She begs to be allowed to cradle Lincoln. Dr. Leale, somewhat stunned but knowing it can do no harm, agrees.

Keene lifts the president's head into her lap and calmly strokes his face. Before becoming an actress she worked for a time as a restorer of old paintings, so she is more than familiar with the world of art and sculpture. She knows that this moment is Michelangelo's *Pietà* come to life, with her as Mary and Lincoln as Christ. Surrounded on all sides by what can only be described as anarchy, Laura Keene nurtures the dying man. The war years have been hard on her—drink has made her face puffy, and the constant wartime barnstorming has done little to stop her slowly declining popularity. The chestnut-eyed actress with the long auburn hair knows that this moment will put her name in papers around the world, so there is more than a touch of self-indulgence in her actions. But Laura Keene is not maudlin or the slightest bit dramatic as Abraham Lincoln's blood and brains soak into the lap of her dress. Like everyone else in the state box, she is stunned. Just a few minutes before, the president of the United States had been a vibrant and larger-than-life presence. Now everything has changed.

CHAPTER FORTY-SIX

FRIDAY, APRIL 14, 1865
WASHINGTON, D.C.
11:00 P.M.

The president of the United States cannot die on a dirty floor. No one knows how much longer he will live, but he must be moved. Dr. King suggests they move him to the White House, where he can pass the final moments of life in the comfort of his own bed. But Dr. Leale knows better than to attempt a bumpy carriage ride through Washington, D.C., particularly through panicked crowds that will necessitate the driver stopping and starting and turning quite suddenly. "He will be dead before we get there," Leale says firmly.

The young doctor agrees, however, that Lincoln should be resting in a bed, not on the floor. Dr. Taft sends a soldier to scour nearby boarding-houses for an empty room. Four other young soldiers are ordered to lift Lincoln back into the rocking chair and carry the president out of the theater.

But Dr. Leale overrules Taft. The logistics of carrying a rocking chair containing a man with very long legs borders on the absurd. Just getting down to the lobby involves navigating sharp angles, a narrow corridor, two small doorways, and a flight of stairs. A stretcher would be ideal, but none is available. Leale orders the four soldiers to stop gawking and get to work. They will lock their hands beneath the president and form a sling. Two will lift the torso, while two will carry the legs. They will transport Lincoln headfirst. Leale will walk backward, cradling Lincoln's head in his hands.

Laura Keene steps aside. She can't help but marvel at Lincoln's upper body, still possessing the lean musculature of the young wrestler renowned for feats of strength. The youthful power and appearance of his chest is in marked contrast to that famously weathered face. The only clue that this great body is actually dying is that his skin is pale and growing more so by the moment.

The four soldiers—John Corry, Jabes Griffiths, Bill Sample, and Jacob Soles of the Pennsylvania Light Artillery—now slip their hands under that torso and raise Lincoln to a sitting position. Dr. Leale, with help from the other two physicians, dresses the president in his frock coat and buttons it.

"Guards," barks Leale. "Clear the passage."

As if leading a processional, Laura Keene waits for the body to be lifted. She then marches out of the box, followed by the backward-walking Leale, the four soldiers, and Dr. King, who supports a shoulder, if only so he can remain a part of the action. Through the hallway, out into the dress circle, and down the stairs they travel. Mary Lincoln follows in their wake, stunned and shaky as she walks.

∽

Their progress is slow, for two reasons. The first is that theatergoers block the way, desperate for a peek—desperate to be able to say they saw Lincoln's corpse. The faithful make the sign of the cross and mumble a quiet prayer as Lincoln passes before their very eyes.

"Clear the way," Leale barks. Soldiers in the crowd respond, jumping forth to push back the mob. It becomes a wrestling match. Chairs are destroyed. Punches are thrown. Noses are bloodied. A Union officer finally draws his sword and threatens to cut down any man standing in Lincoln's path. This manages to quiet the crowd but only for an instant.

The second reason for the dawdling pace is that the bullet hole in Lincoln's head is clotting at an amazing rate. When this happens, Lincoln appears to be in obvious discomfort from increased pressure against his brain. So despite the anarchy all around him, Dr. Leale

orders the processional halted every few feet. Then he slips his fore-
finger into Lincoln's skull to clear the hole, bringing forth even more
blood but taking pressure off the president's brain.

They finally reach the lobby but don't know where to go next. By
now, soldiers have found the partition usually used to divide the state
box. At seven feet long and three inches thick, it makes a perfect
stretcher for Abraham Lincoln. His body is shifted onto the board.

Dr. Leale and the other two surgeons decide they will carry Lincoln into Taltavul's, right next door. A soldier is sent to clear the
tavern. But he soon comes back with word that Lincoln will not be
allowed inside—and for very good reason. Peter Taltavul is a patriot,
a man who spent twenty-five years in the Marine Corps band. Of all
the people in the crowd on this frenzied night, he is one of the few
who has the foresight to understand the significance of the presidency and how the night's events will one day be viewed. "Don't
bring him in here," Taltavul tells the soldier. "It shouldn't be said that
the president of the United States died in a saloon."

But where should they bring him?

Leale orders that Lincoln be lifted and carried to the row houses
across the street. There is an enormous crowd in front of Ford's. It
will be almost impossible to clear a path through their midst, but it's
vital that Leale get Lincoln someplace warm and clean, immediately.
The pine stretcher is lifted and Lincoln's body is carried out into the
cold, wet night, the procession lit by that murky yellow light from the
tar torches. Lincoln's carriage, with its magnificent team of black
chargers, is parked a few feet away.

Then his bodyguards arrive. Not John Parker, for the instant he
heard that Lincoln was shot he vanished into the night, continuing
his villainy. No, it is the Union Light Guard, otherwise known as the
Seventh Independent Company of Ohio Volunteer Cavalry, that gallops to the rescue. These are the men who have served as Lincoln's
bodyguards during his rides around the city and out to the Soldiers'
Home. They raced over from their stables next to the White House
when they heard about the shooting. Rather than dismount, they
work with other soldiers on the scene to make a double-wide corridor
from one side of Tenth Street to the other. Leale and the men carrying Lincoln make their way down Ford's granite front steps and onto

the muddy road, still not knowing where they will finally be able to bring him but glad to be away from the chaos and frenzy of Ford's.

⁓

Only more chaos awaits them in the street. The violent mob has swelled from dozens to hundreds in mere minutes, as people from all around Washington have sprinted to Ford's Theatre. Many are drunk. All are confused. And no one is in charge.

"Bring him in here," a voice shouts above the madness.

Henry S. Safford is a twenty-five-year-old War Department employee. He has toasted the Union victory every night since Monday, and tonight he was so worn out that he stayed in to rest. He was alone in his parlor, reading, when the streets below him exploded in confusion. When Safford stuck his head out the window to see what was happening, someone shouted the news that Lincoln had been shot. Safford raced downstairs and out into the crowd, but "finding it impossible to go further, as everyone acted crazy or mad," he retreated back to the steps of the Federal-style brick row house in which he rents a room from a German tailor named William Petersen. Safford stood on the porch and watched in amazement as Lincoln's failing body was conveyed out of Ford's. He saw the confusion on Dr. Leale's face as the contingent inched across Tenth Street, and witnessed the way Dr. Leale stopped every few feet and poked his finger into Lincoln's skull to keep the blood flowing. He saw Leale lifting his own head and scanning the street front, searching for someplace to bring Lincoln.

Now Safford wants to help.

"Put him in here," he shouts again.

Dr. Leale was actually aiming for the house next door, but a soldier had tried and found it locked. So they turn toward Safford. "This was done as quickly as the soldiers could make a pathway through the crowd," a sketch artist will remember later. Just moments earlier he had been so enthralled with the happy crowd in front of Ford's that he had impulsively grabbed a pad and begun drawing—"women with wide skirts and wearing large poke bonnets were as numerous as the men. . . . The scene was so unusual and inspiring."

But now he is sketching a melee and the sad scene of "the prostrate form of an injured man."

He will later say, "I recognized the lengthy form of the president by the flickering light of the torches, and one large gas lamp. The tarrying at the curb and the slow, careful manner in which he was carried across the street gave me ample time to make an accurate sketch. It was the most tragic and impressive scene I have ever witnessed."

⁓

Leale and his stretcher bearers carry Lincoln up nine short, curved steps to the front door of the Petersen house. "Take us to your best room," he orders Safford. And though he is hardly the man to be making that decision, Safford immediately realizes that his own second-floor room will not do. He guides the group down to the spacious room of George and Huldah Francis, but it is locked. Safford leads them deeper into the house, to a room that is clearly not Petersen's finest— but that will have to do. He pushes open the door, which features a large glass window covered by a curtain, and sees that it is empty.

The room is that of William Clark, a twenty-three-year-old army clerk who is gone for the night. Clark is fastidious in his cleanliness, so at just under ten feet wide and eighteen feet long, furnished with four-poster bed, table, bureau, and chairs, the bedroom is a cramped though very neat space.

But Lincoln is much too big for the bed. Dr. Leale orders that the headboard be broken off, but it won't break. Instead, the president is laid down diagonally on the red, white, and blue bedspread. The lumpy mattress is filled with corn husks. His head points toward the door and his feet toward the wall. Ironically, John Wilkes Booth often rented this very room during the previous summer. In fact, as recently as three weeks ago, Booth lolled on the very bed in which Lincoln is now dying.

⁓

Everyone leaves but the doctors and Mary Lincoln. She stares down at her husband, still wearing his boots, pants, and frock coat; there are two pillows under his head, and that bearded chin rests on his chest. Now and then he sighs involuntarily, giving her hope.

"Mrs. Lincoln, I must ask you to leave," Dr. Leale says softly.

Mary is like a child, so forlorn that she lacks the will to protest as others make her decisions for her. The first lady steps out of William Clark's rented room, into the long, dark hallway.

"Live," she pleads to her husband before she leaves. "You must live."

CHAPTER FORTY-SEVEN

SATURDAY, APRIL 15, 1865
WASHINGTON, D.C.
MIDNIGHT TO DAWN

D
r. Leale strips Lincoln's body. He, too, marvels at the definition of the muscles on the president's chest, shoulders, and legs. This is clearly the body of a man who has led a vigorous life. Dr. Leale searches the body for signs of another wound but finds none. The area around Lincoln's eyes and forehead is becoming swollen and black and blue, like a boxer's face after a tough fight.

Moving down the long and slender frame, Leale is disturbed to feel that Lincoln's feet are now icy to the touch, which he immediately treats by applying a mustard plaster to every inch of the front of Lincoln's body, from shoulders down to ankles. "No drug or medicine in any form was administered to the president," he will later note. "But the artificial heat and mustard plaster that I had applied warmed his cold body and stimulated his nerves."

He then covers the president with a blanket as Dr. Taft begins the process of removing the ball from Lincoln's head. Taft inserts his index finger into the wound and pronounces that the bullet has penetrated beyond the fingertip.

Meanwhile, Lincoln's pockets are emptied and his belongings carefully cataloged: an Irish linen handkerchief with the embroidered letter *A*; money, both Confederate and U.S.; newspaper clippings; an ivory pocketknife; and a pair of gold-rimmed glasses whose broken frame the president had mended with string.

More brandy and water is poured between Lincoln's lips. The Adam's apple once again bobs during the first spoonful but not at all for the second. With great difficulty, the doctors gently turn Lincoln on his side so that the excess fluid will run from his mouth and not choke him.

Lincoln is battling to stay alive. This is quite clear to each doctor. A normal man would be dead by now.

∽

The surgeon general of the army, Dr. Joseph Barnes, arrives and takes control of the scene. Barnes is closely followed by future surgeon general Charles H. Crane. Dr. Leale has been bold and aggressive these past few hours since the shooting. He now explains his course of action in great detail to two of the most powerful and well-regarded physicians in America. Both men agree with Leale's assessment and treatment, much to the young physician's relief.

The human brain is the most complex structure in all the world's biology, a humming and whirring center of thought, speech, motor movement, memory, and thousands of other minute functions. It is protected on the outside by the skull and then by a layer of connective-tissue membranes that form a barrier between the hard bone of the cranium and the gelatinous, soft tissue of the brain itself. Lincoln's brain, in which a Nélaton's probe (a long, porcelain, pencil-like instrument) is now being inserted in hopes of finding the bullet, contains vivid memories of a youth spent on the wild American frontier. This brain dazzled with clarity and brilliance during great political debates. It struggled with war and the politics of being president, then devised and executed solutions to the epic problems of the times. It imagined stirring speeches that knit the country together, then made sure that the words, when spoken, were uttered with exactly the right cadence, enunciation, and pitch. It guided those long slender fingers as they signed the Emancipation Proclamation, giving four million slaves their freedom. Inside his brain, Lincoln imagined the notion of "One country, one destiny." And this brain is also the reservoir of Lincoln's nightmares—particularly the one in which, just two weeks earlier, he envisioned his own assassination.

Now, thanks to a single round metal ball no bigger than a marble, Lincoln's brain is finished. He is brain-dead.

∽

Dr. Leale realizes that he is no longer needed in that cramped bedroom. But he does not leave. Emotion supersedes professional decorum. Leale, like the others, can barely hold back his tears. He has noticed that Lincoln is visibly more comfortable when the wound is unclogged. So he sits next to Lincoln's head and continues his solitary vigil, poking his finger into the blood clot every few minutes, making sure there's not too much pressure on Lincoln's brain.

A light rain is falling outside, but the crowd is eager for news and will not leave. In the room next door, Secretary of War Stanton has arrived and now takes charge, acting as interim president of the United States. Word of the assassination has brought a crowd of government officials to the Petersen house. The police investigation is beginning to take shape. It is clear that Booth shot Lincoln, and many believe that the actor also attacked Seward in his bed. Vice President Andrew Johnson, whose luck held when his assassin backed out, now stands in the next room, summoned after learning of Lincoln's plight.

All the while, Dr. Leale maintains his vigil by the dim candlelight. The occupants of the bedroom change constantly, with clergymen and officials and family members stepping in for a moment to pay their respects. More than sixty-five persons will be allowed inside before the night is through. The most frequent presence is Mary Lincoln, who weeps and even falls to her knees by the bedside whenever she is allowed a few moments with her husband. Leale takes care to spread a clean white handkerchief over the bloody pillow whenever she is about to walk in, but the bleeding in Lincoln's head never ceases, and before Mary Lincoln departs the handkerchief is often covered in blood and brain matter.

At three A.M., the scene is so grisly that Mary is no longer admitted.

The various doctors take turns recording Lincoln's condition. His respiration is shallow and fast, coming twenty-four to twenty-seven times a minute. His pulse rises to sixty-four at five-forty A.M., and hovers at sixty just a few moments later. But by then Leale can barely feel it.

Another doctor makes notes on Lincoln's condition:

"6:30—still failing and labored breathing."

"6:40—expirations prolonged and groaning. A deep, softly sonorous cooing sound at the end of each expiration, audible to bystanders."

"6:45—respiration uneasy, choking and grunting. Lower jaw relaxed. Mouth open. A minute without a breath. Face getting dark."

"6:59—breathes again a little more at intervals."

"7:00—still breathing at long pauses; symptoms of immediate dissolution."

With the president's death imminent, Mary Lincoln is once again admitted. Dr. Leale stands to make room. She sits in the chair next to Lincoln and then presses her face against her husband's. "Love," she says softly. "Speak to me."

A "loud, unnatural noise," in Dr. Leale's description, barks up from Lincoln's lungs. The sound is so grotesque that Mary collapses. As she is carried from the room she steals one last glimpse of her husband. She has known him since he was just a gangly country lawyer and has shared almost half her life with him. This will be the last time she sees him alive.

"I have given my husband to die," she laments, wishing that it could have been her instead.

Dr. Leale can't find a pulse. Lincoln's breathing becomes guttural, then ceases altogether before starting again. The room fills with a small army of elected officials, all of whom wish to witness the historic moment of Lincoln's death. Outside, it is dawn, and the crowds have grown even larger, with everyone waiting for a sliver of news.

In the bedroom, Robert Lincoln sobs loudly, unable to control his grief. He stands at the head of the bed and looks down at his father. Dr. Barnes sits in the chair, his finger on Lincoln's carotid artery, seeking a pulse. Dr. Leale has moved to the other side of the bed and wedged himself against the wall. He once again holds Lincoln's hand, simultaneously using his index finger to feel for a pulse on Lincoln's wrist.

There is no death rattle. Lincoln draws his last breath at seven twenty-one. His heart beats for another fifteen seconds, then stops altogether at ten seconds past seven twenty-two A.M.

More than twenty men are packed into the bedroom. Nobody says a word for five long minutes. Dr. Barnes reaches into his vest pocket for a pair of silver coins, which he places over Lincoln's eyes—one of which is now completely black and blue. Dr. Leale, meanwhile, folds the president's arms across his chest and carefully smooths his hair.

He barely hears Secretary Stanton rumble, "Now he belongs to the ages."

Sketch created at the deathbed of President Lincoln

Part Four

THE CHASE

John Wilkes Booth in portrait

CHAPTER FORTY-EIGHT

SATURDAY, APRIL 15, 1865
MARYLAND COUNTRYSIDE
EARLY MORNING

John Wilkes Booth and David Herold, the most wanted men in the United States of America, have successfully fled into the Maryland countryside. They met up at the rendezvous spot in the dead of night. With no sign that Atzerodt or Powell managed to escape Washington, Booth and Herold pushed on with their flight, galloping their horses south, toward Virgina. However, Booth's leg injury is so severe, and their horses so tired, that they were forced to find a place to rest. They are now hiding in the house of the eminent physician and Confederate sympathizer Dr. Samuel Mudd.

Somewhere in Washington, George Atzerodt and Lewis Powell are still on the loose.

The authorities don't know any of that yet—no numbers, no identities, and no motives. But even before Lincoln breathed his last, they began the intricate process of unraveling the mystery of his death.

Investigators stumble upon Atzerodt's trail first. After failing to carry out the assassination of Vice President Johnson, the carriage painter spent the night wandering aimlessly about Washington, getting thoroughly drunk in a number of bars and making sure to dispose of the knife he was supposed to use to kill the vice president. Other than plotting against the president of the United States, he has committed no crime. Atzerodt has a reputation for being dim, but he is canny enough to know that once he threw his knife into a gutter, the only obvious piece of evidence connecting him with the conspiracy was being seen publicly on Booth's horse. It might take days for authorities to make that connection. If he maintains a low profile and keeps his wits about him, there is every chance that he can get out of Washington and get on with a normal life.

Atzerodt is all too aware that returning to his room at Kirkwood House would be a very stupid idea. So just before three A.M. he checks into the Pennsylvania House hotel, where he is assigned a double room. His roommate, at a time when Atzerodt needs to be as far away from the long arm of the law as possible, is a police lieutenant named W. R. Keim. The two men know each other from Atzerodt's previous stays at the Pennsylvania House. They lie on their backs in the darkness and have a short conversation before falling asleep. Keim is stunned by the slaying of Lincoln. As drunk as he is, Atzerodt does an artful job of feigning sadness, saying that the whole Lincoln assassination is a terrible tragedy.

Lieutenant Keim never suspects a thing.

∞

But events are already conspiring against Atzerodt. Even as he sleeps off his long, hard night of drinking and walking, detectives sent to protect Andrew Johnson are combing through Atzerodt's belongings at Kirkwood House. A desk clerk remembers seeing a "villainous-looking" individual registered in room 126. Atzerodt took the only room key with him when he fled, so detectives have to break down the door to investigate. Quickly canvassing the empty room, they come up with the first solid leads about Lincoln's murder. In the breast pocket of a dark coat hanging on a wall peg, they discover a ledger book from the Ontario Bank in Montreal. The name written inside the cover is that of John Wilkes Booth, whom scores of eyewitnesses have already identified as Lincoln's killer. The book confirms the connection between Atzerodt and Booth.

A quick rifling of the bed produces a loaded revolver under the pillow and a Bowie knife hidden beneath the covers. And that is just the beginning. Room 126 soon becomes a treasure trove of evidence:

a map of southern states, pistol rounds, a handkerchief embroidered with the name of Booth's mother, and much more.

Investigators now have two suspects: Booth and Atzerodt. Warrants are issued for their arrests.

∽

At the same time, an anonymous tip leads investigators to raid Mary Surratt's boardinghouse on H Street in the dead of night. Nothing is found, but Surratt's behavior is suspicious enough that detectives decide to keep an eye on her and the house. A similar anonymous tip leads police to room 228 at the National Hotel—Booth's room—which is quickly ripped apart. Booth has left behind an abundance of clues—among them a business card bearing the name "J. Harrison Surratt" and a letter from former conspirator Samuel Arnold that implicates Michael O'Laughlen. More and more, it is becoming obvious that John Wilkes Booth did not act alone.

∽

A few blocks away, detectives question Secretary of State Seward's household staff, which adds two more nameless individuals to the list: the man who attacked Seward and his accomplice, who was seen waiting outside. This brings the number of conspirators to six: Booth, Atzerodt, O'Laughlen, Arnold, and Seward's two unknown attackers. John Surratt becomes a suspect because police are watching his mother.

The detectives, thrilled at their brisk progress, are sure they will arrest each and every member of the conspiracy within a matter of days.

Meanwhile, Washington is in a state of shock. Flags are flown at half-mast. Vice President Andrew Johnson is sworn in as the seventeenth president of the United States. Secretary of State Seward is not dead, as is widely rumored. But he is very badly injured.

He will be in a coma through Saturday but will awaken on Easter Sunday. Gazing out the window, he will see the War Department's flags at half-mast and immediately know what has happened. "The president is dead," Seward will sigh.

When his nurse insists that this is not the case, Seward will hold his ground. "If he had been alive he would be the first to call on me," he will say, "but he has not been here, nor has he sent to know how I am, and there's the flag at half-mast." Then he will turn his head from the window, tears streaming down his cheeks, their salt mingling with the blood of his still-fresh wounds.

∽

But now it is still Saturday morning. Black crepe replaces the red, white, and blue bunting on government buildings. Liquor outlets are shut down so that angry Washingtonians don't find yet another excuse to begin drinking and perhaps, in their drunken anger, start looting. Multiracial crowds gather in front of the Petersen house, grateful to merely be in the presence of the hallowed ground where Lincoln died. Just across the street, Ford's Theatre has instantly gone from a Washington cultural hub to a pariah; the good fortune of having Lincoln attend *Our American Cousin* will soon put the theater out of business. The government will decree that the building may never again be used as a place of public amusement.

The cast of *Our American Cousin* is so afraid of being attacked by angry mobs that the actors and actresses lock themselves inside the theater after the shooting. One of their own, Harry Hawk, has already been taken into police custody for sharing the same stage as Booth.

Throughout the nation, as the news spreads, Abraham Lincoln's worst fears are being realized. Outraged northerners mourn his loss and openly rant about revenge, while southerners rejoice in the death of the tyrannical man who wouldn't give them the freedom to form their own nation. The Civil War, so close to being finally over, now seems on the verge of erupting once again.

∽

Believing that catching Lincoln's killer will help quell the unrest, Secretary of War Stanton spends Saturday expanding the search, making the hunt for Lincoln's killers the biggest criminal dragnet in American history. Soldiers, cavalry, and every imaginable form of law enforcement throughout the northern states are called off every other task and ordered to devote all their energies to finding John Wilkes Booth and his band of killers. In the same manner that Grant attempted to besiege Petersburg by throwing a noose around the city, Stanton hopes to throw a giant rope around the Northeast, then slowly cinch the knot tighter until he squeezes out the killers. He also sends a telegram to New York City, recalling Lafayette Baker, his former spymaster and chief of security. The strange connection between Stanton and Baker now becomes even stronger.

Why does Stanton call for Baker, of all people?

⚬⚬

As all this is going on, George Atzerodt wakes up at dawn on Saturday morning, still drunk after just two hours of sleep. He is somehow oblivious to the fact that people might be looking for him. Nor does he have any idea that the man who assaulted Secretary Seward, Lewis Powell, is also still stuck in Washington, hiding out in a cemetery after being thrown from his horse. Atzerodt knows he must get out of Washington, but first he needs money to fund his escape. He has no plan, and he is under no delusion that he will find a way to meet up with John Wilkes Booth; nor does he want to.

Atzerodt leaves the Pennsylvania House and walks across the city to nearby Georgetown, where he makes the unusual gesture of calling on an old girlfriend. He tells her he is going away for a while, as if she might somehow want to come along. And then as mysteriously as he appeared, Atzerodt leaves the home of Lucinda Metz and pawns his revolver for ten dollars at a nearby store. He uses the money to buy a stagecoach ticket into Maryland, taking public transportation at a time when all common sense cries out for a more inconspicuous means of escape.

But now fate is smiling upon George Atzerodt. Nobody stops the stagecoach as it rolls out of Washington and into Maryland. Even when the stage is halted and searched by Union soldiers miles outside the capital, nobody suspects that the simple-witted Atzerodt is capable of being resourceful enough to take part in the conspiracy. In fact, Atzerodt is so unassuming that the sergeant in charge of the soldiers actually shares a few glasses of cider with the conspirator.

In this way, George Atzerodt stumbles deeper and deeper into the countryside, on his way, he believes, to safety and freedom.

CHAPTER FORTY-NINE

John Wilkes Booth is miserable. Flat on his back on a bed in the country home of Confederate sympathizer Samuel Mudd, Booth screams in pain as the thirty-one-year-old doctor cuts off his boot and gently presses his fingers into the grossly swollen ankle. As if shattering his fibula while leaping to the stage wasn't bad enough, Booth's horse threw him during his thirty-mile midnight ride through Maryland, hurling his body into a rock. Booth is sore, hungover, exhausted, and experiencing a new and nagging anxiety: that of the hunted.

After the assassination, Booth and David Herold rode hard all night, stopping only at a small tavern owned by Mary Surratt to pick up some Spencer rifles she'd hidden for them. Herold was glib, boasting to the Confederate proprietor that they'd killed the president. But he also had his wits about him, buying a bottle of whiskey so Booth could enjoy a nip or two to dull the pain. Then they rode on, ten more hard miles on tree-lined country roads, for Booth every mile more painful than the last. It was the actor's leg that made them detour to Mudd's house. Otherwise they would have reached the Potomac River by sunrise. With any luck, they might have stolen a boat and made the crossing into Virginia immediately.

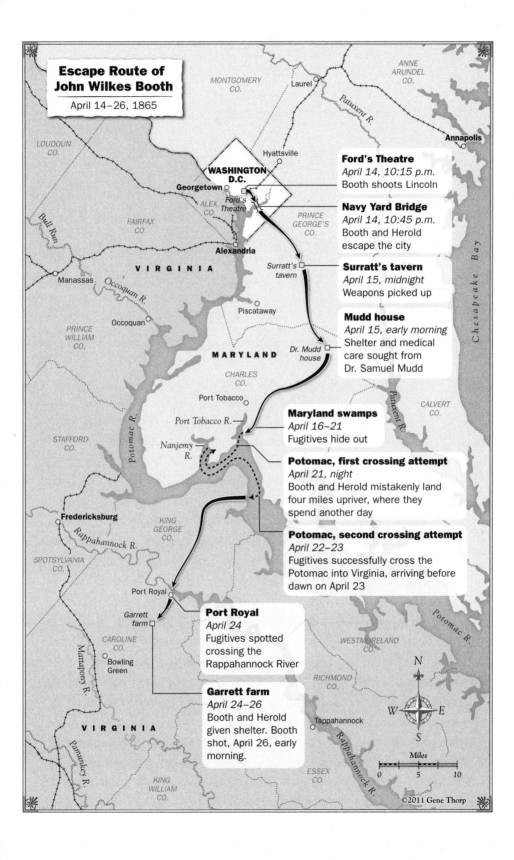

Escape Route of John Wilkes Booth

April 14–26, 1865

Ford's Theatre
April 14, 10:15 p.m.
Booth shoots Lincoln

Navy Yard Bridge
April 14, 10:45 p.m.
Booth and Herold
escape the city

Surratt's tavern
April 15, midnight
Weapons picked up

Mudd house
April 15, early morning
Shelter and medical
care sought from
Dr. Samuel Mudd

Maryland swamps
April 16–21
Fugitives hide out

Potomac, first crossing attempt
April 21, night
Booth and Herold mistakenly land
four miles upriver, where they
spend another day

Potomac, second crossing attempt
April 22–23
Fugitives successfully cross the
Potomac into Virginia, arriving before
dawn on April 23

Port Royal
April 24
Fugitives spotted
crossing the
Rappahannock River

Garrett farm
April 24–26
Booth and Herold
given shelter. Booth
shot, April 26, early
morning.

MONTGOMERY CO.
Laurel
ANNE ARUNDEL CO.
Patuxent R.
Annapolis
LOUDOUN CO.
Hyattsville
WASHINGTON D.C.
Georgetown
Ford's Theatre
PRINCE GEORGE'S CO.
FAIRFAX CO.
ALEX. CO.
Alexandria
Bull Run
VIRGINIA
Manassas
Occoquan R.
Surratt's tavern
Chesapeake Bay
Occoquan
Piscataway
PRINCE WILLIAM CO.
MARYLAND
Dr. Mudd house
CHARLES CO.
Patuxent R.
CALVERT CO.
Port Tobacco
Port Tobacco R.
STAFFORD CO.
Potomac R.
Nanjemy R.
Fredericksburg
KING GEORGE CO.
Rappahannock R.
SPOTSYLVANIA CO.
Port Royal
Garrett farm
WESTMORELAND CO.
Potomac R.
CAROLINE CO.
Bowling Green
RICHMOND CO.
Mattapony R.
Tappahannock
N
W E
S
VIRGINIA
Pamunkey R.
KING WILLIAM CO.
ESSEX CO.
Rappahannock R.

Miles
0   5   10

©2011 Gene Thorp

Dr. Samuel Mudd

Still, they're close. Very close. By choosing to take shelter at Mudd's rather than stay on the main road south to the Potomac, they have veered off the fastest possible route. But Mudd's two-hundred-eighteen-acre estate is just north of Bryantown, south and east of Washington, and fully two-thirds of the way to the Potomac River.

Booth's pants and jacket are now spattered with mud. His handsome face, so beloved by women everywhere, is unshaven and sallow. But more than anything else, John Wilkes Booth is helpless. Almost overnight he has become a shell of himself, as if assassinating Lincoln has robbed him of the fire in his belly, and the pain of his shattered leg has transformed him from daredevil to coward. He is now completely dependent upon David Herold to lead their escape into the South. At a time when Booth needs all his wiles and resources to complete the second half of the perfect assassination, he is too distraught and in too much agony to think straight.

Dr. Mudd says he's going to splint the leg. Booth lies back and lets him, despite the knowledge that this means he will no longer be able to slip his foot into a stirrup. Now he must ride one-legged, half on and half off his horse—if he can ride at all.

◦◦◦

Mudd finishes splinting the leg, then leaves Booth alone to get some rest. The actor is in an upstairs room, so if anyone comes looking, he won't be found right away. He wraps a shawl around his neck and face to conceal his identity, and he has plans to shave his mustache. But otherwise, he does absolutely nothing to facilitate his escape. The pain is too great. It will take a miracle for Booth to travel even one mile farther.

He rolls over and closes his eyes, then falls into a deep sleep, sure that he is being hunted but completely unaware that more than a thousand men on horseback are within a few miles of his location—and that Lafayette Baker is now on the case.

CHAPTER FIFTY

Lafayette Baker is in his room at New York's Astor House hotel when he hears that Lincoln has been shot. The disgraced spy, who was sent away from Washington for tapping Secretary Stanton's telegraph lines, is not surprised. His first thought, as always, is of finding a way to spin this tragedy for his own personal gain. Baker loves glory and money. He understands in an instant that the man who finds Lincoln's killer will know unparalleled wealth and fame. Baker longs to be that man.

It's noon on Saturday when a telegram arrives from Stanton, summoning him to "come here immediately and find the murderer of our president."

If Baker were an ordinary man and not prone to weaving elaborate myths about himself, that telegram would be a very straightforward call to battle. But Baker is so fond of half-truths and deception that it's impossible to know if he is traveling to Washington as a sort of super-sleuth, handpicked by Stanton to find Lincoln's killers, or if he is traveling to Washington to find and kill Booth before the actor can detail Secretary Stanton's role in the conspiracy. Whatever the case, at a time when Baker could have been anywhere in the world, Stanton knew exactly where to find the fired spy so that he could be summoned to the capital.

Lafayette Baker takes the overnight train to Washington, arriving at dawn. The city is in chaos, and he will later describe the looks on people's faces as "inexpressible, bewildering horror and grief." Baker travels immediately to the War Department, where he meets with Stanton. "They have killed the president. You must go to work. My whole dependence is upon you," the secretary tells him. The entire detective forces of New York, Baltimore, Philadelphia, and Boston have traveled to Washington and are devoting their considerable professional talents to finding the killers. But Stanton has just given Baker carte blanche to move in and take over the entire investigation.

One of Baker's specialties is playing the part of the double agent. Even though there is evidence that Baker and Booth are somehow connected to each other through the 178½ Water Street, New York, address, Baker claims that he knows nothing about the case or about the suspects. His first act is to post a reward for $30,000 leading to the arrest and conviction of Lincoln's killers. He also has photographs of John Surratt, David Herold, and John Wilkes Booth plastered all around town.

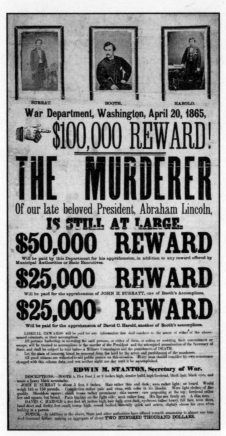

*One of several reward posters for
the capture of John Wilkes Booth*

CHAPTER FIFTY-ONE

SATURDAY–SUNDAY, APRIL 15–16, 1865
MARYLAND COUNTRYSIDE

David Herold needs a buggy. It's the most obvious solution to John Wilkes Booth's plight. With a buggy they can travel quickly and in relative comfort. He asks Dr. Mudd to loan them his, but the doctor is reluctant; secretly harboring fugitives is one thing, but allowing the two most wanted men in America to ride through southern Maryland in his personal carriage would surely implicate Mudd and his wife in the conspiracy. Their hanging— for that is surely the fate awaiting any Lincoln conspirator—would leave their four young children orphans.

Instead, Mudd suggests that they ride into Bryantown to pick up some supplies and check on the latest news. With Booth still passed out upstairs, Herold agrees to the journey. But as they draw closer and closer to the small town, something in Herold's gut tells him not to take the risk. A stranger like him will be too easily remembered by such a tight-knit community. He is riding Booth's bay now, because it's too spirited for the actor to control with his broken leg. Herold lets Mudd go on without him, then wheels the mare back to the doctor's home.

Good thing. The United States cavalry now has Bryantown surrounded. They're not only questioning all its citizens, they're not letting anyone leave, either.

This is the sort of savvy, intuitive thinking that separates David Herold from the other members of Booth's conspiracy. Atzerodt is dim. Powell is a thug. And Booth is emotional. But the twenty-two-year-old Herold, recruited to the conspiracy for his knowledge of Washington's backstreets, is intelligent and resourceful. He was educated at Georgetown College, the finest such institution in the city. He is also an avid hunter, which gives him a full complement of the outdoor skills that Booth now requires to escape, the additional ability to improvise in dangerous situations, and an instinctive sixth sense about tracking—or, in this case, being tracked.

But now Herold is just as exhausted as Booth. He didn't endure the same extreme adrenaline spike last night, if only because he didn't kill anyone. But he experienced a definite and sustained rush as he galloped over the Navy Yard Bridge, then along the dangerous darkened roads of Maryland. He's had time to think and to plan, and he knows that constant forward movement is the key to their survival. Otherwise, Herold has no doubt that the cavalry will be on their trail in no time.

∾

Clearly, they cannot stay at Dr. Mudd's any longer. Just before dusk, Herold rouses Booth and helps him down the stairs and up into the saddle. Herold guides them south through the countryside, aiming for the Zekiah Swamp, with its quicksand bogs and dense stands of old-growth hardwoods. The few trails that exist are almost impossible to see in the dark, and the pair are soon lost and frustrated. They turn back toward Mudd's farm but remain out of sight, plotting their next move.

The next twelve hours bring an enduring awareness that they are neither safe nor welcome anywhere.

Easter Sunday dawns hard and bleak. Herold and Booth are camped in a stand of pines a quarter mile off the main road. A cold front is racing across Maryland, and they shiver in the damp swampy air, just a few short miles from the final obstacle to their escape into Virginia, the Potomac River. Booth isn't wearing a boot on his injured leg, and his foot and ankle are in pain and quite cold from walking on swampy ground in the thin shoes he took from Mudd. Yet Herold doesn't dare make a fire. Beside him, Booth is curled up in the fetal position, head resting on one hand. Each man clutches his revolver as a stiff wind bends the towering pines. The last sympathizer they visited, the wealthy owner of forty slaves in this still-lawless region, promised to send a man to ferry them across to safety. The rescue signal will be a soft whistle, a pause, and then another soft whistle.

So now they wait. Hour after brutally cold hour, they wonder who will deliver them from this hell. Booth says little, except to cry out in pain or mutter something about not being taken alive. He still has some fight in him. Now and then they hear the jangle of bridles from the nearby road. And all the while, a gnawing little voice in Herold's gut tells him that they have been betrayed—that the whistle, when it comes, will be their only warning before United States cavalry confirm their position and ride in with guns blazing.

Late Sunday afternoon they hear the first whistle. Then a second. Confederate sympathizer Thomas Jones calls out to them in a low voice, announcing that he is walking into their camp.

CHAPTER FIFTY-TWO

There is nothing dashing or heroic about the man who has come to save the lives of Booth and Herold. Thomas Jones is a broken man, a forty-four-year-old smuggler who has done time in prison, outlived his wife, and lost his home. He now earns his living by transporting everyone from secret agents to diplomats across the Potomac River to the South. On average, he makes the crossing three times a night. He is so skilled that northern newspapers secretly enlisted his help to get their product into the South during the war. A favorite technique employed by the silver-haired and low-key Jones is to begin his first crossing just before dusk, when the angle of the sun makes it impossible for sentries on the opposite shore to see small craft on the water. It is a brazen and brilliant tactic. Clearly, if any man can get Booth and Herold to safety, it's Thomas Jones.

On his first visit to the campsite he merely wanted to get a look at the men he would be helping, to see if they were mentally and physically capable of enduring what might be a very long wait until it is safe to cross.

His second visit comes one day later. It's also the second day in the pine forest for Booth and Herold. They once again hear the whistle from the trees. Booth is even worse today, the pain in his leg so severe that he doesn't do much more than whimper. Herold stands, carbine pointed toward the sound of approaching footsteps, until Jones finally appears in their thicket, his pockets overflowing with ham, butter, bread, and a flask of coffee. In his hands he holds the one thing Booth wants to see more than any other: newspapers.

Cavalry are combing the countryside, he cautions the killers, and he reminds them to be patient. It might take several days before things die down. No matter how cold it gets, no matter how extreme the conditions, they must be prepared to hunker down in the woods until the coast is clear. As soon as it is, he'll let them know.

Booth argues that their lives are in danger and that they can't stay here any longer. But the thunder of hoofbeats from the nearby road stops him short—it's Union cavalry and far too close for comfort.

"You see, my friend," Jones whispers. "You must wait." He tells them to kill the horses, lest their whinnying give the killers away.

Prior to the assassination, Booth would have continued to argue and then done as he pleased. But now he quietly gives in. "I leave it all with you," he says to Jones.

Jones departs quickly. His visits are uplifting to Booth and Herold, a welcome break from the monotony of sitting still for hours and hours out in the open. They don't even dare build a shelter, for fear the noise will attract unwelcome attention. Jones doesn't just bring food and newspapers; he also offers hope, his cool confidence suggesting that all will be well, just so long as they are patient.

With a sigh, Booth turns his attention to the newspapers. He reads about the extent of the search. But his melancholy soon turns to rage as he learns that his monumental actions are not being applauded. Far from it. He is being labeled a scoundrel and a coward for shooting Lincoln in the back. Washington newspapers assail him as the war's ultimate villain and note that any "kindly feeling" toward the South or its sympathizers has disappeared, thanks to his actions. Booth's achievement is described in the Richmond papers as "the most deplorable calamity, which has ever befallen the people of the United States." And finally, the nation's most staunchly anti-Lincoln paper, the *National Intelligencer,* is now crying out that Lincoln was a true American hero. The very newspaper that the actor had once hoped would print the letter explaining his actions is instead portraying him as an abomination.

Booth, overcome with despair, sets the papers aside. As is his new habit, he regales Herold with a monologue on the killings—regrets, desires, and misunderstandings. Then he takes out his diary and begins keeping a journal of their time in the wilderness. In it, he writes his reflections on killing Lincoln, just to make sure that his point of view is properly recorded for posterity. "I struck boldly and not as the papers say. I walked with a firm step through a thousand of his friends, was stopped, but pushed on," Booth writes. "I can never repent it, though we hated to kill. Our country owed all her troubles to him, and God simply made men the instrument of his punishment."

Booth writes and rants and writes some more. Then he sleeps. Then he awakens and writes some more. There's nothing else to do with his time. So it is with the world's two most wanted men, bored to tears in a Maryland swamp.

CHAPTER FIFTY-THREE

—

Mary Surratt has been a suspect since the night Lincoln was shot. An anonymous tipster alerted Washington police that the boardinghouse on H Street was the hub of the conspiracy. Detectives questioned her at two o'clock that morning, even as Lincoln lay dying. The widow was forthcoming about the fact that John Wilkes Booth had paid her a visit just twelve hours earlier and that her son John had last been in Washington two weeks earlier. When a thorough search of the house turned up nothing, the police left. No arrest was made.

Now they are back. One of her boarders, Louis Weichmann, has volunteered volumes of information to the authorities about the comings and goings of Booth and the conspirators at Mary Surratt's boardinghouse. This eyewitness information has confirmed not only that Booth is at the heart of the plan but that Mary Surratt is complicit.

It is well past midnight when police surround the house. She answers a knock at the door, thinking it is a friend. "Is this Mrs. Surratt's house?" asks a detective.

"Yes."

"Are you Mrs. Surratt?"

"I am the widow of John H. Surratt."

"And the mother of John H. Surratt Jr.?"

"Yes."

"Madam, I have come to arrest you."

Three policemen step inside. Mary's twenty-two-year-old daughter, Anna, is also taken into custody. Just before they are led outside, Mary asks permission to kneel in prayer. She is a devout Catholic and prays "the blessing of God upon me, as I do in all my actions."

The house is quiet. Her words echo through the half-lighted rooms as the detectives awkwardly wait for Mary to finish praying and rise to her feet.

Then there's another knock on the door.

When the detectives open it, they are shocked by the sight of a six-foot-two man with a pickax slung over his shoulder, wearing a shirt-sleeve on his head like a stocking cap. His boots are coated with mud and he is unshaven. As he steps inside, they see that there appears to be blood on his sleeves. The detectives quickly close the door behind him.

Lewis Powell, starved and famished after three days of sleeping in the woods, instantly realizes he has made a grave error. "I guess I am mistaken," he quickly tells the detectives, turning to leave.

The police send Mary and Anna Surratt out the door, where carriages wait to take them to jail. Then they focus their attention on the tall stranger with the pickax.

Powell gives his name as Lewis Payne and fabricates an elaborate story, saying that he has come to Mary Surratt's at her behest, in order to dig a ditch for her in the morning. The police press him, asking about Powell's address and place of employment. When he can't answer in a satisfactory manner, they arrest him. At the police station he is strip-searched, and an unlikely collection of items, including cash, a compass, a pocketknife, and a newspaper clipping of Lincoln's second inaugural address, are found in his pockets.

So far, all evidence points to "Payne's" involvement in the assassination. His height and rugged build clearly match the description of Secretary Seward's attacker. The police summon the young black servant who had given the description to the station. William Bell has been interrogated a number of times since the attacks, so as he is called back to the station once again his attitude is weary. The late hour does not help.

However, when a lineup of potential suspects is paraded into the room before him, Bell becomes instantly euphoric. He marches right up to Powell and presses his finger against the lips of the man who mocked him, insulted him with a racial slur, and very nearly killed his employer and several members of the family and staff. "He is the man," Bell proclaims.

This is the last moment in Lewis Powell's life when he is able to move his arms freely and walk without hearing the clank of chains. Manacles are placed on his wrists. A ball and chain will be attached to each ankle in the days to come, the unyielding iron cutting deeply into his flesh every time he takes a step. A canvas hood will soon be placed over his head, with only a small hole through which he can draw breath and eat.

And yet there is much worse to come for Lewis Powell.

CHAPTER FIFTY-FOUR

The military sweep through southern Maryland is ongoing and intense. Searches of towns and homes have turned up nothing, and it is clear that the time has come to scour more daunting terrain for Booth and Herold. A combined force of seven hundred Illinois cavalry, six hundred members of the Twenty-second Colored Troops, and one hundred men from the Sixteenth New York Cavalry Regiment now enter the wilderness of Maryland's vast swamps.

"No human being inhabits this malarious extent" is how one journalist describes this region. "Even a hunted murderer would shrink from hiding there. Serpents and slimy lizards are the only living denizens. . . . Here the soldiers prepared to seek for the President's assassins, and no search of the kind has ever been so thorough and patient."

The method of searching the swamps is simple yet arduous. First, the troops assemble on the edge of bogs with names like Allen's Creek, Scrub Swamp, and Atchall's Swamp, standing at loose attention in the shade of a thick forest of beech, dogwood, and gum trees. Then they form two lines and march straight forward, from one side to the other. As absurd as it seems to the soldiers, marching headlong into cold mucky water, there is no other way of locating Booth and

Herold. Incredibly, eighty-seven of these brave men will drown in their painstaking weeklong search for the killers.

"The soldiers were only a few paces apart," the journalist reports, "and in steady order they took to the ground as it came, now plunging to their armpits in foul sluices of gangrened water, now hopelessly submerged in slime, now attacked by legions of wood ticks, now attempting some unfaithful log or greenishly solid morass, and plunging to the tip of the skull in poisonous stagnation. The tree boughs rent their uniforms. They came out upon dry land, many of them without a rag of garment, scratched and gnashed, and spent, repugnant to themselves, and disgusting to those who saw them."

The soldiers detain anyone with anti-Union leanings. For many of the arrested, their only crime is either looking or behaving suspiciously. Taking them into custody is the best possible way to ensure that no suspect is overlooked.

Hundreds of these suspects soon fill Washington's jails.

But not a single trace of Booth or Herold can be found anywhere.

࿐

Back in Washington, Lafayette Baker follows their progress. Since arriving in the capital two days earlier, Baker has distanced himself from the other investigators, "taking the usual detective measures, till then neglected," of offering the reward, circulating photos of the suspects, and sending out a small army of handpicked detectives to scour the countryside. But he is hampered by the lack of railroads and telegraph lines through the rough and lawless countryside. There is, however, a telegraph line at Point Lookout, a former Union prisoner of war camp at the mouth of the Potomac River. To keep himself informed of all activities in the area, he dispatches a telegraph operator by steamship to that location and orders him to tap into the existing line.

Now, safe in the knowledge that he has established the broadest possible dragnet, Baker waits for that telegraph line to sing.

CHAPTER FIFTY-FIVE

The moment Dr. Samuel Mudd has been dreading for two days comes while he is in the fields, working his crops. The cavalry unit galloping up his driveway is not there by accident. There are at least two dozen riders, not including his cousin George. It was George to whom Mudd confided that two strangers had spent the night of Lincoln's assassination in his home. They spoke after Easter services, even as Booth and Herold were still very much in the vicinity. Mudd took pains to state that his life was in danger, should these two men ever come back. The story was a cover, intended to make it look as if he had no knowledge of the strangers' identities. It was Mudd's hope that George would act as an intermediary, alerting the police to the fact that his Good Samaritan cousin might just have "accidentally" aided the men who killed Lincoln.

George, however, is a devoted Union sympathizer. Instead of the police, George has brought the cavalry, with their rifles, sabers, and no-nonsense military bearing. The riders dismount. Lieutenant Alexander Lovett is in charge and quickly begins a line of questioning to determine exactly who and what Samuel Mudd saw that night.

Mudd is not a brave man and is quickly rattled. His lips turn blue, even as his face turns chalk white. The story he fabricated and rehearsed in his head so many times suddenly eludes him. Rather than present himself as eager for the "entire strangers" to be captured, Mudd is vague and contrary. He mentions that one stranger had a broken leg and that he had done the neighborly thing by splinting it before sending the men on their way. When Lovett asks him to repeat parts of the story, Mudd frequently contradicts his own version of events.

Lieutenant Lovett is positive that Samuel Mudd is lying. But he does not arrest him—not now, at least. He is determined to find evidence that will link Mudd to the two strangers. He bawls the order to mount up, and the cavalry trots back out to the main road.

Mudd, his heart beating in relief, can only wonder when they will return.

CHAPTER FIFTY-SIX

THURSDAY, APRIL 20, 1865
MARYLAND COUNTRYSIDE
4:00 A.M.

George Atzerodt has chosen to escape via a northeast route, rather than push south like Booth and Herold. This takes him into a much more pro-Union territory, where the Lincoln assassination has people demanding vengeance on the perpetrators. On the surface, Atzerodt's plan is an act of genius, allowing one of the most wanted men in America to literally hide in plain sight.

But the increasingly unbalanced George Atzerodt is not a genius. His escape is not a premeditated act of egress but a random wandering from home to home, accepting sanctuary and comfort wherever he can find it. He dawdles when he should be making continuous progress. After four days on the run he makes a critical mistake, boldly supporting Lincoln's assassination while eating dinner with strangers. His statements quickly make their way to U.S. marshals.

Now, as Atzerodt takes refuge at a cousin's house in the small community of Germantown, Maryland, twenty miles outside of Washington, a cavalry detachment knocks at the door. Entering the house, they find Atzerodt sharing a bed with two other men. "Get up and dress yourself," a sergeant commands.

There is no fight, no attempt to pretend he shouldn't be arrested. George Atzerodt goes meekly into custody, where he is soon fitted with wrist shackles, a ball and chain on his ankle, and a hood over his head, just like Lewis Powell.

Less than three months later, George Atzerodt—the twenty-nine-year-old drifter who stumbled into the conspiracy and stumbled right back out without harming a soul—hangs by the neck until dead.

CHAPTER FIFTY-SEVEN

Friday, April 21, 1865
Washington, D.C.
7:00 a.m.

One week after the assassination, even as John Wilkes Booth is still alive and hiding in a Maryland swamp, the body of Abraham Lincoln is loaded aboard a special train for his return home to Illinois. General Ulysses S. Grant supervises the occasion. The body of Lincoln's late son Willie rides along in a nearby casket. Abraham Lincoln once confided to Mary that he longed to be buried someplace quiet, and so it is that the president and his dear son are destined for Springfield's Oak Ridge Cemetery.

But even after the burial, Lincoln's body will never quite be at rest. In the next 150 years, Lincoln's casket will be opened six times and moved from one crypt to another seventeen times. His body was so thoroughly embalmed that he was effectively mummified.

The funeral, which is quite different from the actual burial, of course, was held on Wednesday, April 19. Six hundred mourners were ushered into the East Room of the White House. Its walls were decorated in black, the mirrors all covered, and the room lit by candles. General Ulysses S. Grant sat alone nearest his dear departed friend, next to a cross of lilies. He wept.

Mary Lincoln is still so distraught that she will spend the next five weeks sobbing alone in her bedroom; she was notably absent from the

The president's funeral procession down Pennsylvania Avenue

list of recorded attendees. The sound of hammers pounding nails all night long on Tuesday, creating the seating risers for the funeral guests, sounded like the horrible ring of gunfire to her. Out of respect for her mourning and instability, President Andrew Johnson will not have the platforms torn down until after she moves out, on May 22.

Immediately after the funeral, Lincoln's body was escorted by a military guard through the streets of Washington. One hundred thousand mourners lined the route to the Capitol, where the body was once again put on view for the public to pay their last respects.

And now, two days later, there is the matter of the train. In a trip that will re-create his journey to the White House five years earlier—though in the opposite direction—Lincoln's special train will stop along the way in twelve cities and pass through 444 communities. In what will be called "the greatest funeral in the history of the United States," thirty million people will take time from their busy lives to see this very special train before its great steel wheels finally slow to a halt in his beloved Springfield.

The unfortunate mementos of his assassination remain behind in Washington: the Deringer bullet and the Nélaton's probe that pinpointed its location in his brain will soon be on display in a museum, as will the red horsehair rocker in which he was shot. He also leaves behind the messy unfinished business of healing the nation. And while Abraham Lincoln has gone home to finally get the rest he has so long deserved, that unfinished business will have to wait until his murderer is found.

CHAPTER FIFTY-EIGHT

Friday, April 21, 1865
Maryland countryside
Noon

Samuel Mudd is not home when Lieutenant Lovett and the cavalry return. Lovett sends farmhand Thomas Davis to find him. Mudd is having lunch nearby and quickly returns to his farm to face Lovett.

The terror of their previous encounter returns. He knows that Lovett has spent the previous three days searching the area around his property for evidence. Mudd's face once again turns a ghostly white. His nervousness is compounded as Lovett questions him again, probing Mudd's story for discrepancies, half-truths, and outright lies.

This time Lovett does not ride away. Nor is he content to search the pastures and outer edges of the farm. No, this time he wants to go inside Mudd's home and see precisely where these strangers slept. Lovett gives the order to search the house.

Mudd frantically gestures to his wife, Sarah, who walks quickly to him. He whispers in her ear, and she races into the house. The soldiers can hear her footsteps as she climbs the stairs to the second floor, then returns within just a moment. In her hands are two items: a razor and a boot. "I found these while dusting up three days ago," she says as she hands them to Lovett.

Mudd explains that one of the strangers used the razor to shave off his mustache. The boot had come from the stranger with the broken leg.

Lovett presses Mudd on this point, asking him if he knew the man's identity.

Mudd insists that he didn't.

Lovett cradles the long riding boot in his hands. It has been slit down one side by Mudd, in order that he might pull it from Booth's swollen leg to examine the wound.

Lovett asks if this is, indeed, the boot the stranger wore.

Mudd agrees.

Lovett presses Mudd again, verifying that the doctor had no knowledge of the stranger's identity.

Mudd swears this to be truth.

And then Lovett shows Mudd the inside of the riding boot, which would have been clearly visible when Mudd was removing it from the stranger's leg.

Mudd's world collapses. His story is shattered in an instant.

For marked inside the boot, plain for all to see, is the name "J. Wilkes."

Dr. Samuel Mudd is under arrest.

And while Lieutenant Lovett has just made a key breakthrough in the race to find John Wilkes Booth and David Herold, the truth is that nobody in authority knows where they are.

∽

Lafayette Baker, however, has a pretty good idea.

Baker keeps a host of coastal survey maps in his office at the War Department. With "that quick detective intuition amounting almost to inspiration," in his own words, he knows that Booth's escape options are limited. When news of the discovery of the abandoned riding boot makes its way back to Washington, Baker concludes that Booth cannot be traveling on horseback. And though traveling by water is more preferable, once Booth is flushed from the swamps—for that is surely where he is hiding—he won't follow the Maryland coastline. There are too many deep rivers to cross, and he would be easily spotted. Lafayette Baker also deduces that Booth won't head toward Richmond if he gets across the Potomac because that would lead him straight into Union lines.

Lafayette Baker is already convinced that John Wilkes Booth must aim for the mountains of Kentucky. "Being aware that nearly every rod of ground in Lower Maryland must have been repeatedly passed over by the great number of persons engaged in the search," he will later write, "I finally decided, in my own mind, that Booth and Herold had crossed over the river into Virginia. The only possible way left open to escape was to take a southwestern course, in order to reach the mountains of Tennessee or Kentucky, where such aid could be secured as would insure their ultimate escape from the country."

It's as if he already knows Booth's plan.

To get to Kentucky, Booth must cross the great breadth of Virginia, following almost the exact same path General Lee took in his escape from Petersburg. But he has no horse, which means traveling by water or on the main roads in a buggy, and he must cross treacherous territory to get south of Richmond.

Baker studies his maps, searching for the precise spot where Booth might cross the Potomac. His eyes zoom in on Port Tobacco. "If any place in the world is utterly given over to depravity, it is Port Tobacco," he will quote a journalist as saying in his memoirs. "Five hundred people exist in Port Tobacco. Life there reminds me, in connection with the slimy river and the adjacent swamps, of the great reptile period of the world, when iguanodons and pterodactyls, and plesiosauri ate each other."

Lafayette Baker is wrong—but not by much.

CHAPTER FIFTY-NINE

Six days. Six long, cold miserable days. That's how long Booth and Herold have now been in the swamp, scratching at wood ticks, shivering under thin, damp wool blankets, and eating just the one meal a day provided by Thomas Jones. The silence has been almost complete, save for the times when Union warships on the Potomac fire their big guns to salute their fallen president.

The newspapers delivered daily by Jones continue to be a source of information and misery, as it becomes more and more clear that Booth's actions have condemned him. Booth would rant about that injustice if he had the energy. The fact is, he and Herold long ago tired of speaking in a whisper. And even if they hadn't, they have nothing to talk about.

The sizzle of happiness that accompanied killing Lincoln is long gone. Booth is a man accustomed to the finest things in life, and his miserable existence in the swamp has him longing for the tender flesh of Lucy Hale, a bottle of whiskey, a plate of oysters, and a warm bed.

Booth is just settling in for another night in the swamp when he hears the first whistle. Herold hears it, too, and is on his feet in an instant. Grabbing his rifle, Herold warily approaches the sound and returns with Jones. "The coast seems to be clear," Jones tells them, his voice betraying the sense of urgency. "Let us make the attempt."

Their camp is three miles from the river. Getting to the Potomac undetected means traveling down well-used public roads. Despite the darkness, they might run into a cavalry detail at any moment, but it is a chance they have to take.

Booth can't walk, so Jones loans him his horse. Herold and Jones help Booth into the saddle. The actor clings precariously to the horse's mane, desperate not to fall off.

Jones tells them to wait, then walks ahead to make sure the coast is clear. Only when he whistles that all is well do they follow. This is how they travel to the river, the ever vigilant Jones utilizing the smuggling skills he honed so well during the war to lead them to safety. Their pace is frustratingly slow to Booth, who wants to canter the horse as quickly as he can manage to the river, but Jones is taking no chances.

∽

When they approach Jones's house, Booth begs to be allowed inside for a moment of warmth. He badly wants to get to the river, but he is also addicted to creature comforts. After six days out in the cold, something as simple as standing before a roaring fireplace feels like a version of heaven. Jones won't hear of it, reminding them that his servants are home and could possibly give them away. Instead, Jones walks inside and returns with hot food, reminding the two fugitives that this might be the last meal they eat for a while.

They press on to the river. Jones has hidden a twelve-foot-long boat at the water's edge, tied to a large oak tree. The bank is steep, and Booth must be carried down the slope. But soon he sits in the stern, grasping an oar. Herold perches in the bow. The night is still dark, for the moon has not risen. A cold mist hovers on the surface of the wide and treacherous Potomac. Safety is just across the river in Virginia, where the citizens are solidly pro-Confederacy. It's so close they can see it. But getting there means navigating unseen currents and tides that can force them far downriver—or even backward. The river is two miles wide at this point and constantly patrolled by Union warships. Some are merely heading into Washington's Navy Yard after time at sea, while others are specifically hunting for two men in a small boat. It is common naval practice for ships to douse their running lights at night, all the better to thwart smugglers. Booth and

Herold might actually run headlong into a ship without even seeing it in the total darkness.

"Keep to that," Jones instructs Booth, lighting a small candle to illuminate Booth's compass and pointing to the southwesterly heading. The actor has carried the compass since the assassination, just for a moment such as this. "It will bring you into Machodoc Creek. Mrs. Quesenberry lives near the mouth of this creek. If you tell her you come from me, I think she will take care of you."

"God bless you, my dear friend," says Booth. "Good-bye."

They shove off. Jones turns his back and returns home, his work complete. No other man has risked as much, nor shown as much compassion for Booth and Herold, as Jones. He did not do it because he applauded the assassination—in fact, Jones is disgusted by Booth's action. Rather, he helped the two men out of compassion for men in trouble and a last-ditch bout of loyalty to the Confederacy. His deeds will go unpunished. When his part in the conspiracy will be revealed later on, the testimony will come from a non-white resident of southern Maryland and thus will be ignored.

Booth and Herold, meanwhile, paddle hard for the opposite shore. That is: Herold paddles hard. Booth sits in the back and dangles his oar in the water under the pretense of steering.

Herold paddles for several hours against a daunting current, but they're going the wrong way. Booth's compass may be a prized possession, but it's useless if not utilized properly.

∽

Things go from bad to worse. The fugitives almost paddle headlong into the *Juniper*, a Federal gunboat. And yet if anyone on the deck of the eighty-footer sees them they don't cry out.

Finally, they land, four miles upriver from where they departed, still in Maryland. Their escape is not going well. They are forced to hide themselves and their boat in the brush for yet another day.

And so, after one last, long twenty-four hours of hiding from the thousands of soldiers now combing the countryside looking for them, John Wilkes Booth and David Herold once again set out under cover of darkness rowing hard for Virginia. This time they make it.

Next stop: Kentucky.

CHAPTER SIXTY

Monday–Tuesday, April 24–25, 1865
Virginia-Maryland border
Day

amuel H. Beckwith is in Port Tobacco, the "Gomorrah," in Lafayette Baker's words, of Maryland. He is the telegraph operator specially detailed by Baker to keep the detective apprised of all actions in the Booth dragnet. Now he telegraphs a coded message back to Washington, stating that investigators have questioned local smugglers and learned that Booth and Herold have gone across the Potomac River.

The evidence is, in fact, erroneous. It refers to a group of men smuggled into Virginia on Easter Sunday, not Booth and Herold. Lafayette Baker immediately reacts, however, sending twenty-five members of the Sixteenth New York Cavalry by the steamship *John S. Ide* from Washington downriver to Belle Plain, Virginia. All of the men have volunteered for the mission. The senior officers are Baker's cousin Lieutenant Luther Baker and Colonel Everton Conger, a twenty-nine-year-old, highly regarded veteran of the Civil War.

Lafayette Baker sees them off. "I want you to go to Virginia and get Booth," he says and then puts his cousin in charge, despite the lower rank.

The *Ide* pushes back at two P.M., for a four-hour voyage. It arrives at the simple wharf and warehouse along the shore just after dark. The men immediately spur their horses down the main road of Belle Plain, Virginia, and then into the countryside, knocking on farmhouse doors and questioning the occupants. They stop any and all riders and carriages they encounter, pressing hard for clues as to Booth's whereabouts.

But nobody has seen Booth or Herold—or, if they have, they're not talking. By morning the cavalry squad is in Port Conway, more than ten miles inland from the Potomac. Exhausted, their horses wrung out from the long night, the soldiers are starting to feel as if this is just another futile lead. Conger has promised them all an equal share of the more than $200,000 in reward money awaiting those who capture Booth. This spurred them to ride all night, but now the prize seems unattainable. They are growing fearful that the *Ide* will return to Washington without them, leaving them to wait days for another ship.

During their trip south, Lieutenant Luther Baker made the rather wise decision to give the command back to Conger. "You have been over the ground," he told the veteran.

Then, just as they are about to give up and go home, on the shores of the Rappahannock River, at a ferry crossing known as Port Royal, two men positively identify photographs of Booth and Herold. They passed through the previous day and were traveling with a small group of Confederate veterans.

By this time, the twenty-five cavalry soldiers are exhausted, "so haggard and wasted with travel that they had to be kicked into intelligence before they could climb to their saddles," Lieutenant Baker will later recall.

But climb into their saddles they do, for hours and hours of more searching.

c✏͜ɔ

At two o'clock in the morning, at a handsome whitewashed farm three hundred yards off the main road, they finally come to a halt. The ground is soft clay, so their horses' hooves make no sound. The soldiers draw their carbines from their scabbards as Lieutenant Baker dismounts and opens the property's main gate. He has no certain knowledge of anything nefarious. It is just a hunch.

Fanning out, the riders make a circle around the house and barn.

In a very few minutes, Lieutenant Baker's hunch will make history.

CHAPTER SIXTY-ONE

Until just a few hours ago, John Wilkes Booth was happier and more content than at any time since killing Lincoln. His broken leg notwithstanding, his three days in Virginia, with its pro-Confederate citizens and custom of hospitality, have made him think that escape is a likely possibility. He even disclosed his identity to a group of former southern soldiers he met along the road. To everyone else who's asked, he's a former soldier who was injured at Petersburg and is on his way home.

He's spent the last day at the farmhouse of Richard Garrett, whose son John just returned home from the war. The Garretts do not know Booth's true identity and believe his story about being a former soldier. He's enjoyed hot meals and the chance to wash and sleep. But an hour before sunset came word that Federal cavalry were crossing the ferry over the Rappahannock River.

Booth reacted to the news with visible fear. The Garretts, seeing this, grew suspicious and insisted that both men leave. Booth and Herold refused, though not in a belligerent manner. Not knowing what to do and not wanting to create a problem with the two armed strangers, John Garrett sent them to sleep in the barn. Now Booth and Herold hide in a forty-eight-by-fifty-foot wooden structure, filled with hay and corn. Tobacco-curing equipment is stored inside, and thick cedar beams provide sturdy structural support. Worried that Booth and Herold plan to steal their horses and escape in the night, John and his brother William sleep outside the barn, armed with a pistol.

Booth doesn't realize the Garrett brothers are outside guarding the barn; nor does he know that the cavalry is surrounding the house. All he is sure of is that at two A.M. the dogs begin barking. Then a terrified John Garrett steps into the barn and orders the men to give up their weapons. The building is surrounded, he tells them.

"Get out of here," Booth cries, "or I will shoot you. You have betrayed me."

∽

Garrett flees, locking the barn door behind him. Booth and Herold are now trapped inside, with no idea how many men are out there. Then Herold says he wants out. He's sick of this life and wants to go home. He's done nothing wrong and wishes to proclaim his innocence.

"Captain," Booth calls out, not knowing the proper rank to use. "There is a man here who very much wants to surrender."

Then he turns to Herold in disgust: "Go away from me, damned coward."

Herold exits through the main door, wrists first. He is immediately taken away and arrested by the soldiers.

Lieutenant Baker calls to Booth, telling him that the barn will be set on fire within moments unless Booth surrenders. "Well, Captain," Booth cries out, his old sense of the dramatic now fully returned, "you may prepare a stretcher for me. Draw up your men. Throw open the door. Let's have a fair fight."

Then Booth hears the crackle of burning straw and smells the sickly sweet wood smoke of burning cedar. "One more stain on the old banner!" he yells, doing his best to sound fearless. No one quite knows what that statement means.

He looks across the barn and sees Lieutenant Baker opening the door. The actor hefts his loaded carbine, preparing to take aim.

Just as Abraham Lincoln felt a slight instant of pain and then nothing at all when Booth shot him, now Booth hears the crack of a rifle and feels a jolt in his neck, and then nothing. Sergeant Boston Corbett has fired a bullet and it slices through Booth's spinal cord and paralyzes him from the neck down. John Wilkes Booth collapses to the floor of the barn, the flames now climbing higher and higher all around him.

Boston Corbett, in his own way, is as much a zealot as Booth. Only his passion is religion. Incredibly, years before, Corbett cut off his own testicles with a pair of scissors after experiencing a moment of lust. Booth has now been shot by a man very much like himself: a rebellious fanatic. Corbett actually disobeyed orders when taking aim at the actor. Baker and Conger pull John Wilkes Booth from the barn moments before it is completely engulfed in flames. The actor is still alive.

As with Lincoln, the decision is made not to transport him, for any movement will surely kill the actor. But he is dead by morning anyway. His limp body is hurled into the back of a garbage wagon.

The flight—and life—of John Wilkes Booth has come to an end. He is just twenty-six years old.

PUBLISHED BY J.L.MAGEE, 305 WALNUT ST PHIL.ª

THE MURDERERS DOOM. MISERABLE DEATH OF J.WILKES BOOTH, THE ASSASSIN OF PRESIDENT LINCOLN.
Shot through the head by Sergeant Boston Corbett in a barn on Garrett's Farm, near Port Royal, near the Rappahannock. April 25, 1865.

CHAPTER SIXTY-TWO

Two and a half months later, the rounding up of Lincoln's killers has become a national pastime. Secretary of War Stanton has personally taken charge of identifying the larger conspiracy that has grown out of Booth's single gunshot, pushing Lafayette Baker from the limelight. While some in the Confederate South now call Booth a martyr and hang pictures of him in their homes as they would for any family member, northerners are even more determined to see every last one of his co-conspirators found—and killed. The jails are full of men and women who have been trapped in the spider's web of the Stanton investigation. Some have absolutely nothing to do with Lincoln's death, like James Pumphrey, the Confederate-sympathizing owner of a stable, who spent a month behind bars. No one is immune from suspicion. Federal agents scour their list of suspects, making sure no one is overlooked. One missing suspect is twenty-one-year-old John Surratt, whose mother, Mary, provided Booth and his conspirators with weapons and lodging.

Mary herself sits inside the old Arsenal Penitentiary awaiting her fate. She's been locked up since her arrest on April 17. The trial of all the co-conspirators, including Mary, began on May 10, and some 366 witnesses were called before it was over, seven weeks later. From the beginning, the public viewed all the conspirators as clearly criminals. Certainly the drunken George Atzerodt and the brutish thug who attacked the Sewards, Lewis Powell, look the part. But Mary Surratt is different. Standing five foot six, with a buxom figure and a pretty smile that captivates some of the journalists in attendance, Mary has initially engendered some sympathy, and many Americans wonder if her life should be spared.

⚬

But Mary's physical appearance, like that of her co-conspirators, began to change as the trial stretched into its sixth and seventh weeks. She suffered severe cramping, excessive menstruating and constant urinating from a disease known as endometriosis. She was barely tended to by her captors, or given the freedom to properly care for herself. Her cell was called "barely habitable" by one eyewitness, and court proceedings were stopped on more than one occasion due to her condition.

The other conspirators underwent physical change for a very different reason. Stanton insisted they wear a thick padded hood over the heads. Extra cotton padding was placed over the lids, pressing hard against the eyeballs. There was just one hole, but it didn't line up evenly with the mouth, making eating and breathing a challenge. Underneath the hoods the heat was intense, and the air stifling. All the sweating and the bloating of the skin from the heavy hoods conspired to make each conspirator look more and more swollen and rabid with each passing day. Over time they resembled not so much men, but crazed apparitions.

⚬

After deliberating for three days, the nine-member jury finds Mary Surratt, Lewis Powell, George Atzerodt, and David Herold guilty. They will be hanged. As for Dr. Samuel Mudd, Michael O'Laughlen, Ned Spangler, and Samuel Arnold, their punishment will be the remote penitentiary of Fort Jefferson in the Gulf of Mexico.

There is no one willing to speak up for the men who will hang. But Mary Surratt's priest comes to her defense. So does her daughter,

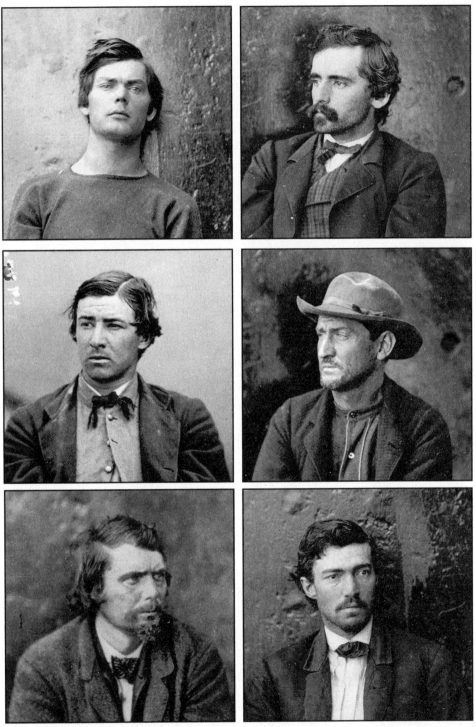

*Guilty! Sentenced to hang (left column): Lewis Powell, David Herold,
George Atzerodt, and Mary Surratt (not pictured). Sentenced to prison
(right column): Samuel Arnold, Ned Spangler, Michael O'Laughlen,
and Dr. Samuel Mudd (not pictured)*

Anna—though not her missing son, John. Mary Surratt's attorney frantically works to get an audience with President Andrew Johnson so that he might personally intervene on her behalf. Her supporters say she was just a lone woman trying to make ends meet by providing weapons for Booth and his conspiracy and point out that she didn't pull the trigger and was nowhere near Ford's Theatre.

There is hope. Not much, but a little. The other three sentenced to hang are all part of Booth's inner circle. Not so with Mary Surratt. Although Johnson will not speak to him, her attorney continues to argue to the fringe of President Johnson's outer circle, those who actively prevent him from speaking with the president, that her life should be spared.

⁂

Mary Surratt spends the night of July 6 in prayer, asking God to spare her life.

In the morning, she refuses breakfast, and even at ten A.M., when her visitors are told to leave so that her body can be prepared, Mary is still hoping. She wears a black dress and veil. Her ankles and wrists are manacled. And then she is marched out into a blazing summer sun. She looks up at the ten-foot-high gallows, newly built for the execution of her and the other conspirators. She sees the freshly dug graves beneath the gallows—the spot where her body will rest for all eternity.

Mary Surratt, Lewis Powell, George Atzerodt, and David Herold climb the gallows staircase. They are seated in chairs on the platform at the top. Their hands and arms are tied to their bodies—the men's with ropes, Mary's with white cloth. Their legs are tied together at the ankles and knees so that they won't kick wildly after the hangman springs the door.

"Mrs. Surratt is innocent!" Powell cries out, just before a white cotton hood is placed over his head.

Outside the prison, Mary's supporters gather. Time is short. But there is still hope. Soldiers stand atop the penitentiary walls, just in case a last-minute rider approaches with a pardon. Inside the penitentiary, one hundred civilians have won the right to watch Lincoln's killers die. The muggy air is thick with anticipation.

All it takes is one word from President Johnson. Mary Surratt continues to pray.

"Please don't let me fall," she says to an executioner, getting vertigo as she looks down on the crowd from atop the tall, unstable gallows. He puts the white hood over her head, and then she stands alone, terrified that she might topple forward over the edge of the gallows before the pardon can arrive.

The death sentences are read in alphabetical order by General Winfield Scott Hancock, another old friend of Generals Grant and Lee from their days in Mexico.

Each trapdoor is held in place by a single post. At the bottom of the scaffold stand four hand-selected members of the armed forces. It is their job to kick away the posts on the signal from the hangman. Suddenly, that signal is given.

The trapdoors swing open. Mary Surratt, like the others, drops six feet in an instant. But unlike the others', her neck does not break, and

she does not die right away. The forty-two-year-old mother and widow, whose son would not come to her rescue out of fear for his own life, swings for five long minutes before her larynx is crushed and her body stops fighting for air.

Stanton lets the bodies dangle in the wind for twenty more minutes before pronouncing that he is satisfied. The corpses are buried in the hard prison yard.

Mary Surratt becomes the first and only woman ever hanged by the United States government.

AFTERWORD

The saga of Lincoln's assassination went on long after he died. Indeed, it continues to this day, as historians and amateur sleuths alike debate a never-ending list of conspiracy theories. The full truth may never be known.

As for the other key figures in the dramatic events of April 1865, their fates are now part of the historical record.

The body of **John Wilkes Booth** was returned to Washington on the *John S. Ide*. Booth's dentist and his personal physician were both brought on board and testified that the body was that of Booth. It was photographed, and then the surgeon general, Joseph Barnes, who had tended to Lincoln in the president's final hours, performed an autopsy while the ship was sailing. The cause of death was determined to be a "gunshot wound in the neck," with the added notation that paralysis was immediate after Booth was shot, "and all the horrors of consciousness of suffering and death must have been present to the assassin during the two hours he lingered."

Dr. Barnes removed the third, fourth, and fifth cervical vertebrae from Booth's neck. These clearly showed the path of the bullet as it entered, then exited the body. The vertebrae are now housed at Walter Reed Army Medical Center, in the National Museum of Health and Medicine—although they are not on public display. Dr. Barnes then turned his completed autopsy over to Secretary of War Edwin

Stanton, who also took control of the photographs made of the corpse, and of Booth's diary, which was handed to him by Lafayette C. Baker.

Curiously, the photographs soon disappeared. And when Baker was later called upon to verify that Booth's diary actually belonged to the killer, he was astonished to see that "eighteen leaves," or pages, had been cut from the journal—allegedly by Secretary Stanton. Neither the photographs nor the missing pages have ever been found, casting more suspicion on Stanton's possible role in a conspiracy.

The secretary of war wished the Booth situation to be handled with as little public outcry as possible, and this meant forbidding a public funeral. On Stanton's orders, Lafayette Baker staged a mock burial, wrapping the body in a horse blanket and publicly hurling it into the Potomac. However, this was just a ruse to conceal the body's actual location. After the crowd on shore watched Baker dump a weighted object into the river, the ship traveled around a bend to the site of the old penitentiary, on the grounds of the Washington Arsenal. The assassin was buried in an anonymous grave beneath the prison's dirt floor, his body concealed inside the gun box that served as his casket. When, two years later, the penitentiary was shuttered and leveled, Booth's remains were moved to the family plot at Green Mount Cemetery in Baltimore, where they remain to this day.

Despite all evidence that Booth is actually dead and was buried in the grave bearing his name, various legends have maintained that he escaped into the South and lived a long life. In December 2010, Booth's descendants agreed to exhume the remains of Edwin Booth to see if DNA from his body is a match for the DNA in the vertebrae housed at Walter Reed. As the chief historian for the Navy Medical Department noted, "If it compares favorably, then that's the end of the controversy. If it doesn't match, you change American history." As of this writing, the outcome of that investigation is still pending.

∽

Mary Lincoln never recovered from Abraham Lincoln's assassination. She insisted on wearing only the color black for the rest of her life. Mary lingered in the White House for several weeks after the shooting, then returned home to Illinois, where she spent her time answering the many letters of condolence she had received from around the world, and also lobbying Congress for a pension. This was granted in 1870, for the sum of $3,000 per year. However, just when it appeared that Mary was recovering from her considerable grief, in 1871 her eighteen-year-old son, Tad, died of a mysterious heart condition. This brought on a downward spiral of mental instability, dramatized in spending sprees, paranoia, and delusions—once she almost jumped out of a building after wrongly believing she saw flames consuming the structure. Her only remaining son, Robert, had her committed to a mental institution in 1875. She spent a year there, during which she engaged in a letter-writing campaign to the *Chicago Tribune* that so embarrassed Robert he had her released. Mary moved to the south of France for four years, living in exile in the town of Pau before returning to Springfield. She died in 1882, at the age of sixty-three. She is buried alongside her husband.

∽

Robert Todd Lincoln went on to a stellar career as an attorney and then public official. He served as secretary of war from 1881 to 1885, during the James Garfield and Chester Arthur administrations, and served as U.S. minister to Great Britain from 1889 to 1893, under Benjamin Harrison. Although he was not present at Ford's Theatre when his father was assassinated, he was an eyewitness to Garfield's assassination in 1881 and nearby when President William McKinley was assassinated, in 1901.

John Wilkes Booth would have been enraged to know that Robert Lincoln and **Lucy Lambert Hale** spent the afternoon of Lincoln's assassination together, studying Spanish. It's possible that Lucy could have mentioned this upcoming appointment to the assassin during their final moments together that morning, fueling his jealousy. In the end, it doesn't matter, because Lucy Lambert Hale will forever be linked with John Wilkes Booth.

Secretary Stanton, out of respect for her father's position, refused to let her be called upon to testify at the trial. However, there were rumors that she was smuggled aboard the *Ides* to view Booth's body and wept openly at the sight. This has never been confirmed. Regardless, the intimacy of their relationship soon became widespread knowledge in Washington, D.C., and she was only too happy to escape to

Spain for the next five years while her father served as ambassador. Lucy and Robert Todd Lincoln continued to maintain a friendly relationship, but she chose to marry William Chandler in 1874. She bore one child, a son, at the age of forty-four. William Chandler went on to serve as secretary of the navy. Their grandson Theodore Chandler would become a highly decorated World War II navy admiral who was killed when kamikazes attacked his ship in the Pacific. Lucy Lambert Hale died of natural causes in 1915, at the age of seventy-four.

Robert Todd Lincoln died at his home in Vermont at the age of eighty-two, though not before being present for the dedication of the Lincoln Memorial in Washington, D.C., in 1922. He is buried in Arlington National Cemetery.

∽

Laura Keene would regret cradling Lincoln's head in her lap that night in Ford's Theatre. The assassination linked her troupe with the killing, and the attendant notoriety was hard on her already floundering career. The actress was eminently resourceful, however, and left America to barnstorm through England before returning in 1869 to manage the Chestnut Street Theatre in Philadelphia. She later took to lecturing on the fine arts and publishing a weekly art journal. Laura Keene died of tuberculosis on November 4, 1873, in Montclair, New Jersey. She was believed to be forty-seven, although she was often vague about her actual birthdate and may have been three years older.

∽

Edwin Stanton did not live long after the death of Abraham Lincoln, and those years he did live were fraught with controversy. Stanton clashed repeatedly with President Andrew Johnson over the process of Reconstruction. Johnson's vengeful policies toward the South were in direct contrast with what Lincoln had hoped for, and despite their earlier animosity toward each other, Stanton was keen to see Lincoln's wishes put in place. Tensions between Stanton and Johnson got so bad that in 1868 the president fired Stanton as secretary of war and replaced him with Ulysses S. Grant. Stanton refused to leave the office and was vindicated when the Senate voted that Johnson's actions were illegal. Johnson tried once again to replace Stanton, this time with General

Lorenzo Thomas. Stanton barricaded himself in his office to avoid being removed. The Senate, which had openly clashed with Johnson over other key issues, now began impeachment hearings, stating that Johnson did not have the authority to remove the secretary of war. Though Johnson escaped removal from office by one vote in the Senate, Stanton was the clear winner in the case. He retired soon after the vote, only to be nominated as a justice to the Supreme Court by the newly elected president, Ulysses S. Grant. Edwin Stanton died before he could take the oath. The end came on Christmas Eve 1869; at the age of fifty-five, Stanton died from a sudden and very severe asthma attack. Did he have any part in the assassination of Abraham Lincoln? To this day, there are those who believe he did. But nothing has ever been proved.

✎

Few men could have successfully followed Abraham Lincoln as president, but **Andrew Johnson** proved particularly inept. His Reconstruction policies were bitterly divisive, to the point that he warred openly with members of his own party. He dodged impeachment but was not reelected to office in 1868. Later in life, Johnson was reelected to the Senate, but soon afterward he died from a stroke, on July 31, 1875.

✎

Lafayette Baker became an instant celebrity for finding Lincoln's killer. The red-bearded detective wrote a best-selling memoir in 1867, *History of the United States Secret Service.* In the book, he detailed his role in finding John Wilkes Booth. Several of his claims, including that he'd handed Booth's diary to Edwin Stanton, led to a congressional investigation into his role in the disappearance of the diary. Soldiers had given Baker the diary upon returning to Washington with Booth's body. Baker then gave it to Stanton, who locked it in a safe for almost two years, never telling investigators that he had the crucial piece of evidence in his possession. The publication of Baker's memoir provoked a great public demand for Stanton to produce the diary. He did so reluctantly, but eighteen pages were missing. The secretary of war denied being responsible for excising the pages. The investigation ended without a formal placement of blame.

In 1960, a controversial amateur historian named Ray Neff came upon a description of the Lincoln assassination in a copy of *Colburn's United Service Magazine*, a British military journal. The article was dated February 5, 1868. Lafayette Baker was the author. Neff claims to have deciphered a coded message from Baker within the story. The substitution code revealed a message that reads thus: "It was on the 10th of April, 1865, when I first knew that the plan was in action. I did not know the identity of the assassin, but I knew most all else when I approached Edwin Stanton about it. He at once acted surprised and disbelieving. Later he said: 'You are a party to it, too.' "

Baker, decoded by Neff, goes on to add: "There were at least eleven members of Congress involved in the plot, no less than twenty Army officers, three Naval officers, and at least twenty-four civilians, of which one was a governor of a loyal state. Five were bankers of great repute, three were nationally known newspapermen, and eleven were industrialists of great repute and wealth. Eighty-five thousand dollars were contributed by the named persons to pay for the deed. Only eight persons knew the details of the plot and the identity of others. I fear for my life."

There is no consensus about whether Neff's hidden message is authentic. What we do know for sure is that Stanton did not hesitate to ask the previously disgraced Baker to lead the Booth investigation— this at a time when the secretary of war had every single detective in the nation at his disposal—and that Baker magically pinpointed Booth's actual location when the thousands of soldiers and detectives combing the woods and swamps could not.

It should be noted that Neff's hypothesis and his entire body of work have been repudiated and dismissed by the vast majority of trained historians and assassination scholars. *Civil War Times*, which originally published his findings about the cipher messages, later denounced him. Once Neff became involved with the movie *The Lincoln Conspiracy* and began promoting bizarre theories about Booth's escape and a later second life in India, he became even more ostracized from mainstream scholars.

The fact remains, however, that Stanton's withholding of Booth's diary was suspicious, as is the subject of the eighteen missing pages. No one has adequately explained this behavior, thus allowing some conspiracy theorists to continue to wonder if he had a larger role in Lincoln's assassination.

Baker became increasingly paranoid after the congressional investigation, certain that he would be murdered. And he was right! Just eighteen months after the investigation, he was found dead in his home in Philadelphia. While Baker was at first believed to have died from meningitis, evidence now points to a slow and systematic death by poisoning. Again, this evidence comes from Ray Neff. The Indiana State University professor used an atomic absorption spectrophotometer to analyze strands of Baker's hair. The results showed that arsenic had been slowly introduced into his system during the last months of his life. Comparing the rising levels of arsenic with diary entries made by Baker's wife, Neff noted a correlation with visits from Wally Pollack, Baker's brother-in-law, who was in the habit of bringing imported German beer to Baker's house whenever he came calling. Pollack, not incidentally, also worked under Secretary Stanton as a War Department employee. The suspicion is that Pollack poisoned Baker by mixing small amounts of arsenic into the beer. Whether or not he acted alone is a matter of conjecture.

⁓

Abraham Lincoln's irresponsible bodyguard **John Parker** never presented himself for duty or tried to help in any way on the night of the assassination. Incredibly, Parker was not held accountable for shirking his duties. In fact, the first time he was seen after the assassination was when he showed up at a Washington police station the next morning in the company of a known prostitute. Formal police charges of dereliction of duty were pressed against Parker, but once again he was acquitted. Three years later, after many attempts to remove him from the police department, Parker was finally booted for "gross neglect of duty." He went on to work as a carpenter and machinist. He died of pneumonia on June 28, 1890, at the age of sixty.

⁓

Lincoln's responsible bodyguard **William Crook** had a more esteemed career, working in the White House for more than fifty years—a time that spanned administrations from Abraham Lincoln's to Woodrow

Wilson's. However, it was his relationship with Lincoln that he trea-
sured most, and his 1910 memoirs provide a vivid insight into the journey to Richmond and the events of April 14. Critics have accused
Crook of padding his own part, but the book makes for compelling
reading. William Crook died in 1915 from pneumonia, at the age of
seventy-seven. He was buried in Arlington National Cemetery, in a
service attended by President Wilson.

✍

After the war, **Robert E. Lee** applied for a pardon for his acts against
the United States. Secretary of State William H. Seward did not file
the pardon but instead gave it to a friend as a souvenir. The document
wasn't discovered for more than one hundred years. President Gerald
R. Ford officially reinstated Lee as a U.S. citizen in 1975.

Marse Robert was buried not at his beloved Virginia home, Arlington, which was confiscated during the war and redesignated as a U.S.
military cemetery, but at Washington and Lee University, in Lexington, Virginia. He died on Columbus Day 1870, at the age of sixty-
three.

✍

Lee's counterpart on the Union side, **General Ulysses S. Grant,** had an
admirable career after the war ended. He remained in the army, helping to implement Reconstruction policies that guaranteed the black
vote. He saw his popularity soar in the North. Elected president in
1868, he served two terms in office. Grant's later years were filled with
travel and, later, financial upheaval. After losing his entire fortune to
bad investments in the early 1880s, he sat down to, with the help of
editor Mark Twain, write his memoirs. Considered by many to be one
of the best military autobiographies in history, Grant's life story was a
best seller. Royalties from the book guaranteed his family a comfortable life long after he died of throat cancer, on July 23, 1885.

The question "Who is buried in Grant's tomb?" seems an obvious
one, for Ulysses S. Grant is buried in this enormous mausoleum in
New York's Riverside Park. However, so is **Julia Grant**. She died on
December 14, 1902, at the age of seventy-six, and now lies alongside
her husband.

ༀ

After being discovered alive on the battlefield that day after the battle for High Bridge, **Colonel Francis Washburn** was immediately transported to a field hospital, then home to Massachusetts, where he died one week after Lincoln did. Coincidentally, he passed away on the exact same day as the Confederacy's **General James Dearing,** his opposite on the field of battle. They were the last two casualties of High Bridge.

ༀ

Two officers present at Sayler's Creek, **General James "Pete" Longstreet** and **General George Armstrong Custer,** followed remarkably different paths after the Civil War. Longstreet's longtime friendship with Grant figured prominently in his embrace of pro-Union Reconstruction efforts, much to the chagrin of diehard rebels, who soon began an active series of revisionist attacks on the great southern general, attempting somewhat successfully to impugn his reputation as a leader and paint him as a coward. By the time Longstreet died, in 1904, at the age of eighty-two, he had served as a diplomat, a civil servant, and a U.S. marshal. A house fire consumed all of his Civil War memorabilia, leaving almost no legacy other than his autobiography to set his wartime record straight.

General Custer continued to fight, using the same aggressive, impulsive tactics that served him so successfully at Sayler's Creek. In his time he would become far better known for his battles on America's western frontier and for his friendships with other larger-than-life figures, such as Buffalo Bill Cody. In June 1876, Custer and his Seventh Cavalry were sent to Montana to force Sioux and Cheyenne Indians back to their reservations. On the morning of June 25, his scouts reported that a small band of warriors were camped along the Little Bighorn River. Behaving in much the same fashion as he did at Sayler's Creek, Custer split his cavalry into three columns and attacked without making a preliminary study of the terrain.

The results were disastrous. Custer and his men were soon cut off, surrounded by a vastly superior force of Oglala Sioux under the legendary warrior Crazy Horse. Custer ordered his men to shoot their horses and stack the bodies to shield them from incoming rifle fire, but within an hour every last man was dead. When the Battle of the Little Bighorn was over, the bodies of the slain soldiers were stripped and mutilated, thanks to an Indian belief that the soul of a mutilated body would wander the earth without rest for eternity. Scalps were taken, stomachs slit open, eardrums punctured, and genitals dismembered. In the case of Custer's brother Tom, who had won his second of two congressional Medals of Honor at Sayler's Creek, his heart was cut out and eaten. Another brother, twenty-seven-year-old Boston, was also killed and scalped.

Strangely, the only body left unmutilated was that of George Armstrong Custer. When U.S. soldiers later came upon the battlefield, they described Custer's face as being a mask of calm. A round .45-caliber bullet hole in his left temple and another just below his heart were the only signs of violence—and point to the likelihood that he was killed by a long-range rifle shot.

Initially, Custer was buried in a shallow grave on the battlefield, next to his brother Tom. News of the devastating defeat was quickly conveyed to Fort McPherson, Nebraska, then on to Washington, D.C., by telegraph. Ironically, word of Custer's defeat arrived in the nation's capital on July 4, 1876—America's first centennial. In its own way, the death of Custer was as traumatizing as that of Lincoln, emboldening the United States Army to seek revenge against the Indians in the same way Lincoln's assassination had northerners seeking revenge against the South. Custer was just thirty-six when he died. His body was later relocated from the Little Bighorn and buried at the United States Military Academy at West Point.

_ɔײַ_

William Seward would live just seven more years after being attacked in his own bed on the night of Lincoln's assassination, but in that time he would undertake an activity that would leave an even longer-lasting legacy than the heinous attack. In 1867, while still serving as secretary of state and still bearing the disfiguring facial scars of the knife attack, he purchased Alaska for the United States. What soon became known as "Seward's Folly" would later be seen as a huge asset when silver and gold and oil were discovered in the new territory. Seward died on October 10, 1872. He was seventy-one.

∽

Major Henry Reed Rathbone, present in the box on the night Lincoln was shot, later married his date from that evening, **Clara Harris**. Unfortunately for Harris, Rathbone later went insane and killed her with a knife. He was institutionalized for the remainder of his life.

∽

Boston Corbett, the man who shot John Wilkes Booth, received a handsome reward for the killing, even though he'd disobeyed orders. He left the military soon afterward, first working as a hatter, then serving as assistant doorman for the Kansas state legislature. It appears that the mercury used in making hats, which was well known for causing insanity (giving rise to the term "mad as a hatter"), caused him to become mentally unstable. In 1887 he, too, was sent to an insane asylum, after brandishing a revolver in the legislature. He escaped, then moved north to Minnesota, where he died in the Great Hinckley Fire of 1894. He was sixty-two.

∽

Dr. Samuel Mudd, Samuel Arnold, and **Michael O'Laughlen** were all given life sentences for their roles in the assassination conspiracy. **Ned Spangler,** the besotted sceneshifter, received a six-year sentence. All were sent to the Dry Tortugas, a baking-hot group of islands west of the Florida Keys. Their jailers, black Union soldiers, had complete power over the daily movements of these white supremacists. O'Laughlen died of fever while in prison, at the age of twenty-seven. Spangler, Mudd, and Arnold were pardoned in 1869 by Andrew Johnson and lived out their days as law-abiding citizens.

The man who helped John Wilkes Booth and David Herold escape into Virginia, **Thomas Jones,** was circumspect about his role in the assassination for many years. He was taken into custody shortly after Booth was killed and spent seven weeks in the Old Capital Prison before being released. Even though he became a justice of the peace after the war, the tight-lipped former member of the Confederate Secret Service was ever after wary of persecution for aiding John Wilkes Booth and David Herold. That changed in 1893, when he wrote a 126-page book telling his side of the events. Jones died on March 5, 1895, at the age of seventy-four.

≈

Perhaps the most shadowy figure in the Lincoln conspiracy, **John Surratt,** Mary Surratt's son, could have been instrumental in reducing his mother's sentence by showing that her part in the assassination was that of passive support instead of active participation. But rather than give the testimony that might have spared her life, John Surratt fled to Montreal, Canada, immediately after the assassination, where he followed the news of his mother's trial and execution. Surratt then fled to England under an assumed name and later continued on to the Vatican, where he served in the Papal Zouaves. He was discovered and arrested but escaped. Another international search for Surratt soon found him in Alexandria, Egypt. Arrested again, he was brought back to the United States to appear before a judge. Amazingly, the jury deadlocked on his involvement. John Surratt was free to go. He died in 1916 at the age of seventy-two.

≈

Mary Surratt's body was reburied in the Catholic cemetery at Mount Olivet in Washington, D.C., where it remains to this day. The petition to spare Mary's life never got to President Andrew Johnson; his assistant Preston King kept the information away from Johnson. But apparently that action preyed on King's conscience. A few months later, King tied a bag of bullets around his neck and leapt from a ferryboat in New York's harbor; he was never seen again. He was fifty-nine years old.

EPILOGUE

The last days of Abraham Lincoln's life included perhaps the most dramatic events in the nation's history. It is eerie that Abraham Lincoln found much solace in the play *Julius Caesar*, by William Shakespeare, given that the two great men met their ends in the same way. Caesar was betrayed by his countrymen, as was Lincoln. Both men died within months of their fifty-sixth birthday, before they could complete their life's work. Just as the story of Julius Caesar has been told and retold for centuries, the tragedy that befell Lincoln should be known by every American. His life and death continue to shape us as a people, even today. America is a great country, but like every other nation on earth it is influenced by evil. John Wilkes Booth epitomizes the evil that can harm us, even as President Abraham Lincoln represents the good that can make us stronger.

Appendix

RE-CREATION OF
HARPER'S WEEKLY

The April 29, 1865, edition of *Harper's Weekly* was entirely devoted to the assassination and death of Abraham Lincoln. The edition went to the printers just hours after word reached Washington that John Wilkes Booth had been located and shot dead. This gives the writers' words an urgency and heartfelt emotion that allow modern readers to gain a very real sense of how the nation was reacting to Lincoln's death. On the day that it came out, Lincoln's funeral train was traveling from Cleveland to Columbus, Ohio, and the trial of the conspirators had not yet begun. The nation was still very much at a loss over how to deal with this national tragedy. Here we reprint the entire text of the article "The Murder of the President" as it appeared in that edition.

HARPER'S WEEKLY.

JOURNAL OF CIVILIZATION.

VOL. IX.—No. 435.]   NEW YORK, SATURDAY, APRIL 29, 1865.   [SINGLE COPIES TEN CENTS. / $4.00 PER YEAR IN ADVANCE.

Entered according to Act of Congress, in the Year 1865, by Harper & Brothers, in the Clerk's Office of the District Court for the Southern District of New York.

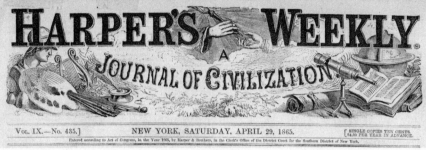

THE MURDER OF THE PRESIDENT.

The Fourteenth of April is a dark day in our country's calendar. On that day four years ago the national flag was for the first time lowered at the bidding of traitors. Upon that day, after a desperate conflict with treason for four long, weary years—a conflict in which the nation had so far triumphed that she breathed again in the joyous prospect of coming peace—her chosen leader was stricken down by the foul hand of the cowardly assassin. Exultation that had known no bounds was exchanged for boundless grief. The record upon which had been inscribed all sorts of violence possible to the most malignant treason that ever sought to poison a nation's heart had been almost written full. But

not quite full. Murder had run out its category of possible degrees against helpless loyalists in the South, against women and children whose houses had been burned down over their heads, and against our <u>unfortunate prisoners,</u> who had been tortured and literally <u>starved to death</u>. But there still remained one victim for its last rude stroke—one victim for whom, it was whispered in rebel journals South and North, there was still reserved the dagger of a BRUTUS. Beaten on every field of recognized warfare, treason outdid its very self, and killed our President.

The man who lent himself to traitors for this vile purpose was JOHN WILKES BOOTH, who sold himself, it may be, partly for the pieces of silver, but chiefly for the infamous notoriety attaching to such an act. There was an ancient villain who deliberately purposed to perpetuate the memory of his name among men by an act of awful sacrilege—a sacrilege so striking as never to be forgotten—and he burned the temple of the Ephesian Diana. EROSTRATUS gained his end, and has been remembered accordingly. A memory far more detestable is in store for JOHN WILKES BOOTH, who dared, by the commission of an infinitely greater sacrilege, to bring a whole people to tears.

He was the third son born in America of the eminent English tragedian JUNIUS BRUTUS BOOTH. There were three brothers, JUNIUS BRUTUS, Jun., EDWIN, and JOHN WILKES, all of whom inherited a predilection for the stage. EDWIN, however, is the only one of these who has attained a very eminent position as an actor, and he is probably surpassed by no living man. In justice to him it is proper here to state that he is true and loyal, and exacts our sincerest sympathy. The elder BOOTH, father of these three actors, died thirteen years ago. He passed the quieter portion of his life upon his farm, in Harford County, some thirty miles from Baltimore. JOHN WILKES BOOTH, the murderer, was born in 1839,

and is now only twenty-six years of age. He went upon the stage at the early age of seventeen, simply as JOHN WILKES. As stock actor he gained a fair reputation, and afterward assuming his full name, he began a more ambitious career. But, partly on account of his dissolute habits, he never achieved a marked success. He performed chiefly in the South and West. He has appeared but few times before a New York audience. In person he bears considerable resemblance to his father. His eyes are dark and large; his hair of the same color, inclined to curl; his features finely molded; his form tall, and his address pleasing. He abandoned his profession recently on account of a bronchial affection. It is said that he has frequently threatened to kill President LINCOLN. His companions have been violent Secessionists, and there are doubtless many others involved to a greater or less degree in his crime. The attempt to assassinate Secretary SEWARD was made probably by an accomplice. It is supposed that Secretary STANTON and ANDREW JOHNSON were to have been added to the list of victims. The latter, at least, received on Friday a card from BOOTH, but was not at home.

Those who were acquainted with BOOTH'S movements on the fatal Friday say that his manner was restless. He knew that the President and his party intended to be present at Ford's Theatre in the evening. He asked an acquaintance if he should attend the performance, remarking that if he did he would see some unusually fine acting. It was the general expectation that General GRANT would form one of the President's party, and there are many who suppose that a blow was intended for him as well as the President. The latter had passed the day in the usual manner. In the morning his son, Capt. ROBERT LINCOLN, breakfasted with him.— The Captain had just returned from the capitulation of ROBERT E. LEE, and the President listened with great interest to his narration of the detailed circumstances. After breakfast he conversed for an hour with Speaker COLFAX about his future policy as to the rebellion which he was about to submit to his Cabinet. At 11 o'clock the Cabinet met. Both the President and General GRANT were present. Having spent the afternoon with Governor OGLESBY, Senator YATES, and other leading citizens of his State, he went to the theatre in the evening with Mrs. LINCOLN, in order to unite in the general expression of popular joy for our late victories. The party consisted of Mrs. Senator HARRIS and daughter, and Major HENRY RATHBONE, Of Albany. They arrived at ten minutes before nine o'clock, and occupied a private box over-looking the stage. The play for the evening was The American Cousin.

BOOTH came upon his errand at about 10 o'clock. He left his horse in charge at the rear of the theatre, and made his way to the President's box. This box is a double one, in the second tier at the left of the stage. When occupied by the Presidential party the separating partition is removed, and the two boxes are thus thrown into one. We give an accurate plan of the box on page 259.—According to Major RATHBONE'S statement, the assassin must have made his preparations in the most deliberate manner beforehand. Of this fact there are at least four proofs, as we shall see: Stealthily approaching the dark passageway leading to the box, BOOTH, after having effected an entrance, closed the hall door, and then, taking a piece of board which he had prepared for the occasion, placed one end of it in an indentation excavated in the wall, about four feet from the floor, and the other against the moulding of the door-panel a few inches higher. He thus made it impossible for any one to enter from without; and securing himself against intrusion in that direction, he proceeded to the doors of the box. There were two of those. Here also the villain had carefully provided before hand the means by which he might, unnoticed himself, observe the position of the parties inside. With a gimlet, or small bit, he had bored a hole in the door-panel, which he afterward reamed out with his knife, so as to leave it a little larger than a buck-shot on the inside, while on the other side it was sufficiently large to give his eye a wide range. To secure against the doors being locked (they both had spring-locks), he had loosened the screws with which the bolt-hasps were fastened. In regard to the next stage of BOOTH'S movements there is some degree of uncertainty. He had been noticed as he passed through the dress-circle by a Mr. FERGUSON, who was sitting on the opposite side of the theatre. This man knew BOOTH, and recognized him. He had been talking with him a short time before. FERGUSON states that when BOOTH reached the door of the corridor leading from the dress-circle to the boxes he halted, "took off his hat, and, holding it in his left hand, leaned against the wall behind him." After remaining thus for the space of half a minute, "he stepped down one step, put his hand on the door of the little corridor leading to the box, bent his knee against it," when the door opened and BOOTH entered. After his entrance to the corridor he was of course invisible to FERGUSON, and, before the fatal shot, was probably seen by no one but the sentry at the door of the corridor. The latter he is said to have passed on the plea that the President had sent for him. What passed before the shot is only conjecturable. He made his observations, doubtless, through the aperture in the door provided for that purpose. And here we come upon another proof of a deliberately-prepared plan. The very seats in the box had been arranged to suit his purpose, either by himself or, as is more likely, by some attaché of the theatre in complicity with him. The President sat in the left-hand corner of the box, nearest the audience, in an easy armchair. Next to him, on the right, sat Mrs. LINCOLN, Some distance to the right of both Miss HARRIS was seated, with Major RATHBONE at her left and a little in the rear of Mrs. LINCOLN. BOOTH rapidly surveyed the situation. The play had reached the second scene of the third act. Mrs. LINCOLN, intent on the play, was leaning forward, with one hand resting on her husband's knee. The President was leaning upon one hand, and with the other was adjusting a portion of the drapery, his face wearing a pleasant smile as it was partially turned to the audience. As to the act of assassination, there are two conflicting statements. According to one, BOOTH fired through the door at the left, which was closed. But this seems to have been unnecessary; and it is far more probable that he entered rapidly through the door at the right, and the next moment fired. The ball entered just behind the President's left ear, and though not producing instantaneous death completely obliterated all consciousness.

Major RATHBONE hearing the report, saw the assassin about six feet distant from the President, and encountered him; but BOOTH shook off his grasp. The latter had dropped his weapon—an ordinary pocket-pistol—and had drawn a long glittering knife, with which he inflicted a wound upon the Major; and then, resting his left hand upon the railing, vaulted over easily to the stage, eight or nine feet below. As he passed between the folds of the flag decorating the box, his spur, which he wore on the right heel, caught the drapery and brought it down. He crouched as he fell, falling upon one knee, but quickly gained an upright position, and staggered in a theatrical manner across the stage, brandishing his knife, and shouting, "Sic semper tyrannis!" He made his exit by the "tormentor" on the opposite side of the stage, passing MISS KEENE as he went out. The villain succeeded in making his escape without arrest. In this he was probably assisted by accomplices and by MOSBY'S guerillas.

The President was immediately removed to the house of Mr. PETERSON, opposite the theatre, where he died at twenty-two minutes past seven the next morning, never having recovered his consciousness since the fatal shot. In his last hours he was attended by his wife and his son ROBERT, and prominent members of his Cabinet. His death has plunged the nation into deepest mourning, but his spirit still animates the people for whom he died.

A DIRGE.

LOWER the starry flag
Amid a sovereign people's lamentation For him
the honored ruler of the nation;

Lower the starry flag!

Let the great bells be toll'd

Slowly and mournfully in every steeple, Let them make known the sorrow of the people;

Let the great bells be toll'd!

Lower the starry flag,
And let the solemn, sorrowing anthem, pealing, Sound from the carven choir to fretted ceiling; Lower the starry flag!

Let the great bells be toll'd,

And let the mournful organ music, rolling, Tune with the bells in every steeple tolling;

Let the great bells be toll'd!

Lower the starry flag;

The nation's honored chief in death is sleeping, And for our loss our eyes are wet with weeping; Lower the starry flag!

Let the great bells be toll'd;

His honest, manly heart has ceased its beating, His lips no more shall speak the kindly greeting;

Let the great bells be toll'd!

Lower the starry flag;

No more shall sound his voice 'in scorn of error, Filling the traitor's heart with fear and terror; Lower the starry flag!

Let the great bells be toll'd;

He reverenced the gift which God has given, Freedom to all, the priceless boon of Heaven, Let the great bells be toll'd!

Lower the starry flag;

Hit dearest hopes were wedded with' the nation, He valued more than all the land's salvation;

Lower the starry flag!

Let the great bells be toll'd;

His name shall live on History's brightest pages, His voice shall sound through Time's remotest ages; Let the great bells be toll'd!

A NATION'S GRIEF.

AH! Grief doth follow fast on Victory! The victors' shout is lost in silence, deep—Too deep for our poor human utterance. The jubilant flags that only yesterday Were the bright heralds of a nation's gain, Now droop at half-mast for her woeful loss. Our foremost Hero fallen, sore at heart we lie Prostrate, in tears, at our dear Lincoln's grave!

The dust of our great Leader, kissed to rest, And folded to our hearts, is there inurned, Beyond the breath of scandal, in sweet peace. Wounded with his wound, our hearts receive The mantle of his spirit as it flies.

His words remain to us our sacred Law: Do we not hear them from the Capitol?—

"Malice toward none, with charity for all!"

The blow at Sumter touched us not so much With grief, or awe of treason, as this last—This cruelest thrust of all at his dear head, Which with spent rage the baffled serpent aimed. It is the world's old story, told again,

That they who bruise the serpent's venomed head Must bear, even as Christ did, its last foul sting, Taking the Savior's Passion with His Crown!

With malice toward none, with charity for all, with firmness in the right, as God gives us to see the right, let us strive on to finish the work we are in, to bind up the nation's wounds, to care for him who shall have borne the battle, and for his widow and his orphans; to do all which may achieve and cherish a just and a lasting peace among ourselves and with all nations."—Last Words of President Lincoln's Second Inaugural.

HARPER'S WEEKLY. SATURDAY, APRIL 29,1865.
Abraham Lincoln.

GREATER love hath no man than this, that a man lay down his life for his friends. ABRAHAM LINCOLN has done that. He has sealed his service to his country by the last sacrifice. On the day that commemorates the great sorrow which Christendom reveres, the man who had no thought, no wish, no hope but the salvation of his country, laid down his life. Yet how many and many a heart that throbbed with inexpressible grief as the tragedy was told would gladly have been stilled forever if his might have beat on. So wise and good, so loved and trusted, his death is a personal blow to every faithful American household; nor will any life be a more cherished tradition, nor any name be longer and more tenderly beloved by this nation, than those of ABRAHAM LINCOLN.

On the 22d of February, 1861, as he raised the American flag over Independence Hall, in Philadelphia, he spoke of the sentiment in the Declaration of Independence which gave liberty not only to this country, but, "I hope," he said, "to the world for all future time." Then, with a solemnity which the menacing future justified, and with a significance which subsequent events revealed, he added, "But if this country can not be saved without giving up that principle, I was about to say I would rather be assassinated upon this spot than surrender it." The country has been saved by cleaving to that principle, and he has been assassinated for not surrendering it.

Called to the chief conduct of public affairs at a time of the greatest peril, he came almost unknown, but he brought to his great office a finer comprehension of the condition of the country than the most noted statesmen of all parties, and that sure instinct of the wiser popular will which made him the best of all leaders for a people about to maintain their own government in a civil war. Himself a child of the people, he lived and died

their friend. His heart beat responsive to theirs. He knew their wants, their character, their powers, and knowing their will often better than they knew it themselves, he executed it with the certainty of their speedy approval. No American statesman ever believed more heartily than he the necessary truth of the fundamental American principle of absolute equality before the laws, or trusted with ampler confidence the American system of government. But he loved liberty too sincerely for passion or declamation. It was the strong, sturdy, Anglo-Saxon affection, not the Celtic frenzy.

With an infinite patience, and a dauntless tenacity, he was a man of profound principles but of no theories. This, with his insight and intuitive appreciation of the possibilities of every case, made him a consummate practical statesman. He saw farther and deeper than others because he saw that in the troubled time upon which he was cast little could be wholly seen. Experience so vindicated his patriotic sagacity that he acquired a curious ascendency in the public confidence; so that if good men differed from his opinion they were inclined to doubt their own. Principle was

fixed as a star, but policy must be swayed by the current. While many would have dared the fierce fury of the gale and have sunk the ship at once, he knew that there was a time to stretch every inch of canvas and a time to lay to. He was not afraid of "drifting." In statesmanship prudence counts for more than daring. Thus it happened that some who urged him at the beginning of the war to the boldest measures, and excused what they called his practical faithlessness by his probable weakness, lived to feel the marrow of their bones melt with fear, and to beg him to solicit terms that would have destroyed the nation. But wiser than passion, more faithful than fury, serene in his devotion to the equal rights of men without which he knew there could hence-forth be no peace in this country, he tranquilly persisted, enduring the impatience of what seemed to some his painful delays and to others his lawless haste; and so, trusting God and his own true heart, he fulfilled his great task so well that he died more tenderly lamented than any ruler in history.

His political career, from his entrance into the Illinois Legislature to his last speech upon the Louisiana plan of reconstruction, is calmly consistent both in the lofty humanity of its aim and the good sense of its method, and our condition is the justification of his life. For the most malignant party opposition in our history crumbled before his spotless fidelity; and in his death it is not a party that loses a head, but a country that deplores a father. The good sense, the good humor, the good heart of ABRAHAM LINCOLN gradually united the Democracy that despised the "sentimentality of abolitionism," and the abolitionism that abhorred the sneering inhumanity of "Democracy," in a practical patriotism that has saved the country.

No one who personally knew him but will now feel that the deep, furrowed sadness of his face seemed to forecast his fate. The genial gentleness of his manner, his homely simplicity, the cheerful humor that never failed are now seen to have been but the tender light that played around the rugged heights of his strong and noble nature. It is small consolation that he dies at the moment of the war when he could best be spared, for no nation is ever ready for the loss of such a friend. But it is something to remember that he lived to see the slow day breaking. Like Moses he had marched with us through the wilderness. From the height of patriotic vision he beheld the golden fields of the future waving in peace and plenty out of sight. He beheld and blessed God, but was not to enter in. And we with bowed heads and aching hearts move forward to the promised land.

President Johnson.

No President has entered upon the duties of his office under circumstances so painful as those which surround ANDREW JOHNSON. The pause between the death of Mr. LINCOLN and the indication of the probable course of his successor is profoundly solemn. But there can be but one emotion in every true American heart, and that is, the most inflexible determination to support President JOHNSON, who is now the lawful head of a great nation emerging from terrible civil war, and entering upon the solemn duty of pacification.

ANDREW JOHNSON, like his predecessor, is emphatically a man of the people. He has been for many years in public life, and when the war began he was universally hailed as one of the truest and sturdiest of patriots. His former political association with the leaders of the Southern policy, his position as a Senator from a most important border State, indicated him to the conspirators as an invaluable ally, if he could be seduced to treason. If we are not misinformed, JOHN C. BRECKINRIDGE under-took this task; and how he failed—how ANDREW JOHNSON upon the floor of the Senate denounced treason and traitors—is already historical. From that moment he was one of the firmest friends of the Government, and most ardent supporters of the late Administration. His relations with Mr. LINCOLN were peculiarly friendly; and when the news of ROSECRANS's victory at Mill Spring reached the President at midnight, he immediately sent his secretary to tell the good news to Mr. JOHNSON.

He was appointed Military Governor of Tennessee upon the national occupation of that State, and for three years he has stood in that exposed point at the front, a faithful sentry. Formerly a slaveholder, and familiar with the public opinion of the border, he early saw the necessity of the emancipation war policy; and although in his addresses at the beginning of the war he spoke of it as still uncertain and prospective, his views ripened with those of the country, and when the policy was declared he supported it with the sincerity of earnest conviction.

His provisional administration of government in Tennessee, which was for some time debatable ground, was firm and faithful. By the necessity of the case he was the object of the envenomed hostility of the rebels and the bitterest opposition of the enemies of the Administration. The most serious charge of his exercise of arbitrary power was the severe oath as a qualification for voting which Governor JOHNSON approved before the Presidential election. When the remonstrants appealed to President LINCOLN, he replied that he was very sure Governor JOHNSON would do what was necessary and right. And while the opposition at the North was still loudly denouncing, JEFFERSON DAVIS, in one of his furious speeches in Georgia, after the fall of Atlanta, declared that there were thirty thousand men in Tennessee eager to take up arms the moment the rebel army appeared in the State. It was to prevent those thirty thousand from doing by their votes what they were ready to do by

their arms that the oath was imposed. JEFFERSON DAVIS furnished the amplest justification for the action of Governor JOHNSON. President LINCOLN was reproached for the too conciliatory character of his "Border State policy." Let it not be for-gotten that at the time when he was thought to be too much influenced by it he appointed Mr. JOHNSON Governor of Tennessee. That Governor JOHNSON'S course in the State was ape proved by the unconditional loyal men there is shown by the adoption of the new free constitution and the opening of the new era under the administration of Governor BROWNLOW.

Of a more ardent temperament than Mr. LINCOLN, whose passionless patience was sublime, Mr. JOHNSON has had a much sharper personal experience of the atrocious spirit of this rebellion. He has seen and felt the horrors of which we have only heard. The great guilt of treason is vividly present to his mind and memory, and his feeling toward the leaders who are morally responsible for this wasting war is one of stern hostility.

But the Governor of Tennessee in a most critical period of civil war is

now President of the United States at a time when the war in the field is ending and the peace of a whole country is to be secured. What is the great truth that confronts him at the opening of his new career? It is that the policy of his predecessor had been so approved by the mind and heart of the country, had so disarmed hostility and melted prejudice, that the spirit of that policy has almost the sanctity of prescription.

That President JOHNSON will so regard it we have the fullest confidence. That what every loyal man sees, so strong and devoted a patriot as he will fail to see, is not credible. That the successor of ABRAHAM LINCOLN will adopt a policy of vengeance is impossible. Of the leading traitors, as he said a fortnight since, he holds that the punishment should be that which the Constitution imposes. "And on the other hand," he added, "to the people who have been deluded and misled I would extend leniency and humanity, and an invitation to return to the allegiance they owe to the country." These are not the words of passion, but of humanity and justice. They express what is doubtless the conviction of the great multitude of loyal citizens of the country. With a modest appeal for the counsel and assistance of the gentlemen who were the advisers of Mr. LINCOLN, and with calm reliance upon God and the people, he addresses himself to his vast responsibilities amidst the hopes and prayers and confidence of his country.

Mr. Seward.

THE bloody assault upon Secretary SEWARD, a "chivalric" blow struck at a man of sixty-five lying in his bed with a broken arm, has shown the country how precious to it is the life of a man who has been bitterly traduced by many of his former political friends since the war began. Before the shot was fired at Sumter, Mr SEWARD tried by some form of negotiation to prevent the outbreak of civil war. He was then—does Mr. HORACE GREELEY remember?—as-sailed with insinuations of treachery. Will Mr. HORACE GREE-LEY inform us how it was treacherous to try to prevent the war by negotiation with intending rebels, if, while the war was raging, it was patriotic to urge negotiation with rebels in arms? Will he also tell us whether it was more disloyal to the Union to recognize American citizens not yet in rebellion, or after they had slain thousands and

thousands of brave men in blood and torture to call them "eminent Confederates?" Will he teach us why Mr. SEWARD was to be held up to public suspicion because he communicated with Judge CAMPBELL and recommended Mr. HARVEY as Minister to Portugal, while Mr. GREELEY calls one of the basest panders to this scourging war, a man who does his fighting by sending criminals from Canada to burn down theatres and hotels in New York full of women and children, "a distinguished American" of the other party in our civil war?

For four years Mr. SEWARD, as Secretary of State, has defended this country from one of the most constantly threatening perils, that of foreign war. His name in England is not beloved. But seconded by his faithful lieutenant, Mr. ADAMS, he has maintained there the honor of the American name, and persistently asserted the undiminished sovereignty of the Government of the United States. In France, with the cool, clear, upright man who so fitly represented the simplicity and honesty of a popular Government, he has managed our relations with a skill that has protected us from most

serious complications in Mexico. Engaged with the most unscrupulous and secret of modern diplomatists, Louis NAPOLEON, he has with admirable delicacy of skill prevented his interference in our domestic affairs. His dispatches have been free from bluster or timidity. They all show, what his life illustrates, a perfect serenity of faith in the final success of free institutions and the strength of a popular Government.

Like every man in the country, Mr. SEWARD has been taught by the war. None of us are the same. The views of every man have been modified. The course of some organs of public opinion–of the New York Tribune, for instance—is wonderful and incredible to contemplate. There have been times when Mr. SEWARD was thought by some to be a positive hindrance to the war, a nightmare in the Cabinet. The Senate, with questionable friendship to the country, upon one occasion is understood to have asked his removal. But the President could ill spare so calm a counselor and so adroit a statesman. That they often differed is beyond dispute, but the President knew the sagacity and experience of the Secretary, and the Secretary said the

President was the best man he ever knew.

Such was the confidence and mutual respect of the relation between them that the country will regard Mr. SEWARD'S continuance in the Cabinet as a sign of the perpetuity of the spirit of President LINCOLN'S policy. Meanwhile, that he and his son, the able and courteous Assistant Secretary, lie grievously smitten by the blow that wrings the heart of the nation, a tender solicitude will wait upon their recovery. WILLIAM HENRY SEWARD has too faithfully and conspicuously served human liberty not to have earned a blow from the assassin hand of slavery. The younger generation of American citizens who, in their first manhood, followed his bugle-call into the ranks of those who strove against the infamous power whose dying throes have struck life from the President and joy from a triumphing nation, will not forget how valiant and beneficent his service has been, nor suffer the name so identified with the truest political instruction of this country to be long obscured by the clouds of calumny.

GREAT PAN IS DEAD.

THE New York Tribune, in a late issue, after reprinting the infamous rebel offer of a reward of a million of dollars for the assassination of Mr. LINCOLN, Mr. JOHNSON, and Mr. SEWARD, says: "such facts and the corresponding editorials of the rebel journals countenance the popular presumption that the late murderous outrages in Washington were incidents of a comprehensive plot whereto the rebel leaders were privy. The burglarious raid on St. Albans, the attempts simultaneously to fire our great hotels, and other acts wholly out of the pale of civilized warfare, tend to strengthen this conviction."

In the next column the Editor speaks of the men who plotted the raid and the arson as "certain distinguished Americans" of the other "party to our civil war."

Does not the editor of the Tribune see that nothing can more profoundly demoralize the public mind than to call the men who plot arson and massacre "distinguished Americans?" ABRAHAM LINCOLN and GEORGE WASHINGTON were distinguished Americans. Has the editor no other epithets for GEORGE N. SANDERS and JACOB THOMPSON and CLEMENT C. CLAY? Is there no such thing as crime? Are there no criminals? Is the assassin of the President a man impelled by "the conflict of ideas" to a mistaken act? Is there no treason? Are there no traitors? Does the editor of the Tribune really suppose that because it is not the wish nor the duty of the American people to visit the penalty of treason upon every man at the South who has been in rebellion, it is therefore the duty of wise and honest men to invite JEFFERSON DAVIS and WIGFALL into the Senate of the United States, or ROBERT E. LEE, BEAUREGARD, and JOE JOHNSTON into the army?

The Editor of the Tribune may bow down to the ground and grovel before "eminent Confederates;" but it is not from them that the pacification of the South is to proceed. The first step in peace is to emancipate the people of the South from their servile dependence upon the class of "gentlemen" which has first deluded and then ruined them. How can it be done if we affect that respect which no honest man can feel? If there is one suffering Union man in Alabama who has been outlawed and hunted and starved, who has lain all day cowering in swamps and woods, and at night has stolen out and crept for food to the faithful slaves upon the plantations—who has seen his house destroyed, his children murdered, his wife dishonored—who has endured every extremity of suffering, and still believed in God and the flag of his country—and who now, following WILSON's liberating march, has come safely to our lines at Mobile—if there be one such man, who knows that his cruel agony and the waste and desolation of his land have come from "the leaders" of his section, and sees that when they are worsted in battle it is the Editor of the New York Tribune who hastens to fall prostrate before the meanest of them and salute them as "distinguished Americans" and "eminent Confederates," it is easy to believe that such a man should be overwhelmed with dismay as he contemplates the hopeless postponement of pacification which such a spectacle reveals.

Exactly that base subservience to the arrogance of a slaveholding class which has enabled that class to seduce and betray the people of their States is reproduced in the tone of the editor of the Tribune when speaking of it. Is JEFFERSON DAVIS a distinguished American?"

Is he any more so than AARON BURR and BENEDICT ARNOLD? No men despise such fawning more than those it is intended to propitiate. It is not by such men as JACOB THOMPSON and CLEMENT C. CLAY and HUNTER and BENJAMIN and SEMMES, it is by men unknown and poor, by men who have seen what comes of following the counsels of the "leaders," by men who have been tried by blood and fire in this sharp war that peace is to come out of the South. The men whom the editor of the Tribune calls by names that justly belong only to our best and dearest are the assassins of the nation and of human liberty. They would have wrought upon the nation the same crime that was done upon the President. They would have murdered the country in its own innocent blood. Not from them conies regeneration and peace. Let them fly.

But from the long-abused, the blinded, the down-trodden, the forgotten, the despised—from the real people of the South, whom riches and ease and luxury and cultivation and idleness and, all worldly gifts and graces sitting in high places, drugged with sophistries, and seduced with blandishments, and

threatened with terrors, and besotted with prejudice, and degraded with ignorance, and ground into slavery—these, all of them, white and black as God made them, are the seed of the new South, long pressed into the ground, and now about to sprout and grow and blossom jubilantly with peace and prosperity. Old things have passed away. The Editor of the Tribune is still flattering the priests whose power has gone. Great Pan is dead. Why should one of the earliest Christians swing incense before him?

THE FLAG ON SUMTER.

THE old flag floats again on Sumter! Four years ago it was the hope, the prayer, the vow of the American people. Today the vow is fulfilled. The hand of him who defended it against the assault of treason, of him who saluted it sadly as he marched his little band away, now, with all the strength of an aroused and regenerated nation supporting him, raises it once more to its place, and the stars that have still shone on undimmed in our hearts now shine tranquilly in triumph, and salute the earth and sky with the benediction of peace.

To be called to be the orator of a nation upon

such a day was an honor which might have oppressed any man. To have spoken for the nation at such a moment, worthily, adequately, grandly, is the glory of one man. It will not be questioned that Mr. BEECHER did so. His oration is of the noblest spirit and the loftiest eloquence. It is in the highest degree picturesque and powerful. Certainly it was peculiarly fit that a man, fully inspired by the eternal truth that has achieved the victory, should hail, in the name of equal liberty, the opening of the era which is to secure it.

Even amidst the wail of our sorrow its voice will be heard and its tone will satisfy. Even in our heart's grief we can feel the solemn thrill of triumph that the flag which fell in weakness is raised in glory and power.

THE FOLLY OF CRIME.

EVERY stupendous crime is an enormous blunder. The blow that has shocked the nation exasperates it, and in killing ABRAHAM LINCOLN the rebels have murdered their best friend. His death can not change the event of the war. It has only united the loyal people of the country more closely than ever, and disposed them to a less lenient policy toward the rebellion. Whatever the

intention or hope of the murder, whether it were the result of a matured plot or the act of a band of ruffians, whether it were dictated by the rebel chiefs or offered to their cause as a voluntary assistance by the hand that struck the blow, the effect is the same—a more intense and inflexible vow of the nation that the rebellion shall be suppressed and its cause exterminated.

There is no crime so abhorrent to the world as the assassination of a public man. Even when he is unworthy, the method of his death at once ameliorates the impression of his life. But when he is a good and wise man, when he is spotless and beloved, the infamy is too monstrous for words. There is but one assassin whom history mentions with toleration and even applause, and that is CHARLOTTE CORDAY. But her act was a mistake. It ended the life of a monster, but it did not help the people, and she who might have lived to succor and save some victim of MARAT, became, after his death, MARAT'S victim. All other assassins, too, have more harmed their cause than helped it. Their pleas of justification are always confounded by the event. That plea, where it has any dignity whatever, is the riddance of the world of a bad

or dangerous man whose life can not be legally taken. It is to punish a despot—to bring low a tyrant. But the heart recoils whatever the excuse, the instinct of mankind curses the assassin.

In our own grievous affliction there is one lesson which those who directly address public opinion would do well to consider. Party malignity in the Free States during the war has not scrupled to defame the character of Mr. LINCOLN. He has been denounced as a despot, as a usurper, as a man who arbitrarily annulled the Constitution, as a magistrate under whose administration all the securities of liberty, property, and even life, were deliberately disregarded and imperiled. Political hostility has been inflamed into hate by the assertion that he was responsible for the war, and that he had opened all the yawning graves and tumbled the bloody victims in. This has been done directly and indirectly, openly and cunningly. In a time of necessarily profound and painful excitement, to carry a party point, the political opponents of Mr. LINCOLN have said or insinuated or implied that he had superseded the laws and had made himself an autocrat. If any dangerous plot has been exposed, these organs of public opinion had sneered at it as an invention of the Administration. If theatres and hotels full of men, women, and children were to be wantonly fired, the friends of the Administration were accused of cooking up an excitement. If bloody riots and massacres occurred, they were extenuated, and called "risings of the people," as if in justifiable vengeance, and as if the oppression of the Government had brought them upon itself.

This appeal has been made in various ways and in different degrees. A great convention intimated that there was danger that the elections would be overborne by Administration bayonets. Judge COMSTOCK, formerly of the Court of Appeals in this State, addressing a crowd in Union Square, declared that if a candidate for the Presidency should be defrauded of his election by military interference he would be borne into the White House by the hands of the people. Of the Administration thus accused of the basest conceivable crimes ABRAHAM LINCOLN was the head. If there were a military despotism in the country, as was declared, he was the despot. If there were a tyranny, he was the tyrant.

Is it surprising that somebody should have believed all this, that somebody should have said, if there is a tyranny it can not be very criminal to slay the tyrant, and that working himself up to the due frenzy he should strike the blow? When it was struck, when those kind eyes that never looked sternly upon a human being closed forever, and the assassin sprang forward and cried, Sic semper tyrannis, was it not a ghastly commentary upon those who had not scrupled to teach that he was a tyrant who had annulled the law?

The lesson is terrible. Let us hope that even party-spirit may be tempered by this result of its natural consequence.

A SUGGESTION FOR A MONUMENT.

IT is very possible that the great affection of the people of the United States for their late President will lead to a general desire to erect some national monument to his memory. Should this be so, there is one suggestion which will doubtless occur to many besides ourselves. It is that no mere marble column or memorial pile shall be reared, but that the heart-offerings of the people shall be devoted to the erection of a military hospital, to be called the LINCOLN HOSPITAL, for soldiers and sailors—a retreat for the wounded and permanently invalid veterans of the war.

When, in the happier days that are coming, the wards shall be relieved of the lingering monuments of the contest, the foundation would remain for the public benefit. The soldiers and sailors had no more tender and faithful friend than ABRAHAM LINCOLN. He never forgot them; nor did he fail always to pay to them in his public addresses the homage which his heart constantly cherished. To a man of his broad and generous humanity no monument could be so appropriate as a Hospital.

DOMESTIC INTELLIGENCE. OUR SUCCESSES IN NORTH CAROLINA.

GENERAL STONEMAN captured Salisbury, North Carolina, on the 12th inst., securing 1165 prisoners, 19 pieces of artillery, 1000 smallarms, and eight Stands of colors. The plunder found there was enormous, embracing 1,000,000 rounds of ammunition, 1000 shells, 60,000 pounds of powder, 75,000 suits of clothing, 35,000 army blankets, with large quantities of bacon, salt, sugar, rice, wheat, and 7000 bales of cotton. All that was not immediately available was destroyed. Stoneman's raid in East Tennessee and North Carolina has been one of the most important and des-

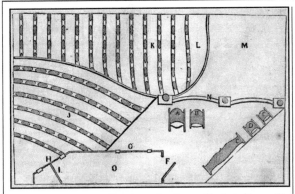

0. Dark Corridor leading from the Dress Circle to Box.—H. Entrance to Corridor. I. The bar used by Booth to prevent entrance from without.—J. Dress Circle.—K. The Parquette.—L. The Foot-lights.—M. The Stage.—F. Open door to the President's Box.—G. Closed door.—N. Place where Booth vaulted over to the Stage below

PLAN OF THE BOX OCCUPIED BY PRESIDENT LINCOLN AT FORD'S THEATER, APRIL 14, 1865

tructive of the war. He has burned half a hundred important bridges, destroyed about 100 miles of track, captured trains, burned depots, and played the mischief generally with secesh property.

The next day after the capture of Salisbury, Sherman occupied Raleigh, with but little resistance. Governor Vance was taken by our cavalry on the same day. It is said that he was deputed by Johnston to surrender the State, but the power was afterward withdrawn. It is reported that Jeff Davis had joined Johnston at Hillsborough, and was still with him,

CAPTURE OF MOBILE.

Mobile was captured by the national forces on the 12th of April.

On the 20th of March the Sixteenth Corps, under General A. J. Smith, left Dauphin on twenty transports, accompanied by gun-boats, and proceeded up an arm of Mobile Bay to the mouth of Fish River, where the troops were landed at Dauley's Mills. The Thirteenth Corps, under General Granger, left Fort Morgan, and on the 21st of March went into camp on the left of Smith, resting its left wing on Mobile Bay. Three days afterward this corps was followed by General Knipe with 6000 cavalry. On the 25th the Federal line was pushed forward so as to extend from Alabama City on the bay to Deer Park. The first point of attack was Spanish Fort, which is directly opposite

Mobile, and is the latest built and strongest of the defenses of that city. It guards the eastern channel of the bay. On the 27th the bombardment commenced. In the mean time the Monitors and gunboats were laboring hard to overcome the obstructions. They had succeeded so far that the Monitors Milwaukee, Winnebago, Kickapoo, and the Monitor ram Osage moved in line to attack at 3 P.M. An hour afterward a torpedo exploded. under the Milwaukee, and she immediately filled and sunk in eleven feet of water. There were no casualties. There was steady firing all night and the next day. At about 2 o'clock P.M. on the 29th a torpedo struck the port bow of the Osage and exploded, tearing away the plating and timbers, killing two men and wounding several others.

We give on page 268 an engraving illustrating the nature of the torpedoes found in the Bay. Those given in the sketch are those with the mushroom-shaped anchor. The slightest pressure causes explosion.

On the 8th of April an extraordinary force was brought to bear upon Spanish Fort. Twenty-two Parrott guns were got within half a mile of the work, while other powerful batteries were still nearer. Two gunboats joined in the tremendous cannonade. The result was that the fort surrendered a little after midnight. Fort Alexandria followed, and the guns of these two were turned against Forts Tracy and Huger, in the harbor, at the mouth of the Blakely and Appalachee rivers. But these had already been abandoned. The Monitors then went busily to work removing torpedoes, and ran up to within shelling distance of the city.

Shortly after the capture of Spanish Fort, intelligence of the capture and the fall of Richmond was read to the troops, in connection with orders to attack Fort Blakely. Several batteries of artillery, and large quantities of ammunition were taken with the fort, besides 2400 prisoners. Our loss in the whole affair was much less than 2000 killed and wounded, and none missing.

Seven hundred prisoners were taken with Spanish Fort. Mobile was occupied by the national forces on the 12th. In the mean time General Wilson, with a formidable force of cavalry, had swept through the State of Alabama. He left Eastport about the 20th of March, and advanced in two columns, each of

which, at about the same time, fought Forrest's cavalry, one at Marion and the other at Plantersville, which were respectively situated about 20 miles northwest and northeast of Selma. On the afternoon of April 2 Selma was captured, with 22 guns, and all the immense Government works, arsenals, rolling-mills, and foundries at that place were destroyed. It is probable that Montgomery was also captured, but later than the capture of Selma we have no details.

MOURNING IN RICHMOND.

Roger A. Pryor stated in Petersburg that he believed Mr. Lincoln indispensable to the restoration of peace, and regretted his death more than any military mishap of the south. He and the Mayor placed themselves at the head of a movement for a town meeting to deplore the loss on both private and public grounds. General Robert E. Lee at first refused to hear the details of the murder. A Mr. Suite and another gentleman waited upon him on Sunday night with the particulars. He said that when he dispossessed himself of the command of the rebel forces he kept in mind President Lincoln's benignity, and surrendered as much to the latter's goodness as to Grant's artillery.

The General said that he regretted Mr. Lincoln's death as much as any man in the North, and believed him to be the epitome of magnanimity and good faith.

ARREST OF SEWARD'S ASSASSIN.

A man was arrested on the 18th in Baltimore who is supposed to have been the assassin of Secretary Seward. He was recognized as such by the negro servant and Miss Fanny Seward.

FOREIGN NEWS. THE REBEL RAM "STONEWALL."

The rebel ram Stonewall left Lisbon, Portugal, on the 28th of March, having been ordered away by the Portuguese authorities. The national steamers Niagara and Sacramento were forbidden to leave until twenty-four hours should have elapsed. These two vessels, about four hours after the Stonewall left, weighed anchor and moved toward the bar. The commander of the Belem Tower then fired upon them, considerably injuring the Niagara. The captains stated that they were only changing their anchorage-ground, and our consul at Lisbon has demanded that the Governor of Belem Tower should be removed, which demand has been conceded.

NOTES

From a research standpoint, the events before, during, and after the Lincoln assassination were ideal. The many articles and eyewitness accounts were laden with an astounding amount of information. The following list of books, websites, and other archived information reflects the main research sources for this book. It bears mentioning that visits to the Sayler's Creek Battlefield, High Bridge, Appomattox Court House, Ford's Theatre, and the various historical sites along John Wilkes Booth's escape route will add immeasurably to the reader's understanding of all that came to pass in April 1865.

Part One: TOTAL WAR

The siege of Petersburg and Lee's subsequent flight across the Virginia countryside are all very well documented. Some of the most fascinating insights came from the soldiers and generals who were there, many of whom wrote their memoirs and recollections years later. In reading them, one is transported back to that moment in time. The accounts of Sayler's Creek and the Battle of High Bridge, in particular, are vivid portrayals of courage under fire. What follows is a brief list of the books used in our research; thanks to the magic of Google's online books, many of the older titles can be easily accessed: *Red, White and Blue Badge: Pennsylvania Veteran Volunteers*, by Penrose G. Mark; *Confederate Veteran*, by S. A. Cunningham; *Battles and Leaders of the Civil War*, by Robert Underwood Johnson; *Pickett and His Men*, by La Salle Corbett Pickett; *Lee's Last Retreat: The Flight to Appomattox*, by William Marvel; *Four Years Under Marse Robert*, by Robert Stiles; *General Lee: A Biography of Robert E. Lee*, by Fitzhugh Lee; *Military Memoirs of a Confederate*, by Edward Porter Alexander; *Meade's*

Headquarters, 1863–1865, by Theodore Lyman; *Grant,* by Jean Edward Smith; *Lee,* by Douglas Southall Freeman; *Personal Memoirs of U. S. Grant,* by Ulysses S. Grant; *From Manassas to Appomattox: The Personal Memoirs of James Longstreet,* by James Longstreet; *Lee's Lieutenants: A Study in Command,* by Douglas Southall Freeman and Stephen W. Sears; *Tom Custer: Ride to Glory,* by Carl F. Day; *The Military Annals of Lancaster, Massachusetts,* by Henry Steadman Norse; *Biography of Francis P. Washburn,* by Michael K. Sorenson; and *The Memoirs of General P. H. Sheridan,* by General Philip Henry Sheridan. The Virginia Military Institute's online archive (http://www.vmi.edu/archives.aspx?id=3945) offers links to several more firsthand letters. In addition, the very excellent *Atlas of the Civil War,* by James M. McPherson, was always within arm's reach during the writing process; it shows in great detail the battle maps and movements of two great armies.

Part Two: THE IDES OF DEATH

Writing about the chaotic final days of Lincoln's life meant accessing all manner of research, from online documents (such as the *New York Times*'s findings about Lincoln's Baptist upbringing) to websites devoted to the Lincoln White House (in particular, www.mrlincolnswhitehouse.org provided a treasure trove of information about everything from floor layouts to daily life, very often told in first-person accounts). The number of websites and easily accessed online articles is endless, and hundreds were scrutinized during the writing of this book.

The reader searching for an overview of April 1865 is encouraged to read the aptly named *April 1865,* by Jay Winik, which frames the events quite well. Other books of note: *"They Have Killed Papa Dead,"* by Anthony S. Pitch, and *American Brutus,* by Michael W. Kauffman; *Team of Rivals,* by Doris Kearns Goodwin; *Lincoln's Last Month,* by William C. Harris; *Lincoln's Body Guard: The Union Light Guard of Ohio,* by Robert McBride; and *Blood on the Moon: The Assassination of Abraham Lincoln,* by Edward Steers. For a compelling history of Washington, D.C., itself, the reader is encouraged to find a copy of *Washington Schlepped Here,* by Christopher Buckley.

Part Three: THE LONG GOOD FRIDAY

For an hour-by-hour description of April 15, 1865, see the excellent *A. Lincoln: His Last 24 Hours,* by W. Emerson Reck; *The Day Lincoln Was*

Shot, by Jim Bishop; *Lincoln's Last Hours*, by Charles Augustus Leale; and *Abraham Lincoln*, by Carl Sandburg.

Of great interest are titles that offer conflicting viewpoints of the assassination, the motivations, and the people involved. Perhaps the most fascinating aspect of researching the Lincoln assassination was poring over the many very good books dedicated to this topic and the shock of discovering that many disagree completely with one another. *Dark Union*, by Leonard Guttridge and Ray Neff, and *Spies, Traitors, and Moles*, by Peter Kross are two of the more controversial titles.

For information on Mary Surratt, see *Assassin's Accomplice*, by Kate Clifford Larson.

Part Four: THE CHASE

The search for Lincoln's killers and their subsequent trial was vividly portrayed in Kauffman's *American Brutus* and James L. Swanson's *Manhunt*. *Potomac Diary*, by Richtmyer Hubbell, provides fascinating insights into the mood in Washington. *History of the United States Secret Service*, by Lafayette Baker, is a rather verbose and self-aggrandizing account of Baker's exploits. Also of note: *Beware the People Weeping*, by Thomas Reed Turner; *Lincoln Legends*, by Edward Steers; *Right or Wrong, God Judge Me: The Writings of John Wilkes Booth*, by John Wilkes Booth; *The Life of Dr. Samuel A. Mudd*, by Samuel A. Mudd; and *Lincoln's Assassins*, by Roy Z. Chamlee

The arguments of Special Judge Advocate John A. Bingham can be found in *Trial of the Conspirators for the Assassination of President Abraham Lincoln*, by John Armor Bingham. Testimony can be found at http://www .surratt.org/documents/Bplact02.pdf.

INDEX

Page numbers in *italics* refer to illustrations.

About the Authors

Bill O'Reilly is the anchor of *The O'Reilly Factor,* the highest-rated cable news show in the country. He also writes a syndicated newspaper column and is the author of several number-one bestselling books. He is, perhaps, the most talked about political commentator in America.

Martin Dugard is the *New York Times* best-selling author of several books of history. His book *Into Africa: The Epic Adventures of Stanley and Livingstone* has been adapted into a History Channel special. He lives in Southern California with his wife and three sons.

Killing Reagan

Killing Reagan

THE VIOLENT ASSAULT THAT CHANGED A PRESIDENCY

Bill O'Reilly

and

Martin Dugard

HENRY HOLT AND COMPANY   NEW YORK

Henry Holt and Company, LLC
Publishers since 1866
175 Fifth Avenue
New York, New York 10010
www.henryholt.com

Henry Holt® and 🅷® are registered trademarks of Henry Holt and Company, LLC.

Library of Congress Cataloging-in-Publication Data

O'Reilly, Bill.
  Killing Reagan : the violent assault that changed a presidency / Bill O'Reilly and
Martin Dugard. — First edition.
        pages cm
  ISBN 978-1-62779-241-7 (hardcover) — ISBN 978-1-62779-242-4 (e-book)
  1. Reagan, Ronald—Assassination attempt, 1981.   2. United States—Politics and
government—1981–1989.   I. Dugard, Martin.   II. Title.
  E877.3.O74 2015
  973.927092—dc23   2015018751

Henry Holt books are available for special promotions and premiums.
For details contact: Director, Special Markets.

First Edition 2015

Designed by Meryl Levavi Sussman

Printed in the United States of America

10 9 8 7 6 5 4 3 2 1

This book is dedicated to all those
who are caring for an elderly person.
You are noble.

God had a divine purpose in placing this land between two great oceans to be found by those who had a special love of freedom and courage.

—Ronald Reagan

Killing Reagan

Prologue

———◦◦◦———

The man with one minute to live is no longer confused.

Ronald Reagan lapsed into a coma two days ago. His wife, Nancy, sits at the side of the bed, holding the former president's hand. Emotionally and physically exhausted by the ordeal, she quietly sobs as her body rocks in grief. Reagan's breathing has become ragged and inconsistent. After ten long years of slow descent toward the grave due to Alzheimer's disease, a bout of pneumonia brought on by food particles caught in his lungs has delivered the knockout blow. Nancy knows that her beloved Ronnie's time has come.

Counting the former president, six people crowd into the bedroom. There is his physician, Dr. Terry Schaack; and Laura, the Irish nurse whose soft brogue the president is known to find soothing. Two of his grown children stand at the bedside. Ron, forty-six, and Patti, fifty-one, have been holding vigil with their mother for days. They have a reputation for conflict with their parents, but on this day those quarrels have vanished as they lend their mother emotional support. An adopted son from Reagan's first marriage, Michael, has also been summoned, but he is caught in Los Angeles traffic and will miss the president's final breath.

Outside the single-story, three-bedroom house, the foggy Pacific marine layer has burned off, replaced by a warm summer sun. The hydrangea and white camellia bushes are in full bloom. A media horde has gathered on St. Cloud Road in Reagan's posh Bel-Air neighborhood,* waiting with their cameras and news trucks for the inevitable moment when the fortieth president of the United States passes away. The former actor and college football player is ninety-three. Even into his seventies, he was so vigorous that he rode the hills of his Santa Barbara ranch on horseback for hours and cleared acres of thick hillside brush all by himself.

But years ago his mind betrayed him. Reagan slowly lapsed into a dementia so severe that it has been a decade since he appeared in public. The root cause could have been genetic, for his mother was not lucid in her final days. Or it might have been the result of a near-death experience caused by a gunman's bullet twenty-three years ago. Whatever the reason, Reagan's decline has been dramatic. Over the past ten years, he has spent most days sleeping or looking out at the sweeping view of Los Angeles from his flagstone veranda. His smile is warm, but his mind is vacant. Eventually, he lost the ability even to recognize family and friends. When Reagan's oldest child from his first marriage, Maureen, was dying of melanoma in a Santa Monica hospital in 2001, the former president was in the same hospital being treated for a broken hip—yet was too confused to see her.

So now, the man who lies at home in a hospital bed, clad in comfortable pajamas, is a shell of his former self. His blue eyes, the last time he opened them, were dense, the color of chalk. His voice, which once lent itself to great oration, is silent.

---

*A group of Reagan's friends bought the house for $2.5 million while he was still in office and leased it to him with an option to buy—which Reagan did, in December 1989, for $3.0 million. The 7,192-square-foot home sits on a 1.29-acre lot and features a swimming pool, three bedrooms, and six bathrooms. Next door is the former Kirkeby Estate, which served as the setting for the *Beverly Hillbillies* television show. Despite the price of Reagan's home, one real estate agent noted that "it's a very ordinary house—Reagan must be the poorest man in Bel-Air."

Another breath, this one more jagged than the last. Nancy's tears fall onto the bedsheets at the onset of the death rattle.

Suddenly, Ronald Reagan opens his eyes. He stares intently at Nancy. "They weren't chalky or vague," Patti Davis will later write of her father's eyes. "They were clear and blue and full of love."

The room hushes.

Closing his eyes, Reagan takes his final breath.

The former leader of the free world, the man who defeated Soviet communism and ended the Cold War, is dead.

1

—⟨⟨∅∅∅⟩⟩—

Convention Center Music Hall
Cleveland, Ohio
October 28, 1980
9:30 P.M.

The man with twenty-four years to live steps onstage.

Polite applause washes over Ronald Reagan as he strides to his lectern for the 1980 presidential debate.* The former movie star and two-term governor of California is striving to become president of the United States at the relatively advanced age of sixty-nine. His jet-black pompadour, which he swears he does not dye, is held in place by a dab of Brylcreem.† His high cheeks are noticeably rosy, as if they have been rouged—although the color may also have come from the glass of wine he had with dinner. At six foot one and 190 pounds, Reagan stands tall and

---

*There were supposed to be three debates in the 1980 campaign, due to the presence of third-party candidate John Anderson, a Republican congressman from Illinois who ran as an independent. President Carter refused to debate Anderson, giving Reagan and Carter the chance to go head-to-head.

†Reagan's hair was actually brown, but the wet look of his hairstyling made it appear black.

straight, but his appearance does not intimidate: rather, he looks to be approachable and kind.

The governor's opponent is incumbent president Jimmy Carter. At five nine and 155 pounds, the slender Carter has the build of a man who ran cross-country in college. In fact, the president still makes time for four miles a day. Carter is a political junkie, immersing himself in every last nuance of a campaign. He has made a huge surge in the polls over the last two months. Carter knows that with one week until Election Day, the race is almost dead even. The winner of this debate will most likely win the presidency, and if it is Carter, his comeback will be one of the greatest in modern history.* In another reality, a Carter loss would make him the first president in nearly fifty years to be voted out of office after just one full term. Still boyish at fifty-six, but with a face lined by the rigors of the presidency, he now stands opposite Reagan, a man he loathes.

The feeling is mutual. Reagan privately refers to the current president of the United States as "a little shit."

As President Carter stands behind the pale-blue lectern, he makes a sly sideward glance at his opponent. Carter is all business and believes that Ronald Reagan is not his intellectual equal. He has publicly stated that Reagan is "untruthful and dangerous" and "different than me in almost every basic element of commitment and experience and promise to the American people."

At his acceptance speech at the August 1980 Democratic National Convention, Carter made it clear that the upcoming election would be "a stark choice between two men, two parties, two sharply different pictures of what America is and the world is."

The president concluded by adding, "It's a choice between two futures."

Indeed, Carter appears to be the smarter man. He graduated fifty-ninth

---

*One reason Jimmy Carter is behind is that CBS News anchor Walter Cronkite's nightly tally of the number of days the American hostages had been held in Iran helped lower voter confidence in Carter.

Jimmy Carter and Ronald Reagan shake hands as they greet each other before their 1980 presidential debate in Cleveland, Ohio.

in a class of 820 from the U.S. Naval Academy and spent his military career onboard nuclear submarines. The Georgia native with the toothy smile possesses an easy command of facts and figures. He has hands-on experience in foreign and domestic policy and often speaks in soothing intellectual sound bites.

In 1976, Carter defeated his Republican opponent, Gerald R. Ford, in their three debates, and he is sure he will do the same tonight. Political pollster Pat Caddell, the nation's leading authority on presidential elections and a member of the Carter campaign, predicts that Carter will clinch the election with a decisive debate victory.

Two months ago, Reagan's lead in the polls was sixteen points. But if the election were held today, polls indicate Carter would garner 41 percent of the vote and Reagan 40. However, Caddell has strongly warned Carter against debating Reagan. The biggest knock against Reagan politically is the perception that he is a warmonger. Caddell believes that a debate would allow Reagan to counter those fears by appearing warm and collected rather than half-cocked. Once it became clear that Carter was intent on a public debate, his advisers pressed for the long, ninety-minute format that will be used tonight, hoping that Reagan will wear down and say something stupid.

That would hardly be a first. Ronald Reagan is so prone to saying the wrong thing at the wrong time that his campaign staff has been known to call him "old foot-in-the-mouth." Perhaps the worst public gaffe of his career will occur in Brazil. Speaking at a dinner in that nation's capital city of Brasilia, Reagan will hoist his glass, proposing a toast to the people of *Bolivia*.*

But Reagan is no fool and is much more incisive than Carter about the Soviet Union's Communist regime. He despises it. But he has no foreign policy experience to refer to. Reagan memorizes speeches and phrases, rather than immersing himself in heavy study or specific details. While this might not be a problem at most campaign events, where Reagan can read from a prepared speech, it could be trouble here in Cleveland: the rules of the debate stipulate that neither candidate is allowed to bring notes to the stage.

Yet Reagan will not admit to being at a disadvantage. He believes his communications skills will make up for his lesser book smarts. Reagan, in fact, is far different from how most people perceive him. He has an army of close acquaintances but few friends. He freely offers his opinions about public policy but rarely shares deep personal thoughts. Some who work for him think Reagan is distant and lazy, as he so often lets others make tough decisions for him. Others, however, find his manner warm, friendly, and endearing and his hands-off management style liberating.

---

*He immediately attempted to cover the slip by adding, "That's where I'm going," referring to his four-nation swing through South America. In fact, he was not going to Bolivia. His next stop was Colombia, whose capital city is Bogotá. Officials tried to cover for Reagan by changing the transcript of the speech to read "Bogota." When asked why, they replied that it was what Reagan intended to say and refused to alter their correction.

Reagan does not really care what other people think. He confidently marches ahead, rarely showing any self-doubt.

To bring him luck in the debate, Reagan traveled to his native state of Illinois and visited the tomb of Abraham Lincoln this past week. He actually rubbed his nose on the statue of the great political debater, hoping some of Lincoln's brilliance would rub off on him.

Not that Reagan is intimidated. Of Carter he has said condescendingly, "He knows he can't win a debate if it were held in the Rose Garden before an audience of Administration officials, with the questions being asked by Jody Powell," referencing the president's hard-living press secretary.

The truth is that Reagan's campaign has lost whatever momentum it once possessed. "Ronald Reagan's presidential campaign may be running out of steam," wrote the *Wall Street Journal* on October 16.

"I think Reagan is slipping everywhere," one of his top aides told reporters in an off-the-record conversation. "If he doesn't do something dramatic he is going to lose."*

Meanwhile, Carter's aides are almost giddy in their optimism. "The pieces are in place for us to win," they tell *Newsweek* magazine.

At the stroke of 9:30, the debate begins.

Ruth Hinerfeld of the League of Women Voters opens the proceedings with a short speech. She speaks her few careful lines in a hesitant tone before handing the proceedings over to the evening's moderator, veteran journalist Howard K. Smith of ABC News. Smith sits at a desk to the front of the stage, his tie loose and his jacket unbuttoned.

"Thank you, Mrs. Hinerfeld," he says before introducing the four journalists who will launch questions at the two candidates.† The chatter

---

*While this remark is still unclaimed, those within the Reagan and Carter circles believe they were the words of the late Lyn Nofziger (1924–2006), a political veteran who was known for his candor with the press.

†Barbara Walters, ABC News; William Hilliard, Portland *Oregonian*; Marvin L. Stone, *U.S. News & World Report*; and Harry Ellis, *Christian Science Monitor*.

and applause that filled the room just moments ago have been replaced by palpable nervous tension. There is a sensation that tonight may change the course of U.S. history.

▬ ▬ ▬

As both Reagan and Carter well know, the 1970s have been a brutal time for America. In 1974, President Richard Nixon resigned under threat of impeachment after the Watergate affair. The unchecked growth of the Soviet Union's war machine and the American failure to win the Vietnam War have tilted the global balance of power. At home, inflation, interest rates, and unemployment rates are sky-high. Gasoline shortages have led to mile-long lines at the pumps. Worst of all, there is the ongoing humiliation that came about when Iranian radicals stormed the American embassy in Tehran in 1979 and took almost the entire staff hostage. Nearly six months later, a rescue attempt failed miserably, resulting in the deaths of eight American servicemen. One week from today, when Americans go to the polls to pick a U.S. president, the fifty-two hostages will have spent exactly one year in captivity.

The United States of America is still very much a superpower, but an air of defeat, not hope, now defines its national outlook.

The small theater in which the debate will unfold was built shortly after World War I, at a time when America had flexed its muscle on the world stage and first assumed global prominence. But tonight, there is a single question on the minds of many watching this debate:* can America be fixed?

Or, more to the point, are the best days of the United States of America in the past?

▬ ▬ ▬

"Governor," asks panelist Marvin Stone, editor of the magazine *U.S. News & World Report*, "you have been criticized for being all too quick to advocate the use of lots of muscle, military action, to deal with foreign crises.

---

*Three thousand in the auditorium and 80.6 million watching at home on television.

Specifically, what are the differences between the two of you on the uses of American military power?"

Reagan's career as a Hollywood actor has seen him through a number of personal highs and lows. He has experienced failure and divorce, and endured the humiliation of acting in films that made him look ridiculous. But he has also learned poise under fire and the art of delivering a line. Now, as Stone zeroes in on what some see as a glaring weakness in Reagan's résumé, those communication skills desert him. He fumbles for words. Eloquence is replaced by odd pauses. "I believe with all my heart," Reagan says slowly, as if he has forgotten the question completely, "that our first priority must be world peace."

Offstage, in the Carter campaign's greenroom, the president's staff roars with laughter as they watch an uncomfortable Reagan on a television monitor.

There is more to Reagan's answer, but it is clear that he is searching for a way to leave the moment behind and revert to the well-rehearsed lines he has prepared for tonight. "I'm a father of sons," Reagan finally says, finding a way to use one of those scripted answers. "I have a grandson. I don't ever want to see another generation of young Americans bleed their lives into sandy beachheads in the Pacific, or rice paddies and jungles in Asia, or the muddy, bloody battlefields of Europe."

About ten feet away, Carter grips his lectern as if standing at a church pulpit. His eyes are tired and his face pinched.* Naturally peevish, he is tired from staying up late trying to negotiate the release of the American hostages in Iran. The talks are at a delicate point, and he knows that his electoral victory is assured if he succeeds. Carter is so preoccupied with these talks that he initially refused to spend time prepping for the debate. The lack of sleep has made him short-tempered, tense, and difficult to be around. This fatigue also makes it difficult for Carter to hide his utter contempt for Reagan as they share the stage.

---

*The Reagan campaign argued that the lecterns should be side by side, which would accentuate Reagan's height. The Carter campaign refused. On the night of the debate, as one observer noted, the lecterns were "as far as possible apart, without actually going off the stage."

When it comes his turn to field the same question, the president speaks in simple declarative sentences, reminding the audience and the millions watching on television that he is committed to a strong national defense. He mentions the American journalist H. L. Mencken by name and quotes him on the nature of problem solving. It is a literary allusion meant to remind the audience of Carter's intellect, but it is a misstep—Mencken is against religion, suspicious of democracy, and elitist. Carter's mentioning him is a thinly veiled attempt to rally the more left-leaning aspects of the Democratic Party. But the American public, Democrat and Republican alike, is in a patriotic mood. They long for a return to simple, straightforward American values. The words of H. L. Mencken only succeed in making Carter look out of touch.

Stone pounces. The balding editor leans into his microphone. He speaks to the president of the United States as if he were lecturing a cub reporter. "Under what circumstances would you use military forces to deal with, for example, a shutoff of Persian Gulf oil, if that should occur, or to counter Russian expansion beyond Afghanistan into either Iran or Pakistan? I ask this question in view of charges that we are woefully unprepared to project sustained—and I emphasize the word *sustained*—power in that part of the world."

Carter will reach for his water glass eleven times tonight. It is his tell, as gamblers call a nervous tic. Another tell is that Carter blinks constantly when ill at ease.

"We have made sure that we address this question peacefully, not injecting American military forces into combat but letting the strength of our nation be felt in a beneficial way," he answers, eyelids fluttering as if he were staring into the sun. "This, I believe, has assured that our interests will be protected in the Persian Gulf region, as we've done in the Middle East and throughout the world."

This is not an answer. It is an evasion. And while Carter is hoping to appear presidential and above the fray, the fact is that he looks indecisive and somewhat weak.

When it comes Reagan's turn to field the same question, he stumbles again—though only for an instant. His thought process seems to be clearing. Reagan has rehearsed this debate with adviser David Stockman, whose sharp intellect rivals that of Carter. That practice now shows in Reagan's new confidence. Statistics suddenly roll off his tongue. He rattles off the 38 percent reduction in America's military force under the Carter administration, the refusal to build sixty ships that the navy deems necessary to fulfilling its global mission, and Carter's insistence that programs to build new American bombers, missiles, and submarines be either stalled or halted altogether.

The outrage in Reagan's voice will connect to those viewers sick and tired of America's descent into global impotency.

Jimmy Carter reaches for his water glass.

More than one thousand miles west, in the city of Evergreen, Colorado, a twenty-five-year-old drifter pays little attention to the debate. Instead, John Hinckley Jr. fixates on schemes to impress Jodie Foster, the young actress who starred opposite Robert De Niro in the 1976 movie *Taxi Driver*—a film Hinckley has seen more than fifteen times. Even though he has never met her, Hinckley considers Jodie the love of his life and is determined to win her hand.

Hinckley's obsession with the eighteen-year-old actress is so complete that he temporarily moved to New Haven, Connecticut, to stalk her while she attended Yale University. Hinckley is a college dropout, unable to focus on his own studies, yet he had little problem sitting in on Foster's classes. In New Haven, he slid love notes under the door of her dorm room, found her phone number, and, in a brazen move, called Foster and asked her out to dinner. Shocked, she refused. So stunned was Foster by Hinckley's advances and subsequent actions that she will not speak of them for years to come.

Now, nearly penniless and having moved back in with his parents, John Hinckley ruminates over how to make Jodie Foster change her mind.

His plans are grandiose and bizarre. Hinckley has contemplated killing himself right before Foster's very eyes, or perhaps hijacking an airliner.

He has even plotted the assassination of President Jimmy Carter.

The pudgy Hinckley, who wears his shaggy hair in bangs, has yet to see a psychiatrist for the schizophrenia that is slowly taking control of his brain. That appointment is still one week away. But no amount of therapy will ever stop him from thinking about Jodie Foster—and the lengths to which he must go to earn her love. Now, sitting in a small basement bedroom, Hinckley considers suicide.

Bottles of prescription pills cover his nightstand. It will take a few more days to summon his courage, but Hinckley will soon reach for the container labeled "Valium" and gobble a deadly dosage.

Once again, John Hinckley will fail.

He will wake up nauseated but alive, vowing to find some new way to impress Jodie Foster.

Killing himself is not the answer. Clearly, someone else must die.

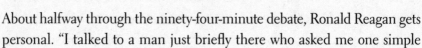

About halfway through the ninety-four-minute debate, Ronald Reagan gets personal. "I talked to a man just briefly there who asked me one simple question," Reagan says gravely. "'Do I have reason to hope that I can someday take care of my family again?'"

Watching from the side of the stage, Nancy Reagan can see that her husband is gaining confidence with every question. This gives her solace, for Nancy was so afraid that her Ronnie would say something foolish that she initially opposed the debate. More than that of any of his advisers, it is Nancy's opinion that matters most to Reagan. They have been married twenty-eight years, and she has been a driving force behind his run for the presidency. Throughout their marriage he has chosen to address her as Mommy, a term of endearment mocked by some journalists covering Reagan.

Nancy Reagan wears a size four dress and has thin legs and thick ankles. Her mother was an actress, her adoptive father an esteemed surgeon, and she grew up determined to find fame.* She relies on sleeping pills and tranquilizers, and sometimes bursts into tears from stress, but there is steel in her voice when she corrects her husband or sees to it that one of the campaign staff is disciplined. Nancy Reagan professes shock when the press portrays her as the conniving Lady Macbeth, but the description isn't entirely off the mark. She is by far the more grating half of the Reagan marriage, and she is determined that this election be won at all costs.

Cheating is not out of the question. Although he does not yet know it, Jimmy Carter's briefing notes for this debate were recently stolen from the White House and secretly handed over to the Reagan campaign. This, of course, has allowed Reagan to know in advance how Carter will respond to every question. Certainly, no one is pointing to Nancy Reagan as having engineered the theft—indeed, reports of the act will not be leaked to the public for three more years, and the real culprit remains in question.† Yet it is well known that, with so much at stake, she doesn't play nice. To Nancy, gaining access to Carter's playbook is a windfall to the Reagan campaign, not a crime.

As the debate continues, Jimmy Carter is not doing himself any favors onstage. "I had a discussion with my daughter, Amy," Carter says, referring to his thirteen-year-old, "to ask her what the most important issue was. She said she thought nuclear weaponry and the control of nuclear arms."

---

*Nancy Reagan was born in New York City on July 6, 1921, as Anne Frances Robbins. Her mother was an actress and her father a used-car salesman. The two split up when the girl who had earned the nickname Nancy was just six. She was sent to live with family in Maryland. Her mother remarried, to a Chicago neurosurgeon named Loyal Davis, who adopted Nancy and gave her his surname. In 1949, after working for a time as a sales clerk, she traveled to Hollywood to pursue her dream of becoming an actress. During that time she dated several prominent names in Hollywood, among them Clark Gable.

†As noted in Craig Shirley's *Rendezvous with Destiny*, the late Paul Corbin, an influential Democrat and friend of the Kennedy family who was bitter about Ted Kennedy losing to Jimmy Carter in the 1980 Democratic primary race, admitted to stealing the playbook shortly after copies were assembled in the White House on the night of October 23. The book was then given to William Casey, the former World War II OSS spy who led the Reagan campaign. Finally, on October 25, the Carter book was handed to the three key players in Reagan's debate prep: James Baker III, David Gergen, and David Stockman. Three years later, when word about the theft was leaked, a ten-month congressional and FBI investigation ensued. Corbin never surfaced as the culprit, and the truth did not come out about his involvement until after his death in 1990. Pat Caddell, when interviewed for this book, said he believes Corbin was given the book by a member of the National Security Council serving in Carter's White House.

In the greenroom, Carter's campaign staff is distraught. While prepping for the debate, Carter told them he planned to use his daughter to make a point. His staff strongly urged him not to.

"In the end," Pat Caddell will later recall, "it came down to 'I'm the president. Fuck you.'"

It is a huge mistake. That the president of the United States is allowing a teenager to decide what matters most to America in a time of such great crisis is laughable. One journalist will later write that the statement was "Carter at his worst: Weak and silly."

But Jimmy Carter does not have that sense. "In the debate itself, it was hard to judge the general demeanor that was projected to the viewers," Carter will write in his diary tonight. "He [Reagan] has his memorized tapes. He pushes a button, and they come out."*

Carter's statement is true. Like all veteran actors, Reagan has mastered the art of memorization. Also, while there are a great number of scripted lines that he has written himself or with his speechwriters to help him score points, Reagan has concocted a simple statement to deride Carter. After the president launches into a detailed and very dry explanation about Reagan's opposition to national health care, Reagan pauses at his lectern. It is obvious that Carter is showing off his intellect in a way that is meant to make Reagan look old, slow, and out of touch. The president's words were specifically chosen to ensure that Reagan's scripted lines could not rescue him and to make it obvious to one and all that Jimmy Carter is the more intelligent of the two.

What follows is Reagan at his best. In four simple words that will be remembered for decades, he succeeds in making President Carter look foolish. They are words that Reagan came up with during the long hours of practice debates but which he has kept to himself, knowing that for maximum effectiveness the line must sound completely spontaneous.

---

*Just moments after the debate ended, a group of journalists came to Jimmy Carter before he could leave the stage. "Are you prepared to claim victory? Did you win it?" Carter refused to answer.

Slowly shaking his head, Reagan turns to Carter and says, "There you go again."

The auditorium erupts in laughter. Reagan's tone is that of a disappointed parent, saddened by a child who has failed to live up to expectations. The words mean nothing and everything. One short sentence captures the mood of a nation that no longer wants detailed policy explanations as to why the economy has collapsed and Americans are being held hostage in a foreign country.

The time for words has passed. Now is the time for action.

The election may be seven days away, but for James Earl "Jimmy" Carter Jr. of Plains, Georgia, it is over. The only man who does not know that is Carter himself. "Both sides felt good about the debate. We'll see whose basic strategy is best when the returns come in next Tuesday," he will write in his diary.

Reagan finishes the debate with a flourish. "Are you better off than you were four years ago?" he says earnestly into the television camera, wrapping up with an emotional appeal to the American people. "Is it easier for you to go and buy things in the stores than it was four years ago? Is there more or less unemployment in the country than there was four years ago? Is America as respected throughout the world as it was? Do you feel that our security is as safe, that we're as strong as we were four years ago? And if you answer all of those questions yes, why then, I think your choice is very obvious as to who you'll vote for."

So obvious, in fact, that the election is a landslide. Ronald Reagan receives 489 electoral votes; Jimmy Carter receives just 49.*

On January 20, 1981, Ronald Reagan is sworn in as the fortieth president of the United States.

John Hinckley Jr. has a new target.

---

*Carter won his home state of Georgia, plus Minnesota, the home state of running mate Walter Mondale. The Carter-Mondale ticket also captured Hawaii, Rhode Island, West Virginia, Maryland, and the District of Columbia.

2

―◦◦◦―

UNIVERSAL STUDIOS
HOLLYWOOD, CALIFORNIA
SEPTEMBER 1950
DAYTIME

The chimpanzee wears a white jumpsuit as she climbs high into the branches of a eucalyptus tree in the front yard of 712 Colonial Street.* "Peggy" is five years old. She was born in the jungles of Liberia and lured into captivity with a bundle of bananas. Since coming to Hollywood, Peggy has been taught to understand 502 voice commands, ride a tricycle, do backflips on cue, and put on a necktie. She has become one of the motion picture industry's top animal performers, commanding a thousand dollars per week in salary. Now, as the cameras roll, she is starring in her first title role. The film is a screwball comedy entitled *Bedtime for Bonzo.*

---

*Not an actual street, but a movie set at Universal Studios. Similar homes on the back lot would be used for many productions in the years to come, including the hit television series *Desperate Housewives.*

Ronald Reagan and Peggy the chimp on the set of Bedtime for Bonzo, *1950*

"Action!" cries director Fred de Cordova.* Peggy instantly obeys trainer Henry Craig's instruction to do what comes naturally for her: climb a tree.

One would think the act will not be quite as easy for her costar. Thirty-nine-year-old Ronald Reagan balances precariously on the top step of an eight-foot ladder leaning against the tree trunk. In his slick-soled shoes, dress shirt, and tie, he is hardly dressed for climbing. His trademark pompadour, meantime, is carefully Brylcreem'd into place. There is no safety rope to halt his fall should Reagan lose his balance, but that is not a problem. Nearly twenty years after his college football career ended, the

---

*Fred de Cordova, a graduate of Harvard Law School, will go on to become Johnny Carson's longtime producer on *The Tonight Show*. In that time, Carson will make several comedic jabs at *Bedtime for Bonzo*.

rugged actor is still lean and athletic. Reagan pulls himself up into the tree with ease, with not so much as a hair out of place.

Just a few years earlier, it would have been ludicrous to imagine Ronald Reagan acting opposite a chimpanzee. He was a star contract player for the Warner Bros. film studio, well on his way to becoming the sort of lead actor who could command any role he wished, like his friends Cary Grant and Errol Flynn.

In every way, Ronald Reagan's life in the early 1940s could not have been better.

But that was then.

▬   ▬   ▬

Ronald Reagan is twenty-six when he steps off the electric trolley at the Republic Pictures stop in Hollywood. The year is 1937. A torrential April rain drenches the young baseball announcer as he strides quickly along Radford Avenue to the studio gate. If Reagan were to lift his head, he would see the legendary "HOLLYWOODLAND" sign just miles above him in the hills, but he keeps his head low, the collar of his raincoat cinched tightly around his throat.

Dutch, as Reagan is known to family and friends, works for radio station WHO in Des Moines, Iowa, covering sports. He has come west to visit the Chicago Cubs spring training camp on nearby Catalina Island, twenty miles off the California coast.* But the storm has shut down the ferries and seaplane service to Catalina, giving Reagan a free day in Los Angeles. Cowboy singing sensation Gene Autry is filming a new Western called *Rootin' Tootin' Rhythm*, and a few of Reagan's friends from back home are playing the roles of Singing Cowhands.† Reagan, who has long fantasized about being a movie star, has come to offer moral support to his pals.

---

*The Wrigley family, who owned the Cubs at the time, also owned a controlling interest in the island, which is why the Cubs trained there.

†They were members of a band called the Oklahoma Outlaws, which had a big following in the Midwest. Autry, who was looking for ways to broaden his national audience, had arranged to bring them to Hollywood.

Reagan will later write that "hundreds of young people—from Iowa, Illinois, and just about every other state"—shared his fantasy. They "stepped off a train at Union Station in Los Angeles . . . they got no closer to realizing it than a studio front gate."

But thanks to his pals, Reagan makes it through the gate and hustles to Autry's soundstage. He enters the cavernous building with klieg lights hanging from high wooden beams. He is immediately intoxicated by the sight of the actors, cameras, lights, and everything else that goes into making a movie. All is quiet as filming begins. Gene Autry himself, dressed in the knee-high boots and gun belt of a cowboy, strums a guitar and sings a lament about life on the prairie. The set is made to look like the parlor of an ornate home. Autry is surrounded by musicians and actors clutching fiddles and guitars, all dressed as cowboys.

"Cut," yells director Mack Wright as the song winds down. Autry stops. Everyone relaxes on the set. A few minutes later, as Wright calls for "action," the scene is repeated.

"I was starry-eyed," Reagan admits to a friend that night. His friend's name is Joy Hodges, and she and her band are performing at the stately Biltmore Hotel in downtown LA. Joy knew Reagan back in Des Moines, and they now enjoy a quiet dinner between sets. The walls are lined with oak, and a marble fountain gurgles in the background. Reagan tells her his dreams of becoming a movie star and how he wishes he could find a way to break into the business.

Joy Hodges, a pretty, raven-haired lady, finds Reagan intriguing.

"Take off your glasses," she commands.

He removes them, and Joy instantly becomes a blur to Reagan.

Hodges, on the other hand, can see him quite clearly—and she likes what she sees. "Studios don't make passes at actors who wear glasses," she warns him before going back onstage for her second set.

Thus, the fairy tale begins. By ten the next morning, Reagan is meeting with Joy's agent, who arranges a screen test for the handsome young man. The test eventually makes its way to Jack Warner, the powerful head of Warner Bros. Pictures. He also likes what he sees and offers Reagan

Up-and-coming movie star Ronald Reagan, 1939

a seven-year contract at two hundred dollars a week—almost three times what he makes at WHO. A hairstylist transforms Reagan's center-parted look into the trademark pompadour he will wear the rest of his life. A tailor ingeniously alters the taper of his collar to create the optical illusion that Reagan's neck is not so thick. Finally, after some deliberation, the publicity department declares that he can keep his real name on-screen.

So it is that by June 1937, just two months after stepping out of the rain at Republic Pictures, Ronald Reagan is acting in his first motion picture. The movie is called *Love Is on the Air*. Appropriately enough, Reagan plays a radio announcer.

Sarah Jane Mayfield—or Jane Wyman, as she is known in Hollywood—knows a thing or two about love. It is early in 1938 as she arrives on the set of the film *Brother Rat*. At the age of twenty-one, she is already married. Her current husband is dress manufacturer Myron Futterman, whom she wed in New Orleans six months ago. Small, with bangs worn high on her forehead and a husky voice that will one day become her trademark, Wyman has struggled to break into Hollywood since coming west from Missouri. But now she finally has gotten her foot in the door through a series of small roles in B movies and is determined to become a star. Her weakness is being impulsive when it comes to love, and she separates from Futterman almost as quickly as she married him.

As Ronald Reagan begins his tenth film in less than a year,* there is no hiding the fact that his *Brother Rat* costar has quickly become infatuated with him. By December 1938, Jane Wyman officially divorces Myron Futterman and takes up with Reagan.

They soon become Hollywood's golden couple, "wholesome and happy and utterly completely American," in the words of gossip columnist Louella Parsons, who, knowing that nothing in Hollywood lasts forever, nevertheless predicts that their union will last thirty years. Wyman and Reagan are married in January 1940, shortly before Reagan begins filming *Knute Rockne All American* with Pat O'Brien. He plays the role of legendary Notre Dame running back George Gipp, uttering the immortal line "Ask 'em to go in there with all they've got, win just one for the Gipper," before dying on-screen. It is his first A film and is soon followed by a costarring role alongside the swashbuckling womanizer Errol Flynn in *Santa Fe Trail*. Just four short years after breaking into Hollywood, Ronald Reagan is now a major star. He and Wyman are soon building a massive new house and spending their evenings at the best Hollywood nightclubs.

---

*Such a pace will be unheard of in years to come, but in an era before television, studios produce hundreds of films each year, and for an actor to go from one picture to another is as simple as walking from one soundstage to a different one next door.

Ronald Reagan and Jane Wyman with baby Maureen

In 1941, Wyman gives birth to a beautiful daughter whom they name Maureen.

World War II is raging. But Ronald Reagan's poor eyesight exempts him from fighting overseas. He stays in California but is eager to contribute to the war effort. Long before moving to Los Angeles, Reagan had joined Iowa's Army Reserve, serving in the cavalry. In May 1937, before making his first motion picture, he was offered a commission as a second lieutenant in the U.S. Cavalry Officer Reserve Corps.

He begins active duty as a second lieutenant in the U.S. Army in April 1942, assigned to making training films and selling war bonds. He secures a top secret clearance, meaning he is often privy to classified information about upcoming American bombing raids. In the process, he learns how such attacks are planned and conducted. Reagan's career up until now has seen him in a series of jobs that do not require leadership or organization. But the army teaches him about taking charge and motivating the men he commands. These are lessons he will use for the rest of his life.

The duties of Reagan's U.S. Army First Motion Picture Unit shift in the waning days of the war. In June 1945, he sends a photographer to a local aircraft factory to take pictures of women working in war production. Pvt. David Conover shoots using color film, a rarity at the time, snapping the indelible image of an eighteen-year-old brunette holding a small propeller. The wife of a young merchant seaman, the fetching girl earns twenty dollars a week inspecting parachutes at a company named Radioplane, which also makes some of the world's first drone aircraft.* She has a wholesome smile, wears a modest green blouse, and has clipped her factory ID badge to the waistband of her pleated gray skirt. Her name is Norma Jeane Dougherty, and these photographs will soon open the doors of Hollywood to her. Eventually, Norma Jeane will divorce her sailor husband and change her name, as she becomes one of the most famous women in the world. As his own career is on the verge of combusting, Ronald Reagan is directly responsible for initiating the fame of Marilyn Monroe.

▰ ▰ ▰

At war's end, Reagan makes a triumphant return to Hollywood. Warner Bros. gives him a new long-term contract worth a million dollars, with a guarantee of fifty-two thousand dollars per movie. Reagan and the petite

---

*Code-named Operation Aphrodite, the drone program featured radio-controlled B-24 bombers that were packed with explosives and flown into position by pilots, who would then bail out as the planes flew on to their targets, guided from afar by a "mother ship." Sometimes, however, the explosives detonated long before the pilots were able to eject. One such fatality was Lt. Joseph P. Kennedy Jr., older brother of future U.S. president John F. Kennedy, who died in a similar naval program known as Operation Anvil.

Wyman live in a five-thousand-square-foot custom home on a knoll over-looking Los Angeles. He spends his off time playing golf with comedians Jack Benny and George Burns, and enjoys steak dinners with Wyman at the exclusive Beverly Club. Also in 1945, Reagan and Jane Wyman adopt a baby boy, whom they name Michael.

Reagan's first movie of the new contract is *Stallion Road*, in which he plays a horseback-riding veterinarian. Reagan's on-screen mount is a midnight black thoroughbred mare named Tar Baby. Reagan likes "Baby" so much that he buys her before filming is completed. To give her a place to gallop, he fulfills a lifelong dream and buys a small ranch in the San Fernando Valley, which he will keep for a couple of years before buying a larger property in Malibu.

Then tragedy strikes. In June 1947, Jane Wyman gives birth prematurely to a young daughter. Reagan is ill in the hospital with pneumonia at the time and cannot be at Wyman's side when Christine Reagan comes into the world. She lives just nine hours. The loss deeply affects his marriage to Wyman.*

Trying to put their lives back together, Ronald Reagan and Jane Wyman pour themselves into their work. Yet, despite all the trappings of success, Ronald Reagan's glory days in Hollywood are numbered. Warner Bros. soon casts him in a series of forgettable pictures that make little money and are scorned by critics. Reagan is perplexed. His Hollywood fairy tale is in danger of coming to an end—and he is powerless to do anything about it.

Reagan is a hardworking, restless man who craves physical activity. He is the son of an all-too-often-drunk Irish shoe salesman and a Bible-thumping mother. Their parenting methods taught young Ron to avoid extremes in behavior, leading him, at times, to appear clueless and shut

---

*Michael Reagan later wrote of Wyman that the death of Christine was "probably the most painful experience of her life, and I don't think she ever truly recovered from it." Wyman's 1951 movie *The Blue Veil* reopened those wounds, as the protagonist dealt with the matter of premature infant death. Filmed in and around St. Patrick's Cathedral in New York City, the film had a profound impact on Jane Wyman's life. The experience brought about a spiritual transformation; three years later, Wyman was baptized into the Catholic Church.

off. Also, it is true: Ronald Reagan is not a great intellect, having struggled to maintain a C average in college. Yet he can memorize paragraphs of script with ease and then recite them again and again on cue. Reagan also is a thinker, craving long periods of solitary meditation—preferably on horseback. He believes that "as you rock along a trail to the sound of the hooves and the squeak of the leather, with the sun on your head and the smell of the horse and the saddle and trees around you, things just begin to straighten themselves out."

Reagan first learned to ride while working as a teenage lifeguard back at Lowell Park in Dixon, Illinois, and lives by the saying "Nothing is so good for the inside of a man as the outside of a horse."

But no long gallop aboard Baby can hide the fact that Ronald Reagan's personal and professional lives are now veering in new and disastrous directions.

Jane Wyman is growing bored with her husband, though he is oblivious to her dissatisfaction. Reagan can often be self-centered and callous. He has a habit of talking down to his wife because he possesses a college degree and she does not. He also likes to be the center of attention; sometimes screening his personal print of the 1942 movie *Kings Row* when guests come over for dinner.*

Jane Wyman is not impressed when friends suggest that Reagan, who is developing a fondness for political activism, run for Congress. "He's very politically minded. I'm not very bright," she answers coolly, when asked if she supports the idea.

Ronald Reagan has also become fond of lecturing. Any topic will do. "Don't ask Ronnie what time it is," Wyman warns fellow actress June Allyson, "because he will tell you how a watch is made."

---

*Of the fifty-three films he made in his career, *Kings Row* was Reagan's favorite. He plays the second lead in the picture, a young man whose legs have been amputated by a villainous surgeon. Reagan's key line, which he uttered spontaneously, happens the moment the young man looks down and sees that his legs are gone: "Where's the rest of me?" It later became the title of his 1965 memoir.

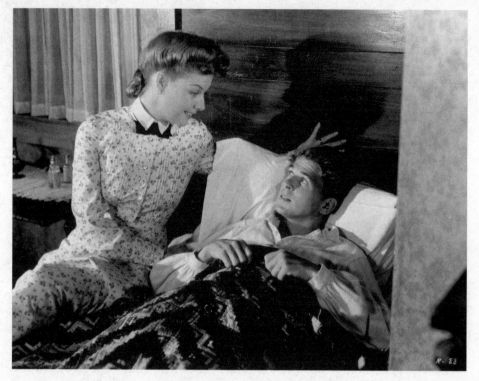

Ann Sheridan and Ronald Reagan in Kings Row, *Reagan's personal
favorite of all his performances*

When a baseball game comes on the radio, Reagan often ignores his
wife and children, turning up the volume and drowning out their words
by pretending to be the broadcaster and calling the game. In that way, he
shuts out his family for hours.

To make matters worse, Reagan resents Wyman's growing level of
celebrity. Her movies, such as *The Yearling*, are earning money, critical
praise, and Academy Award nominations. No longer the star when the two
go out, Reagan must hover at his wife's elbow as *she* basks in the public's
applause.

So it is that Ronald Reagan's newfound political activism, his wife's
growing fame, and the death of their baby daughter combine to drive a
wedge into their marriage. In 1947, Wyman cruelly mocks him during a

lengthy speech he delivers before the Screen Actors Guild membership, foreshadowing the marital split that is soon to come. "Oh, for God's sake, Ronnie," she shouts to actress Rosemary DeCamp, "shut up and go shit in your hat."

The end comes while Wyman is filming *Johnny Belinda* on location in Pebble Beach, California. She begins an affair with costar Lew Ayres. In May 1948, Jane Wyman files for divorce from Ronald Reagan, citing mental cruelty.

"I just couldn't stand to watch that damn *Kings Row* one more time," she explains when the marriage is finally over.

The divorce traumatizes Reagan. He is shattered and sometimes weeps openly, telling friends that the end of his marriage has left him "ashamed." He clings to hope that the relationship can one day be salvaged and still drives the green Cadillac convertible Wyman gave him as a gift before the divorce. But when she publicly declares, "Lew Ayres is the love of my life," it becomes clear that there will be no reconciliation.

Embittered, Reagan begins to behave in a callow fashion. He spends lavishly at Hollywood nightclubs such as Ciro's, the Coconut Grove, and Slapsy Maxie's, drinking too much and conducting a series of sexual affairs with women decades younger than he. His actions do not go unnoticed by the press. *Silver Screen* magazine writes, "Never thought we'd come right out and call Ronnie Reagan a wolf, but leave us face it. Suddenly every glamour gal considers him a super-sexy escort for the evening. Even he admits he's missed a lot of fun and frolic and is out to make up for it."

One of Reagan's liaisons is with actress Penny Edwards, who is just twenty, and another is with the twenty-two-year-old actress Patricia Neal. During a memorable one-night stand in his apartment, Reagan takes the virginity of eighteen-year-old Piper Laurie after first barbecuing her a hamburger. Iron-ically, at the time of their liaison, Reagan was playing the role of Laurie's father in *Louisa*. The actress will later remember Reagan as a "show-off"

in the bedroom, a self-absorbed lover who bragged about his sexual stamina during the act and became impatient when she did not climax. "You should have had many orgasms by now," Reagan scolded Laurie after what she claims was about forty minutes of sex. "You've got to see a doctor about your abnormality."*

Reagan reaches bottom when he wakes up one morning at the Garden of Allah Hotel on Sunset Boulevard and does not know the name of the woman lying next to him. After that, he vows to rein in his behavior.

But he does not. Three years after his divorce, when he proposes marriage to twenty-six-year-old actress Christine Larson by offering her a diamond wristwatch, Reagan is also having relationships with six other women. Larson turns him down.†

Now living on his own in an apartment above the Sunset Strip, Ronald Reagan soon grows apart from his young son and daughter. Three-year-old Michael and seven-year-old Maureen Reagan will long remember their father as loving but also absent from their lives for long periods of time—as was their mother. Both children are sent away to boarding schools by the time they enter the second grade. "There's a distinct difference between the care provided by a parent and the care provided by a paid caretaker," Maureen will say years later. "It was simply one of the prices all of us had to pay for their success."

During this playboy period, Reagan's success has flatlined. He is no

---

*Laurie would go on to win Academy Award nominations for *The Hustler, Carrie,* and *Children of a Lesser God.* Patricia Neal would win an Academy Award for Best Actress in 1963 for *Hud,* costarring Paul Newman. Penny Edwards was never nominated but made a name for herself as Roy Rogers's love interest in six Hollywood Westerns.

†Chief among Larson's reasons for turning him down is her adherence to the Bahá'í Faith, which does not believe in politics. However, that excuse belies the fact that Larson was not in love with Reagan. Among others, she is seeing actors Gary Cooper and Mickey Rooney. She will also go on to have an affair with Lew Ayres, the actor who was involved with Jane Wyman while she and Reagan were still married. In another example of the mattress hopping so common in Hollywood at the time, the legendary lover and Reagan's friend, Gary Cooper, will be rumored to have slept with almost every single leading lady of his lengthy career, including Patricia Neal.

longer viewed as a bankable star by Hollywood standards. To add insult to injury, as his movie career is clearly in its death throes, Wyman wins her first Academy Award and arrives at the ceremony with Lew Ayres as her date, which only makes Reagan's career seem more marginal.* By 1949, Warner Bros. terminates his long-term contract, leaving him without income to pay the bills for the high-flying Hollywood lifestyle to which he has grown accustomed.

Desperate, Reagan accepts the offer to work on *Bedtime for Bonzo*. Animal movies are all the rage in Hollywood in 1950, thanks to the success of the February release *Francis the Talking Mule*. Jimmy Stewart has just finished *Harvey*, about a man and his invisible rabbit companion, on a set just one block down from where Reagan now films *Bonzo*. *Harvey* will open in October and earn Stewart his fourth Academy Award nomination.

As Ronald Reagan now clambers up into the tree after the chimp Peggy (Bonzo), he still believes his career will rebound. The film's other star, Diana Lynn, awaits him in the branches, adding to the comedy's madcap narrative. Meanwhile, Bonzo has jumped off a branch and is now inside the house, somehow managing to call the police. Soon there will be cop cars and fire trucks screaming down Colonial Street, all in a scripted attempt to get everyone down from the tree. This is a far cry from Reagan's days making movies such as *Dark Victory* with major stars such as Humphrey Bogart and Bette Davis, or *Sante Fe Trail* with Errol Flynn. In that movie, Reagan played General George Armstrong Custer, whom he considers a great American hero.

Still, Reagan is a professional. He shows up each morning on time, knows his lines, and is pleasant to his coworkers. There are times, however, when he seems distracted. For there are pressing concerns on his mind.

Ronald Reagan is nearly forty years old. His profession is acting, but politics has set a new fire burning in his belly. The newspapers are full of the amazing events going on in the global fight against communism, as President Harry Truman sends U.S. troops into Korea to stop the Communist

---

*Wyman won Best Actress for *Johnny Belinda* in 1949. She was also nominated for Best Actress in 1947 (*The Yearling*), 1952 (*The Blue Veil*), and 1955 (*Magnificent Obsession*).

advance. Reagan is an ardent supporter of the Democratic president and campaigned for him in 1948. With Truman's time in office due to end if he doesn't run for reelection, Reagan is hoping former army general and World War II hero Dwight Eisenhower will run for president as a Democrat. Even as he deals with Peggy the chimp, Reagan is planning an article for *Fortnight* magazine in which he will explain how to fight communism worldwide. His determination to end the Communist threat is steadfast.

"The real fight with this totalitarianism belongs properly to the forces of liberal democracy, just as did the battle with Hitler's totalitarianism. There really is no difference except in the cast of characters," Reagan will write.

But that is a few months off. For now, Reagan is engaged in far less intellectual fare.

"Cut," director Fred de Cordova yells.

Ronald Reagan climbs down from the tree.

3

⸺ᘒᘒᘒ⸺

Forty-year-old Ronald Reagan gallops Tar Baby over the rolling country-side of his new 270-acre Malibu ranch. He rides English style, wear-ing skintight jodhpurs and knee-high Dehner riding boots. Christmas is just days away. The air is crisp on this winter morning, the skies clear and blue. Reagan's two children, home on break from Chadwick board-ing school, are spending the weekend in the small shingled ranch house back near the barn.

But this weekend is not just a time for a father and his kids. Reagan's latest girlfriend, a thirty-year-old actress named Nancy Davis, has joined them. Though she works very hard to endear herself to his son and daugh-ter, and Maureen and Michael like her very much, Reagan is unsure about this blossoming relationship. He is not ready to be monogamous and is still seeing other women.

Yet Davis is determined to win his heart—by any means necessary. Recently, Davis confessed to Reagan that she might be pregnant. Yet rather than encouraging Reagan to propose marriage, the announcement has the opposite effect. He flees to the home of Christine Larson, the starlet who spurned his offer of marriage earlier this year. Reagan complains to her that he feels trapped by Davis and wonders aloud if she is trying to trick him into marrying her.

But on this day, Reagan does not feel confined. He rides tall and easy in the saddle, feeling the black mare moving beneath him. His connection with Baby is so strong that Reagan now insists upon riding her during on-screen horseback shots. This time last year they were in Tucson, Arizona, filming the Western *The Last Outpost*, which has become a minor success at the box office. The film's horse wranglers warned Reagan that the desert location's heat and dust might prove fatal to the mare. But the actor knows his horse well. Tar Baby survived the grueling shoot without a single problem.

Now, riding on a dirt path lined with sycamores and scrub oak, past Malibou Lake, where he plans to swim in the summer, and the hayfield that parallels distant Mulholland Drive, Reagan finds himself at a curious career crossroads. *Bedtime for Bonzo* was such a box office success that a sequel is in the works. Reagan received mixed notices for his comedic performance, with most reviewers preferring to focus their praise on Peggy the chimp. The *New York Times* called *Bonzo* "a minor bit of fun yielding a respectable amount of laughs, but nothing, actually, over which to wax ecstatic."

Reagan was barely mentioned in the review.

Despite *Bonzo*'s success, he is not offered a role in the sequel.* On top of that, Reagan's tenure as president of the Screen Actors Guild will soon come to an end. It is a time of upheaval and change in Hollywood, and Reagan has been in the thick of the pitched battle between the studios and an emerging Communist presence in the show business community.

---

*The sequel is titled *Bonzo Goes to College*. It stars Edmund Gwenn, best known for his role as Kris Kringle in the classic *Miracle on 34th Street*, for which he won an Academy Award for Best Supporting Actor.

His "double life," as he calls his now-intersecting twin passions of acting and politics, has consumed him. The ranch has been a tonic in these tough times, his Saturday getaway to clear his head from the strife.

Reagan has been the head of SAG for five years. But no year has been more intense than 1951. In addition to acting in three films and attending the Monday night SAG board meetings, he has also traveled around the country speaking on behalf of an anticommunist group known as Crusade for Freedom. The purpose: to raise money for Radio Free Europe. And though Reagan is still very much a Hollywood actor, the words he scripts for himself are those of a seasoned international politician.

Reagan with Tar Baby

"The battleground of peace today is that strip of strategically located countries stretching from the Baltic to the Black Sea," Reagan says in a recorded speech that is replayed to small groups around America. "They are not big countries geographically, but they contain several million freedom-loving people, our kind of people, who share our culture and have sent millions of their sons and daughters to become part of these United States. Some call these countries the satellite nations. More accurately, they're the captive nations of Europe."

Reagan is unaware that Crusade for Freedom is secretly backed by the Central Intelligence Agency, although he would likely be delighted if he knew.

▬ ▬ ▬

Ronald Reagan actually considered joining the Communist Party back in 1938. Many in Hollywood were romanced by the Communists, as Adolf Hitler and his fascist ideology were becoming a threat not just to Europe but to the entire world. The Communists, with their avowed mission of helping the poor and disenfranchised, seemed poised to thwart Hitler's ambitions. But there was more to Reagan's attraction than mere ideology: as a newcomer to Hollywood, just one year into his studio contract, he saw becoming a Communist as a good way to expand his social circle.

"Reagan got carried away by stories of the Communist Party helping the dispossessed, the unemployed and the homeless," screenwriter Howard Fast will claim years later. "Some of his friends, people he respected, were party members, so he turned to them. Said he wanted to be a Communist . . . said he was determined to join."

But actor Eddie Albert, a costar in *Brother Rat*, was just as determined to talk Reagan out of turning red. Albert's motives were deceptive. He leaned far to the left politically and secretly undertook the discussion at the behest of the American Communist Party leadership, who believed the talkative Reagan was a "flake" and did not want him joining their group.

Albert was successful. Reagan's brief flirtation with communism came to an end.

His interest in politics, however, did not cease.

■ ■ ■

It is August 11, 1941, when Ronald Reagan attends his first meeting of the Screen Actors Guild at the union's headquarters on Hollywood Boulevard. He has been invited to serve as an alternate for actress Heather Angel. The Guild is just eight years old at the time, founded to improve working conditions for actors. Reagan's first meeting is more of a social excursion, as he has little knowledge of the Guild's inner workings. Even when Jane Wyman is elected to the board a year later, Reagan remains distant from SAG, involved as he is with the war effort. But he resumes attending meetings in February 1946 as an alternate for horror-movie actor Boris Karloff. In September of that year he is elected third vice president.

By the end of World War II, with Hitler and the German Third Reich defeated, it is clear that Joseph Stalin and the Communists are just as ruthless and just as intent on global domination as the führer was. The Soviet Union, headquarters of global communism, displaces millions of people across Eastern Europe in order to build an empire even bigger than Hitler's. It is also sending spies out around the world to infiltrate other nations and spread propaganda. Reagan soon sees this played out quite clearly in Hollywood. The actor's union is slowly dividing itself into those, like Reagan, who now consider communism a scourge and those who believe that the political system embraced by the Soviet Union is intellectual and fashionable.

"[T]he important thing is that you should not argue with them. Communism has become an intensely dogmatic and almost mystical religion, and whatever you say, they have ways of twisting it into shapes which put you in some lower category of mankind," wrote novelist and screenwriter F. Scott Fitzgerald, describing the ideological tension in Hollywood.

The illusion that communism is a harmless ideology is shattered on September 27, 1946, when the Confederation of Studio Unions goes on strike. The head of the union is Herb Sorrell, a rough-and-tumble former boxer who is also a longtime member of the Communist Party. The strike is funded by the National Executive Council of the Communist Party. "When it ends up," Sorrell predicted, "there'll be only one man running labor in Hollywood—and that man will be me."

This is not a peaceful protest but a violent and militant attempt by the Communists to begin taking control of every major union in Hollywood—and, by proxy, the motion picture industry itself. In addition to the striking union members, Sorrell has enlisted hired thugs from the San Francisco area to provide menace. Cars are overturned in the streets. Police fire tear gas at the picket lines blocking the entrance to the Warner Bros. studio. Great mobs of strikers attack those attempting to cross the picket lines. Actor Kirk Douglas describes a scene of men armed with "knives, clubs, battery cables, brass knuckles, and chains."

Despite the violence, studio head Jack Warner refuses to buckle. He continues making movies. Actors and employees do not cross picket lines to get to work. Instead, they are smuggled into the studio through a Los Angeles River storm drain. For those preferring not to endure the smells and slime of the subterranean entrance, the other option is riding a bus driven straight through the picket lines at Warner's front gate. Scores of police officers are called in to line the route but cannot prevent the strikers from pelting the vehicles with rocks and bricks. Everyone on board the bus is instructed to lie down on the floor to avoid being hit in the head by broken glass and projectiles.

Ronald Reagan, as vice president of the Screen Actors Guild, considers the storm drain a coward's entrance and refuses to lie down on the floor of the bus. No matter that he has two young children and a pregnant wife at home, Reagan puts himself at risk in order to make a statement: he is not afraid.

Each day, arriving for work on a new film called *Night unto Night*, Reagan is the lone person on the studio bus sitting upright, for all to see. When the strikers later escalate their campaign by forcing the Screen Actors Guild to support the strike, an anonymous caller to Reagan's home threatens that he will be attacked and his face burned with acid if he tries to block SAG's pro-strike involvement.

Furious, Reagan refuses to back down. Instead, he buys a pistol and carries it in a shoulder holster wherever he goes. For the rest of his life, Ronald Reagan will be vehemently anticommunist. For him, it is very personal: he will never forget the threats.

Four weeks into the confrontation, on October 24, 1946, Reagan and strike organizer Herb Sorrell sit down at Hollywood's Knickerbocker Hotel. Sorrell is a powerfully built man, fond of using physical intimidation to achieve his goals. But Reagan is no less strong and is uncowed by Sorrell. He angrily accuses the union boss of being responsible for the threats.

"I have to have guards for my kids because I got telephone calls warning what would happen to me," he seethes, before adding, "You do not want peace in the motion picture industry."

Actor Gene Kelly is also at the meeting as a member of SAG's board of directors. He quickly steps in with a joke to keep the peace: "If Mr. Reagan hits Mr. Sorrell I want it understood that this is not the official feeling of this body."*

Kelly's words have their desired effect. The meeting calms until it ends at one thirty the following morning, but nothing is resolved.

By December, with the strike in its third month, Reagan is calling a special meeting of SAG's 350 most elite members. Among them is actor Edward G. Robinson, a man known for playing gangsters on-screen. Robinson is also one of Hollywood's most ardent Communists. In a speech that those in attendance will remember for years to come, Reagan assures the membership of his solid standing as a New Deal Democrat and

---

*Kelly was a man of high ideals who left the Catholic Church when he felt it was not doing enough to halt world hunger, yet donated money to the Provisional Irish Republican Army in its war against Protestants and the British occupation of Northern Ireland. The famous dancer, best known for *Singin' in the Rain*, was once quoted as saying, "I believe in God, the American Way of Life, the freedom of the individual, and everything the Constitution of the United States stands for." To Kelly, this also meant tolerance for the Communists, which made him the perfect middleman for discussions between Reagan and Sorrell.

argues that the Guild should maintain a united stand against the strike. Even Robinson marvels "at Reagan's clear and sequential presentation."

Still, the strike drags on.

The duration of the strike angers Reagan. He is appalled by the Communist union leader's zealous desire to take control of Hollywood. What began as a battle of ideologies has now become Reagan's personal mission. He vows to fight communism, wherever it may be.

▄▄ ▄▄ ▄▄

With Ronald Reagan gaining political confidence, Gene Kelly nominates him for president of the Screen Actors Guild. Veteran actors James Cagney, Robert Montgomery, Harpo Marx, and John Garfield have just stepped down from SAG leadership. Reagan is not present at the time of his nomination, arriving halfway through the meeting to find out that he has won. He is stunned.

The term of office is one year, beginning in 1947. Almost immediately, Reagan is tested by Communist sympathizers attempting to undermine his leadership. "At a mass meeting," Reagan will later write, "I watched rather helplessly as they filibustered, waiting for our majority to leave so they could take control."

A voice in the crowd cries out that the meeting should be adjourned. "I seized on this as a means of ending the attempted takeover. But the other side demanded I identify the one who moved for adjournment."

Reagan is in a bind. While many in the Screen Actors Guild are against the Communists, it is also a career liability to speak out publicly against them. The momentum of the Communist movement is too great, and the possibility of being personally and professionally ostracized from the Hollywood community is very real. Reagan scans the crowd, searching for at least one individual with the backbone to be his ally in this heated moment.

He sees his man. "Why, I believe John Wayne made the motion," Reagan tells the crowd. Wayne is one of Hollywood's best-known tough guys, a former college football player whose starring roles in Westerns and war movies have made him one of the most bankable box office stars in the world. And unlike many Hollywood heroes, who look tall on the screen but are actually diminutive in real life, the gruff Wayne stands at a rugged six foot four.

"I sure as hell did," Wayne roars from the crowd.

The meeting is adjourned.

▰ ▰ ▰

Finally, after thirteen long months, the strike ends. Yet even as the studios emerge victorious, Hollywood's growing embrace of communism continues unabated, drawing the attention of the feared FBI chief J. Edgar Hoover.

In the waning days of their marriage, Ronald Reagan and Jane Wyman are approached by FBI agents Richard Auerbach and Fred Dupuis, who come to their home uninvited on April 10, 1947. The agents ask the couple to "report secretly to the FBI about people suspected of Communist activity."

Wyman and Reagan quickly offer up six names. This will be the end of Wyman's involvement with the FBI, but Ronald Reagan begins meeting frequently with the bureau to provide more names and information. He is given a code name: T-10. Two of the people he names, actresses Karen Morley and Anne Revere, will not work in Hollywood for the next twenty years.*

Ronald Reagan believes this banishment is just, for he knows the women to be Communists—and thinks the Communist Party is an agent of a foreign power.

Reagan will be damned if he will allow the motion picture industry to undermine the moral fabric of the United States of America.

Ronald Reagan will never waver from the belief that informing for the FBI was the right thing to do; nor will he suffer any repercussions for it. "I talked to Ronnie since," Jack Dales, executive secretary of SAG at that

---

*Revere won the Best Supporting Actress award for her role in the movie *National Velvet*. Morley turned to politics after leaving Hollywood, running unsuccessfully for lieutenant governor of New York in 1954. She returned to acting in the 1970s, appearing on television in episodes of *Kojak* and *Kung Fu*.

Reagan testifies before the House Un-American Activities Committee, 1947.

time, will comment years from now. "And he has no doubts about the propriety of what we did."

■ ■ ■

On October 23, 1947, Reagan travels to Washington to appear before the House Un-American Activities Committee, a congressional group trying to root our subversive individuals and practices.* "I believe that, as Thomas Jefferson put it, if all the American people know all of the facts they will never make a mistake," said Reagan, responding to questions from HUAC chief investigator Robert Stripling. "Whether the [Communist] party should be outlawed, that is a matter for the government to decide. As a

---

*Not to be confused with Sen. Joseph McCarthy's Communist investigations, HUAC was originally founded in 1938 to root out Nazi sympathizers. It switched its focus to communism as the Soviet Union rose to power. Thirty-four-year-old Richard Nixon, a newly elected California congressman, was a member of HUAC on the day Reagan testified but was not in attendance.

citizen, I would hesitate to see any political party outlawed on the basis of its political ideology. However, if it is proven that an organization is an agent of a foreign power, or in any way not a legitimate political party—and I think the government is capable of proving that—then that is another matter."

Reagan's appearance before the committee is his first visit to Capitol Hill.

It makes a lasting impression on him.

▬ ▬ ▬

Nearly four years after testifying before Congress, Ronald Reagan guides Tar Baby back to the barn. He hopes soon to add "thoroughbred horse breeder" to the many job titles that currently keep him busy and plans to expand the simple barn into something more elaborate for that purpose.

Reagan leads the mare into her stall and removes her bridle and saddle. Whistling softly to himself, he brushes her torso and flanks. The repetitive movement allows Reagan a contemplative moment.

It is clear that Ronald Reagan needs to make some hard decisions about his future. He gets little respect for his roles as an actor, but he is held in such high esteem for his political activism that when the Friars Club recently honored him they refrained from derogatory jokes and putdowns. Instead, the six hundred members in attendance spent the evening lauding him with sincere speeches about his "stature and dignity," with the legendary singer Al Jolson even going so far as to say that he wished his son would "grow up to be the kind of man Ronnie is."

But with his Guild presidency coming to an end, it seems that Reagan's political days will also cease. All the respect in the world from his Hollywood peers won't pay the bills. He must find a way to revive his career. The mortgage on his ranch alone is eighty-five thousand dollars. Politics doesn't offer that kind of money.

As Reagan steps out of the barn, walking to where Nancy Davis and his children wait inside the small ranch house, he faces a midlife crisis. Reagan well knows the truth: he is a forty-year-old Hollywood has-been on the verge of losing everything. As he enjoys a brief time of quiet and solitude on this cool December morning, he is unsure of what 1952 has in store for him—hardly aware that it is the year in which he will remarry, father a new child, and vote Republican for the first time in his life.*

---

*The battle against communism dogged Ronald Reagan right up to the very end of his term as Screen Actors Guild president. On January 16, 1952, during one of Reagan's final SAG meetings, powerful director Stanley Kramer explained to the board that his recent movie, *Death of a Salesman*, was being picketed by pro-Communist groups who were accusing him of discrimination because he refused to employ Communists. In order to prevent the increasing use of this tactic against other filmmakers, Kramer filed a libel lawsuit. Director John Ford, who gained fame making John Wayne Westerns such as *Stagecoach*, stepped forward to say that he would testify on Kramer's behalf. As a result, Reagan and the SAG board issued a formal resolution backing Kramer and repudiating the Communist pressure. Left unsaid was that during his tenure as president of the SAG board, Reagan had completely shifted the leadership from being sympathetic to communism to openly opposing the ideology and its tactics.

4

————◆◆◆————

"I do," says Ronald Reagan, looking into the large brown eyes of a pregnant Nancy Davis. He is dressed in a black wedding suit with narrow matching tie. Davis, who clutches a fragrant bouquet of orange blossoms and white tulips, does not wear a wedding gown. Instead, she has chosen to wear a gray woolen suit bought off the rack at the I. Magnin department store in Beverly Hills. A single strand of pearls is draped around her neck.

The Rev. John Wells, a Disciples of Christ minister, stands before the small, bare table that represents the altar here at the Little Brown Church. He asks Davis if she, too, agrees to be wed "till death do you part."

"I do," she replies. Nancy Davis has campaigned hard for this moment since setting her sights on Ronald Reagan three years ago. She is undaunted by his flings with other women, accepting his indiscretions while enjoying a few brief affairs of her own.* Davis knows that there are two keys to Reagan's heart: politics and horses. So she has spent hours whitewashing fences at the actor's Malibu ranch and attending the Monday night SAG board meetings to watch him lead the proceedings. "I loved to listen to him talk," Davis will write of their courtship, "and I let him know it."

Standing in the chapel to Reagan's right is his best man, the hard-drinking actor William Holden. The thirty-three-year-old Academy Award nominee for *Sunset Boulevard* has taken a break from filming the World War II drama *Stalag 17* to be at the ceremony. His wife, Ardis, is serving as Davis's matron of honor. The Holdens have been fighting today and are not on speaking terms. That is not an unusual situation in their eleven-year marriage. The main issue between them is infidelity. Holden underwent a vasectomy after the birth of their second son and is fond of bedding his costars without fear of getting them pregnant, thus leaving his wife in a constant state of jealousy and torment.[†]

Even as Ronald Reagan and Nancy Davis recite their vows, awash in apparent marital bliss, the Holdens sit on opposite sides of the tiny church.

Other than these four, and the gray-haired Reverend Wells, who

---

*Nancy Davis has never been married. She was engaged briefly in 1944 to a young naval officer named J. P. White Jr. but broke it off after just a few months. A series of brief affairs followed. "She was what men at that time thought of as 'available,'" a family friend will later recall. After moving from Chicago to New York in 1945 to pursue a Broadway career, Davis had affairs with actor Alfred Drake and producer Max Allentuck. She moved to California and signed with MGM in 1949, where she earned a reputation for being ambitious and allegedly having a torrid affair with producer Benny Thau, a man well known for using the casting couch to further the careers of young actresses. In 1949 Nancy made a list for herself of show business's most eligible bachelors, with an eye to trying to marry one. Ronald Reagan's name was at the top of the list, beginning the three years of pursuit leading to their marriage.

†Ardis Ankerson is a striking brunette who goes by the stage name of Brenda Marshall. Unlike many actresses, she insists that friends and family use her real name rather than her stage name. She is best known for playing Errol Flynn's love interest in the 1940 pirate film *The Sea Hawk*. She made her last film in 1950, preferring to put her career on hold to raise a family. After a number of separations, William Holden and Ardis Ankerson divorced in 1971. Among Holden's lovers during their marriage were costars Grace Kelly, Audrey Hepburn, Shelley Winters, and the French bombshell Capucine. He also had a torrid weeklong affair with Jackie Kennedy in the mid-1950s. Holden, who bragged to a friend that he had played the role of bedroom tutor to the wife of the future American president, commented, "If she goes back to Washington and works her magic with Kennedy he will owe me one."

presides wearing a flowing black robe, there is no one else in attendance for the Reagan-Davis wedding, which makes the Holdens' feud glaringly obvious. The Reagan children, Maureen and Michael, are away at school.

Even though a formal wedding announcement was made on February 21, and gossip writer Louella Parsons spread the word to twenty million people worldwide through her syndicated newspaper column, the ceremony is stunningly casual. There was no limousine to ferry the couple to the church. Instead, Reagan picked Nancy up at her apartment in the Cadillac convertible purchased for him by Jane Wyman.

In addition, there is no formal reception. The group will adjourn to the Holdens' ranch-style home* in nearby Toluca Lake for a quick bite of cake and a splash of champagne before Reagan and Davis drive two hours to Riverside's Mission Inn for their wedding night.

Reagan's initial wedding proposal fell far short of romance. Davis had longed "that Ronnie would take me out in a canoe as the sun was setting and would strum a ukulele as I lay back, trailing my fingers in the water, the way they used to do in the old movies I saw as a little girl."

Instead, Reagan simply pronounced, "Let's get married," over dinner at a Hollywood nightclub shortly after Davis told him she was pregnant. To which she replied, after gazing into his eyes and placing her small hands atop his: "Let's."

Nancy Davis was so eager to marry Ronald Reagan that she willingly accommodated his every wish. If that meant a small ceremony, lacking fanfare or even a hint of the media flashbulbs that might provide a modicum of grandeur—then so be it. Nancy was released from her Metro-Goldwyn-Mayer studio contract just two weeks prior. "I don't want to do anything else except be married. I just want to be Ronnie's wife," she says later.

To Reagan, this anonymous wedding is perfect. His life seems to become more complicated by the day, and he hardly needs a horde of press to remind him that his career is in peril. In addition to dealing with Davis's pregnancy, Reagan was released from his contract with Warner

---

*Neighbors of the Holdens include Bob Hope, Shemp Howard of the Three Stooges, and Frank Sinatra. The Holden home will one day be owned by actor Denzel Washington.

Bros. just five weeks ago. He claims that he wants a small ceremony because the memory of his lavish first wedding to Jane Wyman is still painful. But the truth is that "to even contemplate facing reporters and flashbulbs made me break out in a cold sweat," as Reagan will one day write.

The wedding is so discreet that Reagan has not even invited his mother, Nelle. His father, Jack, died more than a decade ago, but Nelle Reagan now lives nearby, in Southern California. But even though Reagan has a close relationship with his mother, who is a member of the Disciples of Christ denomination, she is not in attendance.

Nancy, on the other hand, has no living relations in Hollywood. Her godmother was Alla Nazimova, the late owner of the legendary Garden of Allah Hotel. Coincidentally, that same den of iniquity was the place where Reagan promised himself that he would stop sleeping around. Thanks to that moment, and to his relationship with Nancy, he is now seen less and less in the nightclubs of Hollywood, preferring to spend weekends at the Malibu ranch.

"It's not that I hunger for somebody to love me," Reagan has confided to Nancy, finally putting the memory of his divorce in the rearview mirror, "as much as I miss having somebody to love."

"I pronounce you man and wife," says Reverend Wells, adjusting his thin wire-frame glasses. Davis is so swept away by the moment that she will not remember saying "I do" or even Ronald Reagan's kiss as their marriage is sealed. Instead, she will recall only the booming voice of Bill Holden as he comes to her side. "Can I kiss the bride?" he asks.

"Not yet," Davis protests. "It's too soon."

But as the svelte Ardis looks on, Holden wraps his arms around Nancy's waist and kisses her passionately on the lips.

Ardis Ankerson has arranged for a photographer to be present at her house as a beaming Nancy Reagan slices wedding cake with her new husband. The three tiers of white frosting, with the small plastic statue of bride and groom perched on top, rests on the Holdens' dining room table. Reagan blinks as the shutter clicks, while Nancy leans in toward the camera with eyes wide open. It is a moment both iconic and timeless, re-created at countless weddings before and since. If not for Ardis possessing the fore-thought to hire a photographer, there would have been no pictures of this moment.

The resulting images are unassuming. Yet one day they will be con-sidered remarkable, for this evening begins a marriage that will change the world.

It is midnight as the newly married Reagans arrive at the Mission Inn, an elaborate structure built to look like an old Spanish mission, with great stucco walls, exposed beams, and a garden courtyard.* A bouquet of red roses waits in their room, compliments of the house.

In Ronald Reagan, Nancy sees a greatness that thus far has eluded him. She will dedicate her life to bringing it forth. Soon, her supplication will vanish and dominance will emerge. Reagan will reluctantly cease his womanizing, although continuing his affair with Christine Larson well past the day his baby daughter, Patti, is born on October 21, 1952.† And while there will be the occasional discreet liaison in the future, Reagan's days as a playboy are in the past. In time, these affairs will come to haunt him. Not a man normally given to regrets, Reagan will rue his behav-ior as his love for Nancy grows deeper. "If you want to be a happy man," he will counsel a friend years from now, "just don't ever cheat on your wife."

---

*President Richard Nixon and his wife, Pat, were married at the Mission Inn. A host of other presidents has visited the historic building: Benjamin Harrison, William Howard Taft, William McKinley, Theodore Roosevelt, Herbert Hoover, John F. Kennedy, Gerald Ford, and George W. Bush. Notably, Kennedy is the only Democrat.

†Reagan is not at the hospital the night Patricia Ann Reagan is delivered by caesarean section. He is in the arms of Larson. However, that relationship comes to an end shortly thereafter, when Reagan shows up at Larson's apartment and a French actor wearing just a small towel answers the door. Nancy will never acknowledge that she is aware of the relationship but will later comment, "When I was back in my room and the nurses brought me our baby for the first time, my first thought was that it was sad that Ronnie couldn't be there." Reagan never provided an excuse for his absence; Nancy just accepted that he wasn't there.

Ronald Reagan and Nancy Davis cutting wedding cake with
William Holden and his wife, Ardis

Nancy Reagan possesses an inner steel that her husband lacks. This quality will soon make her opinions indispensable. She will become his sounding board, tactician, and adviser, prodding and cajoling him to become the man only she believes he can be.

And while Reagan will always be "Ronnie" to his wife, the power in their marriage will slowly shift until Nancy becomes the matriarch known to her husband as Mommy.

Of such odd synergy are great marriages made.

5

The man with a long fifty years to live is in exile.

Ronald Reagan bounds onstage wearing an apron advertising Pabst Blue Ribbon beer. "Vas vils du haben?" he booms in a thick European accent to Ben Cruz, leader of a slapstick group known as the Continentals.

"Vats zoo got under dere?" Cruz says in a bemused voice, pointing at the hem of Reagan's long apron.

Reagan replies, scratching his groin. "Underwear?"

"Under dere," replies Cruz, pointing at the hem of Reagan's long apron. Then, as the audience bursts out in ribald laughter, Reagan and the Continentals break into song, a well-established vaudeville routine.

Reagan's appearance in Las Vegas is such an oddity that after his first show, the *Las Vegas Sun* wrote, incredulously, that "Ronald Reagan, of all people, opened last night at The Last Frontier." But tonight's audience is learning that Reagan can handle the vaudeville stage and is a master showman. His comedic timing, in particular, is impeccable. The three hundred audience members packed into the Ramona Room roar in laughter at his beer vendor shtick. But Reagan is not finished. Quickly, he switches over to an Irish brogue for a series of scripted one-liners. A wave of deep belly laughs fills the room.

Before the show opened there were widespread fears that the Hollywood actor would bomb in front of a live audience. But Reagan is so spectacular, and the subsequent audiences each night love the show so much, that the Last Frontier wants to book him for another month—if not more.

"Reagan opens with some solid humor and the enthusiastic response loosens him to the point he is grinning all over," the show business newspaper *Variety* wrote in a review. "He shines as a Dutch-jargon bartender in a beer selling bit."

Despite the positive press, Reagan is, in fact, terrified. The Last Frontier is an apt name for the casino, because it might just as well describe the slim territory of celebrity to which Ronald Reagan now clings. He can no longer afford a single miscue. He almost backed out of the Las Vegas gig, knowing all too well that if the show failed, his declining career would be all but over.

Even though the show is a hit, Reagan hopes that this is not his future. Nothing about the remote desert town suits him. He is not a gambler. He reads books in his off time or lounges by the pool with Nancy. Sometimes they take day trips to nearby Lake Mead, to indulge his passion for the outdoors. But Reagan longs to be back in California riding Tar Baby and making movies.

However, that choice is not his to make. He now has a wife and child to support, as well as the two children from his previous marriage. Reagan is paying the mortgage on his Malibu ranch and on the new home he and Nancy recently purchased near the Pacific Palisades. He is thousands of dollars in debt and owes a small fortune in back taxes, yet still he insists on living the life of a major movie star: dining at expensive restaurants such as Chasen's and doing little to curb his personal spending habits. Reagan tells friends he will not accept any part that is not up to his personal standards, when the truth is that quality scripts are no longer being sent his way. Instead, he is being asked to narrate public service documentaries for the grand fee of just $240.

So Vegas it is.

Ronald Reagan performs at 8:30 and 11:30 each night, with an extra 1:30 a.m. show on Saturdays. After the beer garden sketch, Reagan and the Continentals rush offstage for a costume change. Meanwhile, tall and handsome Royce and Ramon Blackburn step onstage to perform their song-and-dance act as the Blackburn Twins. The Honey Brothers trio follows with a slapstick acrobatic comedy routine that often finds them close to flying off the stage. Finally, Reagan closes out the performance standing alone, lit by a single spotlight, reciting a monologue about an actor's life.

It's a grind, but the money is extremely good. Reagan is not the only fading celebrity reduced to playing Las Vegas. At the Sands, a casino just down the Strip from the Last Frontier, former movie star Tallulah Bankhead appears onstage almost naked, also reciting dramatic monologues.

Throughout the show, Nancy Reagan sits alone at a small table nursing an ice water. Nancy, who has never smoked cigarettes, is enveloped by thick clouds of tobacco smoke, making it almost impossible for Reagan to see her from the stage. Yet he knows she is there. Despite the oppressive atmosphere, Nancy attends every show, perched in the same spot every night, surrounded by strangers.

Ronald Reagan's career slide has been hard on the ambitious Nancy. As she watches her husband do underwear jokes, she is determined to live a life of fame and fortune. Nancy Reagan was raised in privilege, but she now finds herself in debt. This is intolerable to her. Nancy's entry into Hollywood was facilitated by her mother's friendships with A-list actors Spencer Tracy and Walter Huston, and there was every expectation that her marriage to Reagan would continue to expand those high-level connections.

But now, nursing her ice water, she well understands that she and Ronnie are no longer welcome at the A-list parties. Despite the raucous crowd packing the cavernous Ramona Room on this Saturday night, there is abundant evidence that Reagan is finished in Hollywood. Nancy is three hundred miles away from Los Angeles, sitting alone in a gambling establishment designed to look like an Old West outpost. Outside, a cold winter wind blows across the wide-open desert. She and her husband are so far off the Hollywood grid that they might as well be in Siberia.

Yet Nancy Reagan clings to the hope that Las Vegas will soon lead to something better. America is fascinated by a new medium known as television, which beams entertainment directly inside the homes of people everywhere. As a result of its popularity, more than five thousand movie theaters have closed due to declining ticket sales. Ronald Reagan has done a dozen guest appearances on various television shows, but he is reluctant to pursue TV full-time. "The people who owned movie theaters thought that nobody would buy a ticket to see someone they could see at home in their living room for nothing," he will one day write.

Nancy is not as cautious. The Reagans need money. Television is the future. MCA, the talent agency representing Reagan, is pushing him in that direction—and so is his wife. A few months before heading to Las Vegas, Reagan reluctantly agreed to audition to host a show for the CBS television network titled *General Electric Theater*. It will air every Sunday night for a half hour at 9:00 p.m. The pay is $125,000 per year—more than enough to get the Reagans out of debt and keep the couple current on their mortgage payments. There is no assurance Reagan will get the job, as veteran actors Eddie Albert, Walter Pidgeon, and Kirk Douglas have also been approached for the position.

But should Ronald Reagan be offered the GE job, Nancy will make sure he takes it.

The time is now almost ten o'clock on this Saturday night. In a moment, Nancy will duck backstage to be with her husband for a quick bite of dinner between shows. She is determined to return home as soon as possible—and never come back. She cannot imagine a life of sitting alone each night for three hours of vaudeville, losing contact with Hollywood with each passing day, while minor film celebrities such as Lucille Ball are achieving vast fame and fortune on television.

Nancy Reagan stirs her ice water, hearing the cue that signals the end of the performance.

"You see things and say, 'Why?'" Reagan emotes from the stage, quoting the Irish playwright George Bernard Shaw. A single spotlight illuminates him, alone in his tuxedo, speaking to the audience as if each and every member was a personal friend.

"But I dream things that never were and say, 'Why not?'"

The Ramona Room is silent, but only for an instant. Then the audience leaps to their feet in a standing ovation. The showman grins from ear to ear, basking in what has become a nightly occurrence. If Reagan has learned one thing in Las Vegas, it is that he truly loves a live audience, and they love him back.

One week later, on March 5, 1954, Ronald Reagan turns down an offer to extend his run at the Last Frontier.

Television calls.

▬ ▬ ▬

"I'm Ronald Reagan speaking for General Electric," the actor says into the television microphone. The broadcast is live, taking place on December 12, 1954. "Tonight from Hollywood it is my pleasure to appear in a story entitled 'The Dark, Dark Hours,'" Reagan intones. "Young James Dean, one of the bright new actors in Hollywood, appears with me. And Constance Ford plays my wife on the *General Electric Theater*."

The GE theme music comes up as the camera pulls back. Reagan's introduction completed, the scene changes as the camera lens again zeroes in. Now viewers can see that Reagan is in costume. He's wearing pajamas and a bathrobe. In his role as the kindly Doctor Joe, Ronald Reagan answers the door in the middle of the night to find a thuggish James Dean, playing a character named Bud, imploring Doctor Joe to help a friend who has mysteriously suffered a gunshot wound.

Reagan's skepticism about television is clearly gone. His job as host of *GE Theater* gives him the opportunity to be seen in millions of homes each week, talking about the evening's program and sometimes acting in the dramatic presentation. He is lucky to be in the forefront of top motion picture actors who are now crossing over to television. James Dean—or Jimmy, as Reagan refers to him—is making his second appearance on *GE Theater,* just weeks after starring with former child actress Natalie Wood in an adaptation of Sherwood Anderson's short story "I'm a Fool." Neither Dean nor Wood knows they will soon play opposite each other in the landmark motion picture *Rebel Without a Cause.*

On this night, Reagan plays the hero to Dean's villain, the sort of dashing role that has eluded him for years in motion pictures. By the end of the brief teleplay, Reagan's character has not only wrestled a .32-caliber pistol away from the suicidal Bud but has shown a flash of anger and a knowledge of weaponry that hints at a much darker past. Reagan more than holds his own with Dean, a young actor being hailed as one of the best in Hollywood. The scene concludes with a scowling Reagan shoving a sobbing James Dean, then hugging his family.

Reagan's mastery as a thespian is complete. The viewer is lost in the rage exhibited by his character. The screen goes black. The credits roll.

Then, suddenly, the action shifts to a now-smiling and chipper Ronald Reagan sitting in his dressing room as he once again speaks into the camera. He is still wearing the pajamas and bathrobe, but gone is the brooding and angst so evident just a few seconds ago. Magically, he has returned to a confident, likable persona. "Well," he tells the audience, still winded from his physical interchange with Dean, "I hope you've enjoyed James Dean, Constance Ford, and the rest of us."

In fact, America enjoys *GE Theater* very much—and Ronald Reagan in particular. The show is a smash hit. Reagan's career is back on solid footing, as is his bank account.

But there is more to being the emcee of *GE Theater* than just introducing the night's show and an occasional spot of acting. General Electric is a giant corporation, with plants located in thirty-one states. As part of his contract, Reagan is required to travel to these factories as a goodwill ambassador. It is the thinking of GE's corporate leadership in New York that having the host of their signature television show intermingle with the workers will be good for morale. Afraid of flying, Reagan travels the country by train and then takes time to speak with and listen to each employee he meets.

"At first, all I did was walk the assembly lines at GE plants, or if it didn't interrupt production, I'd speak to them in small groups from a platform set up on the floor of the factories," he will later write.

Reagan is surprised to discover that this clause in his contract is just as fulfilling as his time before the camera. For with every factory he visits, he learns more about the economy and local governments, often accepting invitations to speak to civic groups. The political passion that has lain dormant since his stepping down as president of the Screen Actors Guild three years ago is now being rekindled. Reagan has come to believe that less governmental interference is the best path for America. The long train rides give him plenty of time to ruminate on this and to write careful speeches on stacks of three-by-five cards. He wraps a rubber band around each stack and saves them. Someday his words will be melded into a spectacular thesis that will become known as "The Speech."

It is "The Speech" that will not only change the course of Ronald Reagan's life but also make him a marked man.

On November 18, 1956, a somber Ronald Reagan opens the latest installment of *GE Theater* wearing a coat and tie. James Dean is dead, killed in a car accident one year ago. Due to popular public demand, *GE Theater* is rebroadcasting the production of "I'm a Fool," starring Dean and his *Rebel Without a Cause* costar Natalie Wood. Reagan speaks fondly of Dean but never flashes a smile or a hint of the trademark warmth that has become synonymous with the host of *GE Theater*. Jimmy Dean, he tells his television audience, was a young actor with unlimited potential.

Reagan's monologue on Dean signals that his years as a lightweight

Hollywood actor are coming to an end. He has begun an inexorable journey into ideological warfare and public service that no one, not even Ronald Reagan, could ever have seen coming.

Thus, Reagan's words about James Dean's unlimited potential can also be used to describe him.

6

⸺⦿⦿⦿⸺

As a twenty-eight-year-old mother of two is about to give birth to her third child, she and her husband are hoping that it will be a boy. They are affluent people, with a strong belief in the American dream.

If their child is indeed a boy, it will be named after his father, who, in addition to being president of Ardmore's Optimist Club, is a deeply religious and highly prosperous oilman. There will, one day, be whispers that he is connected to the Central Intelligence Agency, whispers that will be scrutinized very closely.

But all this is in the future, as the hoped-for baby boy enters the world.

Two miles across the Oklahoma town, a brand-new and modern Memorial Hospital is opening to the public. The newborn baby boy could very well have earned the honor of being the first child delivered in this state-of-the-art facility. That would be a mark of distinction, if only in Ardmore. But Jo Ann, as the mother is named, has opted to deliver at a hospital known as the Hardy Sanitarium, which will make the birth unique in another way. The opening of the new hospital will mean that Hardy, a two-story brick building that has been a vital part of Ardmore's fabric for forty-four years, will now close for good on this very day. Rather than being the first baby born in the new hospital, Jo Ann's baby will be the last born at Hardy.

So it is that John Warnock Hinckley Jr. is born in an obsolete mental hospital.

At first glance, the baby appears to be completely normal.

7

—⟨⟨⟨⟩⟩⟩—

The man with three years to live is nervous. Sen. John F. Kennedy steps to the podium and gazes out at eighty thousand Democrats, who are on their feet cheering loudly. The forty-three-year-old patrician from Massachusetts is perspiring lightly. His eyes scan the vast outdoor Los Angeles Coliseum, with its vaulting peristyle arches and Olympic cauldron signifying the Olympic Games held there in 1932. This is a spot reserved for conquering heroes, the same lofty perch where Gen. George S. Patton was welcomed on leave from World War II in 1945.

Just two days ago, the wealthy politician with movie star good looks received the necessary votes to secure the Democratic nomination for president. Now, as the national convention comes to a close with his acceptance speech, bedlam fills the Coliseum. Native Americans in full tribal regalia perform ritual dances on the football field, and low-flying TV news helicopters threaten to drown out Kennedy's words.

With many high-ranking Democrats looking on in person, and famous

Kennedy celebrity backers such as Henry Fonda and Frank Sinatra joining the festivities, John F. Kennedy begins his speech: "With a deep sense of duty and high resolve, I accept your nomination." Kennedy's words are clipped, and he speaks too fast. He has slept very little in the past week, filling his days and nights with political meetings, parties, and rendezvous with would-be girlfriends.* "I accept it with a full and grateful heart—without reservation—and with only one obligation—the obligation to devote every effort of body, mind and spirit to lead our Party back to victory and our Nation back to greatness."

Kennedy now launches into what will become known as the "New Frontier" speech, telling Americans, "Today our concern must be with that future. For the world is changing. The old era is ending. The old ways will not do." As he outlines his vision for the future, Kennedy launches a series of personal attacks on his likely Republican opponent, current vice president of the United States Richard Milhous Nixon.

▬ ▬ ▬

A continent away, Nixon himself cannot sleep. The CBS Television network is broadcasting Kennedy's speech live. Despite its being 11:00 p.m. in Washington, Nixon is riveted to the black-and-white TV in the family room of his Tudor-style home in the city's Wesley Heights neighborhood.[†] He endures every one of his opponent's assaults, taking each slight personally but also knowing that Kennedy does this all the time, as he is fond of hardball politics.

"Mr. Nixon may feel it is his turn now," Kennedy says somewhat sarcastically. Nixon, an acute observer, notes Kennedy's lean face is tense, despite the senator's attempts to appear at ease.

---

*Among them are Judith Campbell and the actress Marilyn Monroe. Campbell, who once dated Frank Sinatra, will go on to become the mistress of mobster Sam Giancana.

†The official residence of the vice president is now the U.S. Naval Observatory in northwestern Washington, DC. However, Congress did not make this official until 1974. Until that time, vice presidents maintained their own private residence. Nixon purchased the five-thousand-square-foot house on Forest Lane in 1957.

"After the New Deal and the Fair Deal—but before he deals, someone had better cut the cards."

The audience laughs.

Kennedy continues: "That 'someone' may be the millions of Americans who voted for President Eisenhower but balk at his would-be, self-appointed successor. For just as historians tell us that Richard I was not fit to fill the shoes of bold Henry II—and that Richard Cromwell was not fit to wear the mantle of his uncle—they might add in future years that Richard Nixon did not measure to the footsteps of Dwight D. Eisenhower."

Nixon is forty-seven years old, but his thick jowls and receding hairline make him look ten years older. He is a man of humble beginnings—unlike Kennedy, who was born into great wealth. In truth, JFK is closer to the commonly held image of a Republican—"fraternity presidents, tax-board assessors, community leaders, surgeons, Pullman porters, head nurses and the fat sons of rich fathers," as one writer described the party faithful.*

Nixon put himself through law school, served in the navy during World War II, then successfully ran for Congress in 1946. He believes strongly in the Republican virtues of fiscal conservatism, small government, and a powerful military. Nixon has a keen political mind. He has watched Kennedy's rise to power closely, recognizing for almost a year that JFK will be his likely opponent for the presidency. Now, mentally cataloguing each item in Kennedy's New Frontier agenda, knowing he must co-opt some of these themes and give them a Republican spin, Nixon concentrates heavily upon his rival.

Nixon's wife, Pat, and two young daughters, Tricia and Julie, are fast asleep, but he has no immediate plans to join them. He listens closely as Kennedy concludes his speech to thunderous applause.

"As we face the coming challenge, we too shall wait upon the Lord,

---

*The writer was Norman Mailer, in a piece for *Esquire* about the 1960 Democratic National Convention titled "Superman Comes to the Supermarket."

and ask that he renew our strength. Then shall we be equal to the test. Then we shall not be weary. And then we shall prevail."

Nixon is not impressed. Those eighty thousand Democrats might seem like a lot, but he well knows the Coliseum can hold many thousands more. Nixon also considers himself a better politician than his rival, and believes he can win the election if he can convince some Democrats to swing away from their party. Nixon needs crossover votes.

"In this campaign I make a prediction," he will tell the audience when he accepts the Republican nomination for the presidency thirteen days from now. "I say that just as in 1952 and 1956, millions of Democrats will join us—not because they are deserting their party, but because their party deserted them at Los Angeles two weeks ago."

Another man is also intensely watching John F. Kennedy.

Sitting in the living room of his lavish Pacific Palisades home, Ronald Reagan is disgusted by what he is hearing. At the conclusion of Kennedy's speech, Reagan gets up and wanders to the floor-to-ceiling windows overlooking the spectacular view of the distant lights of Los Angeles.

Reagan's mind is made up: he will cast his vote for Richard Nixon.

This will come as no surprise to anyone in Hollywood. While still technically a Democrat, Reagan has been heavily influenced by the more conservative views espoused by his wife, Nancy, who grew up in an extremely Republican household and likes to brag that she has been reading the right-leaning *National Review* since its first issue.*

The motion picture industry is deeply divided between liberals and conservatives. A minority of actors such as Reagan and John Wayne openly espouse anticommunist, small-government views. But a much larger contingent, led by singer Frank Sinatra and his Rat Pack, have fallen under

---

*November 19, 1955. The *National Review* was founded by William F. Buckley Jr., a wealthy former CIA operative who believed that conservative commentary was all too often missing from American political debate.

John F. Kennedy's spell. This group includes actors Paul Newman, Joanne Woodward, Elizabeth Taylor, Cary Grant, and Angie Dickinson. While some keep a distance between their personal and professional lives, Sinatra, in particular, has made it clear that he despises not only Ronald Reagan's views but also Reagan himself. "Dumb and dangerous," Sinatra calls Reagan, "and so simpleminded." The singer takes his vitriol a step further by also attacking Nancy Reagan, calling her "a dope with fat ankles who could never make it as an actress."

Despite his career resurgence on television, and the wealth that has allowed him to build this spectacular four-bedroom, 4,700-square-foot home at the end of a long private road in the Pacific Palisades, Ronald Reagan and his wife have become social pariahs. They are rarely invited to the best parties, and even when a dinner offer comes their way, Reagan has a bad habit of lecturing all within earshot about politics. Nancy, for her part, does not help matters by appearing condescending. "We got stuck with them at a dinner party, and it was awful," the wife of screenwriter Philip Dunne once remembered. "Nancy is so assessing—she always looks you up and down before she deigns to speak."

Turning away from the window, Reagan walks past the large stone fireplace and into his small corner office. He sits down and takes pen and paper from a drawer. General Electric has taken great pride in turning his home into "The House of the Future" and has capitalized on that concept by having Reagan film commercials for the *General Electric Theater* from his own kitchen, surrounded by a GE toaster, dishwasher, and electric garbage disposal. But no modern gadget will help Reagan perform the simple task of writing a letter.

Ronald Reagan is not afraid to mail his thoughts to anyone who will read them—as well as many who don't want to. Letter writing from his home office has become the nexus for Reagan's personal conservative movement, and with each letter he sends, his political ambition advances.

With Kennedy's words still echoing in his mind, Reagan picks up his pen and begins writing a letter to Richard Nixon.

"Dear Mr. Vice President," the letter begins. "I know this is presumptuous of me, but I'm passing on some thoughts after viewing the convention here in L.A. . . . I heard a frightening call to arms. Unfortunately, he is a powerful speaker with an appeal to the emotions. He leaves little doubt that his idea of the 'challenging new world' is one in which the Federal Government will grow bigger and do more, and of course spend more."

Ronald Reagan and Richard Nixon first became acquainted back in 1947, when Reagan appeared before Congress. They rekindled that relationship in 1950, when Reagan campaigned for Nixon's opponent in the race for a U.S. Senate seat from California. They've since become friends, and Nixon is actually the reason Reagan still maintains his Democratic Party membership. When Reagan told Nixon he was planning to switch parties in time for the 1960 election, the canny Nixon said he could do more for the Republican Party by remaining a Democrat and using his fame to convince other Democrats to cross party lines with him.

So Reagan remains a Democrat—at least for now. He has no idea that Nixon actually considers him "shallow" and of "limited mental capacity." But even if he did know that, it might not matter. Ronald Reagan simply wants to see John F. Kennedy and his liberal dogma defeated.

Reagan continues his letter: "I know there must be some short-sighted people within the Republican Party who will advise that the Republicans should try to 'out-liberal' him. In my opinion this would be fatal . . . I don't pose as an infallible pundit, but I have a strong feeling that the 20 million nonvoters in this country just might be conservatives."

But Nixon is not planning to take Reagan's advice. In one week's time, he will fly to New York and meet with Republican governor Nelson Rockefeller. After a dinner of lamb chops in Rocky's Fifth Avenue apartment, the two men will stay up all night drafting a more liberal Republican platform. The "Treaty of Fifth Avenue," as it will be dubbed, is designed to appeal to independent and Democratic voters.

Reagan concludes the letter, scalding John F. Kennedy: "Under the tousled boyish haircut is still old Karl Marx—first launched a century ago.

There is nothing new in the idea of a government being Big Brother to us all. Hitler called his 'State Socialism.'"*

Signing the letter "Ronnie Reagan," the actor fervently hopes his offer to campaign for Richard Nixon will be accepted. Though Nixon will lose the 1960 presidential election by less than one percentage point of all votes polled, Reagan will speak on his behalf whenever asked.

▬ ▬ ▬

"Have you registered as a Republican yet?" shouts a voice from the audience. The year is 1962. As Ronald Reagan predicted, Richard Nixon's attempt to "out-liberal" John Kennedy is among the factors that cost him the presidency. Now Reagan is once again campaigning for Nixon, this time as the former vice president runs for governor of California.

Reagan stands before a small crowd of Republican supporters. The fund-raising event is being held in a house just down the street from his Pacific Palisades home. Reagan knows many of those in attendance but does not recognize this voice speaking to him in the middle of the living room.

"Have you registered as a Republican yet?" she asks a second time.

"Well, no. I haven't yet. But I intend to."

The truth is Ronald Reagan no longer has any reason to remain a Democrat. His conservative affiliations have become so notorious that General Electric recently fired him as a spokesman, under pressure from some powerful liberal concerns. So, once again, Ronald Reagan is an unemployed actor searching for his next paycheck. He has absolutely, positively nothing to lose by switching political parties.

---

*Reagan's animosity toward John F. Kennedy will continue even after the young president is shot dead by an assassin's bullet. On November 22, 1963, just a few hours after JFK is assassinated, Ronald and Nancy Reagan will hold a dinner. "Why should we cancel our dinner party just because John F. Kennedy died? Don't be silly," Nancy Reagan told one guest who called to ask if the party was still on. The man, a film producer and former U.S. Army brigadier general named Frank McCarthy, arrived to find Ronald Reagan, John Wayne, and actor Robert Taylor socializing. As a film producer, McCarthy will go on to win the Academy Award for Best Picture in 1970 for *Patton*.

"I'm a registrar," the woman says, standing up and walking toward Reagan with a slip of paper in her hand.

She hands the paper to Reagan. It is a registration form. The woman has already filled in all the blanks, meaning that with a simple swipe of his pen, Ronald Reagan will officially become a Republican.

The registrar hands Reagan a pen.

He signs the form without a moment's hesitation.

As the room erupts in applause, Reagan smiles. There will come a time when few will even remember his thirty years as a Democrat. "I did not leave the Democratic Party," he will tell people, borrowing a line from Richard Nixon. "The Democratic Party left me."

Now, in the first moments of his new life as a Republican, Ronald Reagan gets back to the task at hand.

"Now, where was I?" he asks, before continuing the speech he has been perfecting for the last eight years.

A bitter Richard Nixon strides purposefully onto the stage at the Beverly Hilton Hotel in Los Angeles. The date is November 7, 1962. Despite Ronald Reagan's campaign efforts, Nixon has just lost the election for governor of California, an election he assumed he would win easily.* The governorship was meant to be a job that would keep Nixon in the public eye until 1968. He believed that John F. Kennedy would be president for two terms, so he would wait until then to tender another presidential bid.

Now an exhausted and angry Richard Nixon faces the harsh reality that he is finished. It will be a political near impossibility to recover from this loss.

But before he goes, Nixon has a few words he would like to say.

His face lined with tension, Nixon forces a smile as he looks at the reporters assembled before him. There is no podium, just a cluster of

---

*Polls showed that Richard Nixon would win the 1962 California gubernatorial election. However, Nixon failed to reach out to the more conservative elements of the Republican Party, a blunder that cost him dearly. The incumbent, Pat Brown, won in a landslide, garnering 52 percent of the popular vote to Nixon's 47 percent.

microphones. He is nervous about the speech he is about to give but is attempting to appear jovial. The forty-nine-year-old Nixon considers the media to be his personal enemy and believes that after years of frustrated silence, the time has come to tell them off.

Nixon digs his right hand deep into the pocket of his suit pants. An elaborate chandelier hovers to one side of the room. Reporters sit at a long table in front of him, poised with pencil and paper to write down his words. To his right, television cameras and newspaper photographers prepare to capture this moment of defeat.

"For sixteen years," Nixon begins, "you've had an opportunity to attack me, and I think I've given as good as I've taken."

A hush fills the small ballroom. Nixon has just crossed a line. It is one thing to confront a journalist about his coverage in private, but to do so in public is taboo. And thanks to all those television cameras, this verbal assault is now being filmed for posterity. Pencils scribble frantically as the reporters eagerly await Nixon's next words.

"I will leave you gentlemen now. And, uh . . . You will now write it. You will interpret it. That's your right. But as I leave you, I want you to know—just think how much you're going to be missing. You won't have Nixon to kick around anymore, because gentlemen, this is my last press conference."

Fifty-nine seconds. That's all it takes. Nixon does not field questions. He is whisked from the room and walks quickly out of the hotel, stopping only to shake the hand of a front-desk clerk before stepping into the front seat of a waiting car.

He is thrilled to have gotten the last word.

Yet fate will allow him many more press conferences. And if Richard Nixon thinks the media have gotten the best of him in the past, that is nothing compared to what they will do to him in the future.

Two years later, television cameras again capture a historic moment. The night is October 27, 1964. Ronald Reagan is eagerly anticipating watching himself on television. The occasion is a speech he taped one week

earlier in support of Republican presidential nominee Barry Goldwater.*
At first, Goldwater's people wanted Reagan to deliver the speech live. But
Reagan is by now a canny politician, and although he would have liked
the spontaneous applause and laughter that he knew each line would
engender, he didn't want to take any chances on making a mistake—thus
the live scenario was scrapped.

"Nancy and I went to the home of some friends to watch the broadcast," he will later write of the night that changed his life. Reagan's presentation for Goldwater was so successful that scribes simply dubbed
Reagan's words "The Speech."

Reagan realizes his career is now in public life. After a seven-year
break between films, he has made one last motion picture. He played a
villain in *The Killers*, a movie that sank without a trace at the box office.[†]

Even though the speech is a sensation, Barry Goldwater's advisers did
not want Reagan's talk to air. With the election just one week away, they
were terrified that the conservative themes he was espousing would drive
some voters into the Democratic camp.

As the Reagans sit side by side before the television set in the den of
their friends' home, the black-and-white screen flickers, showing him standing behind a podium draped with patriotic bunting. The edited presentation then cuts to the back of the room, allowing the nation to see the
audience awaiting his words. Some hold placards. Others wear cowboy
hats. All are dressed informally and are meant to look like a homey cross-
section of the American public.

This works perfectly with Reagan's homespun delivery, the gentle,

---

*One young supporter of Goldwater, and an active member of the Young Republican
movement, was a seventeen-year-old Chicago-area young lady named Hillary Rodham.
She was fond of wearing a cowgirl outfit and a straw hat emblazoned with the Goldwater
campaign's AuH_2O slogan (Au is the periodic symbol for gold; H_2O the symbol for water).
Shortly afterward, she would switch her party allegiance to the Democrats, perhaps under
pressure from her liberal friends at Wellesley College.

†Reagan's previous film was 1957's *Hellcats of the Navy*, which costarred Nancy Reagan.
Their final on-camera performance as a couple was the 1958 GE *Theater* episode with the
prescient title "A Turkey for the President."

Reagan in The Killers,
his last movie role

parental voice that he perfected at those GE factories, after-dinner speeches, and countless other conservative venues across the country. "Unlike most television programs, the performer hasn't been provided with a script," he assures the audience as he begins. "As a matter of fact, I have been permitted to choose my own words and discuss my own ideas regarding the choice that we face in the next few weeks."

Then Reagan begins a twenty-seven-minute soliloquy on the virtues of the America in which he truly believes. The Republican presidential nominee, Barry Goldwater, is hardly mentioned. Reagan delivers a dazzling speech full of allusions to the American dream, fiscal conservatism, and small government. He speaks of freedom and the Founding Fathers as if they were brand-new concepts that Americans need to embrace immediately. He talks about poverty, farmers, the Vietnam War, Cuban immigrants, and American veterans. There is no hesitation in Reagan's voice, no fumbling with the words of his self-written script, for this is the summation of what he has believed for years.

"You and I have a rendezvous with destiny," he concludes, his voice at its most earnest and inspirational. "We'll preserve for our children this, the last best hope of man on earth, or we'll sentence them to take the last step into a thousand years of darkness."

≡ ≡ ≡

Ronald and Nancy Reagan drive home in their Lincoln Continental after watching the filmed speech. The fifty-three-year-old Reagan is nervous, unsure if his talk has been a success. Others who watched the speech with them insist that Reagan did his job well, but he is still uncertain.

The October night is partly cloudy, with temperatures in the low seventies. The Reagans park their car, then walk inside the house and go to bed, still not knowing if the speech has been a success or a flop.

It is midnight when the bedside phone rings. The Goldwater campaign is on the other end. Reagan's speech has been such a smash that people from all across the country have called in, pledging support and money for the candidate. "A Time for Choosing," as the speech will come to be known, will be described by reporters as "the most successful national political debut since William Jennings Bryan electrified the 1896 Democratic convention with the 'Cross of Gold' speech."*

---

*Delivered at the Democratic National Convention in Chicago on July 9, 1896. Bryan was a thirty-six-year-old former Nebraska congressman when he delivered the address. His oration was so powerful that the audience screamed in agreement, waving hats and canes. Some audience members threw their coats into the air. The speech, which advocated the use of silver coinage to increase American prosperity, was so effective that Bryan won the nomination. He ultimately lost the general election to Republican candidate William McKinley (who was shot by an assassin's bullet on September 6, 1901, died eight days later, and was succeeded in office by Theodore Roosevelt). William Jennings Bryan ran for the presidency twice more and later in life supplemented his income by delivering the "Cross of Gold" speech during lecture appearances. Bryan is also well known as being the foil for famed attorney Clarence Darrow during the Scopes Monkey Trial, which argued the legality of teaching evolution in schools. Bryan, a devout Presbyterian, argued against the practice. He died in his sleep five days after winning the case.

*Nancy Reagan and Ronald Reagan after winning
the Republican nomination for governor of California in 1966*

"That speech was one of the most important milestones of my life," Reagan will later remember. Until that day, he had been skeptical of any suggestion that he run for political office. Now that is about to change. "A Time for Choosing" will turn out to be, in his words, "another one of those unexpected turns that led me onto a path I never expected to take."

8

―――∾∾∾――

ROTUNDA
STATE CAPITOL BUILDING
SACRAMENTO, CALIFORNIA
JANUARY 2, 1967
12:11 A.M.

Despite making fifty-three films, Ronald Reagan has never known a moment of drama quite like the one he is experiencing right now. Dressed in a black suit with a thin dark tie, he stands, head held high and feet planted twelve inches apart, like a conquering hero from the Western movies he loves so much. His left hand rests on a Bible. A hulking bald man stands in front of him. A glance to his left shows Nancy Reagan prim and straight at his elbow, beaming after plastic surgery to repair her drooping eyelids. Thirty-two television cameras light Reagan's face. "America the Beautiful" echoes in his head, thanks to a choir from the University of Southern California, who serenaded him at the stroke of midnight.

This is Ronald Reagan's greatest moment, a time when at long last he gets to play the leading man. Just two years ago he was hosting yet another television show.* Now he is the newly elected governor of California. There's not a single writer in Hollywood who could have scripted this better.

Reagan raises his right hand, and the swearing-in begins. One hundred fifty guests are closely watching him, waiting for the trademark smile and nod of the head he has used to such populist effect while campaigning.

Yet there is one problem this early morning. The man facing him from two feet away is an annoyance. California Supreme Court justice Marshall McComb is reflecting light off his bald skull directly into Ronald Reagan's eyes. In this, his finest hour, Reagan is forced to squint, barely able to see the man to whom he is speaking.

"I, Ronald Reagan, do solemnly swear that I will faithfully defend the Constitution of the United States," he pledges, repeating the words that McComb has just recited to him. Reagan's voice fills the Rotunda, bouncing off the marble floors and the life-size statue of Spanish queen Isabella looking over him.

Reagan lets his gaze float out over the room. It is impossible not to be distracted. Men, women, and children surround him, watching the proceedings with hushed reverence. Many are standing on tiptoe to better witness the historic moment.

These are Reagan's people. They also represent something of an anachronism. America is descending into turmoil, torn apart by the Vietnam War, a deep racial divide, drug use, and a sexual revolution. But in this room, at this moment, Reagan sees none of that conflict.

Many filling this towering ceremonial space are as conservative as he is. The men wear crisp dark suits. Their hair is cut short, in sharp contrast to the shoulder-length locks so many men are beginning to wear these days. The knee-length dresses worn by the women are a throwback to the more formal styles of the 1950s, and nothing at all like the miniskirts that ride high up a woman's thigh and leave little to the imagination. Recently, when Ronald and Nancy Reagan visited their fourteen-year-old daughter,

---

Death Valley Days, a Western-themed production that ran for 452 episodes from 1952 to 1970. Reagan was the second of four men who hosted the show. He also acted in eight episodes.

Patti, at her boarding school and discovered her in one such short skirt, Nancy was so furious that she stormed out and sat in the car.

Reagan has nothing against the miniskirt. He is still fond of admiring the ladies. "He liked to look at women, no doubt about it," one of his aides will one day recall. "But if he did anything about it, he was very discreet." In truth, Reagan's days of womanizing are mostly behind him. The politically reinvented Reagan prefers to put forth a strong paternal public image.

Of course, no man is perfect. And Reagan still possesses idiosyncrasies that must be kept quiet, such as his trust in astrologers. Both he and Nancy use stargazers in order to divine the future. The conservative folks who admire the Reagans might be troubled if they knew.

Even the details of the swearing-in ceremony have been influenced by Reagan's astrologers. Normally, the gubernatorial inauguration takes place in broad daylight, but Ronald Reagan's stargazers have noted that Jupiter is visible in the nighttime sky at this precise midnight hour. The solar system's largest planet is thought to be a harbinger of fame, prosperity, and power. Rather than tempt fate by holding the inauguration in the morning, when Jupiter is absent, Ronald and Nancy Reagan insist that the ceremony be held at midnight, to reap the full benefit of Jupiter's largesse. This is why a state supreme court justice, chaplain, dozens of members of the press, and a select gathering of invited benefactors and dignitaries now stand in a broad circle around Ronald Wilson Reagan and his beloved wife at this witching hour.*

Reagan knows that in their hearts some in the crowd might doubt his ability to lead, thinking him just an actor. He is also well aware that his political views are at odds with current trends in American and California politics, thus making him a dinosaur in the eyes of many beyond the curved walls of the Rotunda. Reagan's victory notwithstanding, the landslide loss by Barry Goldwater in the 1964 presidential election makes it

---

*When confronted many years later, Ronald Reagan will deny that astrologers played a role in his gubernatorial swearing-in, stating that the unusual midnight ceremony was due to the fact that then governor Pat Brown was making last-minute bureaucratic appointments.

abundantly clear that conservative Republican values are falling out of fashion.

As Justice McComb concludes the lengthy recitation of the oath, Ronald Reagan is keen to begin his new journey. He is absorbing a significant pay cut so that he might hold this position. The forty-four-thousand-dollar governor's salary is so low that the Reagans have had to sell the Malibu ranch.

That is a hardship Reagan will have to endure.*

For, on this cold January night, Ronald Reagan has a secret: The governorship will not be enough. One day Reagan hopes to be president of the United States.

His astrologers think it might be in the stars.

Four months after his inauguration, Ronald Reagan is facing a CBS Television camera in Los Angeles, about to participate in a debate entitled "The Image of America and the Youth of the World." It is 10:00 p.m. at the CBS headquarters in New York, 7:00 p.m. in Los Angeles, and 3:00 a.m. in London, England, where a panel of international college students sits ready to ask questions of Ronald Reagan and his fellow panelist, liberal senator Robert F. Kennedy.

The program will be broadcast live around the world.

Kennedy is in Paris and is the more seasoned political professional. Boyishly handsome at the age of forty-one, RFK is legendary, having served as attorney general under his late brother, the assassinated president John F. Kennedy. In 1964, Bobby, as he is known, was elected U.S. senator from New York. He is cocky and powerful, and tonight he is confident that he will get the best of Ronald Reagan. Kennedy's suit and tie are dark blue;

---

*Reagan's sadness about the sale of the ranch to Twentieth Century–Fox in 1966 was tempered by the $1.9 million selling price, which made him a millionaire for the first time. The property is now part of Malibu Creek State Park, but during the time that Twentieth Century–Fox owned it, the ranch was the location for many motion pictures, including *Butch Cassidy and the Sundance Kid*. It was also the location for the television show *M*A*S*H*.

his demeanor is nonchalant. He thinks so little of Reagan's mental prowess that he barely studied for the intellectual debate.

Reagan is far more cautious. He knows that fifteen million Americans will likely watch this broadcast, as will millions more around the world. So he has prepared for weeks, memorizing statistics about the Vietnam War and the history of Southeast Asia. He cannot afford to appear ill prepared or to let Kennedy make a fool of him, and that concern is etched deeply in Reagan's face. Though he is tanned and rested, his trademark smile is nowhere to be seen. In fact, gazing into the camera, his eyes are cold.

This debate is personal to Reagan. Unbeknownst to the vast audience, he believes it was Bobby Kennedy who pressured General Electric into firing him as host of *GE Theater* back in 1962. RFK allegedly told the giant corporation that no government contracts would come their way if they allowed the conservative Reagan to remain host.*

Ronald Reagan is not a vengeful man, but his memory is long, and now he desperately wants to win this contest and humiliate Kennedy.

"I'm Charles Collingwood," says the CBS host, beginning the proceedings. "And this is *Town Meeting of the World,* the latest in an occasional series of trans-Atlantic confrontations that's been going on [sic] ever since communication satellites made them possible. With me here in the studio of the BBC in London are a group of young people, university students from—one from the United States, but the rest of them from Europe, Africa and Asia. They are all attending universities in Great Britain. They have ideas, all of them, sometimes provocative ones, about the United States, its role and its image."†

---

*Reagan might also have been fired from *GE Theater* because he was speaking out against the Tennessee Valley Authority, in which General Electric had a financial interest. And there was also a drop in the ratings, due to *Bonanza* being moved to a Sunday night slot opposite *GE Theater.* The popular Western won the top spot easily.

†The lone American student on the panel is a former Princeton basketball player and Olympic gold medalist currently attending Oxford University on a Rhodes scholarship. Bill Bradley is twenty-three years old and will one day go on to play ten seasons in the National Basketball Association and serve three terms in the U.S. Senate. He was called upon to speak just once during the Kennedy-Reagan debate, and his comments were notable for his civil tone and a failed attempt to defuse the arrogant hostility of many of his fellow panelists.

The dialogue begins, and the students in London immediately attack. "Senator Kennedy," asks a young man with short bangs, "I'd like to ask you what you think of Dean Rusk's recent claim that the effect of anti–Vietnam War demonstrations in the States may actually be to prolong the war rather than to shorten it."

Kennedy responds timidly, his voice soft. He plans on running for president in one year and is courting the votes of college students who might be watching the broadcast. "I certainly don't think that's why the war is continuing," he says, giving tacit approval to the antiwar protests that some Americans see as unpatriotic. Kennedy glances away from the camera as he talks, looking at notes.

But when it is Reagan's turn to speak, he looks bold and confident: "I definitely think that the demonstrations are prolonging the war," he says emphatically, and then lists the reasons.

Just like that, Reagan is in charge. He dominates the rest of the debate, making Kennedy appear weak and passive. Kennedy does not help matters, allowing the panel to interrogate him as if he were some misguided professor. Sensing weakness, the students grow bolder.

"Answer my question," one demands, cutting RFK off in midsentence. When Kennedy gives him a lengthy response, the student once again interrupts, insisting that Kennedy has not answered the question.

Rather than appear indignant, however, Kennedy mildly accepts the rebuke, despite the fact that he is seething inside. "Who the fuck got me into this?" the deflated Kennedy will demand of an aide as soon as the show ends.

Ronald Reagan gently scolds the students when they interrupt or their statistics are incorrect. An increasingly bolder Reagan espouses freedom, democracy, and the American way. Kennedy apologizes for American foreign policy "mistakes," but Reagan refuses to do so. There is no fear in his eyes as he speaks, no hesitation or hint of backing down when the students harass and attack. A *Newsweek* reporter will write of this evening that "Reagan effortlessly reeled off more facts and quasi-facts about the Vietnam conflict than anyone suspected he ever knew."

As the broadcast enters its second half hour, Reagan veers away from

Vietnam and waxes poetic about the greatness of the United States. His tone is evangelical. Most of the students on the panel have spent the hour painting America as the root of all global evil, and it is to them that he preaches most fervently.

Reagan's hatred of communism has not abated one bit since his days as president of the Screen Actors Guild. If anything, his convictions have become more intense: "I think it would be very admirable if the Berlin Wall, which was built in direct contravention to a treaty, should disappear. I think this would be a step toward peace and toward self-determination for all people, if it were."

As the broadcast winds down, it is Reagan who gets the last word. Among the students on the panel is a young man from the Soviet Union, who lives in a totalitarian state. Reagan's words are aimed directly at him. "I believe the highest aspiration of man should be individual freedom and the development of the individual. That there is a sacredness to individual rights!"

With Reagan's words ringing worldwide, Charles Collingwood ends the broadcast.

In Los Angeles, Ronald Reagan removes the earpiece that has allowed him to hear the students' questions from London. Unlike after the "Time for Choosing" speech of three years ago, there is no question in Reagan's mind that this night has been a triumph. "Political rookie Reagan," *Newsweek* will write, "left old campaigner Kennedy blinking when the session ended."

In Paris, Bobby Kennedy storms out of the studio into the predawn light. Furious at his embarrassing performance, he turns to an aide: "Never again put me on the stage with that son of a bitch."

One year later, it is Bobby Kennedy who is triumphant. Shortly after midnight, he briskly strides through the kitchen of the Ambassador Hotel in Los Angeles, on his way to meet the press. He has just won the highly coveted California Democratic presidential primary. Lyndon Johnson, the

Democrat currently serving as president, announced two months ago that he would not seek another term in office. This leaves the door wide open for the popular and handsome Kennedy. At the age of forty-two, he appears to be just five months away from being elected president.

A crowd of enthusiastic supporters follows Kennedy through the kitchen. Among them are the famous writer George Plimpton and NFL player "Rosey" Grier. An ecstatic Kennedy stops to shake the hand of an immigrant busboy, unaware that an assassin stands just a few feet away.

Suddenly, shots ring out. Bobby Kennedy is hit and immediately slumps to the concrete floor. A single bullet has passed through his brain, entering just behind the right ear. Two other bullets have pierced his upper torso. He is an athletic man who has always taken care of his physical health. And for twenty-six long hours, Kennedy fights for his life. But at 1:44 a.m. on June 6, 1968, Robert Francis Kennedy loses that fight.

Ronald Reagan is on television the day after the RFK assassination, speaking to talk show host Joey Bishop on ABC. "The enemy sits in Moscow," Reagan says, because he believes that it was agents of the Soviet Union who killed Robert Kennedy, as well as his brother John F. Kennedy in 1963. "The actions of the enemy led to, and precipitated, the tragedy of last night."

Four months later, Ronald Reagan smells of Royal Briar cologne as he steps out into the night. A blast of unseasonably cold air chills him as he walks toward the swimming pool, a gin and orange juice cocktail in hand. As on most weekends, Reagan and Nancy have flown down from Sacramento to spend a few days at their Pacific Palisades home in Los Angeles.

But on this night, Nancy has not joined Reagan at this political event in Studio City, a few miles from his home.

Reagan sees a young girl sitting alone by the pool. She appears to be distraught. Slowly, he walks over to see if she is all right.

In truth, it is Ronald Reagan who needs a few kind words. Reagan's first year in office has been a challenge. His personal and political views are not popular. His first real battle came when members of a radical group of African Americans known as the Black Panther Party occupied the California State Capitol Building in Sacramento. In accordance with the Second Amendment to the U.S. Constitution, which allows citizens the right to bear arms, these twenty-four men and six women openly displayed the .357 Magnum pistols and 12-gauge shotguns they carried. California law states that carrying weapons openly in public is legal, and the Panthers were in Sacramento to argue against impending legislation that would revoke this right. The protest ended peacefully, but not before Republicans in the state legislature pushed through a bill that made gun control in California a reality. And it is the gun-loving Reagan himself who gladly signed the bill into law.

A few months later, in a controversy that trails him almost all the way through his first year in the governor's office, Reagan learned that two of his top aides are engaging in homosexual relations. He tries to defuse the situation by quietly letting the men resign. Homosexuality is still illegal in many areas of the country, and there is very little public support for gay rights in most parts of California. But Reagan's Hollywood background infused him with a tolerance for homosexuals. While he will go on record as condemning gay behavior, he is not personally bothered by it. In fact, Carroll Righter, an astrologer on whom he and Nancy depend, is openly gay.

The matter might have subsided if *Newsweek* magazine had not run an item on October 31, 1967, that made Reagan's problem into a national scandal. Making matters even worse, Reagan lied about it, telling the press that the homosexual aides were not fired for their private conduct. By the time the scandal died down, there were many who believed that Reagan's hopes of running for president in 1968 were long gone.

And they were right. In May 1967 it appeared that the battle for president of the United States might be a contest between Ronald Reagan and either Robert Kennedy or Lyndon Johnson. Now Johnson is done, Kennedy is dead, and Reagan's presidential hopes have vanished. In the ultimate irony, the Republican nomination goes to Richard Nixon. In just a few weeks' time, Americans will elect Nixon president over Hubert Humphrey.*

▰ ▰ ▰

Now, on this October night in 1968, taking a break from the Studio City party to clear his head by the pool, Ronald Reagan is relaxed and loose. It helps that Nancy is not here. As much as Reagan adores his wife, she is extremely jealous. Nancy gets outraged if he so much as hugs a woman he knows. Reagan has to be very careful in Nancy's presence.

The young woman sitting before him is just eighteen years old. She looks at Reagan but does not recognize him as the governor. Perhaps feeling some sympathy, Reagan sits down.

The girl's name is Patricia Taylor. Years later she will try to capitalize on her relationship with Ronald Reagan by taping interviews suggesting that intimacy soon followed. Reagan's personal behavior as governor, however, is so exemplary that few question his clearly stated traditional values.

---

*The 1968 election was one of the closest in American history. Nixon beat Democratic nominee Hubert Humphrey by winning thirty-two states and 301 electoral votes. The results were so close that Nixon was not assured of victory for more than fifteen hours after the polls closed on Election Day.

9

WHITE HOUSE
WASHINGTON, DC
AUGUST 9, 1974
7:30 A.M.

A barefoot Richard Nixon wears blue pajamas as he eats his breakfast of grapefruit, wheat germ, and milk. He is alone in his bedroom, having just walked upstairs from the White House kitchen, where he ordered the morning meal. His forty-five-year-old Cuban-born butler Manolo Sanchez delivered the food, opened the drapes, laid out Nixon's clothes for the day, then left the president alone to eat.

Nixon does not sleep with his wife, Pat.* He is prone to talking during the night and gets up at all hours because of insomnia. It's not unusual that Pat Nixon does not sleep with her husband in the White House. The Kennedys and Johnsons before him did not sleep in the same bed, either. Pat

---

*"Pat" Nixon was born Thelma Catherine Ryan in 1912. She earned the nickname Pat as a child because of her family's Irish heritage and because she was born the day before St. Patrick's Day. She is older than her husband by ten months.

Nixon has an adjoining bedroom, separated from her husband's sleeping quarters by a door.

Nixon's high-ceilinged chamber has a fireplace in one corner and two large south-facing windows with views of the Washington Monument. Outside, the morning dawns muggy and overcast. This same bedroom once housed presidents Wilson, Harding, Roosevelt, Truman, Eisenhower, Kennedy, and Johnson.* World-changing decisions have been made within these walls. Yet none of those men has come to the shattering conclusion that Nixon reached just yesterday. In fact, none of the thirty-five men to hold the office of president has ever done what Richard Nixon is about to do.

Nixon strips off his pajamas, showers, and changes into the dark blue suit, white shirt, and maroon tie that Sanchez has laid out for him. He is just moments away from walking downstairs to the Oval Office and affixing his signature to a one-line document: "I hereby resign the Office of President of the United States."

The scandal that would bring down a president begins over two years earlier, on June 17, 1972. Richard Nixon is seeking reelection. His first four years in office have been a triumph, marked by significant efforts to end the war in Vietnam and the historic moment when American astronauts Neil Armstrong and Buzz Aldrin walked on the moon. Sixty-two percent of Americans approve of Nixon's job performance. No matter whom the Democrats select to run against him, he should win the election handily.

Yet the paranoid Nixon is not taking any chances. His reelection committee is undertaking a stealth campaign of political espionage to defeat the Democrats. This operation includes planting eavesdropping devices

---

*Nixon slept in the very bed used by Truman and Eisenhower. It was not until Gerald Ford's residence that a president and First Lady slept in the same bedroom. Pat Nixon's room was officially known as the master bedroom of the White House and was where Abraham Lincoln slept. The room we know as the Lincoln Bedroom was actually an office used by Lincoln and is often said to be the scene of ghost sightings. The White House was completely gutted during the 1948–52 renovation.

in the offices of the Democratic National Committee at the Watergate Hotel complex. On June 18, 1972, the *Washington Post* publishes a curious dispatch noting arrests made at the DNC's offices:

> Five men, one of whom said he is a former employee of the Central Intelligence Agency, were arrested at 2:30 a.m. yesterday in what authorities described as an elaborate plot to bug the offices of the Democratic National Committee here.
>
> Three of the men were native-born Cubans and another was said to have trained Cuban exiles for guerrilla activity after the 1961 Bay of Pigs invasion.
>
> They were surprised at gunpoint by three plain-clothes officers of the metropolitan police department in a sixth floor office at the plush Watergate, 2600 Virginia Ave., NW, where the Democratic National Committee occupies the entire floor.
>
> There was no immediate explanation as to why the five suspects would want to bug the Democratic National Committee offices or whether or not they were working for any other individuals or organizations.

But as the media would reveal over the course of the next 852 days, the Watergate burglars were ultimately working for one very specific individual: Richard Milhous Nixon.

▰ ▰ ▰

More than three thousand miles away, California governor Ronald Reagan is well into his sixth year in office. Reagan has been extraordinarily successful, despite having survived a recall effort during his first term.* Reagan has achieved much as California's leader, cracking down on violent student protests against the Vietnam War, successfully raising taxes in

---

*An anti-Reagan group led by organized labor and the California teachers' unions failed to collect the signatures necessary to recall Governor Reagan. The only successful recall attempt in that state occurred in 2003, when Governor Gray Davis was removed from office and replaced by Hollywood actor Arnold Schwarzenegger.

order to balance the budget, and then issuing a tax rebate. In October 1971, Reagan traveled on one of his four trips to Asia as a special envoy of Richard Nixon to calm foreign heads of state who were nervous about the thawing of relations between the United States and China.

Meantime, Nancy Reagan has also prospered as California's First Lady. She has come to enjoy the trappings of power, such as private jet travel, an aide to carry her purse, and the surprise friendship of singer Frank Sinatra. Once an enemy, Sinatra has become a big supporter of Governor Reagan and a close personal confidant to Nancy.*

Even though her husband has stated publicly that he will not seek a third term as governor, Nancy is not about to give up a life of perks and celebrity adulation. She is working behind the scenes to plan a presidential campaign. The time will come, Nancy believes, when her Ronnie will be ready for the big job.

Her astrologers agree.

But no seer can save Richard Nixon. Nine months after their arrest, the Watergate burglars and the men who helped them plan the break-in of the DNC headquarters are being sentenced. They have all pleaded guilty and have maintained a code of silence as to their motives. All insist they acted without help. At this point, there is absolutely no evidence connecting Richard Nixon or the White House to the break-in.

But John Sirica, the short-tempered, sixty-nine-year-old chief judge for the U.S. District Court for the District of Columbia, is convinced there is more to the story. He stuns the burglars with sentences ranging from thirty-five to forty-five years in federal prison for charges of burglary, conspiracy, and wiretapping. The sentences, however, are provisional: if the defendants break their silence, prison time will be reduced to months instead of years.

The man in charge of security for the Republican National Committee,

---

*Sinatra was furious when President John Kennedy refused to stay at his Palm Springs home because of the singer's alleged Mafia connections. Sinatra switched his allegiance to the Republican Party as a result.

James McCord, a former CIA officer, is the first to crack. "I would appreciate the opportunity to talk with you privately in chambers," he informs Judge Sirica.

▰ ▰ ▰

Five weeks later, on April 30, 1973, President Richard Nixon inhabits an old leather chair in the White House's second-floor Lincoln Sitting Room. Although it is April, flames dance in the fireplace. Nixon enjoys the fire, and even orders it lit during the hot summer months so that he can sit alone and listen to records.

But tonight the Lincoln Sitting Room is silent. Nixon broods and sips from a glass of twenty-year-old Ballantine scotch. Ever since McCord's confession, Judge Sirica's new grand jury investigation into the Watergate scandal has unveiled damning evidence linking the White House to the burglaries. McCord is naming names. Nixon is frantically working to distance himself from those names, even if it means firing men who have long been loyal to him. Just today, he accepted the resignations of three key members of his administration for their role in the Watergate fiasco and fired another.*

The phone rings.

"Governor Reagan on the line," a White House operator tells Nixon.

"Hello," Nixon responds coldly. Nixon has a famously low tolerance for alcohol and gets drunk quickly. Tonight is no exception.

"Mr. President?" says Reagan.

"Hello, Ron. How are you?" Nixon replies in a booming voice.

Reagan's is a courtesy call, one Republican to another. But in truth, the two men are battling for control of their party. Nixon is threatened by Reagan's popularity and his brand of staunch conservatism. He is vehemently opposed to the idea of Reagan succeeding him as president and

---

*Nixon accepted the resignations of advisers H. R. Haldeman and John Ehrlichman, as well as that of Attorney General Richard Kleindienst. He fired White House counsel John Dean for his role in a Watergate cover-up, despite the fact that Dean had been ordered by the White House to lie. This makes an enemy out of Dean, who will subsequently provide very damning testimony against Nixon.

has hand-picked former Texas governor John Connally as the man he will back for the Republican presidential nomination in 1976. Knowing this, Connally is preparing to switch over from the Democratic Party.

"Just fine and how are you?" Reagan responds. His words ring hollow because both men know that Nixon is in trouble. Earlier this evening, Nixon went on national television and lied to the American public, telling the country that he had nothing to do with Watergate. Furthermore, Nixon insisted he would be relentless in finding who was responsible.

"Couldn't be better," Richard Nixon says bitterly, then he immediately changes the subject. "You must have—the time is so far different. You're about only seven o'clock, or eight o'clock there."

"Yes. Yes," Reagan says.

"How nice of you to call." Again Nixon's voice is tinged with sarcasm. In his drunken state, he has a hard time hiding his loathing for Reagan.

"Well, I want you to know we watched," Reagan tells Nixon. "And my heart was with you. I know what this must have been, and all these days and what you've been through, and I just wanted you to know that, uh, for whatever it's worth, I'm still behind you. You can count on us. We're still behind you out here, and I want you to know you're in our prayers."

"How nice of you to say that," Nixon answers. He is determined to change the subject again. "Well, let me tell you this. That we can be— each of us has a different religion, you know, but goddammit, Ron, we have got to build peace in the world and that's what I'm working on. I want you to know I so appreciate your calling and give my love to Nancy. How— how'd you ever marry such a pretty girl? My God!"

Nixon is being disingenuous. He has confided to his staff that "Nancy Reagan's a bitch. A demanding one. And he listens to her."

Ronald Reagan knows none of this. "Well, I'm just lucky," he says, chuckling.

"You're lucky. Well, I was lucky."

"Yes. Yes. You were."

"How nice of you to call. You, you thought it was the right speech though?"

"I did. Very much so. Yes."

"Had to say it. Had to say it."

"Yeah. I know how difficult it was. And I know what it must be with the fellas having to do what they did. And they—"

Nixon cuts him off. "That's right. They had to get out."

"And I can understand—"

Again, Nixon interrupts to change the subject. "Right? Where are you at now? Are you in Sacramento?"

"No. Los Angeles."

"Ha, ha. Good for you to get out of that miserable city."

"Yeah."

"Right. Rod," Nixon says, unintentionally mangling Reagan's name. "Damn nice of you to call."

"Well—"

"OK."

"This too shall pass," Reagan says, trying to console the president.

"Everything passes. Thank you."

"You bet. Give our best to Pat," Reagan concludes.

The line goes dead.

▰ ▰ ▰

Throughout 1973, the evidence that Richard Nixon funded acts of political espionage and engaged in a cover-up continues to grow. A brand-new cloud of scandal settles over the White House when it is revealed that Vice President Spiro Agnew has been taking bribes while in office.* In order to

---

*Spiro Agnew served as vice president from 1969 to 1973. He was very controversial, particularly because he attacked the press, once famously calling journalists "nattering nabobs of negativism." He was accused of taking bribes and kickbacks from contractors during his time as governor of Maryland, a practice that continued into his vice presidency. He was ultimately accused of tax evasion, conspiracy, bribery, and tax fraud. However, he plea-bargained those charges down to just one: income tax evasion, to which he pleaded no contest. The terms of this deal included three years' probation and resignation from the office of vice president of the United States. Agnew never spoke to Richard Nixon again once he left office, but he was in attendance at Nixon's funeral in 1994. Spiro Agnew died of leukemia in 1996 at seventy-seven.

escape prosecution for conspiracy, extortion, and bribery, Agnew resigns on October 10, 1973.

Richard Nixon is torn about a successor. He would like to nominate John Connally for vice president, but the lifelong Democrat switched political parties only five months ago. There is still animosity among Democrats about the defection, and Nixon feels that they will block Connally's congressional confirmation.

The second choice is Nelson Rockefeller, the liberal Republican governor of New York. Given their long-ago Treaty of Fifth Avenue, which led to a blending of their personal political views into a road map sending the Republican Party on a more moderate course, Nixon fears that this choice will alienate the conservative elements of the party.

The third name on Nixon's list is Ronald Reagan. He is extremely popular among Republicans, and, despite conservative philosophies that are far to the right of Nixon's, Reagan has few enemies in Washington and should have little problem getting confirmed.

Reagan has campaigned for Nixon during three elections. He has called to offer condolences at a time of hardship. Reagan and Nixon have exchanged correspondence for more than a decade. They should be friends.

But because of envy on Nixon's part, they are not.

Nixon's nomination for the vice presidency is an old friend: Congressman Gerald Rudolph Ford Jr. of Grand Rapids, Michigan, the minority leader in the House.

Ronald Reagan will not be coming to Washington anytime soon.

All through the 1973 Christmas season, and into 1974, Richard Nixon battles to stay in office. As prosecutors circle ever closer, he denies them access to tape-recorded discussions he had about the Watergate situation. The prosecutors are forced to take the case all the way to the Supreme Court, which rules unanimously on July 24, 1974, that Nixon must turn over the recordings of sixty-four conversations related to Watergate that occurred in the

Oval Office.* It is a crushing defeat for the president, made all the worse three days later, when the House Judiciary Committee files three articles of impeachment against him. There is a chance that Richard Nixon will be not only forced out of office but also sent to prison.

Every night throughout the crisis, comedian Johnny Carson performs a six-minute monologue of topical one-liners on *The Tonight Show*. Carson is "the most powerful single performer in television," one critic says of the late-night talk show host, and it is true, as many in the media take their cues from him.

Carson and other entertainers batter Richard Nixon, causing more and more Americans to believe that their president is indeed a crook. Cries for Richard Nixon to resign are relentless, and so is Johnny Carson: "Tonight's monologue is dedicated to Richard Nixon. I've got a monologue that just won't quit."

Richard Nixon is not a quitter. But by August 7, 1974, it is clear that he has no other choice. He calls Secretary of State Henry Kissinger to explain his decision. The two men, who bonded over ending the Vietnam War, meet in the Lincoln Sitting Room, Nixon's favorite room in the White House. Richard Nixon's mental health has become an issue as the Watergate crisis has dragged on for more than two years. He has hinted at suicide. He drinks too much and often takes sleeping pills to allow himself at least a few hours of peace. But the pills don't always work: Nixon has begun wandering the White House hallways late at night, engaging in

---

*Voice-activated tape recorders were located in the Oval Office, the Executive Office Building office, the Cabinet Room, and in the Aspen Lodge at Camp David. In addition, microphones were placed inside telephones in those locations and in the Lincoln Sitting Room. Nixon was taping the conversations for posterity, knowing that one day historians would be interested in the 3,700 hours of conversations that he taped between the installation of the tape recording system in early 1971 and July 12, 1973, when he stopped recording due to the Watergate scandal. Franklin Roosevelt, John F. Kennedy, and Lyndon Johnson had also made it a habit to tape White House conversations.

loud verbal debates with the paintings of former presidents that hang on the walls.*

But on this evening, Nixon is not in an argumentative mood. Instead, he is defeated and drunk. Kissinger enters the White House to find Nixon slumped in his favorite leather chair. The room is nearly dark. Even though Nixon is still technically the president, his powers are deeply diminished. The military Joint Chiefs of Staff no longer recognize his authority and actually refuse to take orders from him. Secretary of Defense James Schlesinger has even gone to the extreme of planning for the army's Eighty-Second Airborne Division to remove Nixon from office forcibly, if it should become necessary.

Suddenly, Nixon begins to cry. "Pray with me," he says to Kissinger, pushing back his ottoman and sinking to his knees on the light gray carpet.

Kissinger is startled and initially confused. He is Jewish and does not share Nixon's Quaker faith. But above all, Henry Kissinger is an accommodating man and soon joins Nixon on the floor.

Nixon continues to cry as he prays, then falls forward and presses his face into the carpet. "What have I done?" he laments, pounding the floor with his fists. "What has happened?"

Thirty-six hours later, Nixon signs his letter of resignation with a flourish. There is no precedent for his act. Per the Presidential Succession Act of 1792, Nixon addresses the letter to Henry Kissinger, his secretary of state and most trusted adviser.†

---

*Edward Cox, who is married to Nixon's daughter Tricia, had been a staunch defender of Nixon throughout Watergate. But by August 6, 1974, he realized that Nixon was no longer capable of governing. When Michigan senator Robert Griffin told Cox that Nixon seemed completely rational, Cox informed him, "The President was up walking the halls last night, talking to pictures of former presidents—giving speeches and talking to the pictures on the wall."

†The Presidential Succession Act of 1792 (amended in 1886, 1947, and 1967) stipulated which individual would be next in line for the presidency. It was always understood that a president would leave office before the completion of his term only through death, not resignation. However, in the unlikely event resignation should take place, Section 11 of the act requires the president to submit an instrument of resignation in writing to the secretary of state.

Now there is nothing to do but leave the White House. Nixon stops first to say good-bye to his household staff in the West Hall. The cooks and maids form a single line, and Nixon stops to shake each hand. Then it is on to the East Room, where a large crowd of family and supporters waits to hear him deliver one last speech. The U.S. Marine Band plays the theme song from *Oklahoma!* as Nixon enters and steps to the podium, followed by "Hail to the Chief." Nixon's wife, Pat, stands to his left as he pulls out a pair of black-framed glasses and steps to the three microphones. His daughters, Julie and Tricia, also stand on the podium, next to their husbands. The women have all been crying. Nixon speaks for twenty minutes, fighting back tears at times, and concludes his remarks by reminding his audience, "Always give your best, never get discouraged, never be petty; always remember, others may hate you, but those who hate you don't win unless you hate them, and then you destroy yourself."

George H. W. Bush, head of the Republican National Committee, stands in the audience, marveling at Nixon's words. Later he will write in his journal, "The speech was vintage Nixon—a kick or two at the press—enormous strains. One couldn't help but look at the family and the whole thing and think of his accomplishments and then think of the shame and wonder [what] kind of man is this really. No morality—kicking his friends in those tapes—all of them. Gratuitous abuse."

Across the country, Ronald Reagan watches Nixon's resignation unfold on television. All three major networks are carrying the proceedings live. "It is a tragedy for America that we have come to this, but it does mean that the agony of many months has come to an end," Reagan says in a statement to the press.

As Nixon leaves the White House and steps into the Marine Corps helicopter that will fly him away from the presidency forever,* Ronald

---

*Nixon's helicopter takes him to Andrews Air Force Base, where he boards Air Force One with his family. The plane flies to El Toro Marine Corps Station in Orange County, California, where Nixon then travels by car to his home on the ocean in San Clemente. Air Force One is thirteen miles southwest of Jefferson City, Missouri, when Gerald Ford takes the oath of office as president of the United States. As Air Force One carries that designation only when the president is on board, pilot Ralph Albertazzie radios ground control to ask for a new call sign. Thus, Richard Nixon's presidency finally and officially comes to an end.

Reagan is left to wonder if Gerald Ford will ask him to be the new vice president of the United States. Reagan tells reporters he would consider such a request "a call to duty."

But that call never comes.

10

————⟨⟨⟨⟩⟩⟩————

As Richard Nixon flies into self-imposed exile, his plane passes just a few hundred miles north of this sprawling Texas city. Below, in a furnished rental apartment, John Hinckley Jr. lies around, strumming his guitar. The spartan room is tidy, for Hinckley is a fanatic about cleanliness and personal hygiene, often washing his face with such vigor that his father fears "he'd take the skin off."

Hinckley is nineteen years old now, living in Dallas near his elder sister, Diane, while on summer break from college. He works in a local pizza joint called Gordo's, where he sweeps floor and clears tables. Hinckley is already gaining the sixty pounds he will soon add to his five-foot-ten-inch build. His Paul McCartney–type haircut frames his face, bangs sweeping low across the tops of his eyebrows. When he smiles, Hinckley's dull blue eyes come alive. Yet Hinckley rarely smiles; nor does he have any inclination to shed some of his expanding girth. He has little interest in physical fitness or presidential politics—or in anything, for that matter.

While his elder brother, Scott, is being groomed to run their father's oil company, and his sister is newly married and settling down, John has retreated into a world all his own. He speaks with a flat affect, and his gaze often lacks expression. His only solace comes through music.

The truth is John Hinckley is at a loss to explain what is happening in his brain. He has some form of schizophrenia, a mental disorder that causes the mind to distort reality. A combination of inherited traits and environmental factors has altered his genetic makeup, beginning with subtle changes in his teenage years. If left untreated, his condition can tailspin into delusions and violent behavior that will become dangerous to him and those around him.

His parents are currently building a new home in Evergreen, Colorado, a small mountain town populated largely by wealthy conservatives. They moved there from Dallas just a year ago, as John was beginning his freshman year at Texas Tech University. Having no friends in Evergreen, John Hinckley prefers to spend the summer in scorching-hot Dallas before heading back to school in the fall.

But Hinckley has no friends in Dallas, either. This is nothing new. Once, his high school classmates called him "as nice a guy as you'd ever want to meet." He was popular and well liked, a member of the Spanish Club, Rodeo Club, and an association known as Students in Government. But halfway through high school, he abruptly stopped playing sports or taking part in school functions. His mother, Jo Ann, was heartbroken by the sudden change—and confused as to why it happened.

John Hinckley is no longer one to experience happiness. It has been a long time since he has known that emotion. But here in his room, at least he is content. He listens to the Beatles and plays guitar, day after day after day. Today is a Friday. The president of the United States has just quit. The world is in shock. Outside, the sun is shining on yet another baking-hot Texas summer afternoon. But John Hinckley does not notice. Within these walls, each day is just like any other. Friday might as well be Monday. It does not matter.

Hinckley's parents think themselves lucky that their son does not drink, take drugs, or engage in sexual promiscuity. They are deeply religious evangelical Christians, and to know that their son is not violating biblical principles gives them some peace. So they leave him alone.

One day they will look back and realize that their son's withdrawal from society was not normal.

By then, it will be too late.

11

onald Reagan sits on a small cloth-upholstered sofa, his left knee just inches away from touching that of a woman sitting in an adjacent chair. Reagan is now a former governor, having left his office in Sacramento three months ago. The still-handsome sixty-four-year-old senses an immediate chemistry between himself and the forty-nine-year-old Margaret Thatcher, Great Britain's new House of Commons opposition leader.

Thatcher is a homely woman, but Reagan considers her "warm, feminine, gracious, and intelligent"—so much so that he will take the unprecedented step of gushing about the British leader to Nancy Reagan when this meeting ends in two hours. For Margaret Thatcher, the feeling is mutual. "When we met in person I was immediately won over by his charm, sense of humor, and directness," Thatcher will later recall.

Thatcher wears her graying hair swept up in a high wave. Her dress features wide lapels and a zipper down the front, a style not often seen in the staid world of British politics. She is a complex woman, fond of working through the night and unwinding with a glass of whisky. She owns an American-made Ruger handgun for protection, and there is a growing legend that she helped invent soft-serve ice cream back in the days when she was a chemist instead of a member of Parliament.

Thatcher is a new breed of politician, eager to break her nation out of the cradle-to-grave welfare philosophy that has thwarted the British economy since the end of World War II. Though she is dedicated to politics, ideology means more to Thatcher than appearance. In time, she will learn to balance the two, burnishing her image by switching to power suits and a simple strand of pearls. Her favorite color is turquoise, but she often prefers the more powerful appearance of black, white, gray, and navy. She will soon begin dying her hair reddish blond, and, at the suggestion of legendary actor Laurence Olivier, she will hire a voice coach from London's Royal National Theatre to bring her speaking voice down an octave.

In time, Thatcher will earn the nickname Iron Lady, for her habit of imposing her will on Parliament and her staunch opposition to the Soviet Union and socialism.

But all this is yet to come. For now, Margaret Thatcher is more focused on talking policy with the man she has just met but who is obviously her political "soul mate," to use Reagan's words.

Thatcher presents her guest with a pair of cuff links. Reagan opens the small box and tries them on as a photographer snaps the moment for posterity. He wears a dark suit, polka-dot tie, and white shirt. The former governor's successful economic policies have led to an invitation to speak with British businessmen about ways to reduce the size of government and grow the economy. This sort of political proselytizing has become Reagan's primary occupation since moving from the governor's mansion in Sacramento back down to Los Angeles. He will make almost two hundred thousand dollars this year traveling the world giving speeches.* In addi-

---

*Bureau of Labor Statistics adjust this figure to roughly $872,000 in today's currency.

Ronald Reagan presents Margaret Thatcher with a silver dollar medallion,
April 9, 1975.

tion, two ghostwriters help him prepare his weekly syndicated newspaper
column, which goes out to 226 papers in the United States. And he personally writes the Saturday afternoon radio broadcast he delivers to 286
conservative stations nationwide.

When Margaret Thatcher requested the meeting, she hoped Ronald
Reagan might spend forty-five minutes with her. But the two get along so
well that they spend more than double that time in this small chamber
crowded with many tables and chairs.

Thus begins a beautiful friendship.

A few days after Ronald Reagan flies home from London to America, there is staggering news: the capital of South Vietnam, Saigon, falls to the North Vietnamese Army. American television cameras capture vivid images of American military and intelligence personnel being hastily evacuated by helicopter from the rooftop of an apartment building near the U.S. embassy. After two decades, the Vietnam War finally ends in defeat.*

"I have chosen a dark day to write a belated thank you," Reagan says in a letter to Margaret Thatcher on April 30, 1975. "The news has just arrived of Saigon's surrender and somehow the shadows seem to have lengthened."

Reagan's grim mood infects the whole country. Secretary of State Kissinger has compared America to the former Greek city-state of Athens, which suffered a long slide into oblivion. Kissinger also equates the Soviet Union with Sparta, the militaristic Greek state that constantly prepared for war. The rotund Kissinger is pessimistic about America's standing in the world. And he is not alone. Many believe America's decline began with the assassination of John F. Kennedy in 1963, continued through the anti-war protests of the late 1960s, and then accelerated with the chaos of Watergate in the early '70s.

Eight months before the fall of Saigon, new president Gerald R. Ford tried to stanch the bleeding by pardoning Richard Nixon for any and all crimes he may have committed while in office, believing that the nation would not benefit from the prolonged spectacle of a president on trial. "My

---

*The Department of Defense once considered January 1, 1961, as the first official day of the Vietnam War. However, American military advisers were in the country long before that. This meant that the name of U.S. Air Force Technical Sergeant Richard Fitzgibbon Jr., who died in 1956, before the war officially began, could not be listed on the Vietnam Veterans Memorial in Washington, DC. The policy was changed in 1998, shifting the start of the war to November 1, 1955. Fitzgibbon and eight others are now listed on the wall. Fitzgibbon's son was killed in action in Vietnam on September 7, 1965. This makes them one of only three father-and-son service members to die in that conflict. The others were Leo Hester Sr. and Leo Hester Jr.; and Fred and Bert Jenkins.

fellow Americans," Ford had promised in his inaugural address, "our long national nightmare is over."

But it is far from over. And the outrage continues to grow. America, a nation built upon integrity, honesty, and trust, has seen those principles twisted in a way that signals not some future form of greatness but imminent decay.

And no one seems to know how to stop it.

"Ladies and gentlemen," intones a booming offstage voice, "the President of the United States."

A lectern bearing the presidential seal stands in the middle of the speaker's platform. The president steps onstage, only to get tangled in the American flag. He drops the typed speech he is carrying. Quickly scooping up the pages, he steps to the lectern and composes himself. "My fellow Americans," he begins, "ladies and gentlemen, members of the press, and my immediate family."

Then things get worse. The president stumbles over his words, repeating himself again and again, bumbling his way through the address. "I do have two announcements to make," he says, before falling to the ground again. "Whoa. Uh oh. No problem. No problem," he says, gripping the lectern with two hands to right himself.

The date is November 8, 1975. The "president" is actually comedian Chevy Chase, playing the part of Gerald R. Ford. Earlier in the year, while visiting Austria on official business, Ford tumbled down the steps of Air Force One. He was not hurt, and blamed the spill on a bad knee. However, the fallout has been immense. The former University of Michigan football star's perceived clumsiness has become a national joke. A vast national audience roars at Chase's lampooning of a sitting American president. An office that was once revered and respected out of patriotic fervor has become fodder for farce. Gerald Ford's most difficult task since replacing Richard Nixon is restoring dignity to the presidency. He is failing.

Chevy Chase finally stumbles away from the lectern, trips on a folding chair, and falls hard to the ground. "Live from New York, it's Saturday Night," he yells into the camera.*

Nancy Reagan is not one to laugh easily. She is now decidedly unamused that her twenty-two-year-old daughter, Patti, is living with a rock musician and openly smoking marijuana. Nancy is also incensed that her seventeen-year-old son, Ron, recently seduced the thirty-year-old wife of musician Ricky Nelson in Nancy's own bedroom.[†]

"The bad news is you came home early and caught him," older son Michael Reagan reminds his father when he hears the news. "The good news is you found out he wasn't gay."[‡]

"I hadn't thought of that," Reagan responds. "But you're absolutely right. I guess it's a blessing. Thanks, Mike. I must tell Nancy."

But what really gets to Nancy Reagan's inner core is the growing celebrity of First Lady Betty Ford. America may not be completely sold on her husband as president, but the country loves Betty. The fifty-seven-year-old represents a huge relief from the heaviness of the Nixon White House. Betty Ford talks openly about premarital sex, abortion, and equal rights for women. Adding to that, she had a mastectomy just one month after her husband took office, losing her right breast to cancer. She speaks

---

*The amiable Ford is a good sport about the send-up. He and Chase will go on to become friends, and Ford will even host a special comedy symposium at his presidential library in 1986—at which Chase will appear.

[†]Patti Reagan takes her mother's maiden name while in college because her liberal political views clash with those of her father. Beginning in 1974, she has a four-year relationship with Bernie Leadon, a founding member of the Eagles. Together, they write the song "I Wish You Peace," which appears on the Eagles' One of These Nights album.

[‡]The marriage of Kristin and Rick Nelson is already strained at the time, thanks to the constant travel required by his musical career—and to his womanizing. They will reconcile and split several times before finally divorcing in 1982. Rick Nelson left his entire estate to his four children, leaving Kristin Nelson with nothing after he died in a plane crash in De Kalb, Texas, on New Year's Eve 1985. Kristin Nelson is the older sister of television star Mark Harmon.

candidly about the scar it produced, along with the fact that she likes to have sex with her husband "as often as possible."

Nancy Reagan craves that level of celebrity for herself. Betty Ford notices this after dining with the Reagans in Palm Springs during the 1975 Easter vacation. "She's a cold fish," Ford later recalled. "Nancy could not have been colder. Then the flashbulbs went off, and she smiled and kissed me. Suddenly, an old friend. I couldn't get over that. Off camera, ice. On camera, warmth."

The purpose of the dinner was to suggest that Ronald Reagan not challenge Gerald Ford for the 1976 Republican presidential nomination. It is an uncomfortable night. This is not the first time Reagan and Ford have met, but they circle each other as if they are strangers. Aides note that both men are "uptight, unnatural, pathetically polite, and acutely on guard" at the dinner. "Betty Ford and Nancy Reagan hit it off even worse."*

Ford, a lifelong Republican who served in the navy during World War II, considers Reagan little more than a lightweight actor and former Democrat. However, he knows that Reagan represents the conservative vote, and this concerns him. Rather than marginalizing his potential opponent, Ford has chosen to court Reagan. He has twice offered him a spot in his Cabinet, telling the former governor that he can select almost any position he likes. He has also offered Reagan the job as U.S. ambassador to Great Britain, to which Reagan replied, "Hell, I can't afford to be an ambassador."

In addition, Ford asked Reagan to be part of a panel investigating alleged abuses by the CIA. All this is an effort to prevent Reagan from running for president and splitting the Republican Party in two. Suspicious, Reagan keeps his distance from Ford, accepting the spot on the CIA panel in an effort to gain national exposure, but turning down any scenarios that would make him subservient to Ford. Finally, in an effort to gain conservative support, Gerald Ford strongly suggests that Nelson Rockefeller

---

*The quote comes from White House counselor to the president Robert T. Hartmann, who is best known for penning Ford's inaugural address in 1974.

step down as vice president when his term comes to an end.* Rockefeller cooperates, and the path is now open to Reagan running as Ford's new vice president in 1976.

But it is not to be. Believing he has the resources to defeat Ford for the nomination, Reagan makes it clear that he has no interest in the secondary position. Still, he keeps Gerald Ford guessing as to whether or not he will challenge him. "I tried to get to know Reagan, but I failed," Ford will later write. "I never knew what he was really thinking behind that winning smile."

Gerald Ford quickly finds out what is on Reagan's mind. On November 19, 1975, Ford is working in the Oval Office at 4:28 in the afternoon, with Vice President Nelson Rockefeller and Chief of Staff Dick Cheney, when the phone rings. Governor Reagan is on the line.

Ford does not take the call.

Reagan tries again at 4:57 p.m. This time, Ford picks up. Reagan is calling from his suite at the Madison Hotel in Washington, where he and Nancy have just checked in. In the morning, Reagan tells Ford, he is going to announce his candidacy for president at the National Press Club.

"I trust we can have a good contest," Reagan tells Ford.

At first, Gerald Ford is not upset by the news, for he has anticipated Reagan's decision ever since that Easter dinner in Palm Springs. He takes a thirty-minute stroll to gather his thoughts, stopping first at the White House barbershop for a quick trim. By the time he returns to the Oval Office, Ford is convinced that he will breeze to victory.

The *New York Times* echoes Ford's sentiments, writing that a Reagan presidential bid "makes a lot of news, but it doesn't make much sense."

---

*On that same day, November 4, 1975, Ford also appoints Donald Rumsfeld as secretary of defense, Dick Cheney as White House chief of staff, and George H. W. Bush as director of the Central Intelligence Agency. All three men will play pivotal roles in American politics for the next thirty years.

However, a Gallup poll shortly after Reagan's announcement shatters Gerald Ford's illusion.

The poll finds Republican voters favoring Ronald Reagan over Gerald Ford by a margin of 40 to 32 percent.

Let the games begin.

***

"When you leave the platform, turn to your left," a Secret Service agent whispers to Ronald Reagan as he prepares to deliver the first speech of his presidential campaign. The new candidate is in Miami. He and Nancy now have a Secret Service detail, offering round-the-clock protection against would-be attackers.

The whirlwind life of a presidential candidate has already begun for the Reagans. They flew by chartered plane from Washington, DC, down to Florida this morning. After his speech in the main ballroom at the Ramada Inn on Twenty-Second Street, they will be whisked back to Miami International Airport, where they will then fly to Manchester, New Hampshire. Tomorrow it's on to Charlotte and then Chicago, and finally California. This will be life for the Reagans for the next nine months until the Republican National Convention in August. If they are lucky, they will get to continue the nonstop travel into November, when the presidential election is held. While the pace will be frantic, it will be well worth it. The ultimate goal for Ronald Reagan is being elected president of the United States and thus being recognized as the most powerful man on earth.

In Miami, Reagan speaks for twenty minutes. At 2:00 p.m. he steps down from the dais but chooses to ignore the Secret Service's demand that he turn left. Instead, Reagan goes right, hoping to say hello to an old friend he has spied from the stage.

"What the hell do you think you're doing?" campaign chairman Tommy Thomas says to Reagan as he plunges into the audience.

The crowd closes around Reagan. He is unafraid, eagerly shaking hands, working the room like the seasoned politician he has become. All around the governor, people smile and try to catch his eye. Suddenly, a twenty-year-old man with dark hair and dressed in a checkered shirt, who is standing just two feet in front of him, extends his right arm and points a .45-caliber pistol at Reagan's chest.

Before Reagan can react, his Secret Service detail surges past him and tackles Michael Lance Carvin. Reagan himself is thrown to the ground for his protection, the agents shielding his body with their own.

"I feel fine," Reagan later explains to the press.

"I hope it doesn't happen again," a startled Nancy Reagan tells the media. "I think you always have to keep it in the back of your mind."*

Nine months later, Ronald and Nancy Reagan are running through the labyrinthine hallways and tunnels of Kansas City's Kemper Arena. The Republican National Convention is in its final moments, and the Reagans are on their way to the stage. The roar of the crowd echoes down the corridors, and delegates from all over America are in a state of near bedlam as they await the candidate and his wife. This is the first time Ronald Reagan has made an appearance at the four-day convention, and the moment he shows his face, a collective roar shakes the arena.

Reagan is unsteady. "What am I going to say?" he asks Nancy. He has not prepared a speech. The losing candidate is not supposed to speak at

---

*Michael Lance Carvin is an admirer of convicted mass murderer Charles Manson's acolyte, Squeaky Fromme, who tried to assassinate Gerald Ford. The pistol turns out to be a toy replica of an actual pistol. Carvin, who phoned the Denver office of the Secret Service two weeks earlier to make death threats against Gerald Ford, Ronald Reagan, and Nelson Rockefeller, is arrested and later convicted of eight felony charges on April 19, 1976. Carvin is released on bail while awaiting sentencing and promptly flees. Federal agents finally capture him in Lake City, Florida, and Carvin is sent to prison. He is released on January 4, 1982, and resumes a normal life, including getting married and landing a steady job. However, in 1998 he is accused of making death threats against controversial disc jockey Howard Stern. He is sentenced to two years in federal prison, a period reduced to seven months. His current location is unknown.

the convention—and as of last night, Ronald Reagan has officially lost the Republican nomination for the presidency. Gerald Ford's slender margin of 1,187 votes to Reagan's 1,070 has ensured a Ford victory.* As he did so many months ago, Reagan has made it clear that he will not accept the vice presidency if it is offered. So Ford has not offered.

The two candidates were neck and neck at the start of the convention. Ford won fifteen primaries, Reagan twelve. But Reagan committed a major blunder by announcing his running mate before the convention, selecting liberal Republican senator Richard Schweiker. This alienated Reagan's core conservative constituents. He tried to fix the error by suggesting that convention rules be changed to mandate that Ford also name his running mate early. The matter was taken before the Republican Party's Rules Committee, where it was voted down. Ford won the nomination on the first ballot. This is the first time Reagan has ever been beaten head-to-head in an election. He will remain bitter about the loss for years to come.

Gerald Ford's acceptance speech is masterful. He is interrupted by applause sixty-five times. Watching Ford on television, Jimmy Carter's campaign manager, Hamilton Jordan, parses no words in describing the strength of Ford's delivery: "It scares the shit out of me."

Now Gerald Ford concludes his acceptance speech by calling Ronald and Nancy Reagan to the stage in a display of party unification. For Reagan, this will mean he must make a few brief remarks.

---

*The enmity between Reagan and Ford only grew in the months leading up to the convention. Ford cleverly hired Stuart Spencer to run his campaign, well aware that Spencer managed both of Reagan's gubernatorial victories in California. This insider knowledge of Reagan's rhetoric helped Ford win the opening primary in New Hampshire by painting Reagan as keen to levy taxes. Should Ford have lost in New Hampshire, the election might have been over. Yet he continued his string of victories in Massachusetts, Florida, and Illinois. Then, just as Reagan's staffers were suggesting their candidate quit the race, Reagan won the North Carolina primary. He accused Ford of letting the United States fall behind the Soviet Union in the global arms race, which played into America's mourning over the loss in Vietnam. Ford countered with an attack ad suggesting Ronald Reagan would be quick to start a nuclear war. Ford also sowed seeds of discontent among Reagan backers by inviting influential delegates to the White House, campaigning for delegates seeking political office, and allowing key delegates to be seen with him at important celebrations, such as the 1976 U.S. Bicentennial gala in New York.

"Don't worry," Nancy tells him. "You'll think of something."

As the couple steps onto the stage, their appearance once again ignites a furor. "Viva!" Reagan's Texas supporters shout.

"Olé!" respond his California followers, trying to outdo them.

Over and over, they chant the words back and forth. The convention is no longer a political event but a massive party. Reagan lets go of Nancy's hand and moves to the lectern. The stage is a mob, with the Fords, the Rockefellers, and new vice presidential candidate Bob Dole and his wife, Elizabeth, all crowded onto the small space. Reagan still gropes for the words he will say, even as he steps up to the microphone. Nancy is at his side, pressing her white skirt against her thighs because she has chosen to stand atop a grate blowing air up under the garment.

Reagan begins by praising his party. "There are cynics who say that a party platform is something that no one bothers to read and it doesn't very often amount to much. Whether it is different this time than it has ever been before, I believe the Republican Party has a platform that is a banner of bold, unmistakable colors with no pale pastel shades. We have just heard a call to arms, based on that platform.

"And a call to us to really be successful in communicating and reveal to the American people the difference between this platform and the platform of the opposing party, which is nothing but a revamp and a reissue and a rerunning of a late, late show of the thing that we have been hearing from them for the last forty years."

Reagan's remarks provoke roaring applause, followed by hushed silence. Delegates hang on his every word.

There is no script to Reagan's speech, no notes. His impromptu address is dazzling. He veers away from generalities and into his own deeply held political beliefs, until it is as if Ford is not there at all. Reagan speaks of the Communist threat and the vast potential of America. "We live in a world in which the great powers have poised and aimed at each other horrible missiles of destruction—nuclear weapons—that can, in a matter of minutes, arrive at each other's country and destroy virtually the civilized world we live in."

Then Reagan articulates his thoughts on the peace and security of future Americans, and how everyone witnessing this speech can mold the country's future.

"Whether they have the freedoms we have known up until now will depend on what we do here. Will they look back in appreciation and say, 'Thank God for those people back in 1976 who headed off that loss of freedom'?"

His voice rises until Reagan is no longer a politician but a preacher. He stands not at a podium but at a pulpit. And Kemper Arena is his church. "This is our challenge, and this is why we're in this hall tonight."

"We must go forth from here, united," he concludes. "'There is no substitute for victory.'"*

The speech is less than three minutes long, but the applause breaks stretch it to eight. That's all it takes for Republicans to see Reagan's vision, humanity, and charisma.

As Ronald Reagan waves good-bye to the crowd, it is quite clear to many across America that the Republican Party has nominated the wrong man for president.

---

*Reagan is quoting Gen. Douglas MacArthur, in his final address to Congress on April 19, 1951, in which he concluded fifty-two years of military service with the same words. MacArthur also famously uttered the line "Old soldiers never die; they just fade away."

12

Pacific Palisades, California
November 2, 1976
7:30 a.m.

Eleven weeks after former governor Reagan electrified America with his speech at the Republican National Convention, Election Day finally arrives. It is a cool Los Angeles morning, and Ronald and Nancy Reagan rise at seven thirty, taking their breakfast of fresh orange juice, toast, and decaffeinated coffee at the kitchen table.

As Ronald Reagan looks in the mirror to shave, he is pleased with himself. At age sixty-five, he is still an impressive physical specimen. His hair is thick. His teeth are white. Also, his body is toned from a daily regimen of calisthenics and from weekends chopping wood and clearing brush at the ranch. He will later joke that he should write an exercise book about his regimen entitled *Pumping Firewood*.

Nancy Reagan is also in good shape, though her physique comes more from diet than exercise. The Reagans are fastidious about watching how much they eat and drink, preferring a light breakfast and a lunch of soup so that they may indulge in favorite foods such as meat loaf or macaroni

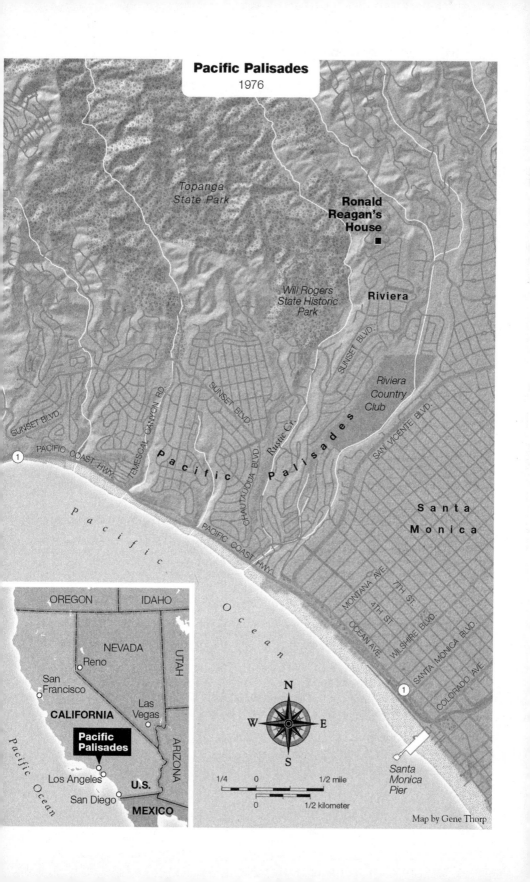

and cheese for dinner. The governor likes also to "hold a few calories back" at dinner so he can enjoy dessert.

After finishing their morning ablutions, the Reagans walk the half mile to the longtime residence of Robert and Sally Gulick. The former World War II navy pilot and his wife have allowed their house to be used as a polling place for more than two decades, and it is here that the Reagans will cast their ballots.

All across America, voters are deciding who will lead them. Either the incumbent president, Gerald R. Ford, or the Democratic candidate, James Earl "Jimmy" Carter, will be the next president of the United States. It is a choice between the man who pardoned the despised Richard Nixon but kept the nation from further chaos or a devoted Christian southern governor who some believe is far more secular than he pretends to be. Neither candidate inspires the nation. Watergate and the Vietnam War have made many Americans cynical. Today will see the lowest voter turnout since 1948.*

The Gulick home, on a tree-lined suburban street, is where many other local celebrities, such as bandleader Lawrence Welk and Los Angeles Dodgers broadcaster Vin Scully, will cast ballots, but the Reagans are the reason the media stand waiting in the street. The former governor gives reporters a friendly hello and walks inside to vote.

Sally Gulick greets the Reagans warmly. The fifty-nine-year-old community doyenne is well known for three things: breeding German shepherds, her annual Army-Navy football game party, and having an avid interest in politics.

In anticipation of the Reagans' arrival, Sally has put out a jar of jellybeans, in case the governor wants to indulge his sweet tooth with his favorite candy. And while a polling place is required to be impartial, Sally

---

*Turnout for the Truman-Dewey race in 1948 was 51.1 percent. Carter-Ford in 1976 was 53.55 percent. The lowest turnout in modern history is 49 percent for the Clinton-Dole contest in 1996. Until 1900, voter turnout in the United States frequently exceeded 75 percent. The highest in recorded U.S. history was 81.8 percent in 1876, when Republican Rutherford B. Hayes of New York lost the popular vote but won the election over Democrat Samuel Tilden of New York by one vote cast by the congressionally appointed Electoral Commission.

Gulick is not above placing a papier-mâché Republican elephant in plain sight.

However, on this day, Ronald Reagan is not a loyal Republican. He has been bitter since the convention, avoiding showing any overt support for Gerald Ford. Later this afternoon he will write a letter to a supporter in Idaho, stating that he has campaigned for Ford in twenty-five states and sent a million letters to back the president's campaign.

But that will be disingenuous. Ronald Reagan did not take losing easily. He has refused to appear in public with Gerald Ford or even to be photographed with the president. Reagan's many campaign speeches were pro-Republican, but focused only on politicians who'd endorsed him during the primaries. Worst of all, in the final days of the campaign, at a time when Ford desperately needed Reagan to make a last-minute swing through the South to secure conservative votes, the governor flat-out refused.

Now, as Reagan pushes the lever casting his vote, he once again refuses Ford.

Stunningly, Ronald Reagan declines to vote for the office of the presidency. He cannot bring himself to cast a ballot for Gerald R. Ford. Neither can Nancy, whose disdain for Betty Ford was clear throughout the Republican convention.*

"I'm at peace with the world," Reagan tells the press as he and Nancy leave the polling place to begin their walk home.

"Will you run again in four years?" a reporter asks.

"I wouldn't rule it out," Reagan answers. "And I wouldn't rule it in."

---

*Nancy Reagan and Betty Ford were a study in contrasts, with Betty's fun-loving persona a polar opposite to Nancy's steely self-control. The press called their appearance at the 1976 Republican National Convention the "battle of the queens" and wrote extensively on their choices of dress and hairstyle. At one point during the convention, an ovation for Nancy Reagan was cut short when the band launched into "Tie a Yellow Ribbon Round the Old Oak Tree," whereupon Betty Ford and singer Tony Orlando got up onstage and danced. Nancy Reagan seethed. The competition did not end at the convention, with Nancy making it a point to write critically of Betty Ford in her 1989 memoir, *My Turn*.

Several hours earlier, and two thousand miles east, Gerald Ford is eating pancakes. He cast his ballot at the Wealthy Elementary School polling place at 7:33 a.m. Michigan time. His hometown of Grand Rapids has just installed new voting machines, and Ford had to be given a tutorial on how to use them. Surrounded by watercolor drawings and a sign saying, "Welcome Mr. and Mrs. Ford" that schoolchildren prepared for this day, Gerald Ford punched out his ballot.

Now Ford sits in Granny's Kitchen Restaurant and indulges in his Election Day superstition. Granny's was where he ate blueberry pancakes the day he was first elected to Congress in 1948, and he keeps coming back.

Gerald Ford is nervous. That is understandable. His fate and future are now out of his hands. In just twenty-four hours, he will know whether he has been reelected or booted from office.

Gerald Ford is a man who has been through intense situations before and knows how to remain cool under pressure. While he was serving aboard the light aircraft carrier USS *Monterey* during World War II, the ship was struck by Typhoon Cobra near the Philippines. The storm was so severe that it sank several destroyers, killing nearly eight hundred U.S. sailors. On the morning of December 18, the pitching *Monterey* was buffeted by screaming winds and seventy-foot waves. Young lieutenant Gerald Ford ventured out onto the exposed flight deck in an attempt to climb a ladder to the ship's wheelhouse in order to secure his duty station. Suddenly, a wave taller than the *Monterey* itself broke over the side of the ship, knocking Ford from the ladder and sending him sliding toward the Pacific Ocean. Ford was powerless to stop his inevitable plummet into the churning sea. At the very last minute, the former University of Michigan football star reached out and grabbed hold of a small metal catwalk. Hanging on for dear life, he pulled himself to safety and worked his way up into the wheelhouse.

Heroic yet humble, Ford speaks infrequently about that terrifying moment. Few of his closest friends even know it occurred.

Now, thirty-two years and a political lifetime after Typhoon Cobra,

Gerald and Betty Ford sit in a small corner booth sipping coffee and awaiting their food. A player piano in the corner puts forth "One Sweet Kiss." An antique sign hangs from the wall advertising "Genuine Ford Parts Used Here." Outside, a crowd of well-wishers peers through the windows, watching the president eat his breakfast.

Soon the Fords will board Air Force One to fly to Washington. There, Ford hopes to take a nap before having dinner with sports broadcaster Joe Garagiola and his wife.

The First Lady has already made peace with this election. In private statements to the press, she pretends to be fine with the outcome, whatever it might be. "Either the president wins," she says, "or if he loses we get to see more of him."

But Betty Ford is hiding her apprehension. Polls show her husband trailing Carter by a slim margin over the last few weeks. Betty, a realistic woman, understands there is a good chance that she and her husband will soon be evicted from the White House.

═ ═ ═

As President and Mrs. Ford fly back to Washington, Nancy Reagan is already planning for the next presidential election. Her husband spends the morning of Election Day in his office, composing handwritten letters to supporters. Then the two of them drive into Hollywood, where she listens as Reagan records a whopping twenty radio commentaries.* In the waning moments of the Republican National Convention, Ronald Reagan made it clear that 1976 would not be his last bid for the presidency. "Nancy and I," he told his campaign staff, "we aren't going to sit back in our rocking chairs and say that's all for us."

Nancy Reagan cried publicly as he spoke on that day, refusing to stand at her husband's side when he said good-bye to his campaign staff because she was so emotional. She turned away from the crowd so no

---

*Reagan normally tapes just fifteen radio spots at a time. He does this with producer Harry O'Connor. Each address is three minutes long and most are written by Reagan himself.

photographer could capture the tears in her eyes. Losing the nomination was hard on her husband but perhaps just as difficult for Nancy. Now she spends many nights alone here in Pacific Palisades as Reagan travels the country to give speeches. When not campaigning, her husband is usually ensconced in his study. Nancy knows Ron's focus is on building his political base. So she is forced to do everything else, taking charge of the family because her husband is too busy. Nancy deals with the drama of her liberal daughter Patti's turbulent life, including her drug use and frequent changes of boyfriend.

Nancy is also concerned that her son, Ron Reagan Jr., is heading in the wrong direction. He wears his hair too long and is developing a passion for ballet dancing. This does not amuse his father, who prides himself on being rugged. Finally, Nancy Reagan watches as the children from Reagan's first marriage, to Jane Wyman, Maureen and Michael, grow more distant by the day, largely because they don't like her.

None of the blame for the family's troubles seems to fall on Ronald Reagan. It is Nancy who accepts the criticism. She knows that her controlling ways have alienated not just the children but also some of her husband's campaign staff.

But she could not care less.

To Nancy Reagan, a troublesome employee is just one more person who has to go. Nancy has terminated numerous staffers. The deed is almost always done by Michael Deaver, a longtime Reagan aide who has become very close to Mrs. Reagan.

Nancy is now fifty-five and still looks as if she is in the prime of her life. She is so devoted to her husband that Betty Ford tells *Time* magazine, "When Nancy met Ronnie, that was it as far as her own life was concerned."

But Nancy Reagan's single-mindedness toward her husband has paid off: Ronald Reagan has become a powerful man. Their income is assured, thanks to Reagan's radio contract and numerous paid speeches around the country. Nancy will never have to work again.

So it is that Ronald and Nancy Reagan end Election Day 1976 by themselves in their home on San Onofre Drive. Since Ron Jr. has left home to begin his studies at Yale, the Reagans are empty nesters. On most nights, they watch an old movie and unwind before going to bed at eleven. But with all three major television networks showing nothing but election returns, the Reagans cannot help but watch.

To them, neither presidential candidate offers the country the necessary ideology and passion. If only Reagan had defeated Ford in the primaries, this would have been their Election Day, and perhaps their night of triumph. Instead, they sit alone in the house, looking out over the lights of Los Angeles and wondering, "What if . . . ?"

But tomorrow is a new day.

As always, Ronald Reagan will spend a few hours in his study, writing his letters and speeches, laying the ideological groundwork to expand his conservative constituency.

But the story is different for Nancy Reagan. She has nothing at all to do. Shopping and socializing with her wealthy friends gets dull after a while.

So Nancy Reagan looks ahead to the day that her husband, Ronald Wilson Reagan, becomes the president of the United States in 1980.

She will see to it.

≡ ≡ ≡

At 3:18 a.m. in Washington, DC, an exhausted Gerald Ford finally goes to bed. He has been watching the election returns for hours, and there is still no clear winner. Thirty-six invited guests have spent the last three hours in the White House watching with Ford. The family's gathering is private, as compared with the giddy scene on ABC, where broadcasters Howard K. Smith and Barbara Walters talk over images of a festive Jimmy Carter party, presided over by his aging mother, Lillian. The matriarch speaks as if she senses victory.

Still, Ford thinks he will win. Too tired to stay awake any longer, he plans to fall asleep and then arise to the news that he has been reelected. He steps out into the hallway with Chief of Staff Dick Cheney, issues a few minor orders, and then walks to his bedroom. The president slips between the sheets, Betty Ford at his side. Good news or bad, in the morning it will all be over.

The fact that the election is this close is testament to Gerald Ford's tenacity. Back in the summer of 1976, as Ronald Reagan divided the Republican Party with his campaign attacks on Ford, Jimmy Carter held a thirty-three-point lead in the polls. America wanted to believe that the smiling small-town peanut farmer would heal the country's maladies.

But Carter almost self-destructed. Against the advice of his counselors, he gave an interview to *Playboy* magazine, hoping to attract voters who might have been put off by his conservative Christian religious views. In that interview, he admitted, "I've committed adultery in my heart many times."*

National headlines ensued, with Carter coming across as somewhat lurid.

The interview was a huge mistake. In attempting to be completely honest, the governor actually lost the support of some women voters and evangelical Christians who thought his admission unseemly.

The gap between Carter and Ford closed even further when the president won the first televised debate in late September. Looking physically robust and in command of the facts, Ford made it clear which candidate was the president and which was not.

Now, as Gerald Ford turns out the light at 3:20 in the morning, he does so with the knowledge that he is on the verge of accomplishing some-

---

*Just as they did with Ford's pratfalls, *Saturday Night Live* was quick to spoof Carter's gaffe. In a skit that aired the night of October 16, 1976, Dan Aykroyd played the part of Carter in a mock interview with a female journalist, Liz Montgomery of the *New York Post*, played by Jane Curtin.

MONTGOMERY: Governor Carter, you have said that the *Playboy* interview may have been a mistake. Do you think you are being too honest with the American people, and do you still lust after women?

GOVERNOR CARTER: Well, I don't think there's such a thing as being too honest, uh, Ms. Montgomery, and just to prove it I'm going to answer honestly how I feel right now . . . I want to say that you're a very attractive woman, and your hair looks kind of silky and kind of soft and, uh, at this moment, in my heart, I'm wearing a leather mask and breathing in your ear.

thing no other presidential candidate has ever done: closing a twenty-point gap in the polls in just eleven weeks' time.

The White House master bedroom goes dark.

Gerald Ford sleeps for five hours.

In the morning, he opens his eyes, hoping for good news.

He doesn't get it.*

---

*Carter narrowly beat Ford in the popular vote, 50 percent to 48 percent. However, he garnered 297 of the electoral votes to Ford's 240, thus sealing his victory.

13

—⁓⦿⦿⦿⁓—

EGYPTIAN THEATRE
HOLLYWOOD, CALIFORNIA
SUMMER 1976
AFTERNOON

Just fifteen miles from the home of Ronald and Nancy Reagan, John Hinckley Jr. sits alone in this aging movie palace watching a new film called *Taxi Driver*. It's a motion picture Hinckley will eventually see more than fifteen times. The twenty-one-year-old drifter, who continues to put on weight, wears an army surplus jacket and combat boots, just like the film's main character, Travis Bickle. Hinckley's hair is now down to his shoulders, and his breath smells of peach brandy, another affectation he has picked up from Bickle, who is played with frightening intensity by actor Robert De Niro.

Screenwriter Paul Schrader based the character of Bickle on Arthur Bremer, the would-be assassin of presidential candidate George Wallace in 1972. Bremer shot Wallace to become famous and impress a girlfriend who had just broken up with him. He had originally intended to kill President Richard Nixon but botched several attempts.*

But it is not De Niro who stirs the most emotion in John Hinckley. Instead, it is the child prostitute Iris who brings him back to the Egyptian Theatre time after time. Portrayed by twelve-year-old Jodie Foster, Iris behaves like an innocent child by day while turning tricks with grown men at night. During the filming of *Taxi Driver*, Foster was so young that she had to undergo a psychological evaluation to make sure she could cope with the troubling subject matter. Her nineteen-year-old sister, Connie, was brought in to be a body double for her in explicit scenes.†

Hinckley does not know these things. Nor does he care. He is falling in love with Jodie Foster, no matter what her age.

Outside the Egyptian, the once-glamorous streets of Hollywood that Ronald Reagan knew when he was a movie star thirty years ago are no more. Hustlers, con artists, pimps, and drug addicts troll the sidewalks. There is an air of menace as solitary men enter cheap X-rated theaters. Street thugs and drug addicts mingle with tourists who buy tacky souvenirs and study the cement sidewalk handprints of the stars at Grauman's Chinese Theatre.

John Hinckley has come to Hollywood to be a star in his own right. He hopes to use his guitar skills to make his fortune, but that has not happened. His squalid accommodation at Howard's Weekly Apartments just off Sunset Boulevard has become a prison. "I stayed by myself in my apartment," he would later write of his months in Southern California, "and

---

*The twenty-one-year-old Bremer attacked Wallace at a campaign rally in Laurel, Maryland, firing four bullets into Wallace's body at close range. One bullet lodged in Wallace's spine, paralyzing him for life. Three other bullets wounded nearby police officers and campaign volunteers. Bremer was sentenced to fifty-three years in prison but was released after thirty-five. He is now a free man.

†Foster won the role over a reported 250 other actresses, including Kim Basinger, Mariel Hemingway, Carrie Fisher, Bo Derek, Jennifer Jason Leigh, Debra Winger, and Eve Plumb, best known for playing Jan Brady on the wholesome television show *The Brady Bunch*. Despite the extensive casting search, Scorcese told Brandy Foster, Jodie's mother, that he had never considered anyone else for Iris.

dreamed of future glory in some undefined field, perhaps music or politics."

The lonely Hinckley keeps to himself, living on fast food and slowly becoming convinced that Jews and blacks are the enemies of white men like him. The more time he spends in Hollywood, the more Hinckley expands his circle of loathing. He now views the city of Los Angeles as "phony" and "impersonal."

Isolated, Hinckley does not even keep in contact with his parents unless he needs money. He has become a drifter, unwilling to finish his studies at Texas Tech or get a job, and would be homeless without their support. John and Jo Ann Hinckley are growing increasingly concerned about their son's behavior, but they support him financially, hoping that

Jodie Foster as Iris in Taxi Driver

one day he will turn his life around and come back to Colorado. Hinckley gives them hope by writing that he is in a relationship with a woman named Lynn. But "Lynn Collins" is not real. She is a myth based on Betsy, Cybill Shepherd's character in *Taxi Driver*—a fact the Hinckleys will not learn for five more years.

There are more lies, such as the one about the rock music demo he fictitiously records. In reality, the only good thing in John Hinckley Jr.'s life right now is up there on the screen at the Egyptian. *Taxi Driver* gives him hope and a sense of purpose. The fog of depression hanging over him lifts. Adopting the same manner of dress and behavior as Robert De Niro's character is empowering for him. In *Taxi Driver*, Hinckley sees a series of clues that will lead him to a better life.

"You talking to me?" Travis Bickle says, alone in a ratty apartment not much different from Hinckley's. Bickle stares at his reflection in the mirror, taunting an imaginary antagonist. "You talking to *me*? Well, I'm the only one here. Who the fuck do you think you're talking to?"*

Hinckley is enthralled as the on-screen action shifts to an attempted political assassination. The scene shows Bickle intending to kill a presidential candidate in order to win the love of a woman. But the Secret Service foil Bickle's effort, and he slips away without firing a shot.

John Hinckley knows the next scene well. It is the final gun battle. Travis Bickle goes to rescue Jodie Foster's character from her pimp, who has sold her to an aging mobster. Jodie is beautiful up there on the screen, her blond hair rolled into tight curls, lips painted a vivid red. A one-man vigilante, Bickle blasts his way down the dingy hallway to where Iris's liaison is being consummated. Blood spatters the walls as the body count rises. The camera pulls in tight to the surprised look on Iris's face as she hears the approaching gunshots. It is her friend, Travis Bickle, who has come to save her. She is not afraid. Quite the opposite. She cries when it appears that Travis might die.

---

*Robert De Niro reportedly stole the line from Bruce Springsteen, who said it onstage in response to fans shouting his name.

As the movie ends and the credits role, Travis Bickle is a hero in the eyes of Jodie Foster's character—and in the eyes of John Hinckley Jr.

And if Bickle can be a hero, then Hinckley can be a hero, too.

There are any number of reasons John Hinckley has fallen in love with that beautiful young girl up there on the screen. She is the one person the solitary Travis Bickle cares enough about to put his own life on the line for—and in real life, her name is Jodie, which is the nickname Hinckley's mother goes by. A delusion is beginning to take shape in Hinckley's disturbed brain: that Jodie Foster might just be capable of falling in love with him.*

The screen grows dark. John Hinckley steps out into the hot California sunlight. He walks the streets, just as Ronald Reagan once did. It was here on Hollywood Boulevard, near the corner of Cahuenga, that Reagan received his star on the Hollywood Walk of Fame in 1960. Hinckley strides over it without even noticing.

In addition to acquiring boots, a jacket, and a newfound thirst for peach brandy, John Hinckley now also keeps a journal, just like Travis Bickle. The only trait he has not borrowed from the taxi driver is a passion for owning guns.

That will soon change.

---

*This condition is known as erotomania, in which an individual believes someone he or she admires is harboring the same feelings toward him/her. It is often associated with mental illness.

14

⟨⊙⊘⊙⟩

President Jimmy Carter is depressed. The White House switchboard wake-up call has not made his real-life nightmare disappear. In fact, it's getting worse. Having his press secretary leak the horrible news to the media in the dead of night was bad enough, but the weight of what he must do now feels like a heavy stone upon his chest.

Carter is a man who likes to micromanage. He dresses quickly, in a dark suit, light blue shirt, and yellow-and-blue tie. The president then picks up the bedroom phone to call his press secretary, Jody Powell. Throughout the last four years, Powell has been very busy, as Carter's presidency has seen one setback after another. Catastrophic inflation has weakened the dollar. Skyrocketing oil prices and long lines to purchase gasoline have shocked and angered the public.* And now there is humiliation overseas.

Jimmy Carter and Jody Powell talk intensely about what the president will say on television in just one hour. An anonymous scheduler keeps track of the president's calls, inserting a *P* next to this moment in the president's daily worksheet, indicating that it was Carter who placed the call to Powell. (An *R* is used when the president receives a call.)

The two men talk for five minutes. Neither has any interest in breakfast. They are used to working under pressure. But even though the day is still young, they are already drained. The speech on television should have been one of celebration, the president of the United States proclaiming jubilant news to the world: *A daring rescue attempt has freed the fifty-two American hostages.* The hostages have been held in Iran by Muslim militants for six harrowing months because of U.S. support for the shah of Iran, who was admitted to the United States for cancer treatment shortly after going into exile. The radicals holding the Americans hostage insisted that he be returned to Iran to be put on trial for crimes committed during his thirty-eight-year reign.

Instead of celebration, though, there is disaster: eight American soldiers and pilots lie dead in the hot sands of the Iranian desert following an aborted rescue attempt, their bodies burned beyond recognition. In a rush to flee without being captured, their fellow soldiers left the dead Americans behind. It is, perhaps, one of the greatest military humiliations in U.S. history.†

But Jimmy Carter's nightmare will not end with a public explanation

---

*The shortage of American gasoline was caused by the overthrow of the shah of Iran in January 1979. The Iranian ruler, Ayatollah Khomeini, cut Iran's oil production, drastically reducing the shipment of crude-oil shipments to the United States. The soaring price of gasoline plunged the American economy into a recession and sent interest rates soaring to as much as 20 percent.

†Operation Eagle Claw was aborted at the behest of its commanders shortly after the would-be rescuers arrived at Desert One, their preliminary staging area in the Iranian Dasht-e Kavir desert, due to mechanical problems with the mission's helicopters. Carter approved their request. However, as the Special Forces units began pulling out of Iran, a helicopter collided with a C-130 transport. The subsequent explosion resulted in the deaths of five air crewmen aboard the C-130 and three from the RH-53D helicopter. The press was informed of the debacle at 1:00 a.m.

of why he authorized the rescue attempt, why he suddenly ordered it aborted, and why eight American servicemen are now dead.

Iranian militants have long threatened to kill the hostages if any rescue attempt were launched. Carter finally called their bluff—only to fail miserably. Now he has to explain the tragedy to the American people.

Jimmy Carter walks downstairs from the second-floor residence. His wife, Rosalynn, a woman known for her frosty demeanor, is on her way home from Austin, Texas, where she was supposed to spend the day campaigning on her husband's behalf. It was shortly after midnight when Jimmy Carter asked his wife to come back to Washington. This would not be a day for campaigning.

Morose, the president steps into the Oval Office at 6:08 a.m. He sits at his desk in this great room and places phone calls to the First Lady and Secretary of Defense Harold Brown. A news camera and microphone are brought into the room. The president straightens his tie. His speech is laid before him on the famous *Resolute* desk.*

Finally, at 7:00 a.m., Carter looks into the camera. He wants to appear in command, but his eyes betray him, showing exhaustion. The president will speak for eight minutes. Afterward, he will receive condolences from former secretary of state Henry Kissinger, who will offer to explain the purpose behind the failed rescue mission to the major television networks on Carter's behalf.

Jimmy Carter never imagined such a moment when he was governor of Georgia. Then, he was a solitary man with huge ambitions, launching a long-shot campaign in 1974 eventually to become president of the United States. Carter has come a long way from his small hometown of Plains, Georgia, but now it is all crashing down.

Carter speaks like a naval officer instead of a politician as he

---

*A gift from Britain's Queen Victoria to the United States in 1880, the desk was made from timbers of the Arctic exploration vessel HMS *Resolute*, which was frozen in ice and later retrieved by American whaling vessels before being returned to Great Britain. It was used by Presidents Kennedy, Carter, Reagan, Clinton, Bush II, and Obama in the Oval Office. The first President Bush used the *Resolute* desk for the first five months of his presidency, then had it moved into his private study.

unemotionally explains his tactics to the nation, hoping his words will save his reelection campaign.

"I canceled a carefully planned operation which was under way in Iran to position our rescue team for later withdrawal of American hostages, who have been held captive there since November 4," he begins.

"Our rescue team knew, and I knew, that the operation was certain to be difficult and it was certain to be dangerous. We were all convinced that if and when the rescue operation had been commenced that it had an excellent chance of success. They were all volunteers; they were all highly trained. I met with their leaders before they went on this operation. They knew then what hopes of mine and of all Americans they carried with them," Carter explains.

"It was my decision to attempt the rescue operation. It was my decision to cancel it when problems developed in the placement of our rescue team for a future rescue operation.

"The responsibility is fully my own."

Carter exhales. It has been a brutal morning. And he fears the worst is yet to come.

Out of respect for the fifty-two captives, Carter has done little campaigning for reelection. He believes this "Rose Garden strategy" of remaining in the White House to deal with the crisis makes him look more presidential—and that it will ultimately win him another term.

That strategy is doomed to fail. And so is Jimmy Carter's presidency.

After his nationwide address on the Iranian hostage-rescue disaster, Carter's job approval rating plunges to 28 percent.

Ronald Reagan takes notice.

Ten months before the failed rescue attempt, Jimmy Carter is responding to the news that Sen. Ted Kennedy plans to run against him for president. "I'll whip his ass," Jimmy Carter tells a group of Democratic members of Congress.

The two men are sworn enemies and will remain that way the rest of their lives. Kennedy, the blue-blooded youngest brother of the assassinated

John and Robert Kennedy, is a forty-seven-year-old senator from Massachusetts. He's a man of many pleasures, drink and women being chief among them. Kennedy is the sentimental favorite among many Democrats who have bestowed sainthood upon his dead brothers.

But Teddy Kennedy is no saint, as the events of a fateful summer night one decade ago clearly showed.

It was 11:15 p.m. on July 18, 1969. The senator was attending a party on Chappaquiddick Island, a short ferry ride from the main hamlet on Martha's Vineyard, Edgartown. Kennedy was restless and decided to leave the party with an attractive young campaign worker, twenty-eight-year-old Mary Jo Kopechne. The fresh-faced Mary Jo was infatuated with Kennedy, and he knew this as he led her to a 1967 Oldsmobile Delmont 88. Kennedy had been drinking but nevertheless got behind the wheel while Mary Jo, a former member of the Robert Kennedy 1968 presidential campaign, sat in the front passenger seat. Strangely, she'd left her purse and her hotel room key behind, as if expecting to return to the party later that night.

Kennedy and Mary Jo drove into the dark. Few people live on Chappaquiddick Island. First, the two made a stop on Cemetery Road, an out-of-the-way location. Suddenly, a police car approached, so Kennedy started up the Olds again.

Later, Ted Kennedy will tell investigators that he was driving Mary Jo Kopechne to the local ferry so she could make the last crossing to Edgartown. But that was a lie; they were driving in the opposite direction from the ferry. Kennedy turned down a dirt road and onto a small wooden bridge that crossed a canal. There were no guardrails, and the car was traveling twenty miles per hour when it suddenly slid off the bridge and into the water. The Oldsmobile flipped upside down in the black current, disorienting Kennedy and Mary Jo. The senator quickly got free of the vehicle and then kicked hard for the surface. In the darkness, he did not see or hear Mary Jo Kopechne.

Kennedy panicked. Not only had he driven a car off a bridge in the dead of night, in the company of a woman who was not his wife, but that woman may also have drowned.

Soaking wet, Kennedy walked up the road until he came to the body

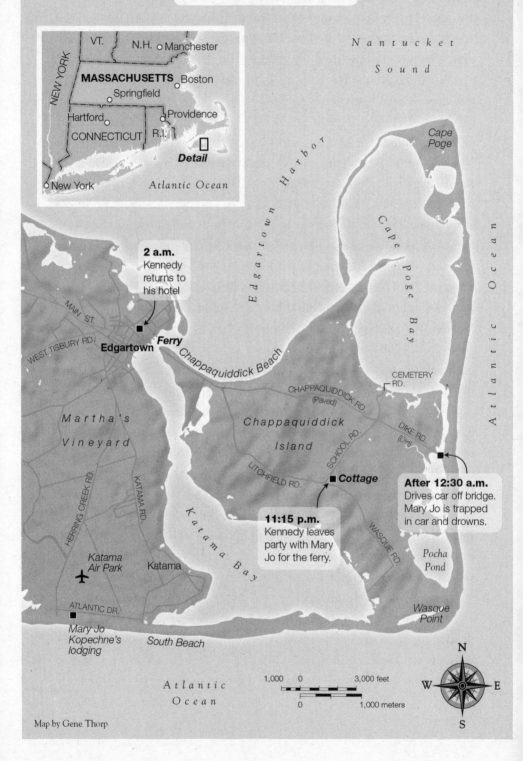

Chappaquiddick Incident
July 18–19, 1969

VT.
N.H. ○ Manchester
NEW YORK
MASSACHUSETTS ○ Boston
Springfield ○
Hartford ○ ○ Providence
CONNECTICUT **R.I.**
Detail
○ New York
Atlantic Ocean

N a n t u c k e t
S o u n d

Cape Poge

E d g a r t o w n   H a r b o r

Cape Poge Bay

Atlantic Ocean

2 a.m.
Kennedy returns to his hotel

MAIN ST.

WEST TISBURY RD.

Edgartown **Ferry**

Chappaquiddick Beach

CEMETERY RD.

CHAPPAQUIDDICK RD. (Paved)

Chappaquiddick Island

DIKE RD. (Dirt)

SCHOOL RD.

Martha's Vineyard

LITCHFIELD RD.

■ **Cottage**

After 12:30 a.m.
Drives car off bridge. Mary Jo is trapped in car and drowns.

HERRING CREEK RD.

KATAMA RD.

K a t a m a   B a y

11:15 p.m.
Kennedy leaves party with Mary Jo for the ferry.

WASQUE RD.

Pocha Pond

Katama Air Park

Katama

ATLANTIC DR.

Mary Jo Kopechne's lodging

South Beach

Wasque Point

Atlantic Ocean

1,000   0   3,000 feet
0   1,000 meters

N
W   E
S

Map by Gene Thorp

of water separating Chappaquiddick from the main part of Martha's Vineyard. He dove into the water and swam five hundred feet to Edgartown. Incredibly, once on land, Kennedy returned to his hotel room, changed into dry clothes, and went to bed. He did not inform police about the accident for nine more hours. When he finally did talk to the authorities, he told them he'd called Mary Jo Kopechne's name many times and made an effort to swim down and find her in the submerged vehicle. Few believed his story.*

Soon, fishermen spotted the wreck, and rescue divers pulled Mary Jo Kopechne's body from the car. Quickly, investigators deduced that she'd initially survived the wreck, finding an air pocket inside the vehicle. Judging from the position of her body, police believed she'd remained alive for some time. Edgartown Rescue Squad diver John Farrar, who pulled Mary Jo's body from the vehicle, told friends that Mary Jo suffocated rather than drowned. The car's doors were all locked, but the windows were either open or shattered, leaving investigators to wonder how the six-foot-two Kennedy could successfully escape while the five-foot-two Mary Jo remained in the vehicle.

In another incredible occurrence, there was no autopsy, in part because the Kopechne family opposed it. Almost immediately, the young woman, whose family lived outside Scranton, Pennsylvania, became the subject of rumor and innuendo.†

One week after Mary Jo Kopechne's death, Sen. Ted Kennedy learned that he would get off easy. An openly sympathetic judge, James Boyle,

---

*Every effort was made to keep Ted Kennedy's name out of the media regarding the accident, but shortly after noon on July 19, 1969, radio station WBZ in Boston broke the story that Kennedy was the driver. The lurid headline in the New York Daily News the next day read, "Teddy Escapes, Blonde Drowns." The scandal was forced out of the headlines later that day, when Neil Armstrong and Buzz Aldrin became the first men to land on the moon. However, the story was quickly revived and followed Kennedy for the rest of his life.

†The body of Mary Jo was buried in Pennsylvania, where in December 1969 a local judge denied a request by the State of Massachusetts to exhume the body for a further inquiry into the cause of death.

quickly wrapped up the case. Kennedy pled guilty to leaving the scene of an accident, and Boyle gave him a suspended sentence, saying, "You will continue to be punished far beyond anything this court can impose."

Now, more than ten years later, Boyle's words ring true. "Chappaquiddick," as the incident has become known, dogs Edward Kennedy as he challenges Jimmy Carter for the presidency. Two months after announcing his candidacy, CBS news interviewer Roger Mudd brings up that ill-fated night during a televised interview. Mudd also asks about the state of Kennedy's marriage.

Ill at ease, the senator fumbles for words. At one point, Mudd appears to accuse him of lying. Kennedy will later state that Mudd duped him into speaking about matters for which he was not prepared.

Making the situation even worse, the interview airs on November 4, 1979, the same day that fifty-two Americans are taken hostage in Iran. Immediately, the nation rallies around their president rather than the callow Kennedy. In primary after primary during the early months of 1980, Jimmy Carter is true to his word, whipping Kennedy's ass again and again, winning thirty-seven primaries to Kennedy's eleven.*

In the mind of Ted Kennedy, Jimmy Carter is a sanctimonious, weak man. "He loved to give the appearance of listening," Kennedy will one day write of visiting the Carter White House as a senator. "You'd arrive about 6 or 6:30, and the first thing you'd be reminded of, in case you needed reminding, was that he and Rosalynn had removed all liquor from the White House. No liquor was ever served during Jimmy Carter's term. He wanted no luxuries nor any sign of worldly living."

Kennedy also seethes about what he believes to be Carter's growing conservatism, thinking it an affront to the democratic ideals for which his brothers fought so hard. "Jimmy Carter," Kennedy will write, "held an inherently different view of America from mine."

---

*Despite the lopsided total, Kennedy's victories in the crucial California and New York primaries kept him in the race.

So it is that, despite the lingering stain of Chappaquiddick and the many primary defeats, Ted Kennedy vows to continue his fight against Jimmy Carter all the way to the Democratic National Convention at New York's Madison Square Garden on August 11. In the same manner in which Ronald Reagan sought to unseat President Gerald Ford with a last-minute bid four years ago, Ted Kennedy and his staff now hatch a plan to take down Carter.

Polls support this plan. When asked, Democratic voters said they'd prefer Ronald Reagan over Jimmy Carter if those two candidates faced off for the presidency. Those same polls, however, show Ted Kennedy defeating Ronald Reagan.

On June 5, 1980, six weeks after Carter's televised national address about the failed hostage rescue, he and Ted Kennedy meet in the White House. Kennedy is giving Carter one last chance to avoid the sort of bruising convention that Ford endured—and that ultimately led to his defeat in the general election. All Kennedy wants is the chance to debate Jimmy Carter on national television, allowing voters to decide who should lead the country. The campaign has been a long one for Kennedy, taking him through forty states in nine months. He estimates that he has flown a hundred thousand miles in that time. He is not yet ready to concede the nomination, particularly against an opponent he despises.

"We were not victorious," Kennedy will write of his mind-set going into the meeting; "nor were we defeated."

Kennedy and Carter meet in the Oval Office, at 4:35 in the afternoon. The senator will remember the meeting as lasting fifteen minutes, when in fact they speak for forty. The president is secure in the knowledge that he has more than enough delegates to win the nomination. Kennedy knows this but is hatching an audacious scheme to steal those delegates and make them his own. Kennedy's plan is to force a shift in convention rules that will allow delegates the freedom to vote for anyone they want, rather than the candidate to which their state's primary results bind them.

By the time the meeting is done, Carter has made his intentions clear: there will be no debate.

▬ ▬ ▬

Two months later, the end finally arrives for Ted Kennedy. His scheme hasn't worked. His campaign staff works the convention floor in a frenzy, determined to find some last-minute way to avoid defeat. But it is not to be. Kennedy has lost his bid for the presidency.

Unbowed, Kennedy gives a concession speech that sounds more like a call to arms. "The commitment I seek is not to outworn ideas, but to old values that will never wear out. Programs may sometimes become obsolete but the idea of fairness always endures," Kennedy tells the convention. "For all those whose cares have been our concern, the work goes on, the cause endures, the hope still lives, and the dream shall never die."

Kennedy is lucid and focused. Many will say it is the finest speech he has ever delivered.

▬ ▬ ▬

Two nights later, as the convention closes, Ted Kennedy has scotch on his breath as Jimmy Carter invites him onto the dais in a display of party unity. Rosalynn Carter stands at her husband's side, looking every bit the "Steel Magnolia" who has had so much influence in the White House. Speaker of the House Tip O'Neill is on the crowded stage, as are a host of Democratic Party big shots.

But it is the body language between Ted Kennedy and Jimmy Carter that the crowd watches closely. Kennedy wears a pin-striped suit and has a look on his face that his staff calls "the smirk." The senator strides purposely to the lectern, making no attempt to heal any lingering wounds from the campaign. He shakes Carter's hand in the most perfunctory manner possible, then immediately walks to the side of the stage, where he can look out over the Massachusetts delegation. As they roar their approval, Kennedy thrusts a triumphant fist into the air.

Unbeknownst to Kennedy, Jimmy Carter follows him. He, too, puts up a victor's fist for the Massachusetts contingent, hoping for a side-by-side display of party unity with his opponent. But as Carter's fist goes up, Kennedy's goes down. There will be no partnership in this campaign.*

In Ronald Reagan's mind, defeating Jimmy Carter for the presidency was just a matter of time.

After accommodating his closest Republican rival, George H. W. Bush, with the vice presidential nomination at the Republican National Convention in New York City, Reagan had a united party at his disposal. Nevertheless, he campaigned hard, crisscrossing the country and denigrating Carter's performance both at home and abroad. He had plenty of ammunition: high inflation, high unemployment, high gas prices, and voter outrage about the Iranian debacle.

On November 4, 1980, the landslide is so great that Jimmy Carter concedes the election before the polls even close in California. He phones his Republican opponent at home to give him the news.†

It is Nancy Reagan who answers the phone. Her astrologer has predicted that she and her husband are in for a long night of awaiting returns. But the stargazer is wrong. Therefore, the call at 5:35 p.m. is such a surprise that Ronald Reagan is in the shower. Nancy calls him to the phone. He steps out half-naked and reaches for the phone.

"Standing in my bathroom with a wrapped towel around me, my hair dripping with water," Reagan will later recall, "I had just learned I was going to be the fortieth President of the United States."

---

*Though often discussed as a candidate, Edward Moore "Ted" Kennedy never again sought the presidency after Carter defeated him in 1980. He went on to serve forty-seven years in the Senate, the fourth longest of any senator in U.S. history. Despite many legislative achievements, his career was tarnished by a propensity for drink and women. He divorced his wife, Joan, in 1982, and married for a second time, to Victoria Reggie, in 1992. After his nephew John F. Kennedy Jr. was killed in an airplane crash in 1999, Ted Kennedy appeared to settle down, adopting the role of family patriarch. He died of brain cancer on August 25, 2009. Ted Kennedy was seventy-seven years old.

†Reagan won the popular vote 50.8 percent to 41.0 percent, with third-party candidate Illinois senator John Anderson getting 6.0 percent. The results were even more punishing in the Electoral College, where Reagan won 489–49. Despite these lopsided numbers, Carter later blamed his loss on the participation of John Anderson in the race.

15

—◦◦◦—

NASHVILLE, TENNESSEE
OCTOBER 9, 1980
12:02 P.M.

Losing the election may have saved Jimmy Carter's life.

It is three weeks before the vote when John Hinckley finally makes up his addled mind. He will assassinate President Carter in order to impress actress Jodie Foster, with whom he has fallen deeply in love. Hinckley's plan comes right out of the movie *Taxi Driver*.

But today the frenzied Hinckley has reluctantly decided to delay the killing. He is now running through the Nashville airport, late for his plane. Over the last month, Hinckley has stalked Carter at appearances in Dayton and Columbus, Ohio; Washington, DC; and now Nashville. In Dayton, he got within six feet of Carter but did not shoot because he was not in "a frame of mind in which I could carry out the act."*

That has not been the case in Nashville. President Carter arrived in

---

*Hinckley made this comment to court psychiatrists when he went on trial for shooting the president.

the city less than an hour ago. He is now onstage at the Grand Ole Opry, speaking to 4,400 local residents. In two more hours, Carter will board Air Force One for the flight to his next campaign stop in Winston-Salem, North Carolina. Hinckley's frame of mind has nothing to do with his inability to murder Jimmy Carter today. The fact of the matter is Hinckley could not get close enough to squeeze off a shot. Security was too tight, so the would-be assassin decided to get out of town.

The handle of Hinckley's oversize gray suitcase is clutched in one fist as he bears down on the security checkpoint. He bought his first handgun just a year ago, and now owns several. Three of them—two .22-caliber pistols and one .38-caliber revolver—are inside his luggage. Hinckley is nervous. His heart races and he feels short of breath as he approaches the X-ray machine.*

"I'm running late," he yells, doing his best to bluff his way through without having his suitcase scanned.

Laura Farmer and Evelyn Braun of the Wackenhut Security Corporation are unfazed. In fact, Sergeant Braun thinks that the pudgy young man looks extremely suspicious. Rather than passing him through, she instructs Mrs. Farmer to pay extra attention to the X-ray of Hinckley's bag.

John Hinckley reluctantly places the suitcase on the conveyor belt. The security officers notice that his hands are shaking.

Laura Farmer studies the video screen as it reveals the contents.

She signals to Nashville airport police officer John A. Lynch, who walks over and opens Hinckley's suitcase. Not only does he find the three handguns, but Hinckley is also carrying fifty .22-caliber bullets and a set of handcuffs.

Hinckley begins to argue, claiming that he is selling the guns, and insists that he is late for his plane.

---

*Hinckley usually checked his luggage, knowing his guns would not be x-rayed. The practice of x-raying carry-on luggage began in 1973, in an effort to curb the extremely high rate of airline hijackings (forty in 1969 alone). At the time, most airlines were opposed to individual passenger screening, and it was not even necessary to show identification when checking in for a flight. The Air Transportation Security Act of 1974 made x-raying carry-on luggage the law. Checked luggage was not x-rayed or searched until 1988, in response to the bombing that brought down Pan Am Flight 103 over Lockerbie, Scotland.

Airport police officer Lynch ignores him. "You have the right to remain silent," he informs Hinckley, officially placing him under arrest.

▬ ▬ ▬

The four years since his first summer in Los Angeles have been largely a haze for John Hinckley. He continued to wander, shuttling from one state to another in an attempt to find himself, often returning to Texas Tech University, in Lubbock, to take a few courses. His grades were Bs and Cs, and Hinckley has been in no hurry to graduate. At school, he woke up each morning and ate a half-pound hamburger from Bill's Lot-A-Burger. Once fastidious about neatness, Hinckley has become a slob. He keeps no food in his simple apartment, where a fine layer of dust from the local sand-storms and a pile of white Lot-A-Burger bags cover the dining table.

In Lubbock, Hinckley often walked into Acco Rentals to talk football with owner Don Barrett. Other days, he sat alone in silence by the pool at the Westernaire Apartments.

But recently, John Hinckley has developed a new passion. He's become enamored of Adolf Hitler and recently purchased a two-volume set of the German dictator's ideological opus, *Mein Kampf,* for thirty dollars at a Lub-bock bookstore. Hinckley even joined the American Nazi Party for a year. He proudly wore the official brown uniform, with its swastika armband and storm-trooper jackboots. But Hinckley was asked to leave the fascist group because he consistently advocated violence.

"Rallies and demonstrations were not enough," neo-Nazi leader Michael Allen explained. "He said he believed violence and bloodshed was [sic] the answer. He advocated illegal acts, and we believe in acting within the law. We don't want his kind in our organization."

Another neo-Nazi official was blunter, saying that Hinckley was "vio-lent, irrational and advocated terrorism."

But this is not the side of his persona John Hinckley wants Jodie Fos-ter to see. Just one month ago, on September 17, Hinckley flew to New Haven, Connecticut, where the actress has begun attending Yale Univer-sity. The image of her beautiful innocence in *Taxi Driver* continues to haunt Hinckley, who still watches the film on a regular basis. He is determined to win Jodie's love, but the journey to Yale proved to be a setback. He wrote her letters and poems, and even managed to speak with her on the phone. But rather than find the attention romantic, Foster was disturbed. She told Hinckley he was rude and dangerous, and ordered him never to call her again.

Initially, Hinckley was devastated. He attempted suicide by swallowing antidepressants but failed. Rather than try again, Hinckley vowed to renew his pursuit of Foster by imitating Travis Bickle's strategy for romancing women: political assassination.

So it is that John Hinckley spent what little money he had on handguns and airfare, following the president of the United States around the country, hoping to put a bullet in his head.

Within an hour of his arrest in Nashville, John Hinckley stands before Judge William E. Higgins. The location is not a courtroom but a small office in police headquarters. He is being charged with possession of a firearm.

A terrified Hinckley can only imagine what will happen next. He has never been in jail before. With President Carter just a few miles away at the Grand Ole Opry, it is logical that Judge Higgins or the FBI would question Hinckley about his guns and his intent. Even though it might appear to be a coincidence, the president's presence in Nashville demands that those questions be asked.

But on this day, John Hinckley is in luck. The FBI is so overwhelmed by Jimmy Carter's visit to Nashville that every last agent has been tasked with ensuring his safety. So there is effectively no interrogation of Hinckley.

Judge Higgins's verdict is swift: John Hinckley will be punished to the maximum letter of the law. He is immediately ordered to pay a $50 fine, along with $12.50 in court costs. He also loses his guns.*

John Hinckley walks out of Judge Higgins's courtroom a free man.

---

*Hinckley was charged with possession of concealed weapons. Carrying a gun without a permit was not against the law in Tennessee at the time.

He immediately returns to the airport, where he takes the next plane to Dallas.

■ ■ ■

In 1980 the Secret Service has a computer file listing the four hundred individuals most likely to attempt a presidential assassination. There is also a secondary list of the more than twenty-five thousand people who might be capable of carrying out such a killing.

Despite his troubles in Nashville, John Hinckley does not make either list.

Four days after his arrest, Hinckley enters Rocky's Pawn Shop at 2018 East Elm Street in Dallas. There, in a strip mall whose tenants include a bail bondsman and a dive bar, he purchases two snub-nosed pistols of the same model. Its official name is the RG-14 .22-caliber revolver. In police parlance, the gun is known as the Saturday Night Special.

The intensity of John Hinckley's quest for the love of Jodie Foster ratchets up. His compulsion has now overwhelmed him.

16

❦

R onald Reagan stares at the elephant in the room. It stands thirteen feet tall and measures twenty-seven feet from trunk to tail. It took thirteen four-inch bullets to kill him. The Fénykövi elephant, as the regal animal is known, is poised for battle in the center of this festive rotunda. Its flanks are draped in patriotic red, white, and blue bunting, making it the very symbol of the Republican Party.*

The other symbol of the party stands at a lectern bearing the official seal of the president of the United States of America. Ronald Wilson Reagan gazes out over the hundreds of supporters dressed in formal wear who have come to celebrate his inauguration. He wears white tie and tails. Nancy Reagan, on his right, is draped in a white satin sheath that

---

*At the time of its shooting by Hungarian big-game hunter Joseph Fénykövi on November 12, 1955, it was the largest-ever African elephant in recorded history. On March 6, 1959, Fénykövi donated the preserved hide of the elephant to the Smithsonian, where a team of taxidermists labored for sixteen months to prepare it for display.

took a team of dressmakers four weeks to embroider. Her full-length Maximilian mink coat and alligator handbag are backstage, watched over by the Secret Service. Unbeknownst to the crowd, Nancy's outfit for the evening costs close to twenty-five thousand dollars.*

This is the Reagans' ninth inaugural ball of the evening. And with midnight just moments away, they still have one more to go. The festivities began the previous night, at the inaugural gala organized by Frank Sinatra. Johnny Carson was the emcee, introducing performances by Sinatra and comedian Bob Hope, who poked fun at Reagan's Hollywood days by joking that the new president "doesn't know how to lie, exaggerate or cheat—he's always had an agent for that!"

Tonight is even more glamorous. Priced at a steep five hundred dollars a ticket, seats are in such demand that the press will compare these formally dressed men and women to "drunken soccer fans" as they battle for their places at the table, where swordfish and chateaubriand are washed down with California wine and Kentucky bourbon. Hundreds of corporate titans have flown in from all over the country—so many, in fact, that their private jets have disrupted normal flight patterns at Washington's National Airport this morning. As limousines clog the city streets, California socialite and longtime Nancy Reagan confidante Betsy Bloomingdale actually gets out of her stretch limo to direct traffic at Dupont Circle. A mink stole draped around her shoulders, the fifty-eight-year-old Bloomingdale doesn't have time for gridlock.

Indeed, so many women have worn expensive furs to these inaugural balls that the press will report coatracks looking like "giant furry beasts." The Washington caterer Ridgewells will serve four hundred thousand hors d'oeuvres at the various parties tonight. Lavish consumption is on display, something Jimmy and Rosalynn Carter would never have allowed.

Throughout the night, Ronald Reagan remains unfazed. "I want to thank all of you," he tells the crowd at the Smithsonian. His voice is growing hoarse after hours of speeches, but though he is just weeks away from

---

*More than sixty-eight thousand dollars in today's money.

turning seventy years old, the new president shows no signs of fatigue. "Without you there wouldn't be this successful inaugural."

Four years ago, Jimmy Carter did not feel it appropriate to celebrate his inauguration with even one formal ball, let alone ten. No partying for the man from Plains. Instead, Carter's 1977 inaugural address was somber, pointing out America's limitations as a nation. The tone of pessimism and defeat that marked Carter's first day in office came to define his entire presidency.

If Ronald Reagan's first day in office is any indication of what is to come, the United States of America is in for a far more upbeat presidency. He and Nancy spent last night at Blair House, the official state residence where presidents-elect sleep the night before their inauguration.* The first couple is rested and ready to take full advantage of the celebration.

The Reagans have been in Washington for a week, adapting to the capital's routine after more than a year living out of suitcases on the campaign trail. With their new life comes intense public scrutiny. A litany of personal facts is finding their way into the media. Given his age, many wonder about Reagan's health. Despite a medical history that includes a shattered femur suffered in a celebrity baseball game thirty years ago, the worst of his maladies right now is minor arthritis in his right thumb and chronic hay fever. He continues to work out each night, using a small exercise wheel before taking an evening shower. To some doctors, for a man about to enter his eighth decade, Reagan is an amazing physical specimen.

In fact, the biggest physical problem Reagan has right now might be his hair color. It has become a national mystery. The president says he does not dye his dark hair, but many are skeptical.[†]

---

*Blair House is a 120-room, 60,600-square-foot mansion across the street from the White House. Built in 1824, it was originally the home of Surgeon General of the U.S. Army Joseph Lovell. Francis Preston Blair Sr., adviser to several presidents, including Abraham Lincoln, purchased the home in 1836. The United States bought the property in 1942 to avoid having guests of the president sleep in hotels.

[†]Gerald Ford once noted that Reagan's hair was "prematurely orange." This occasional side effect is often seen as evidence of the use of Clairol hair dye, and in 2009 a former Clairol executive stated to the New York Times that the Reagans brought their own personal hair colorist into the White House. However, it has never been confirmed.

There is no question that Ronald Reagan is a vain man. He is almost deaf in his right ear, thanks to standing too close to gunfire while filming a series of movies about the Secret Service in the late 1940s. But Reagan refuses to wear a hearing aid. Also, he can get testy at times. Some of his campaign staff whisper about Irish rages. In one case, candidate Reagan became so annoyed with his speechwriters that he took off his glasses and threw them against the wall. Such outbursts are rare, but Reagan's closest confidants know that when they see his jaw tighten, it is time to back off.

The Reagans are often pedestrian in their tastes. Reagan's favorite Christmas carol is "Silent Night," and his favorite song is the "Battle Hymn of the Republic." He enjoys lasagna and hamburgers for dinner, followed by a dessert of brownies or carrot cake. When watching television, the Reagans prefer *The Waltons* and *Little House on the Prairie*, shows built around wholesome values.

Ronald Reagan's political hero is no longer Franklin Delano Roosevelt; he's been replaced by former Republican president Calvin Coolidge. "He [Coolidge] wasn't a man with flamboyant looks or style, but he got things done in a quiet way," Reagan will write of the man whose picture he will hang in the White House Cabinet Room. "He came into office after World War I facing a mountain of war debt, but instead of raising taxes, he cut the tax rate and government revenues increased, permitting him to eliminate the wartime debt."

This kind of analysis surprises observers in Washington, many of whom don't think that Ronald Reagan has a first-rate intellect. He has long studied the nuances of domestic and foreign policy and possesses a stunning ability to recollect the most minute facts for the purposes of a speech or debate. But Reagan often hides his knowledge in order to present himself as a simple man of humble opinions, an image he believes makes him more appealing to regular voters.

Yet Reagan does not pander. While many politicians use religion as a campaign theme, the Reagans rarely go to church, and the new president does not make an issue out of his belief in God. However, his spirituality does influence him. On October 11, 1979, Reagan sends a letter to a writer for a pro-life Catholic magazine, in response to an article about Reagan's views on abortion. "To answer your questions; I have a very deep belief that interrupting a pregnancy means the taking of a human life. In our Judeo-Christian tradition, this can only be justified as a matter of self-defense."

But expressions like that for Ronald Reagan are rare. His experience in the secular state of California imbued him with a practical political strategy, so he mostly avoids the emotional issue of religion.

Nancy Reagan, on the other hand, avoids very little. She is known to blurt out her personal thoughts. When her son, Ron, attacks Jimmy Carter as having "the morals of a snake," Nancy publicly defends her boy.* In December, just one month after the election, she stands up against gun control by admitting to owning a "tiny little gun." Coming shortly after the assassination of singer John Lennon, the comment strikes many as callous, and there is public outrage over the incident in liberal circles. Reacting to the heat, Nancy fires her newly appointed press secretary for not "protecting" her from the media backlash.

Sensing blood, the press descends on Nancy Reagan. Soon, she is being described as being cheap and self-absorbed. *Tonight Show* host Johnny Carson refers to her as the "Evita of Bel-Air," comparing her to the imperious wife of Argentinian dictator Juan Perón, Eva, who longed for her own unlimited power.

In truth, Nancy Reagan is much more interested in high fashion and copies the dress and look of two icons: Jackie Kennedy and England's Duchess of Windsor. To cover the cost of such extravagance, the incoming First Lady expects designers to give her clothing and handbags gratis— under the pretense that they are merely being "borrowed."

≡ ≡ ≡

---

*Ron Reagan Jr. made these comments in an interview with *New York* magazine in December 1980.

Nancy Reagan wears one of those outfits now, a three-thousand-dollar dress, coat, and hat by the Cuban-born designer Adolfo, as she and Ronald Reagan are driven from Blair House to the White House shortly before noon on Inauguration Day. There they are met by a somber Jimmy Carter and his wife. Per tradition, the two men ride together in a limousine for the short two-mile journey to the Capitol building for Reagan's swearing-in. They sit side by side in the backseat but do not speak. Instead, each man looks out the window, waving to the crowds on his side of the limo. "He was polite," Reagan will later write of that stony ride. "He hardly said a word to me as we moved slowly toward the Capitol, and I think he hesitated to look me in the face."

Nancy Reagan and Rosalynn Carter are driven in a separate limousine, directly behind their husbands. Rosalynn Carter wears a dull brown skirt and coat with a matching scarf knotted at her throat, making her look somewhat dowdy next to Nancy in her fire-engine red outfit. Today is the end of a dream for Rosalynn, who grew up poor, with a widowed mother who took in sewing to make ends meet. The differences between her and Nancy Reagan, with her debutante past and wealthy stepfather, are many. Rosalynn has attempted to be kind to Nancy throughout the transition, as her husband has been to Ronald Reagan, for the Carters well remember the courtesies extended to them by the Ford family as they were leaving office four years ago.

However, Nancy Reagan has managed to annoy Rosalynn. She has visited the White House several times, intent most of all on gauging the amount of closet space so that her enormous wardrobe will have a home. Mrs. Carter tolerated having Nancy snoop around, even though the White House was still very much the Carter home. But when Nancy requested that the Carter family move out a week before the inauguration, Rosalynn drew the line. Her answer was a firm no. The Carters remained the White House's official residents until just a few minutes before noon on Inauguration Day.

Nevertheless, the transition of presidential power is well under way. The recorders who tally every moment of a president's day stopped recording Carter's activities one week ago. The Carters' furniture is being

*Ronald and Nancy wave from the presidential limousine
on Inauguration Day, 1981.*

removed from the White House, replaced by that of the Reagans. Leaving office is hard on Jimmy Carter, for he is exhausted from staying up all night in a last-minute attempt to free the hostages in Iran. It is an act for which he will receive little credit. The Iranian militants would not set the Americans free until Reagan was sworn in, due to Carter's support for the shah of Iran.*

The Reagans have brought California's weather with them. Tens of thousands of people stand in shirtsleeves and light jackets on this

---

*On January 19, 1981, the Algiers Accord resulted in the freeing up of $7.9 billion in Iranian assets that had been frozen by the United States once the hostage crisis began. This paved the way for the hostages' freedom.

fifty-six-degree day. The crowds stretch from the Capitol Building all the way down to the National Mall to the Lincoln Memorial. American flags and red, white, and blue bunting seem to be everywhere, imbuing this day with a jubilant sense of patriotism. Later on, once word gets out about the newly freed American hostages, yellow ribbons will be tied around every available tree, only heightening the festive atmosphere.*

But not everyone is joyful. There are many in the media who despise Ronald Reagan. Terms such as *lightweight, B-movie actor,* and even *dangerous* are sometimes used to denigrate him, both privately and in print. Ever since the failed Nixon administration, it has become commonplace in the media to disrespect Republican politicians.

Despite many preconceived notions and his familiar television persona, the press and most of the American people do not really know Ronald Reagan. He reveals himself to very few people. He is wary of the media and easily guided by the strong personality of Nancy, who has more influence than any of his advisers—though even she is often frustrated by his unwillingness to share his feelings. Ronald Reagan is passive in many ways. He can be stubborn when he chooses to put his foot down but often allows others to make decisions for him. He craves approval and applause, thanks to growing up the son of an alcoholic father who gave him little of either. He often appears disengaged, preferring the company of his own thoughts to time with family and friends. He is a loyal man but has put little effort into fatherhood, often ignoring his children when they need him most. Reagan's world revolves around his conservative ideals and Nancy, with whom he has been known to get annoyed but rarely angry.

This is the real Ronald Reagan. But the public man is a far different story. To millions of his supporters, the new president is a benign father figure, a man who makes them proud to be Americans. And Reagan himself is proud of that image.

---

*This American tradition of welcoming home prisoners of war and soldiers was revived by the 1973 song "Tie a Yellow Ribbon Round the Ole Oak Tree," by Tony Orlando and Dawn. The practice dates to the nineteenth century, when American women wore a yellow ribbon to show their faithfulness to a husband or sweetheart serving in the U.S. Cavalry.

Vice President George H. W. Bush is sworn in first. The choice of running mate was a savvy move on Reagan's part, as it was Bush who proved the toughest opponent during the 1980 Republican presidential primaries. A longtime party workhorse, the World War II bomber pilot has served as a congressman from Texas, envoy to China, director of Central Intelligence, and chairman of the Republican National Committee. At six foot two, he stands an inch taller than Reagan and shares a similar athletic background. His eyes are blue, and he adds styling mousse to his gray-brown hair to keep it in place. "Poppy," as he was nicknamed in his youth, is known for being a gentle yet tough man.

Bush now steps into the thankless role of vice president with the same aplomb he brought to each of his previous jobs. Reagan has plans to make great use of George Bush and his many skills, in a manner normally unseen between a president and a vice president. Unlike Reagan, who can be privately aloof, Bush makes friends easily. He still keeps in touch with schoolmates and navy buddies he met decades ago. The same holds true in Washington, where Bush is deeply connected inside the Beltway. Reagan's practical side will not allow him to let such qualities go to waste.

At the stroke of noon, the new vice president steps away from the lectern. It is now Ronald Wilson Reagan's turn to take the oath of office. He wears a gray vest and tie under his black suit as he places his hand on a Bible that once belonged to his mother. A poised Nancy Reagan is at his side, resplendent in her matching red dress, coat, and hat. In what is a political first for Reagan, all four of his grown children are in attendance, standing with the other invited guests just behind him. And in what is a harbinger of things to come, none of the children is smiling.

A burst of sunshine plays on Reagan's face as Chief Justice Warren Burger reads him the oath. "I, Ronald Wilson Reagan, do solemnly swear . . ."

The oath takes just forty seconds. Reagan relishes each phrase, repeating words for dramatic impact and adding a pause here and there for emphasis.

"May I congratulate you, sir," the chief justice says, reaching over to shake Reagan's hand. As a twenty-one-gun salute echoes throughout Washington, DC, Reagan kisses his wife on the cheek. They turn together and look out on the thousands of Americans who have traveled to Washington to be here with them in person to witness this historic moment. Tonight there will be fireworks in the nation's capital. In New York, the Statue of Liberty will be bathed in spotlights. For the next twelve hours, Ronald and Nancy Reagan will be celebrated with a dazzling succession of parades, parties, and speeches. Then, finally, will come the humbling moment when Ronald Reagan steps into the Oval Office for the first time.*

As the most powerful man in the world, Ronald Reagan is preparing himself for the job by bringing in many political veterans. His chief of staff will be James Baker III, a fellow former Democrat who ran the presidential campaigns of Gerald Ford and then George H. W. Bush four years later. Reagan is willing to overlook that indiscretion for the sake of an organized and efficient White House. He likes that Baker is a no-nonsense manager known for his crisp analysis.

Reagan's deputy chief of staff, and the second man in what will become known as the Troika, will be Michael Deaver, a member of his California gubernatorial staff and a man whom both Ronald and Nancy Reagan prize for his loyalty.

And the third man upon whom Reagan will rely for advice in times of doubt is Edwin Meese, an attorney who served as chief of staff during the California governorship. His official title is counselor to the president, but the forty-nine-year-old Meese's actual job description goes much deeper than merely giving legal advice. He and Reagan know each other so well that Meese is often considered the president's alter ego. However, knowing that such a role can carry too much clout in the White House, Meese has made it a point to meet with Baker in order to sharply define their roles. It is a balance of power that will be tested much sooner than either man is anticipating.

Thanks to his capable team, Reagan is confident that he can run the country. He is so eager to begin changing America that this afternoon he

---

*This occurred at precisely 5:08 p.m. on January 20, 1981.

will sign his first executive order. With the swipe of a pen, he will order a federal hiring freeze. Within a week he will also lift price controls on oil and gasoline, simultaneously setting in motion his personal idea of a free-market economy and making his many donors from the gas and oil industry billions of dollars richer.*

"It is time for us to realize that we are too great a nation to limit ourselves to small dreams," he preaches in his inaugural address. "We're not, as some would have us believe, doomed to inevitable decline. I do not believe in a fate that will fall on us no matter what we do.

"I believe in a fate that will fall on us if we do nothing."

The last inaugural ball winds down well past midnight, but at nine o'clock the same morning, Ronald Reagan sits down at the *Resolute* desk in the Oval Office and scans his list of scheduled meetings. He wears a coat and tie, as he will each and every time he sets foot in this legendary work space.

Reagan is firmly in command. Or so it seems to those around him.

Little does he know the violence that lies ahead.

---

*It was Richard Nixon who introduced the price controls on gasoline, in an attempt to stimulate greater domestic oil production. Carter instituted a levy known as a "windfall tax" against the oil companies during his administration, which promptly led to a decrease in domestic output. He later signed an executive order that would phase out price controls by October 1981. Reagan's lifting of the controls before that scheduled date caused production to soar, leading to a 50 percent drop in the price of oil.

17

STAPLETON AIRPORT
DENVER, COLORADO
MARCH 7, 1981
6:00 P.M.

John Hinckley shuffles off the United Airlines flight from New York, eyes glazed from fatigue and face unshaven. He has spent a week on the East Coast in yet another futile attempt to win Jodie Foster's love. "Dear Mom and Dad," the twenty-five-year-old wrote in a note just seven days ago. "Your prodigal son has left again to exorcise some demons. I'll let you know in a week where I am."

But Foster once again rejected Hinckley, and yesterday morning at four thirty, a broke and incoherent Hinckley phoned his parents, begging for a ticket to fly home. He is unaware that Jodie Foster has given his love letters to the Yale University campus police, who are currently launching an investigation into his whereabouts.

Hinckley is among the last passengers to disembark. His fifty-five-year-old father, Jack, is waiting. His mother has not made the drive into the city from Evergreen because she is so distraught about her son that she has spent the day sobbing. The entire Hinckley family has been devastated by John's behavior. His sister, Diane, and elder brother, Scott, both phoned yesterday to encourage their parents to place John in a mental hospital. "He just keeps going down," Scott Hinckley told his father. "John doesn't seem like he can cope anymore."

But coping is the least of it. If Jack and Jo Ann Hinckley were the sort of people to pry, they would find a handgun, bullets, and paper targets in the shape of a man's torso in a small green suitcase hidden in their son's bedroom closet. But they do not believe in snooping into their son's belongings or his personal business. They have no idea why John impulsively flew back to New York City, and certainly no knowledge of the grandiose scheme to court Jodie Foster.

This does not mean that Jack and Jo Ann are completely hands-off parents. It was through their urging that their troubled son has begun seeing a Colorado psychiatrist about his failing mental health. Dr. John Hopper, however, does not see anything greatly wrong with John Hinckley. In their sporadic sessions together over the last five months, Hopper has seen no signs of delusion or other symptoms of mental illness. John Hinckley trusts Hopper enough to confess that he is "on the breaking point" mentally, but rather than be alarmed, the psychiatrist thinks him a typical socially awkward young man who exaggerates his obsessions. Hopper treats Hinckley by attaching biofeedback electrodes to his forehead and thermometers to his fingers in an effort to teach him relaxation techniques.

Relaxation, Hopper believes, is vital to curing Hinckley.

The psychiatrist also believes that Jack and Jo Ann Hinckley are mostly to blame. He believes they coddle their son, not holding him accountable for his behavior. They allow him to live at home and don't force him to find a job. So Hopper has encouraged them to draw up a contract to set in motion the wheels of John Hinckley's independence. By March 1, he is to have a job; by March 30, he is to have moved out of the house. "Give John one hundred dollars," Dr. Hopper told the Hinckleys, "and tell him good-bye."

Technically, John Hinckley has remained true to the contract. He beat the deadline for finding employment, landing a menial position with the local Evergreen newspaper. But he walked away from that job when he flew to New York. Now, in the busy Denver airport, a heartbroken Jack

Hinckley must perform a most gut-wrenching act of parenting: he must tell his son good-bye.

Jack Hinckley guides John to an unused boarding gate. "Have you eaten anything?" he asks.

"I bought a hamburger in New York, and ate again on the plane," John replies.

They sit down. Jack is direct, telling his son that he is no longer welcome in their home. "You've broken every promise you've made to your mother and me. Our part of the agreement was to provide you with a home and an allowance while you've worked at becoming independent. I don't know what you've been doing these past months, but it hasn't been that. And we've reached the end of our rope."

John Hinckley is shocked. Even at age twenty-five, he is so accustomed to having his parents solve his problems that his father's words stun him.

Jack presses two hundred dollars into John's hands. "The YMCA is an inexpensive place to live," he says softly.

"I don't want to live at the Y."

"Well, it's your decision, John. From here on you're on your own."

The two men walk to the airport garage, where John Hinckley Jr. parked his white Plymouth Volare seven days ago. Jack Hinckley has brought along antifreeze, knowing that the car has been sitting in the winter cold all week. He empties the jug into the engine and then stands back as his son turns the key in the ignition.

"I watched him drive slowly down the ramp," Jack Hinckley will later write of that moment.

"I did not see my son face-to-face again until we met in prison."

Three weeks later, John Hinckley parks the white Volare in his parents' driveway. He has been living at a dive called the Golden Palms Hotel, thirty minutes away in Lakewood.

Jack is at work, so it is Hinckley's mother who answers the door. John is flying to California to start his new life, and Jo Ann Hinckley has agreed to drive him to the airport. The date is Wednesday, March 25, 1981. At this same moment, Ronald Reagan is taking advantage of one of the great perks that come with being president, flying by helicopter to Marine Corps Base Quantico, where he will spend two hours on horseback.

Mother and son barely speak during the hour-long ride into Denver. She does not want him to leave but forces herself to stick with what she and her husband now call the Plan.

John parks in front of the Western Airlines terminal. Jo Ann violates the Plan by giving him one hundred dollars. "He looked so bad and so sad and in absolutely total despair," she will later recall. "I thought he would take his own life."

But John Hinckley's flirtation with suicide has passed. He has a very different form of killing on his mind. "Mom," he tells her, saying good-bye once and for all to his former life, "I want to thank you for everything you've ever done for me."

Jo Ann Hinckley knows something is wrong. Her son never speaks with such formality. But the Plan must be obeyed, so she overrules her intuition and does nothing to stop John from leaving. If not for the Plan, the course of history might have been changed.*

"You're very welcome," Jo Ann tells her son. Her voice is intentionally cold because she knows she will start sobbing if she lets down her guard. Then, without a kiss or hug or even a handshake, she gets in the Volare and drives away.

Little does she know, her son is carrying one of his RG-14 .22-caliber Saturday Night Specials in his luggage.

It has become a vital part of *his* plan.

---

*Dr. John Hopper will be sued by Hinckley's many victims, saying that Hopper should have known he was dangerous and placed him in a hospital. The case was dismissed.

18

WHITE HOUSE
WASHINGTON, DC
MARCH 3, 1981
1:22 P.M.

Seated inside the Diplomatic Reception Room, President Ronald Reagan makes small talk with CBS anchorman Walter Cronkite as a sound engineer adjusts their lapel microphones. The two men sit opposite each other on simple wooden chairs. Behind them, the iconic Frederic Remington bronze sculpture *Broncho Buster* perches on a credenza. Reagan's legs are crossed, and he rests his hands on his knees to keep them still as he speaks. Both men are dressed in dark suits, with Reagan's maroon tie in subtle contrast to the blue and yellow favored by the newsman.

Walter Cronkite has been a major figure in broadcasting for forty years, and Reagan has specifically chosen him to conduct his first interview since taking office six weeks ago. The anchorman has personally known each president since Herbert Hoover and has an opinion on each.* Cronkite finds Reagan to be "a lot of fun to be with, the kind of guy you really like to have as a friend."

Despite that admiration, Cronkite has a job to do. In this instance, he must ask Reagan tough questions in an attempt to reassure the world that the president does not plan on waging a nuclear war against the Soviet Union. So far Reagan has done little to dispel that notion, taking the same hard-line stance against the Soviets that he took against Communists in Hollywood almost four decades ago.

The situation has grown worse in the past week. On February 24, Soviet leader Leonid Brezhnev gave a three-hour speech in front of a Communist Party gathering in Moscow. The seventy-four-year-old Brezhnev is a short, overweight man with enormous bushy eyebrows who has ruled his nation for almost seventeen years. During that time, he has pursued a ruthless path of aggression against the United States and the rest of the West, secretly building a nuclear arsenal and military that now dwarf those of America and NATO.† This is in violation of several treaties between the two nations designed to keep world peace. Since the Nixon administration, the United States has pursued a policy of détente, in which the Soviet Union has often played the part of the aggressor and America has usually acceded to its demands in an effort to keep the peace.

It is a policy that Ronald Reagan abhors, and he is determined that

---

*Cronkite considers Hoover's presidency to have been "damned" by the Great Depression and Franklin Roosevelt to be a man of great charisma and personal strength. He considers Harry Truman one of the great presidents and was surprised by Dwight Eisenhower's total recall about the World War II D-Day landings more than a decade later. He thought John F. Kennedy handsome and sometimes arrogant; Lyndon Johnson larger than life; Richard Nixon an oddball; Gerald Ford a nice, straightforward guy; and Jimmy Carter to have been the smartest president he ever met.

†The Soviet Union had no nuclear warheads at the end of World War II, when Gen. George Patton urged Gen. Dwight D. Eisenhower and Undersecretary of War Robert Patterson to prolong that conflict by pushing for a show of strength against the encroaching Russian influence. Patton believed the Soviet Union was just as dangerous as the Third Reich. By 1981, as Reagan takes office, the Soviets have 32,146 nuclear warheads aimed at America, and the United States has 9,000 fewer aimed at Russia.

Brezhnev understand that. "It has been a long time since an American president stood up to the Soviet Union," he says to his son Michael in 1976. "Every time we get into negotiations, the Soviets are telling us what we are going to have to give up in order for us to get along with them, and we forget who we are."*

At the time of Brezhnev's speech at the Kremlin, many within the KGB fear that the Soviet Union can no longer keep up with the United States economically or militarily.† A nation can be militarily successful for only so long. At some point, the economy must also be powerful, and this is where the Soviets are failing. The Cold War, that decades-old ideological conflict between capitalism and communism, could soon come to an end—and communism could lose.

For this reason, Brezhnev's speech included an invitation that Ronald Reagan sit down at the negotiating table. Pretending to seek peace, Brezhnev was again bluffing. He wanted to bully the untested American president.

But Ronald Reagan is in no mood to be bullied—not by Leonid Brezhnev, nor by Walter Cronkite.

From the very first question, Cronkite attempts to put Reagan on the defensive. He asks about the "crisis" in American foreign policy, drawing comparisons between the United States military advisers in El Salvador and the early days of America's involvement in Vietnam.

Reagan fires back in a cordial yet firm tone of voice. "No, Walter," referring to the newsman by his first name, "the difference is so profound."

The president continues for a full minute, rattling off the details of

---

*Reagan made this comment from his hotel suite during the 1976 Republican National Convention. He was lamenting his loss to Ford and the missed opportunity to implement his own foreign policy. His words continued: "I wanted to become president of the United States so I could sit down with Brezhnev. And I was going to let him pick out the size of the table, and I was going to listen to him tell me, the American president, what we were going to have to give up. And I was going to listen to him for maybe twenty minutes, and then I was going to get up from my side of the table, walk around to the other side, and lean over and whisper in his ear, 'Nyet.' It's been a long time since they've heard 'nyet' from an American president."

†KGB, for Komitet gosudarstvennoy bezopasnosti, translates from the Russian as "Committee for State Security."

the growing Communist threat in Central America thanks to military groups controlled by the Russians and Cubans.

Cronkite replies with another pointed question about the "wisdom" of Reagan's foreign policy. Reagan responds instantly, his command of the facts absolute. Back and forth they go for twenty minutes, two master communicators making sure their message is heard. And while Cronkite is speaking to the American people, Ronald Reagan is talking directly to Leonid Brezhnev. Every word of this interview, right down to each comma, will be transcribed and scrutinized in Moscow. Reagan wants the Russians to know one thing above all else: he is not Jimmy Carter.

Soon enough, the subject turns to Brezhnev's demand for a summit meeting.

"You might have overdone the rhetoric a little bit by laying into the Soviet leadership, calling them liars and thieves," Cronkite states, referring to a comment Reagan made at his first press conference. "The world, I think, is looking forward to some negotiations to stop the arms race, to get off this danger point."

But Reagan does not budge.

"I do believe this," Reagan begins, distancing himself from a détente that he considers phony. "It is rather foolish to have unilaterally disarmed, you might say, as we did by letting our defensive [*sic*], our margin of safety, deteriorate, and then you sit with the fellow who's got all the arms. What do you have to negotiate with?"

Leonid Brezhnev is not pleased.

The Soviet leader sits in his Kremlin office on this cold winter day, craving the cigarettes that doctors are forcing him to quit. The last time he met with an American president was a year and a half ago, at the Hofburg Palace in Vienna, Austria. There, after signing an arms-control treaty that limited the Soviet Union and United States to the same number of missiles and long-range bombers, a jubilant Brezhnev embraced Jimmy Carter, kissing him on both cheeks. To the millions worldwide watching this display on television, Brezhnev seemed to want to appear both charming and lighthearted.

Soviet leader and Reagan nemesis Leonid Brezhnev in his Kremlin office

"He has the Slavic love of physical contact—back slapping, bear hugs, and kisses," Secretary of State Henry Kissinger wrote in a confidential memo to President Gerald Ford in 1974. "His anecdotes and imagery, to which he resorts frequently, avoid the language of the barnyard. His humor is heavy, sometimes cynical, and frequently earthy.

"Brezhnev is a nervous man, partly because of his personal insecurity, partly for physiological reasons traced to his consumption of alcohol and tobacco," Kissinger continued. "You will find his hands perpetually in motion, twirling his gold watch chain, flicking ashes from his everpresent cigarette, clanging his cigarette holder against an ashtray. From time to time, he may stand up behind his chair or walk about. He is likely to interrupt by offering food and drink. His colleagues obviously humor him in these nervous habits."

But Brezhnev has a notorious dark side. Until recently, he womanized constantly, despite being married for more than fifty years. Physical ailments, however, have left him bloated and unable to speak without slurring, making sexual liaisons only a memory. His condition is so bad that the television broadcast of his February 24 speech to the Communist Party

Congress was suddenly terminated after just six minutes. At this point, Brezhnev often seems incoherent, so much so that many Russians now mock him.

But they do so secretly. Brezhnev may be in poor health, but he still wields the power to make men disappear into the gulags of snowy Siberia or to vanish altogether.* After Brezhnev overthrew former Soviet dictator Nikita Khrushchev in 1964, sending him into house arrest on a farm outside Moscow, he made it clear that his role model was the ruthless Joseph Stalin, the World War II leader who murdered tens of millions of Russians and foreigners over the course of his brutal thirty-one-year reign.

Brezhnev is on a less extreme course. He and his KGB chief, the equally barbaric sixty-six-year-old Yuri Andropov, are fond of imprisoning dissidents and either declaring them insane or sending them to forced-labor gulags. There, the prisoners live on thin soup and hard black bread, laboring to chop down trees in temperatures as cold as seventy below zero. Soviet guards are known to shoot them on sight if they attempt to flee the barbed wire ringing their forest prisons.

Brezhnev copied the gulags from Joseph Stalin. So far, he has murdered approximately two million people in the camps. He is dedicated to Stalin's belief that communism should rule the world and that all brutality is permissible in this quest.

Sensing weakness in the West, Leonid Brezhnev has sent Soviet troops into Vietnam, Egypt, and Afghanistan and to the Chinese border—and those are just the nations where these forces are in the open. Soviet troops can also be found hidden within Angola, Cuba, Central America, and a host of smaller nations in which Brezhnev plots to spread global domination. Wherever the Soviets go, atrocities follow. The body count extends far beyond military intrusions. In Afghanistan, children are routinely maimed,

---

*Gulag is short for *Glavnoe Upravelenie Lagerei*, or "main camp administration." Though often thought to have existed only above the Arctic Circle, in Siberia, they were located throughout the Soviet Union. These were prison, labor, and psychiatric camps designed to break the will of dissidents through torture, hard labor, and exposure to extreme cold. Sentences were determined in advance by Brezhnev's hierarchy. Trials were conducted in secret, with no chance for an appeal.

mutilated, and murdered by a nefarious device known as the "butterfly" mine. Dropped by Soviet helicopters, millions of these explosive devices flutter to earth like small insects. But when a child tries to capture one of these delicate figures, the liquid explosive inside detonates, instantly severing their hands.

Ronald Reagan knows all this and despises the Communist leadership. He also understands he has four, perhaps eight, years to implement his strategy to reduce the Soviet threat. Brezhnev is intent on maintaining power for as long as he lives. He has marginalized his political rivals, keeping them on the fringes of power. For example, a fifty-year-old up-and-comer named Mikhail Gorbachev has just been named a voting member of the Soviet Politburo but is limited to a role in the Secretariat for Agriculture.

Brezhnev "has given his regime such strength and stability that a move to oust him, short of his physical incapacitation, seems almost inconceivable," the *New York Times* reports.

But the Soviet boss knows he must stay strong to maintain power. Now deeply angered by Ronald Reagan's comments to Walter Cronkite, Brezhnev feels his lighthearted manner vanish. He furiously dictates a nine-page personal letter to Reagan. "The Soviet Union has not sought, and does not seek superiority," he seethes. "But neither will we permit such superiority to be established over us. Such attempts, as well as attempts to talk to us from a position of strength, are absolutely futile . . . to attempt to win in the arms race, to count on victory in an atomic war—would be dangerous madness."

Ronald Reagan receives Brezhnev's letter at the White House on March 6. It is a Friday, and he is looking forward to a weekend at the Camp David presidential retreat for a dose of the outdoors. He knows Brezhnev, having met him at Richard Nixon's home in San Clemente, California, years ago, when he was still governor of California. World peace is contingent upon Reagan finding some way to relate to his Soviet counterpart. It is a delicate thing, to know that the fate of the world hangs on your next action.

"I didn't have much faith in Communists or put much stock in their word," Reagan will later write. "Still, it was dangerous to continue the East-West nuclear standoff forever, and I decided that if the Russians wouldn't take the first step, I should."

As he so often does in moments like these, Reagan consults with his advisers. This time, he turns to Secretary of State Alexander Haig, who has been insisting since the inauguration that he be given a more vital role in foreign affairs. Speaking in the Oval Office, he suggests to Haig that it might be good for Reagan himself to write Brezhnev a personal letter in reply.

But Haig is appalled. He knows the Soviets well from his years in the military as NATO commander, during which he often squared off against the Soviet-led Warsaw Pact allies. In Haig's estimation, Brezhnev's letter is typical Soviet rhetoric. He suggests that Reagan allow *him* to draft the return letter.

Ronald Reagan defers to Haig. He considers his secretary of state his chief adviser on foreign affairs. Nineteen days later, on March 25, Haig sends his draft of the letter to the White House.

That date is notable because it is the same day that John Hinckley is dropped off at the airport in Denver by his mother. Also on that Wednesday, Ronald Reagan flies by helicopter to Quantico for an afternoon of horseback riding.

"It felt great," Reagan writes in his journal that evening. "We should do this often."*

As he has done so frequently over the years, Reagan uses the time astride the small brown mare to sort out his thoughts. Haig has been a nettlesome presence in the White House, constantly wheedling power where he can find it, often at the expense of Vice President George Bush. The letter that Haig has drafted reflects that temerity. Reagan considers Haig's words inflammatory and not at all diplomatic.

---

*Reagan begins keeping a journal on the very first day of his presidency. He will not miss a single entry over the course of his administration. Several days after the incident, he even took the time to write about the day he was shot.

The president sends the letter back to the State Department, asking for a new draft. Five days later his request is fulfilled.

But once again, it is not the letter Reagan has in mind. The date is March 30, 1981. Ronald Reagan has been in office sixty-nine days. But no letter will be written that day.

Instead, an act of pure evil intervenes.

19

—⦿⦿⦿—

PARK CENTRAL HOTEL
WASHINGTON, DC
MARCH 30, 1981
9:00 A.M.

John Hinckley is hungry. He turns off *The Today Show* in his AAA-approved budget hotel room and steps out onto the corner of Eighteenth and G Street. The sky is overcast. A light rain settles on Hinckley's well-worn beige jacket as he strolls three blocks to the K Street McDonald's. He did not sleep well last night, troubled by how to play out his Jodie Foster obsession once and for all. Money is also on his mind. Once again, Hinckley is almost broke. After spending $47 on his room last night, and then spending a dollar for breakfast, he has less than $130 to his name. This is barely enough for a ticket back home to Denver, but John Hinckley does not care. He will never return to that home again.

On his way to breakfast, Hinckley turns into the local Crown Books. He browses, looking for literature about his two favorite topics: the Beatles and political assassination.

But little interests Hinckley this morning. He leaves the bookstore,

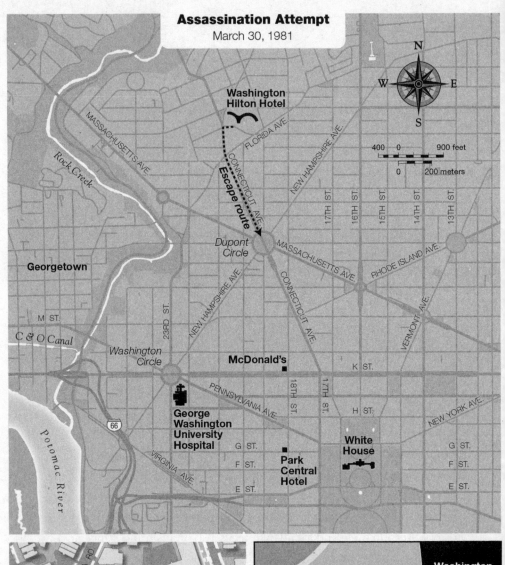

Assassination Attempt

March 30, 1981

Washington Hilton Hotel

Escape route

FLORIDA AVE.

MASSACHUSETTS AVE.

CONNECTICUT AVE.

Rock Creek

NEW HAMPSHIRE AVE.

17TH ST.

16TH ST.

15TH ST.

14TH ST.

13TH ST.

Dupont Circle

MASSACHUSETTS AVE.

RHODE ISLAND AVE.

Georgetown

CONNECTICUT AVE.

NEW HAMPSHIRE AVE.

23RD ST.

M ST.

VERMONT AVE.

C & O Canal

Washington Circle

McDonald's

K ST.

18TH ST.

17TH ST.

NEW YORK AVE.

66

PENNSYLVANIA AVE.

George Washington University Hospital

G ST.

H ST.

G ST.

VIRGINIA AVE.

Park Central Hotel

White House

F ST.

F ST.

Potomac River

E ST.

E ST.

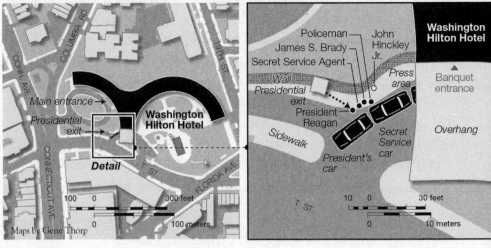

CONN. AVE.

COLUMBIA RD.

19TH ST.

Main entrance →

Washington Hilton Hotel

Presidential exit →

CONNECTICUT AVE.

Detail

T ST.

FLORIDA AVE.

100   0   300 feet

0   100 meters

Maps by Gene Thorp

Policeman   John Hinckley Jr.

James S. Brady

Secret Service Agent

Press area

Washington Hilton Hotel

Wall

Presidential exit

▲ Banquet entrance

President Reagan

Sidewalk

President's car

Secret Service car

Overhang

T ST.

10   0   30 feet

0   10 meters

crosses the street to McDonald's, orders an Egg McMuffin, and sits down in a booth to plan his day. Unlike most Washington tourists, Hinckley does not envisage hours of sightseeing. Instead, he will either take the train to New Haven and shoot himself dead in front of Jodie Foster, or he will murder Ted Kennedy, if only to add his name to the notorious list of assassins who have stalked and killed a member of that political dynasty.

If that target is not available, he might enter the U.S. Senate chamber and try to kill as many lawmakers as possible. And there is one other scenario in Hinckley's mind: assassinating President Ronald Reagan.

No matter which of the four schemes he chooses, Hinckley has the means to pull it off. Nestled within his large suitcase back at the Park Central Hotel are his snub-nosed pistol and forty-three lethal bullets.

Hinckley sits alone in the McDonald's for an hour. He cannot make up his mind. Shortly before eleven he walks back to the Park Central, stopping along the way to buy a copy of the *Washington Star*.

At the same moment, two blocks away in the White House, President Ronald Reagan is just concluding a ceremonial fourteen-minute meeting in the Cabinet Room with a group of Hispanic leaders. It has been a long morning, beginning with a breakfast for his political appointees in the Blue Room at 8:34, then a fifteen-minute session with his top advisers. Four more meetings round out the morning, each with a cast of dignitaries and administration officials. Among them is a relatively new face: James Brady. As Reagan's recently hired press secretary, Brady has the job of dealing with the media, using wit and intelligence to get the president's message to the public.

The husky Brady, a political veteran from Illinois, is forty years old. Nancy Reagan initially opposed him for the high-profile position, thinking him too old and too heavy. But Brady's sense of humor and his candor impressed the president and have made him popular with the Washington press corps.

Brady is hoping to tighten his bond with Ronald Reagan in the coming months by spending time with him. This afternoon, Reagan is due to give a short speech at the Washington Hilton, but Brady is unsure if he will attend. The president will not be taking questions from the press, and Brady's time might be better spent at the White House.

As James Brady deliberates, Ronald Reagan spends thirty minutes alone in the Oval Office, tinkering with his upcoming speech. The audience will be liberal union members who oppose his politics, but Reagan is confident he can win them over with his Irish charm.

Finally, at 11:24 a.m., Ronald Reagan slips out of the Oval Office and walks along the Colonnade, next to the Rose Garden, then takes the elevator upstairs to his private residence. There, he changes into a new blue suit before sitting down to a lunch of soup and fruit. Nancy Reagan is attending a luncheon in Georgetown, so the president dines with an old friend from California, the openly gay interior decorator Ted Graber.

▬ ▬ ▬

As the president eats lunch, John Hinckley is taking a shower. He is deep in thought as the water beats down on him. An item on page A-4 in the *Washington Star* has caught his eye. Under the heading "President's Schedule," the piece mentions that Ronald Reagan will be giving a speech at the Washington Hilton this afternoon. This presents Hinckley with a dilemma: should he murder the president or kill himself in front of Jodie Foster? He has already decided against murdering Ted Kennedy or shooting up the Senate Chamber. Now, with his options down to just two, Hinckley soaks under the shower spray, trying to make up his mind.

"It was in the shower," he will later explain, "that I debated whether to detour to the Hilton or go up to New Haven. I was thinking, should I go over to the Hilton with my little pistol and see how close I could . . . well, see what the scene was like."

Hinckley rinses off the soap and turns off the water.

His mind is made up. He is going to the Hilton.

He towels off and gets dressed in a pair of simple trousers, a shirt, and ankle-high boots. His wallet contains $129 in cash along with two library cards, a Texas driver's license, a chess club membership, and folded magazine photos of Jodie Foster. There is no guarantee he will fire his gun this afternoon, but if he does get close enough to squeeze off a round, John Hinckley wants Jodie Foster to know he is doing it for her. He sits down at a small wooden desk and composes a letter to his beloved: "Dear Jodie," he writes. "There is a definite possibility I will be killed in my attempt to get Reagan. This is why I am writing you this letter now.

> As you well know by now I love you very much. Over the past seven months I've left you dozens of poems, letters and love messages in the faint hope that you could develop an interest in me. Although we talked on the phone a couple of times, I never had the nerve to simply approach you and introduce myself. Besides my shyness, I honestly did not wish to bother you with my constant presence. I know the many messages left at your door and in your mailbox were a nuisance, but I felt that it was the most painless way for me to express my love for you.
>
> I feel very good about the fact that you at least know my name and how I feel about you. And by hanging around your dormitory, I've come to realize that I'm the topic of more than a little conversation, however full of ridicule it may be. At least you know that I'll always love you.
>
> Jodie, I would abandon the idea of getting Reagan in a second if I could only win your heart and live out the rest of my life with you, whether it be in total obscurity or whatever. I will admit to you that the reason I'm going ahead with this attempt now is because I cannot wait any longer to impress you. I've got to do something now to make you understand, in no uncertain terms, that I'm doing all of this for your sake!
>
> By sacrificing my freedom and possibly my life, I hope to change your mind about me. This letter is being written only an hour before I leave for the Hilton Hotel. Jodie, I'm asking you to please look into your heart and at least give me the chance, with this historical deed, to gain your respect and love.
>
> I love you forever—John Hinckley.

He adds the time, 12:45 p.m., to his signature and then places the letter in an envelope. This will be left behind in his suitcase for investigators should he succeed in murdering the president.

John Hinckley stands and removes the Saturday Night Special from his suitcase, along with boxes of ammunition. Several types of bullets soon litter his bedspread. Hinckley has the choice of normal, round-nosed bullets or six rounds of an especially brutal bullet designed to blow a hole in the target by exploding on impact, spewing hot shrapnel.

Appropriately, these bullets are known as "Devastators."

He chooses them.

Armed and dangerous, Hinckley then takes a cab for the short ride to the Washington Hilton. He is nervous and has to urinate, so he asks the driver to stop at the Holiday Inn across the street. Hinckley uses the restroom and then hurries back to the entrance of the Hilton. A small crowd of seven journalists and a dozen eager spectators await Ronald Reagan's arrival. A padded black rope has been hung across the sidewalk by hotel security to keep the crowd a safe distance from the president.

Pistol snug in his jacket pocket, John Hinckley joins the crowd.

The time is 1:46 p.m.

At almost the exact same time, Ronald Reagan and his fifteen-vehicle motorcade depart the White House for the Hilton. Reagan's 1972 Lincoln Continental, with its backward-opening "suicide doors," is nicknamed Stagecoach. The president, whose Secret Service code name is Rawhide, a reference to the Westerns he loves, rides in the backseat with Secretary of Labor Raymond Donovan.

Trailing behind are several limousines carrying members of the White House staff; the president's personal physician, Dr. Daniel Ruge; and a bevy of Secret Service agents. It is a 1.3-mile drive to the Hilton.

Press secretary James Brady is also in the caravan. At the last moment he decided to make the trip in order to hear what Reagan will say.

At 1:51 p.m., the presidential motorcade arrives at the Hilton.

John Hinckley stands in the crowd of spectators behind the security rope, watching the motorcade approach. The main entrance of the Hilton is behind him. The president will not enter through this door. Instead, he will use the canopy-covered VIP entrance just forty feet away.

The assassin feels an unlikely burst of excitement at the prospect of seeing Reagan in person. Hinckley pats the pistol in his right pocket.* Ample time at the rifle range has prepared him for what is to come. He knows the .22-caliber Rohm must be fired at close range for peak accuracy, and the spot where he now stands is well within the pistol's optimal range of ninety feet.

Hinckley surveys the scene, seeing ABC newsman Sam Donaldson, among others. More than two dozen Secret Service agents stand ready to protect the president. Hotel security and Washington police also crowd around the Hilton, including two police officers facing the crowd on the other side of the security rope. Hinckley notices that there are some Secret Service agents on nearby rooftops.

Suddenly, President Reagan's limousine glides past the security rope and comes to a halt just outside the VIP entrance. An agent steps out the front passenger door and hustles to open Reagan's door on the right rear side of the vehicle. Quickly, the president emerges into the afternoon drizzle, taking a moment to wave to the crowd.

DC police officers Herbert Granger and Thomas Delahanty are working the security rope and should be facing toward the crowd, looking

---

*A button featuring the image of his hero John Lennon is in his left pocket. Lennon was shot dead by an assassin just four months previously. Hinckley attended a vigil for Lennon shortly afterward. His father, Jack Hinckley, was actively involved in a Christian relief organization known as World Vision during the mid-1970s. Some believe the global missionary group was engaged in espionage on behalf of the U.S. government. The Catholic human rights group Pax Christi accused World Vision of being "a Trojan horse for U.S. foreign policy." The fact that Lennon's assassin, Mark David Chapman, also worked for World Vision has led some to suggest a link between the two shootings. However, a link between the two assassination attempts and World Vision has never been proven.

for signs of trouble. Instead, they crane their necks to the left to see the president.

This is the perfect time for John Hinckley to shoot.

But he does not. Hesitating, he responds to the president's wave with a wave of his own. It is not an assassin's kiss but rather the goofball motion of a confused man.

"He was looking right at me and I waved back," Hinckley will recall. "I was kind of startled."

In the blink of an eye, Reagan is inside the building.

◼ ▰ ◼

The time is 2:02 p.m. The president is introduced by Robert A. Georgine, the forty-eight-year-old head of the AFL-CIO's Building and Construction Trades Department. Reagan bounds onto the stage to the strains of "Hail to the Chief" and then launches into his speech. As always, the nearsighted Reagan has removed one contact lens, which will allow him to read the printed text with one eye while scanning the crowd with the other.

Ronald Reagan enjoys public speaking. It comes easily to him. He begins his speech, as usual, with a joke.

◼ ▰ ◼

John Hinckley hears laughter coming from the ballroom. He has left the security rope to step inside the Hilton and wander around the lobby. "Should I? Should I?" he asks himself repeatedly, feeling the heft of the Saturday Night Special in his pocket. He is having second thoughts about killing Ronald Reagan. If he were to leave right now and go back to his hotel room, nobody would be the wiser. He could burn his letter to Jodie Foster and slide the .22-caliber back into his luggage. Rather than die in a hail of Secret Service bullets or spend the rest of his life in prison, John Hinckley could simply walk away. "I just wasn't that desperate. I just wasn't that desperate to act," he will later state. "Also, it was raining. And I wasn't going to stand around in the rain."

Hinckley makes up his mind: he will go back to the spectator area and wait. If Reagan does not appear in ten minutes, Hinckley tells himself, he will leave.

The time is 2:19 p.m. Ronald Reagan has five minutes left in his speech.

Meanwhile, less than two miles away, Nancy Reagan is lunching at the Georgetown home of Michael Ainslie. The president of the National Trust for Historic Preservation is hosting the First Lady and the wives of several Cabinet members after a brief morning tour of the Phillips Collection museum of art.

But at 2:20 p.m., Nancy Reagan suddenly tells Secret Service agent George Opfer she is not feeling well. It's nothing specific, just a general feeling of anxiety. The worried First Lady says her good-byes and is driven back to the White House.

John Hinckley is back in the spectator area outside the Hilton. He works his way to the very front of the crowd, so that the black rope presses against his belly and his right shoulder is against the hotel's façade. Three Washington police officers stand on the other side of the rope, facing him. Hinckley later remembers that they, as well as Secret Service agents, turned away from the crowd when President Reagan appeared.

The would-be assassin notices immediately that the Secret Service has moved Ronald Reagan's limousine to facilitate an easier departure from the hotel. Rather than being parked just outside the VIP entrance, it is now standing so close to the security rope that the right rear bumper almost touches the spectator area. Ronald Reagan will enter the Lincoln not forty feet but just ten feet away from where John Hinckley now stands.

All at once, Hinckley is jostled. Newsmen are pushing to get a better position in order to ask Reagan questions. Hinckley is outraged, shouting to the other spectators that the media should not be allowed to push their way to the front of the crowd. But then it becomes clear to him that the press is providing a vital distraction.

Everyone is paying attention to the media.

No one is paying attention to John Hinckley.

▬   ▬   ▬

Ronald Reagan finishes his speech at 2:24 p.m. The applause is polite, which disappoints him, for it is not the robust ovation he was hoping to hear. "Speech not riotously received," he will later write in his diary. "Still it was successful."

As part of his daily routine, Reagan places a checkmark next to each item on his agenda once it is concluded. The speech to the Building and Construction Trades Department having just earned its checkmark, the president leaves the stage and immediately follows his Secret Service escort to the car. Press secretary James Brady stands just inside the VIP door with Michael Deaver as Reagan approaches. A wave of Secret Service agents rushes past Brady, taking up their positions near the limousine. Agent Tim McCarthy is tasked with opening the right rear door for Reagan.

James Brady steps out of the VIP entrance before his boss, walking next to Deputy Chief of Staff Deaver. The president has chosen not to take questions, so Brady will now speak with the reporters himself. "Deal with them," Deaver says tersely as he heads toward the car that will ferry him back to the White House.

James Brady steps closer to the crowd, as Ronald Reagan walks out the hotel door. Secret Service agent Jerry Parr follows one step behind. It is his job to protect the president, so he now moves slightly to Reagan's left, placing his body between him and the crowd of spectators. If something were to happen within the first few steps outside the VIP door, Parr would immediately force Reagan back inside the safety of the hotel.

The first fifteen feet to the presidential limousine pass without incident. Parr is no longer thinking about pulling Reagan back. Now he is focused on moving the president forward into the car.

Agent McCarthy opens the right rear door of the limo. Like Press Secretary James Brady, McCarthy attended the University of Illinois at Urbana–Champaign. In a light blue suit, the former college football player is just shy of thirty-two. Brady stands ten feet from him, walking quickly to the security rope to meet with the press. McCarthy stands ready to close the door behind Reagan, unsure if the president will linger to wave to the crowd before getting inside the car.

The time is 2:27 p.m.

≡ ≡ ≡

John Hinckley sees Ronald Reagan clearly. He also sees the small crowd of agents—"body men," in Secret Service parlance—accompanying the president. Hinckley notices James Brady moving toward the rope line. Things are happening very quickly.

The president raises his right arm and waves to the crowd. A woman calls out from the spectator area as if she knows him. A friendly Reagan motions in her direction. Normally the president wears a bulletproof vest when appearing in public, but the walk from the door to the car is so short that the Secret Service did not think he needed it today.

John Hinckley braces his right arm against the rough stone wall, dropping his hand into his pocket. Quickly, he pulls the gun out.

Later Hinckley testifies that his head tells him, "Put the gun away."

But he does not.

Tomorrow, the worldwide media will take one look at this loner and describe him as a deranged gunman, as if he has no idea what he is doing. But John Warnock Hinckley is a cold-blooded killer, a man who has trained himself in the art of murder.

Just as he has done so many times at the firing range, Hinckley grasps the butt of the pistol with two hands for maximum stability. He bends his knees and drops into a shooter's crouch, then extends both arms and pulls the trigger.

The first bullet hits James Brady square in the head, just above the left eye. He falls face-first to the sidewalk, his blood dripping through a sidewalk grate.

The second shot strikes Washington Metro police officer Thomas K. Delahanty in the neck, ricocheting off his spine and lodging against the spinal column. He falls to the ground in agony, screaming.

The third shot goes wild, hitting no one.

The fourth shot strikes Secret Service agent Tim McCarthy in the torso. He, too, falls to the sidewalk, seriously wounded, a bullet lodged in his liver.

The fifth shot bounces off the limousine.

The sixth also hits the Lincoln, but ricochets—piercing Ronald Reagan's body under his left arm. The bullet enters his lung, coming to rest just one inch from his heart.

The president of the United States staggers.

▬ ▬ ▬

It takes just 1.7 seconds for Hinckley to fire all six Devastators.

The assassin is immediately punched in the head by a nearby spectator, then gang-tackled by the crowd. Hinckley is buried beneath several hundred pounds of angry citizens as Secret Service agents try to take him

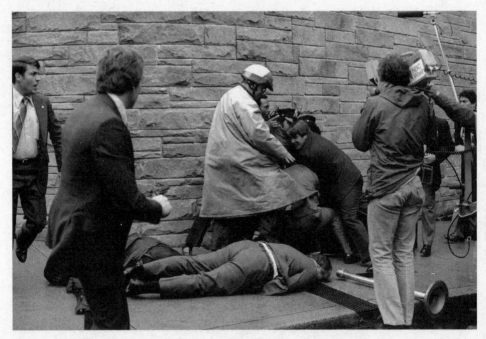

John Hinckley Jr. being tackled by Secret Service agents and other onlookers after his attempt to assassinate Ronald Reagan, March 30, 1981

alive. Ironically, their job is to now protect Hinckley with the same vigor they devote to protecting the president.

As Hinckley is subdued, three men are fighting for their lives.

One of them is Ronald Wilson Reagan.

▬ ▬ ▬

At the sound of the first bullet, agent Jerry Parr grabs Reagan by the waist, shoving him hard into the back of the limo. The two men land in a heap, with Parr on top. As Reagan's face hits the armrest dividing the backseat, an intense wave of pain shoots through his body.

"Jerry," he cries. "Get off. I think you broke one of my ribs." The president is angry, believing Parr was unnecessarily rough.

Parr is not interested in delicacy. He needs to get the president to safety immediately. Long ago, as a boy, it was the 1939 Ronald Reagan movie *Code of the Secret Service* that inspired Parr to become an agent. Now, through a brutal coincidence, Jerry Parr has become the most important person in Reagan's life. "White House," he barks at Agent Drew Unrue, who sits at the wheel. "Let's get out of here! Haul ass!"

Parr climbs off the president. Neither man knows that Ronald Reagan has been shot. But as Reagan tries to sit up, he is "almost paralyzed by pain." He coughs hard, sending a stream of bright red blood onto his hand.

"You not only broke a rib," he tells Parr as the presidential limousine races to the safety of the White House, "I think the rib punctured my lung."

"Were you hit?" asks a concerned Parr.

"No, I don't think so."

Parr runs his hands over the president's shoulders, chest, and head. He sees no sign of blood. Reagan can barely sit up, his face ashen. He begins pressing his left arm against his chest as if having a heart attack. Reagan tastes blood and tells Parr that he might have also cut his mouth. The agent looks closely, seeing that the bright red blood on Reagan's lips contains numerous air bubbles, which is the sign of a lung injury.

"I think we should go to the hospital," Parr tells Reagan.

"Okay," Reagan answers, still believing that Parr broke his rib.

■■ ■■ ■■

At the same time, in the third-floor White House solarium, Secret Service agent Opfer calmly enters the room and interrupts Nancy Reagan's conversation with the White House's chief usher. "There was a shooting," Opfer informs the First Lady. "The president is going to the hospital."

Immediately distraught, Nancy Reagan is led out of the White House. Her Secret Service code name is Rainbow, in reference to the many colors of her fiery personality. But there is no evidence of that on display right now. She is quiet and terrified. A car is brought around, and Nancy's frustration intensifies as the two-limousine motorcade gets caught in Washington gridlock on its ten-block journey. "I'm going to get out and walk," she yells. "I need to walk. I have to get there."

Traffic begins to flow, and fifteen minutes after leaving the White House, Nancy Reagan's limousine pulls up to the George Washington University Hospital. As soon as the vehicle stops at the emergency entrance of the gray cinder-block building, she sprints toward the emergency room. Waiting at the door is Deputy Chief of Staff Mike Deaver.

"He's been hit," Deaver tells her.

"But they told me he wasn't hit," replies a shocked Nancy Reagan. "I want to see my husband," she pleads.

■■ ■■ ■■

It takes Ronald Reagan's limousine four minutes to get to the hospital. He walks through the front door under his own power, then passes out and collapses hard to the floor. He is immediately transported to the emergency room. "I feel so bad," Ronald Reagan tells the paramedic, who quickly begins cutting the clothes off the president's body. "I feel really awful. I can't breathe."

This is the first indication that something is very wrong with Ronald Reagan. At first, doctors believe Reagan may die. Now an attempt to take his blood pressure has not yielded a systolic reading, meaning that his heart is barely pumping.

All around Reagan, the emergency room is a frantic scene of doctors, nurses, and well-armed Secret Service agents. Dr. Joseph Giordano, a surgeon who heads the hospital's trauma team, is inserting a clear plastic chest tube into Reagan, hoping to drain the blood from his chest cavity. "This better go well," Giordano tells himself as he slices open the president's skin.

"He was seriously injured," Giordano will later remember. "He was close to dying."

Ronald Reagan is a seventy-year-old man who has just suffered a devastating trauma. Not only was he shot, but he was thrown bodily into a car, and his head slammed hard into an armrest. His body may not have the ability to endure much more.

Reagan is conscious throughout the trauma procedure. Once he is stabilized, the next step will be surgery to remove the bullet. Spotting Jerry Parr just before being wheeled to the operating room, Reagan shows the first signs that he might make it: "I hope they're all Republicans," he tells the Secret Service agent who saved his life less than thirty minutes ago.

"Mr. President," Dr. Giordano, a lifelong Democrat, tells Reagan, "today we are all Republicans."

＝ ＝ ＝

A pained but lucid Ronald Reagan is being prepped for surgery. Lying on the gurney, he looks up to find Nancy Reagan gazing down at him. She is unsteady. Blood loss has made her husband's skin the palest white she has ever seen. A nurse removes the president's oxygen mask from his mouth. "Honey," he tells her, hoping that a joke will erase the fear from her face, "I forgot to duck."

Nancy fights tears as she bends down to kiss him. "Please don't try to talk," she whispers.

Later, Nancy will remember this moment with sadness and fear. "I saw him lying naked, with strangers looking down at his naked body and watching the life ebb from him, and as a doctor's daughter I knew that he was dying," she will recount to her friends.

But Ronald Reagan is experiencing another reaction. He will later write of the joy this moment gives him. "Seeing Nancy in the hospital gave me an enormous lift. As long as I live, I will never forget the thought that rushed into my head as I looked up into her face. Later, I wrote it down in my diary: 'I pray I'll never face a day when she isn't there . . . [O]f all the ways God had blessed me, giving her to me was the greatest—beyond anything I can ever hope to deserve."

Reagan is wheeled into surgery. Nancy clings to the bed's handrail the whole while, walking with the team of doctors and the now surgically gowned Secret Service agents who will accompany her husband into Operating Room Two.

"Who's minding the store?" Reagan asks Ed Meese as the gurney passes the White House counselor.

At the double doors leading into the surgery center, Nancy is told she cannot accompany her husband any farther.

The time is 3:24 p.m.

All she can do is wait.*

▬ ▬ ▬

At 4:00 p.m., Ronald Reagan lies unconscious on the operating table. A rib spreader pulls his fifth and sixth ribs apart, allowing Dr. Ben Aaron to see clearly inside Reagan's chest. The seventh rib is indeed fractured, thanks to the bullet glancing off it. More troublesome is the blood filling the chest cavity. The president has lost half his total blood supply. Tubes running into Reagan's body fill him with new blood, antibiotics, and hydration fluid.

Dr. Aaron's goal is to remove the bullet from Reagan's body, but there is a big problem. While he can trace its path through the half-inch-wide hole it has left in the tissue and lung, he cannot find the location of the .22-caliber round.

Using his fingers, Aaron reaches inside the president's body and feels for the bullet, delicately working around Reagan's slowly beating heart as

---

*Eighteen years before, First Lady Jacqueline Kennedy suffered through the same ordeal, entering a hospital emergency room to await the outcome of surgery on her husband after JFK was shot. Jackie Kennedy first handed doctors pieces of his skull she'd retrieved from the presidential limousine, then stood patiently in a corner of the trauma room as doctors tried to revive him. Her pink suit was still drenched in the blood of her husband.

he does so. "I might call it quits," the surgeon says, frustrated he can find no sign of the bullet.

⬛ ⬛ ⬛

Frustration also reigns one mile away, at the White House.

"Who is running the government in the absence of President Reagan?" a journalist asks Deputy Press Secretary Larry Speakes on live television.

All across America, millions are glued to their TV sets as regular programming has been interrupted. A somber America awaits news about the severely wounded Ronald Reagan.

But if viewers are looking for reassurance, Speakes's words do not provide it.

"I cannot answer that question at this time," he responds.

One floor below where the press conference is taking place, members of Ronald Reagan's Cabinet huddle in the White House Situation Room, horrified at Speakes's response. Even worse, they know something that the press secretary does not: the Soviets are taking advantage of Reagan's condition by moving their submarines alarmingly close to America's East Coast. A nuclear missile could strike Washington in just eleven minutes. Secretary of Defense Caspar Weinberger has ordered America's bomber crews to go on high standby alert. Yet with the president now unconscious and Vice President George H. W. Bush in the air somewhere over Texas, no one at the White House has the direct authority to respond to the Soviet threat.*

Fearing the worst, National Security Adviser Richard Allen has ordered that the special briefcase known as "the football," which contains the nuclear launch codes that could begin World War III, be brought to him. It now sits on a conference table here in the Situation Room, safely concealed beneath a small pile of papers.

Suddenly, Gen. Alexander Haig takes charge. The secretary of state, who has long sought to expand his power, appoints himself temporary president.

---

*Vice President George H. W. Bush was slated to give a speech in Austin, Texas. When news came that Reagan had been shot, he returned to Washington.

"The helm is right here," he declares to the startled Cabinet members. "And that means in this chair, right now, constitutionally until the vice president gets here."

Haig, an intimidating man, looks around, daring anyone to dispute him. Constitutionally, the general is incorrect. Speaker of the House Tip O'Neill should be next in line. But no one in the Situation Room cares to defy the former four-star army general who fought in Vietnam and Korea.

"How do you get to the press room?" he asks, rising from his chair.

The room goes silent. Before anyone can stop him, Haig races upstairs and barges into the press center. Knees buckling, voice cracking, and hands grasping the lectern so hard his knuckles turn white, Alexander Haig proclaims his authority to the nation on live TV.

"As of now, I am in control here in the White House."

▬ ▬ ▬

Nancy Reagan is not in control. She is desperately praying. She sits in the hospital chapel along with the wives of Press Secretary James Brady and Secret Service agent Tim McCarthy. All three of their husbands are currently in surgery. The women are unaware that the media will soon report that James Brady is dead.

The women are not alone in this small second-floor sanctuary. White House chief of staff James Baker kneels in prayer, while Mike Deaver and Ed Meese join the vigil. They are as close to the president as any group of advisers could be, and the wait is torturous.

▬ ▬ ▬

Finally, at 5:25 p.m., thanks to a set of X-rays that show the bullet's location, Dr. Aaron feels the dime-size chunk of metal. The surgeon plucks the bullet from Reagan's lung with his fingertips.

"I've got it," he tells the surgical team, which includes a member of the Secret Service, who now steps forward to retrieve the bullet as evidence.

Dr. Aaron now turns his attention to the nonstop internal bleeding that still might kill Ronald Reagan.

Finally, at 6:46 p.m., an unconscious Reagan is closed up and wheeled from the operating room. The greatest crisis has passed, but danger remains.

Within an hour, Reagan is awake, though groggy. A breathing tube in his throat makes it impossible for him to talk, so he scribbles a note to his nurse. "If I'd had this much attention in Hollywood, I'd have stayed there."

≣ ≣ ≣

Twenty miles away, at Andrews Air Force Base, the plane carrying Vice President George H. W. Bush has finally touched down on the runway. His return marks the end of Alexander Haig's self-declared three-hour reign as leader of the free world. And while Haig was legally wrong to

Alexander Haig briefs the press in the aftermath of the attempted assassination of Ronald Reagan.

declare himself in charge, his blunt behavior has had one positive effect: Soviet forces are backing down.

In the White House Situation Room, National Security Adviser Richard Allen breathes a sigh of relief that there will be no need to open the special briefcase containing the nuclear launch codes.

Not today, at least.*

▬ ▬ ▬

Meanwhile, John Hinckley sits in a Washington, DC, interrogation room. He complains that his wrist might be broken; there are also cuts and bruises on his face from being shoved to the concrete sidewalk. But for the most part, Hinckley is calm as Detective Eddie Myers of the Washington Metro Police Department's Homicide Division interrogates him.

"How do you spell 'assassinate'?" Myers absentmindedly asks a fellow officer during the questioning.

"A-s-s-a-s-s-i-n-a-t-e," Hinckley answers, grinning.

The FBI has requested Hinckley be given a physical, including retrieving a sample of his pubic hair.

"Pubic hair?" the grizzled Myers asks in disbelief. "For Chrissakes. He didn't fuck Reagan, he shot him."†

▬ ▬ ▬

It is not until morning that Ronald and Nancy Reagan are allowed to see each other again. She has spent a long night alone in the White House, sleeping at the side of his bed, hugging one of her husband's T-shirts to feel his presence. At 10:00 a.m., Nancy enters the intensive care unit with Patti and Ron Reagan, who have made the flight to Washington upon hearing of the shooting. Although Michael and Maureen Reagan have

---

*Haig never recovered from the public perception that he had become unglued in this time of crisis. He was fired as secretary of state fifteen months later and ran unsuccessfully for president in 1988.

†The FBI asked for the physical examination as a precautionary technicality. The exam was performed by Dr. William J. Brownlee.

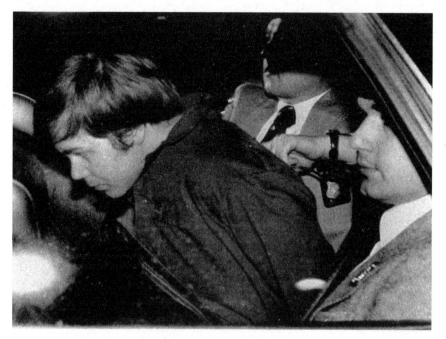

*John Hinckley Jr. in police custody following the shooting of Ronald Reagan
and three others, March 30, 1981*

traveled to the hospital, they are not ushered in until Nancy's children have had their moment.*

Ronald Reagan is oblivious to any sibling rivalry. He sees his family and is deeply moved. His breathing tube has been taken out, allowing him to joke and visit with Nancy and his children. He knows the shooting has changed his life forever.

"Whatever happens now I owe my life to God," he will write in his diary, "and I will try to serve him in every way I can."

---

*Maureen Reagan has just announced her candidacy for the U.S. Senate from California, against her father's wishes. Several weeks before the shooting, Michael Reagan was accused by California investigators of felony stock fraud. He will be cleared of the fraud charges in November. Without her father's backing, Maureen's Senate bid is ill-fated, ending when she finishes fifth in a field of thirteen candidates during the primary election. The protective Nancy Reagan sees both actions as a betrayal on the part of Reagan's children from his first marriage.

20

House of Representatives
Washington, DC
April 28, 1981
7:00 P.M.

The president who was nearly killed is bathed in applause. Members of Congress leap to their feet in bipartisan support of the man who was hit by an assassin's bullet a little more than four weeks ago. Ronald Reagan is visibly thinner and frail but is walking easily under his own power.

The roar continues as Reagan strolls to the podium and shakes hands with Vice President George Bush, who also serves as president of the Senate. Reagan greets the rotund white-haired Speaker of the House, Massachusetts congressman Tip O'Neill. The president then turns to address the Congress.

But the ovation will not end.

Reagan grins. He is genuinely thrilled by the outpouring of warmth. His cheeks and forehead are red, thanks to hours spent enjoying the sun in the White House Solarium during his recovery. He wears a well-tailored dark blue suit with a gray-and-blue-striped tie.

Referring to the shooting, Reagan launches an unexpected joke: "You wouldn't want to talk me into an encore." Laughter erupts.

After three full minutes, the applause finally dies down, and Reagan begins his remarks. The purpose of the speech is to gain congressional approval for his economic recovery program. However, almost immediately, he detours from the details of that plan to speak from the heart.

"Mr. Speaker," Reagan begins, "distinguished Members of the Congress, honored guests, and fellow citizens: I have no words to express my appreciation for that greeting.

"I'd like to say a few words directly to all of you and to those who are watching and listening tonight, because this is the only way I know to express to all of you on behalf of Nancy and myself our appreciation for your messages and flowers and, most of all, your prayers, not only for me but for those others who fell beside me."

At the mention of her name, all eyes shift to Nancy Reagan. She sits in the front row of the congressional balcony, wearing a bright red dress. The murder attempt has rattled her so deeply that she has stricken the word *assassination* from her vocabulary. Her public approval rating is one of the worst a First Lady has ever experienced, for many consider her a controlling ice queen. But what the public does not know is that Nancy Reagan sobbed at the hospital after her husband was shot. Even now, there are moments when she completely breaks down emotionally.

Nancy knows the little things about her husband that every wife knows: that Ronald Reagan likes his eggs soft-boiled for precisely four minutes; that his favorite soup is a hardy combination of beef broth and lean ground hamburger served with a slice of French bread; and that the bumps on his left hand are caused by a hereditary disease that forces his pinky finger to curl permanently into his palm.*

Nancy Reagan is one of the few who saw how pale and feeble her

---

*Known as Dupuytren's contracture, this disorder is found most often in older males of northern European descent, which is why it is also known as Viking disease.

Ronald and Nancy Reagan at George Washington University Hospital during his recovery

husband was in the hours after the shooting. For the first time, with those great dark circles under his eyes and haggard wrinkles, he looked like an old man. She saw the same frailty when he returned to the White House, walking in small, hesitant steps, his arms punctured by intravenous injections. In those days, he slept on a hospital bed in the Lincoln Bedroom, reliant on pain pills to get through the day and night. Nancy has even given up her own nightly sleeping pill to make sure that she will hear her husband should he cry out.

The First Lady's obsession with her husband's well-being extends to the public arena. Nancy Reagan now works with Deputy Chief of Staff Michael Deaver to regulate the president's schedule. Fearing that he will be overscheduled, Nancy decides whom Reagan will and will not see. This practice will continue throughout Reagan's presidency. Nancy's behavior is so hands-on that Deaver will one day state, "I always imagined that when I died there would be a phone in my coffin and at the other end of it would be Nancy Reagan."

She also watched with trepidation on April 16 as Ronald Reagan made his first public appearance since the shooting—taking a stroll around the Rose Garden before photographers. The nation marveled at his vigor and quick recovery, but Nancy knows it was all a carefully orchestrated façade, designed to reassure Americans that their seventy-year-old president was still very capable of leading the country.

On this evening, Nancy supervises her husband's meticulous pre-speech preparation. It begins with Ronald Reagan styling his hair immediately after stepping out of the shower. Reagan combs his still-wet locks forward until they hang over his eyes in long bangs. Then he applies a dab of Brylcreem in order to hold his hair in place and maintain the "wet look." Only then does the president sweep his hair back, deftly combing it into the trademark pompadour that takes years off his appearance.

"I never realized how much your face is changed when you comb your hair up in that pompadour," Michael Deaver once said to Reagan, after witnessing the hairstyling ritual. At first, with the hair hanging down on Reagan's face, Deaver was concerned that "Reagan looked eighty years old."

But with each stroke of the comb, youth magically reappears.

"Oh, yes," the president told Deaver. "It takes all the lines right out of my face."

Nancy has seen the combing ritual many times, just as she has seen countless makeup artists try to coax her husband into their chair before a big television appearance or a speech under bright lights. But harkening back to his old Hollywood days, Ronald Reagan refuses to wear makeup. That red-rouged appearance he now displays on the congressional podium is all natural.

These are the peculiarities of a man who has long charted his own course, and after his near-death experience Nancy is thankful for the gift of being able to witness them at all. Not that the shooting is entirely behind the first couple. Nancy alone knows that even now, basking in the relieved applause of his political friends and rivals, Ronald Reagan is summoning all his strength and concealing a great deal of pain in order to give this address.

Nancy needs strength as well. She knows America does not like her. The press has been ruthless, disapproving of what they perceive to be her power over the president. The criticism nettles her, but Nancy endures it. She can be a vain, selfish, and even deluded woman, far too reliant on fortune-tellers. But she is also very clever. And her loyalty and love for Ronald Reagan are absolute.

The president feels Nancy's approval as his speech transitions from the personal to the patriotic. "The warmth of your words, the expression of friendship and, yes, love, meant more to us than you can ever know," Reagan tells America and the Congress. "You have given us a memory that we'll treasure forever. And you've provided an answer to those few voices that were raised saying that what happened was evidence that ours is a sick society."*

Reagan pauses for dramatic emphasis.

"Well, sick societies don't produce men like the two who recently returned from outer space."

The president is referring to astronauts John Young and Robert Crippen, who successfully piloted a new craft known as the Space Shuttle on its inaugural voyage into the heavens during Reagan's convalescence. *Columbia*'s journey forever changes manned space flight. What Crippen and Young accomplished is, indeed, revolutionary.† It seems that the entire

---

*After the shooting, it was Senator Bill Bradley (D-NJ) who proclaimed from the Senate floor that America was a "sick society."

†*Columbia* was launched April 12, 1981, twenty years to the day after Soviet cosmonaut Yuri Gagarin became the first man in space. Designed as a reusable platform, the Space Shuttle rocketed into space and landed back on Earth with wheels down, like a traditional airplane. Its versatility allowed its crew to actually live in space. The astronauts could float free of the spacecraft to explore and to deliver supplies to the International Space Station. They could even make repairs of existing satellites. In the words of the National Aeronautics and Space Administration (NASA), the Space Shuttle "fundamentally changed our understanding of the universe."

world has undergone a major transition in the twenty-nine days since John Hinckley opened fire.

The days of Reagan's recovery also marked the end of an era, when the last top American World War II general, Omar N. Bradley, died at the age of eighty-eight. Just one day later, on April 9, a frightening new epoch begins when the first confirmed diagnosis of a disease that will come to be known as AIDS takes place in San Francisco. And just four days previously, Reagan penned his long-delayed letter to Soviet premier Leonid Brezhnev, opening a new epoch of relations between the two nuclear superpowers.*

But the greatest changes to Reagan since the assassination attempt are more personal. In addition to allowing Nancy to assume control of his schedule, he surprised her one recent Sunday morning by suggesting they go to church. In the past, religion has been mostly politically expedient to the president. After the shooting, however, Ronald Reagan has become a man who understands his own mortality and is determined to draw closer to God.

"Sick societies," Reagan continues, "don't produce young men like Secret Service agent Tim McCarthy, who placed his body between mine and the man with the gun simply because he felt that's what his duty called for him to do."

Agent McCarthy, the recipient of John Hinckley's fourth bullet, checked out of George Washington University Hospital on April 7. He will spend the rest of his life joking that the Devastator round ruined his new woolen suit. More important, the Secret Service will soon begin showing new agents videotape of the Reagan assassination attempt, pointing to the way

---

*Reagan expressed a willingness to sit down at the negotiating table with Brezhnev, as the Soviet premier had demanded. However, Reagan also made it clear that "a great deal of tension in the world today is due to Soviet actions." He took Brezhnev to task for the Soviet nuclear and military buildup and for its ongoing attempts to use force directly and indirectly to increase its sphere of influence.

McCarthy shifted his body into a linebacker crouch, with arms up and legs slightly wider than shoulder width, to protect the president. In doing so, Tim McCarthy exposed himself to the bullet. The round spun McCarthy as it entered the right side of his abdomen, knocking him to the ground. In a split second, the .22-caliber slug hit a rib, punctured a lung, passed through his diaphragm, and came to rest in his liver. The surgery at George Washington to remove the bullet lasted a little more than an hour.

As Ronald Reagan speaks to Congress, Tim McCarthy has no regrets about what transpired. The devout Catholic father of two young children is a product of his rigorous training and is already making plans to get back on the job.

In this way, McCarthy and Ronald Reagan are two very similar Irishmen.

▬ ▬ ▬

Ronald Reagan continues his speech: "Sick societies don't produce dedicated police officers like Tom Delahanty."

▬ ▬ ▬

Officer Delahanty is also of Irish descent. He is considered an "exemplary officer" by his superiors, having received more than thirty commendations during his seventeen years on the force. But the Washington Metropolitan cop earned instant retirement when John Hinckley's second bullet struck him in the neck. His injuries make it impossible for him to stay on the job.

Delahanty wasn't supposed to be at the Hilton on March 30. When the forty-five-year-old Pittsburgh native reported for work that fateful morning, he assumed that he would be doing his usual job with a canine division in Washington's Third District.

But Delahanty's dog was suffering from heartworms. Kirk, as the mixed-breed canine is known, lives with Delahanty and his wife, Jane, in suburban Maryland. Delahanty chose to leave him home for the day and then accepted an assignment from the department's Special Services Division specifically to work the Hilton detail.

Secret Service protocol stipulates that an agent never turn his back on a crowd when a president is present. But Tom Delahanty and the other Metro police working the Hilton never received that training. This may have saved his life. The bullet that went into his neck as he turned to gawk at President Reagan would have hit him in the throat had he been facing the shooter.

That is small solace for Delahanty. The bullet lodged in the lower left neck, dangerously close to his spinal column. Doctors at Washington Hospital Center initially decided against removing it, and only upon learning that the unexploded Devastator might detonate at any minute did the surgeons reverse that decision. As a safety precaution, they performed the operation wearing bulletproof vests.

However, by the time Delahanty was released from the hospital on April 10, the Devastator had left its mark. Irreversible nerve damage to his left arm means he must retire from the force. The department is also retiring Kirk, who will live out his days with Tom and Jean Delahanty.

Even in retirement, though, the incident haunts Officer Delahanty. He clearly proved himself to be far better in the protection of President Reagan than John F. Parker, the Washington Metro policeman who went drinking before President Abraham Lincoln was shot in Ford's Theater in 1865. Yet the Secret Service is now saying that Hinckley could have been stopped. All it would have taken was for Delahanty and the other Metro Police officers on the rope line to continue facing the crowd as Ronald Reagan departed the Hilton.

It is a question that will dog Thomas Delahanty the rest of his life.

Ronald Reagan pauses for emphasis. His eye contact with Congress is intense. He is firmly in control of the speech. "Sick societies don't produce . . . able and devoted public servants like Jim Brady."

As Ronald Reagan speaks his name, Press Secretary James Brady lies in a bed at George Washington University Hospital, his head resting at a twenty-degree angle to ease the pressure on his damaged brain.

Brady was pronounced dead by the media after John Hinckley shot him in the left side of the forehead. But those early reports were erroneous. Even as President Reagan speaks, Jim Brady is beginning a recovery process that will last a lifetime. The bullet that struck him was the only Devastator to explode on impact, sending shards of metal into his brain.

"The bear," as Brady calls himself, was comatose when the Secret Service brought him into George Washington University Hospital. Parts of his skull were missing, and his brain was visible. His eyes were swollen shut, and his breathing was rapid and shallow. Nerves were severed by the passage of the bullet, and a blood clot was forming on his brain.

The trauma team cut off Brady's blue business suit and stashed it in a plastic bag beneath the gurney. A catheter was installed, as were intravenous lines to replenish fluid and blood. But it appeared to be all for naught. James Brady's brain was swelling dramatically, squeezing the brain stem out through the bottom of the skull.

But Brady was in luck. He is right-handed, and while the bullet destroyed those portions of the brain that govern left-handed function, it spared those areas specific to right-handed behavior. He was also shot at a time of day when the hospital was at full staff, including a brain surgeon, allowing him to receive immediate assistance.

Within ten minutes, the trauma team stabilized Brady's condition.

But at 5:13 p.m., as word of Brady's grave condition leaked, Dan Rather of CBS News told America, "It is now confirmed that Jim Brady has died."

This was news to Sarah Brady, who was sitting with a social worker outside the emergency room.

It was also news to Dr. Arthur Kobrine, who was leading the surgical team then removing pieces of Brady's skull to relieve pressure on the brain.

Remarkably, the operation was a success. And though James Brady was still suffering in the hospital, he was alive. Amazingly, he will eventually recover a great portion of his brain function.

James Brady, the fourth Irish American shot by Hinckley, is also now forcibly retired. For the rest of the Reagan administration, the person taking his place will always be known as "acting" press secretary, out of respect for Brady.

Ronald Reagan is almost finished. "Sick societies don't make people like us so proud to be Americans and so very proud of our fellow citizens."

With those words, Reagan publicly puts the assassination behind him.

"Now, let's talk about getting spending and inflation under control and cutting your tax rates."

Three months later, standing in the Rose Garden at 10:55 on a sultry Washington summer morning, Ronald Reagan shows that he has rebounded from the shooting—and is not a man to be taken lightly.

"This morning at 7 a.m.," the president tells reporters, "the union representing those who man America's air traffic control facilities called a strike. This was the culmination of seven months of negotiations between the Federal Aviation Administration and the union. At one point in these negotiations agreement was reached and signed by both sides, granting a $40 million increase in salaries and benefits. This is twice what other government employees can expect. It was granted in recognition of the difficulties inherent in the work these people perform. Now, however, the union demands are 17 times what had been agreed to—$681 million. This would impose a tax burden on their fellow citizens which is unacceptable."

In Moscow, the Soviet leadership is watching this speech very carefully, even though it is a domestic matter. They are still unconvinced of Ronald Reagan's toughness. They do not know what sort of man he truly is. He may have survived an assassination attempt, but until now his leadership has not been tested by political crisis.

Shortly after Reagan won the election, the leadership of the Professional Air Traffic Controllers Organization demanded a 100 percent pay increase. These federal employees are not just responsible for the safety of America's skies but are also vital to national security, thanks to the military jets that rely on their guidance. PATCO was the rare union, along with the Teamsters, that supported Reagan during the election, and he sympathizes with their pay request. But it is too much. Such an enormous raise at a time when he is committed to cutting taxes is impossible.

So Reagan delivers an ultimatum: "If they do not report for work within 48 hours, they have forfeited their jobs and will be terminated."

A total of thirteen thousand air traffic controllers are now on strike. Their goal is to bring America to its knees, forcing Reagan to surrender. The threat of a major air disaster looms, an event that could destroy public faith in the president.

This is what the Soviets are watching so closely. If Reagan backs down, they will know how to negotiate with him in the future.

Understanding he is being personally challenged, Reagan is furious at the union. It has crossed the line. He may appear affable and easygoing, but he has a long history of holding tight to his convictions. In his mind, there can be no backing down. As he tells Secretary of Transportation Drew Lewis, quoting the words of his presidential idol, Calvin Coolidge, "There is no right to strike against the public safety, by anybody, anywhere, at any time."

In defiance of Reagan, more than eleven thousand air traffic controllers ignore his warning and continue to walk the picket lines. Forty-four hours later, Reagan makes good on his promise.

They are fired.

All of them.

"I'm sorry," Reagan tells the press. "I'm sorry for them. I certainly take no joy out of this."

Later, Reagan will reflect on this day with a sense of justification: "I think it convinced people who thought otherwise that I meant what I said."

Especially the Soviets.

George Shultz, who will one day serve as Reagan's secretary of state, will call this "the most important foreign policy decision Reagan has ever made."

The brutal firings send a signal worldwide: Ronald Reagan is back, and he is just getting started.

21

⟶◦◦◦⟵

House of Commons
London, England
April 3, 1982
11:19 a.m.

Margaret Thatcher is terrified. Heart racing, but appearing calm on the outside, the British prime minister rises to speak. She is dressed immaculately, in a dark-blue suit accompanied by her trademark pearl necklace and earrings. Thatcher's reddish-brown hair, held in place by copious amounts of hair spray, rises several inches off her forehead and rings her face like a lion's mane. French president François Mitterrand likes to say that Thatcher has "the eyes of Caligula and the mouth of Marilyn Monroe," in reference to her cunning and her offbeat look. Those traits are very much in evidence today.

Mrs. Thatcher leans forward, her weak chin and blue eyes on full display. For the first times in fifteen years, Parliament is meeting on Saturday. Both sides of the chamber are filled, the elected members sitting comfortably on benches padded in green leather. They have come to debate whether Britain will go to war. But there is another issue at stake today, one that few in this room will say out loud: Margaret Thatcher's political career could be all but over.

"We are here," Thatcher begins, "because for the first time in many years, British sovereign territory has been invaded by a foreign power."

And it is all her fault.

Just yesterday, the Falklands, a collection of mountainous, windswept islands in the South Atlantic that Britain has controlled for nearly 150 years, were invaded by hundreds of Argentine commandos, infantry, and armored vehicles. Margaret Thatcher knew the Argentine military government had been rattling its sabers over the Falklands to deflect the public's attention from the country's wretched economy. But she did not take the threat seriously, believing the islands insignificant and of no military value.

"I thought that they would be so absurd and ridiculous to invade the Falklands that I did not think it would happen," she will later tell a board of inquiry, adding that when she realized the invasion was imminent, "it was the worst, I think, moment of my life."*

Eight thousand miles away from London, the British Union Jack no longer snaps in the South Atlantic wind. It has now been replaced by the blue-and-white Argentine triband. In response, patriotic outrage seethes on the streets of Britain, almost all of it directed at Thatcher. In desperation, the Iron Lady has reached out to Ronald Reagan, asking the United States to help Britain retake the Falklands. But her fellow world leader and ideological soul mate is refusing. In fact, Reagan even suggests that Great Britain relinquish its claims to the Falklands, seeing the islands as a vestige of Britain's colonial past.

But Reagan is being shortsighted. This is about more than the Falkland Islands. This is about salvaging national pride at a time when Britain's global status is sinking and when its "special relationship" with the United States is overwhelmingly lopsided in America's favor. To allow a

---

*The Argentines call the islands the Malvinas and have laid claim to them since the nineteenth century, protesting British occupation multiple times since.

nation such as Argentina, and its arrogant military ruler, General Leopoldo Galtieri, to dictate terms is unthinkable to the British population.

No, this is a time for war, even if Margaret Thatcher and Great Britain must go it alone.

Thatcher has been prime minister for almost three years, and her conservative policies are fast losing popularity. The daughter of a grocer seems to have forgotten her humble beginnings.* Her greatest success has been in cutting taxes for the rich while trimming services for the poor. Up until now she has shown little interest in foreign affairs and has been a lackluster leader on both the domestic and international stages. Her nation's mood matches her dour performance. With unemployment hovering in double digits, the people of Britain are defeatist and cynical, a far cry from the plucky can-do spirit that buoyed Great Britain in World War II. Opinion polls show that if an election were held today, Margaret Thatcher would lose to her liberal opponents in a rout.

Yet Thatcher has no intention of altering her policies. "This lady's not for turning," she has publicly announced. "People are prepared to put up with sacrifices if they know those sacrifices are the foundation of future prosperity."

British press secretary Bernard Ingham would later describe Thatcher as "macho in a man's world, determined to work men under the table; fierce in argument, asking no quarter and giving none; in the back row when tact was handed out; impetuous; secretive; inspirational, and utterly dedicated, with a constitution as tough as old boots."

Now that constitution will be sorely tested. On the surface, Margaret Thatcher appears ill suited to lead Great Britain into battle. But lead she must.

---

*Thatcher was born Margaret Roberts, in the eastern England town of Grantham. Her father, Alfred Roberts, served as town alderman, a lay minister, and mayor of Grantham, in addition to owning two grocery stores. He was accused on several occasions of groping, fondling, and taking other sexual liberties with his young female employees, which was one plot thread of a thinly veiled 1937 satirical novel of Grantham, *Rotten Borough*. Some believe these accusations were false, spread by political opponents of his daughter. Neither of Margaret Thatcher's parents lived to see her rise to prime minister. Alfred Roberts died in 1970; Thatcher's mother, Beatrice, died in 1960.

With little political opposition, the Iron Lady launches a most audacious scheme to get the Falklands back. She orders the head of the navy, Admiral of the Fleet Sir Henry Leach, to prepare an attack.* Within a day, an armada of British warships will set sail for the Falklands.

▬ ▬ ▬

Four days after Margaret Thatcher's combat force sets sail from southern England, Ronald Reagan tiptoes into the Caribbean Sea. American warships are anchored offshore. The aquamarine ocean in Barbados is churning, with waves crashing onto the beach. Reagan begins to swim, though cautiously, knowing that he is not at full strength. It has been almost a year to the day since his release from the hospital after the assassination attempt. Part of Reagan's fitness regime now includes weightlifting and stretching, and as he emerges from the surf after the brief swim, he is proud of the five pounds of muscle he has added to his upper body.

There are indications, however, that Ronald Reagan's health is not what it used to be. Reporters noted earlier in the week that he was completely exhausted by just two days of meetings with Caribbean leaders. And while Reagan made a point of venturing into the water for his swim, aware that photographers down the beach were capturing the moment, his vigorous session of backstroke and freestyle alongside his Secret Service bodyguard was brief.

Ronald Reagan walks up the white sand to where Nancy sits with their hostess, former Hollywood actress Claudette Colbert.† Nancy wears a strapless green-and-black bathing suit with a straw hat, while Colbert is

---

*Shortly after the crisis began, Leach insisted that Thatcher back a swift counterattack. "If we do not," Leach explained to the prime minister, "or if we pussyfoot in our actions and do not achieve complete success, in another few months we shall be living in a different country whose words count for little." Thatcher agreed.

†The French-born Colbert was born Emilie Chauchoin. She is best known for her role opposite Clark Gable in the 1934 comedy, *It Happened One Night*, for which she won the Best Actress Oscar. A staunch conservative Republican, Colbert died at Bellerive on Barbados on July 30, 1996. She had lived there alone ever since her husband of thirty-two years, a California surgeon named Joel Pressman, passed away in 1968 at the age of sixty-seven.

clad in a white beach outfit. The actress did her own swim this morning, preferring thirty minutes of backstroke in the pool at the estate she has named Bellerive. *National Review* editor William F. Buckley Jr. and his wife, Pat, have joined Colbert and the Reagans for lunch.

Despite the state of world affairs, the president considers this a day off. He and Nancy flew to Barbados on official business, but the weekend is to be a time of sun and relaxation. Their get-together with Colbert and the Buckleys will stretch from just past noon until almost midnight. First, a cocktail hour, and then a dinner of curried chicken in Colbert's turquoise-colored dining room. Later, the Reagans will return to a private residence six miles away to sleep.

Yet world matters do not simply vanish because Reagan is in the mood to relax. Those warships anchored within view of Colbert's two-story villa are American navy communications ships, along with a hospital vessel standing by to treat Reagan should something once again go horribly wrong. Secretary of State Alexander Haig is currently in London, meeting with Margaret Thatcher about the Falklands, and Reagan is waiting on a report. While pretending to be neutral, the president is a firm backer of the British and has little sympathy for the Argentine dictator Galtieri, whom he considers a drunk. However, Reagan does believe the Argentine leader to be an ally in the war against communism. Evidence of this can be found in Argentina's military and financial support for a group known as the Contras, who are currently fighting the Marxist regime in Nicaragua. Since 1979 the United States has also backed the Contras. It is a policy that will soon lead to the greatest scandal of Reagan's presidency.

But there is another reason Reagan is adopting a tone of neutrality in the Falklands situation. The Soviet Union is courting Galtieri by threatening to join Argentina in the conflict against the British. Reagan does not want this to happen, so he is cautious in his public statements.

Secretary of State Haig's report from London is flashed to the White House Situation Room shortly after the Reagans finish lunch in Barbados. "The Prime Minister has the bit in her teeth, owing to the politics of a unified nation and an angry parliament," Haig reports. "She is clearly prepared to use force."

Reagan spends part of the afternoon thinking of his response. He finally writes back to Haig just before dusk. The larger problem facing the president is not the Falklands crisis but that he is still in the process of formulating his own foreign policy. In his one year in office there have been stirrings of unrest in Poland, delicate communiqués with the Soviet leadership, and an escalating crisis between Israel and Lebanon that now threatens to blossom into full-scale war.

"The report of your discussions in London makes clear how difficult it will be to foster a compromise that gives Maggie enough to carry on, and at the same time meets the test of 'equity' with our Latin neighbors," Reagan responds to Haig. "There isn't much room for maneuver in the British position."

Then, knowing his words mean war, Ronald Reagan gets dressed for happy hour.

On April 25, less than three weeks after sailing from England, British Special Forces and Royal Marines retake South Georgia Island.* The weather is terrible, a combination of force-ten gales and driving snow. Two British helicopters crash while attempting to rescue a group of commandos stranded on a glacier in the severe weather, and initial reports back to London indicate the loss of seventeen British soldiers. Thatcher weeps at the news, only to be told hours later that all the men survived. South Georgia Island is taken without a single casualty. "Rejoice!" she urges the citizens of Great Britain as the news breaks. "Just rejoice!"

But the Argentines are resolute. They still hold the islands' main city, Stanley, even as a full-scale British invasion looms. Argentine president Galtieri's nation, like Great Britain, is engulfed in patriotic fervor. Galtieri,

---

*First explored in 1775 by British sea captain James Cook, South Georgia was named for King George III and has been a British protectorate ever since. The remote island earned lasting fame in 1916, when Antarctic explorer Ernest Shackleton's ship *Endurance* was crushed by ice and he saved the lives of his crew by piloting a small boat across the Southern Ocean to the safety of a South Georgia Island whaling port. After his death in 1922, Shackleton was buried on South Georgia Island. Somewhat poignantly, one of the British vessels involved in retaking the island in 1982 is a modern vessel also christened *Endurance*.

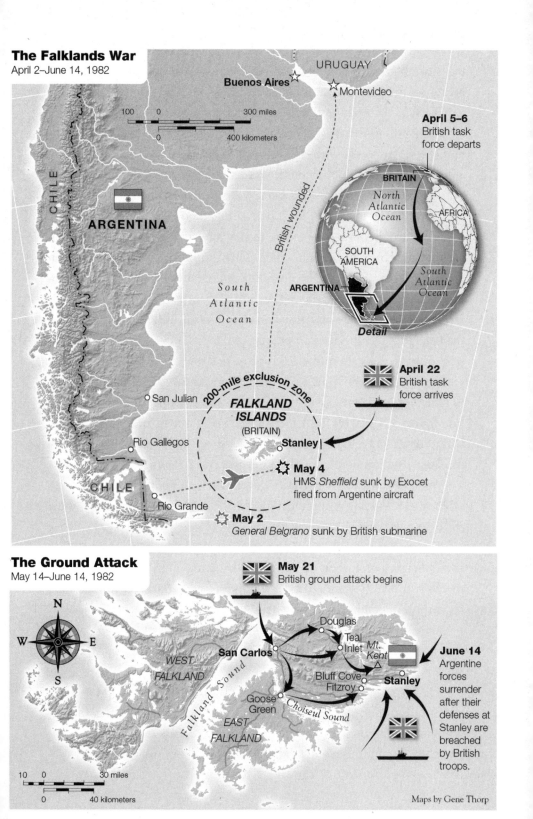

The Falklands War
April 2–June 14, 1982

URUGUAY

Buenos Aires ☆

☆ Montevideo

100 0   300 miles

0   400 kilometers

April 5–6
British task
force departs

BRITAIN

North Atlantic Ocean

AFRICA

CHILE

ARGENTINA

SOUTH AMERICA

ARGENTINA

South Atlantic Ocean

Detail

British wounded

South Atlantic Ocean

○ San Julian

200-mile exclusion zone

FALKLAND ISLANDS
(BRITAIN)

○ Rio Gallegos

Stanley

April 22
British task
force arrives

May 4
HMS *Sheffield* sunk by Exocet
fired from Argentine aircraft

CHILE

○ Rio Grande

May 2
General Belgrano sunk by British submarine

The Ground Attack
May 14–June 14, 1982

May 21
British ground attack begins

N
W   E
S

Douglas ○

Teal
Inlet

Mt. Kent △

June 14
Argentine
forces
surrender
after their
defenses at
Stanley are
breached
by British
troops.

WEST FALKLAND

San Carlos

Falkland Sound

Bluff Cove ○
Fitzroy ○

Stanley

Goose
Green ○

Choiseul Sound

EAST FALKLAND

10 0   30 miles

0   40 kilometers

Maps by Gene Thorp

the silver-haired former combat engineer, refuses to back down. He's been in office just four months, and this test of his administration will be either his greatest triumph or his political undoing.

On April 30 the British declare a "total exclusion zone" around the Falklands. Any vessel found within a two-hundred-nautical-mile radius around the islands will be considered a ship of war and will be subject to immediate attack. Three days later, with Margaret Thatcher's complete approval, the Argentine cruiser *General Belgrano* is sunk by a British torpedo. Its two escort vessels refuse to stay and rescue the survivors, cowardly fleeing back to the mainland. Three hundred twenty-three sailors are sent to their graves in the icy South Atlantic waters.

Two days after the *Belgrano* is sunk, Argentina gets its revenge. The HMS *Sheffield* is part of a British task force patrolling seventy miles off the Falklands. "Shiny Sheff," as it is known for its highly polished stainless-steel fittings, is a state-of-the-art Type 42 destroyer.

At 7:50 a.m. on May 4, an Argentine patrol aircraft picks up the *Sheffield* on its radar. Two hours later, a pair of Super Etendard Argentine fighter jets take off from an air force base at the tip of South America. With French-made Exocet antiship missiles affixed to the bottom of their fuselages, the jets home in on the unsuspecting *Sheffield*.

Argentine pilots Lt. Armando Mayora and Lt. Cmdr. Augusto Bedacarratz use caution when approaching the ship, flying just a few feet above the ocean to avoid being detected.

Despite their stealth, radar operators on board the aircraft carrier HMS *Invincible* pick up the Etendards when the planes are 180 miles away. But the British fleet has undergone a number of false alarms in the past few days, thinking they see planes where none exists. The officer in charge of *Invincible*'s electronics ignores the sighting, telling his radar operators that they are "chasing rabbits." No warning is sent to *Sheffield* or any other British vessel in the vicinity.

On board the *Sheffield*, the mood is calm. The crew is not at battle stations, and the ship's officers are chatting with their superiors in London via satellite phone. The electromagnetic effects of the phone interfere with the ship's Type 965 radar, making it all but useless.

So it is that both Argentine planes fly within twelve miles of the *Sheffield* before launching their Exocets. Pilots Mayora and Bedacarratz fire their missiles and then split up to avoid detection. The Exocets' rocket propellant ignites both missiles one second after launch. The missiles drop to just six feet above the Atlantic and race toward the unsuspecting ship at seven hundred miles per hour.

"The sea was very calm," British sublieutenant Steve Iacovou will later remember. "We were looking out to sea and I thought it looked like a torpedo was on its way because the sea was shimmering and shaking."

With no time to undertake defensive measures, the crew takes cover. "Missile attack. Hit the deck!" is quickly broadcast throughout the ship.

One Exocet lands harmlessly in the sea.

The other does not.

The missile pierces the *Sheffield*'s hull on the starboard side. Quickly, a fifteen-foot hole opens up and the seawater pours in. Luckily for the men of the *Sheffield*, the missile is a dud, and the 165-kilogram warhead does not explode. However, flames from the rocket propellant ignite everything in the Exocet's path. Diesel fuel stored in the Forward Auxiliary Machine Room detonates, sending thick clouds of acrid black smoke throughout the vessel. The heat is so intense that all efforts to fight the fire are in vain. The blaze rages unabated, asphyxiating and burning all those trapped belowdecks. Amazingly, the *Sheffield* remains afloat, and the crew struggles to guide her into port. The order to abandon ship is given six days later, and the empty ship is towed into port. The *Sheffield* becomes the first British vessel sunk in combat since World War II.

"Twenty officers and ratings [enlisted men] died," the official report will read. "Some personnel, in the Galley area, were killed on impact."

This is the message that is read aloud to the House of Commons at 10:56 p.m. on May 4. Margaret Thatcher sits with her head bowed as British defense secretary John Nott tells the members of Parliament the sad news. The one thing she has feared more than any other was the loss of a ship. Now that has come to pass.

The prime minister does not reveal her emotions until she returns to 10 Downing Street, whereupon she breaks down. Margaret Thatcher weeps. Going to war was easy. But knowing that her decisions cost young men their lives, and that mothers throughout Great Britain are now learn-ing the news that they have lost a son, is devastating. Her own boy, twenty-two-year-old Mark, and her husband, Denis, comfort Thatcher in the sitting room at 10 Downing Street as she sobs.*

"What are you making all this fuss for?" Denis asks bluntly as the prime minister's crying continues. He is not always fond of being a politi-cian's spouse, having suffered a nervous breakdown and abandoned his wife for two months early in her career. Fond of a large drink and a laugh, Denis was unsure of whether to divorce Margaret Thatcher or remain mar-ried to this workaholic woman with the buckteeth and frizzy hair who talks politics nonstop. In the end, he came back home, but Denis Thatcher is not one to mince words. "When there's a war on you've got to expect things to not go right all the time."

The next morning, the Iron Lady is stunned to get a message from Ron-ald Reagan, who once again suggests that the British consider leaving the Falklands to the Argentines. Reagan believes the conflict is not worth the price.†

Margaret Thatcher's mourning is replaced by rage. British soldiers and sailors are dying due to her decisions. Hundreds more are being wounded. In a scathing response, she makes one thing very clear: Great Britain is not backing down.

The men of the *Sheffield* will not have died in vain.

---

*Great Britain's version of the White House, 10 Downing Street is the official residence and workplace of the prime minister. While appearing relatively modest from the outside, it contains more than one hundred rooms and offices, along with the third-floor living quarters. Originally a collection of three houses built by Sir George Downing in 1682, it was first used for official state business in 1732 by Sir Robert Walpole and is within walk-ing distance of the Parliament, Buckingham Palace, and Trafalgar Square.

†Among the few countries that backed Great Britain were Ireland, New Zealand, and Argentina's antagonist neighbor, Chile.

▬ ▬ ▬

It is Memorial Day in Washington, DC. Ronald Reagan started his day at Arlington National Cemetery, in a moment of remembrance for the many Americans who lost their lives in war. Now he places a phone call to Margaret Thatcher.

"Margaret?"

"Yes, Ron?"

"Could you hear me all right?

"We could hear you very well. Can you hear me?"

"Yes, seems a little echo, but I guess that goes with the line we're on."

Ronald Reagan and Margaret Thatcher are speaking via the transatlantic hotline linking the White House with 10 Downing Street. It is 6:03 p.m. in Washington, close to midnight in London. Four more British ships have been sunk since the *Sheffield* went down, including her sister ship, the HMS *Coventry*. More than two hundred British servicemen have lost their lives on land and sea, but British troops have successfully retaken many parts of the Falklands. The war will not be over, however, until the British capture the capital city of Stanley.

"Could I impose and be presumptuous and give you some thoughts right now on the Falklands situation?" asks President Reagan.

"Yes, of course," Thatcher replies with a curt tone.

"I want to congratulate you on what you and your young men are doing down there. You've taken major risks and you've shown that unprovoked aggression does not pay."

Thatcher thanks the president and then listens in stony silence as Reagan puts forth a plan for a cease-fire to avoid "complete Argentinian humiliation." He hopes for a withdrawal of British troops and for peace to be maintained by a United Nations peacekeeping force. Thatcher is having none of it.

"Just supposing Alaska was invaded," she asks furiously.

"I have to say that I don't think Alaska is a similar situation."

"More or less so," Thatcher replies, not backing down an inch.

"It was always my understanding or feeling that you had in the past been prepared to offer independence to the islands."

With that, Reagan completes the last full sentence he will utter in this conversation. Despite the tone of civility, and the awareness that Great Britain is the weaker partner in their special relationship, Margaret Thatcher is uncowed by Ronald Reagan. Even as she speaks, British wounded are beginning the long journey back to Britain. Some maimed, some severely burned, they will bear the marks of the Falklands War the rest of their lives. Margaret Thatcher feels the emotional burden of their sacrifice and that of those who have fallen. She has slept little since the war began. The prime minister's official study is a short, seventeen-step walk up a staircase from her private apartment. She ascends those steps each night to listen to the BBC World News with her personal assistant, Cynthia Crawford. For the workaholic Thatcher, this is the closest she comes to an actual friendship. Crawford will remember: "We used to sit on the bedroom floor—the heating would have gone off and there was a two-bar electric fire in the bedroom—kick off our shoes and relax. . . . She had practically no sleep for three months. Just catnapping. She was so incredibly strong and determined. Not once did she flag."

After so many of these anxious nights, Margaret Thatcher has absolutely no intention of buckling under the suggestions of Ronald Reagan or any international peacekeeping body. She is not a woman fond of small talk, and her sense of humor is so dry that most people miss it. In a word, Margaret Thatcher is a serious woman.

So she lets the U.S. president know what's on her mind.

"Ron, I'm not handing over the island," Thatcher tells him. "I can't lose the lives and blood of our soldiers to hand over the islands to a contact. It's not possible." She continues: "You are surely not asking me, Ron, after we've lost some of our finest young men, you are surely not saying, that after the Argentine withdrawal, that our forces, and our administration, become immediately idle? I had to go to immense distances and mobilize half my country. I just had to go."

"Yes," says Reagan before Thatcher can cut him off.

She then launches into a long rant about Britain's territorial rights.

Theirs is a friendship strong enough to endure this disagreement, so she plunges forward with abandon.*

"Margaret—" Reagan says, trying to get in a word during her tirade.

"Well—" He tries again.

"Yes—"

"Yes, well—"

"The point is this, Ron," Thatcher concludes. She has never been one to bully, unlike many politicians. However, she is relentless in making her point. "We have borne the brunt of this alone . . . we have some of our best ships lost because for seven weeks the Argentines refused to negotiate reasonable terms."

"Well, Margaret, I'm sorry I intruded," Reagan says before hanging up.

"You haven't intruded at all. And I'm glad you telephoned."

Margaret Thatcher hangs up the hotline. Two weeks later, Stanley falls and Argentina surrenders. "She required guts to do it—her single greatest quality—and she deserved some cross-party support," liberal British leader David Owen will comment of the war. "Thatcher's personal resolve made all the difference between victory or defeat." Owen continued: "Thatcher would not have remained prime minister if General Galtieri's forces had not been thrown off the Falklands."

In the process, the British prime minister has emerged as a global force.

Her nation, as she has suggested, rejoices.

---

*"They disagreed over the Falklands, but that didn't hurt their friendship at all," Nancy Reagan will later comment.

22

Ronald Reagan is struggling. As he presides over a mid-morning meeting of his speechwriters, the president strains to hear the words they are saying. Age is taking its toll. Weakened physically since the assassination attempt, he continues to go deaf in his right ear. His left ear is only marginally better. Reagan tries to keep this a secret, but everyone in the room is well aware that the president's hearing is impaired.

Seated in a cream-colored chair with his back to the fireplace, Reagan crosses his legs and pretends to listen as his six-person team sits on two couches in the center of the room. They are there to discuss the president's upcoming speaking engagements, but the Oval Office's poor acoustics are making it difficult for Reagan to decipher what is being said. To make matters even worse, the three men and three women often talk over one another.

Looking on silently, Reagan tries to follow the conversation by reading lips and watching body language to see if a direct question is aimed his way. The meeting is brisk and efficient, just fifteen minutes long. But during longer policy sessions with his senior advisers, Reagan has been known to grow so bored that he gives up all attempts to follow the proceedings, spending his time doodling on a yellow legal pad. This may not be normal behavior for most presidents, but the seventy-two-year-old Reagan knows he must husband his energy carefully in order to make it through the busy days.

Today, for example, began with breakfast. He dined with Nancy in the second-floor residence, eating his usual bran cereal, toast, and decaffeinated coffee. He said good-bye to Nancy with his usual gusto, pulling her to him as if they would be separated for months instead of mere hours. The president then took an elevator down to the first floor, where he was met by Secret Service agents. He then walked to the armored door of the Oval Office, via the West Wing Colonnade, where he began his workday.

After a series of morning meetings, Ronald Reagan will have a formal lunch with West German chancellor Helmut Kohl to discuss the growing Soviet threat.

By two thirty in the afternoon, his work will be done. This being a Friday, the Reagans will fly to Camp David for the weekend. But the time of their departure is always subject to change. As with all the president's travel arrangements, an astrologer living in San Francisco must first approve. Nancy Reagan keeps the Vassar-educated socialite Joan Quigley, fifty-six years old, on a three-thousand-dollar-per-month retainer secretly to provide astrological guidance. Nancy remains deeply superstitious, making sure to sleep with her head facing north, and constantly knocks on wood. But her dependence on Quigley runs much deeper. Very few members of the White House staff know that Nancy's astrologer controls much of the president's calendar.

To make sure that White House operators do not eavesdrop on their conversations, Nancy has a private phone line in the White House, and another at Camp David, connecting her directly to the stargazer. "Without her approval," Deputy Chief of Staff Michael Deaver will one day write of Quigley, "Air Force One does not take off."

But there is one item on today's agenda so minor that Quigley has not been consulted, and Ronald Reagan's personal assistant Kathy Osborne has not typed it into the schedule. Sometime during the day, Reagan will take a moment to affix his signature to a proclamation naming April 10–16 as National Mental Health Week. The purpose is "to seek and encourage better understanding of mental disorders" and to bring "welcome hope to the mentally ill."

⬛ ⬛ ⬛

Eight miles away, in southeast Washington, DC, John Hinckley is finding that it pays to be mentally ill. Rather than suffer a heinous punishment for his attempted assassination of the president and near murder of three other men, Hinckley has been found not guilty of all crimes by reason of insanity. Thus, he spends his days in St. Elizabeth's Hospital, a century-old brick psychiatric facility. There, Hinckley has a soft life. He resides in a fourth-floor room, eats in the cafeteria, attends therapy sessions, shoots pool, plays his guitar, and watches TV. He can listen to any music he likes, and his hair remains long and shaggy. There are no shackles on his wrists or ankles. The only significant difference between this new life and his previous one is that Hinckley can no longer travel impulsively. His monetary woes are a thing of the past.

Shockingly, Hinckley still pines for Jodie Foster, telling the *New York Times* in a bizarre letter, "My actions of March 30, 1981 have given special meaning to my life and no amount of imprisonment or hospitalization can tarnish my historical deed. The shooting outside the Washington Hilton hotel was the greatest love offering in the history of the world. I sacrificed myself and committed the ultimate crime in hopes of winning the heart of a girl. It was an unprecedented demonstration of love. But does the American public appreciate what I've done? Does Jodie Foster appreciate what I've done?"

Hinckley continues: "I am Napoleon and she is Josephine. I am Romeo and she is Juliet. I am John Hinckley Jr. and she is Jodie Foster. The world can't touch us."

⬛ ⬛ ⬛

Ironically, one of the first things Ronald Reagan did when he came into office was slash federal funding for the treatment of mental illness, trimming the budget for the National Institute of Mental Health and repealing the Mental Health Systems Act of 1980. Yet, as the definition of mental impairment grows over time to include not just the insane or psychotic like John Hinckley but also those whose faculties are diminished by age, there are signs that the president himself may be sliding into this spectrum. The *New York Times* reported as early as 1980 that his "penchant for contradictory statements, forgetting names and general absent-mindedness" were considered by some to be a sign of Alzheimer's disease. This very specific form of dementia displays itself as confusion, impaired thought, and impaired speech.

In truth, Ronald Reagan can be sharp at times. Often, he spins entertaining yarns, adding dialects and jokes to his presentations. But on other occasions, the president gets lost mid-story. Sometimes he will tell a tale about some event in his life, when in fact he is confusing it with a movie role he once played. His staff is fond of saying that Reagan "has his good days and his bad days," and they know that the president tends to think more slowly in the evening than in the afternoon. In addition, Reagan has developed an "essential tremor," a slight shaking of the hands and nodding of the head. Though not a sign of brain impairment, it will grow worse with age.

Ronald Reagan has admitted to journalists that his mother died of "senility" and said that should such a condition ever affect him, he will resign the office of president of the United States.

But today, as his speechwriters rise promptly from their seats at 10:10 and file out of the Oval Office, nobody is realistically suggesting that Ronald Reagan is senile.

Or that he should resign.

Not yet.

23

WHITE HOUSE SITUATION ROOM
WASHINGTON, DC
OCTOBER 26, 1983
1:28 P.M.

Relief has arrived. Ronald Reagan wears a brand-new hearing aid, allowing him to make out the voice on the other end of the transatlantic hotline quite clearly.*

"Margaret Thatcher here."

The prime minister has excused herself from a parliamentary debate to take Reagan's call. The Iron Lady, just as Reagan's mother, will eventually live out the last dozen years of her life in a state of dementia.

But that confusion is seventeen years away.

Right now, Margaret Thatcher is completely furious.

Yesterday, on Reagan's orders, American troops invaded the former British colony of Grenada, an island in the south Caribbean. On Octo-

---

*Reagan began using a hearing aid in his right ear in September 1983. He began wearing one in his left ear in 1985.

ber 19, Marxist commandos overthrew the government, and there are fears that the new Grenadian leaders are aligned with Fidel Castro. The Cuban dictator has long sought to spread communism throughout the Western Hemisphere. Even as Reagan talks with Thatcher, there are civil wars under way in Nicaragua and El Salvador. Under the pretense that the lives of eight hundred Americans attending medical school in Grenada are at risk, eight thousand American marines, Navy SEALs, and Army Rangers have invaded the island.* Reagan's popularity among U.S. voters is soaring, and the president has bipartisan support in Congress for this bold move.

Unfortunately, Ronald Reagan never informed the Thatcher government. In fact, his advisers told Margaret Thatcher's foreign secretary there would be no attack. That information was then relayed to the British press. In the hours leading up to the American assault, Thatcher attempted to phone the president to warn him against military action but was told he was unavailable.

Ronald Reagan lied to the British, and now Thatcher wants an explanation.

"If I were there, Margaret, I'd throw my hat in the door before I came in," the president sheepishly apologizes.[†]

"There's no need to do that," Thatcher answers in a calm but firm voice. She knows not to antagonize the American president because there is too much at stake. Soviet president Leonid Brezhnev died almost a year ago, and since that time the Cold War has intensified. The threat level of nuclear war between the United States and the Soviet Union, now

---

*There is evidence that the invasion was planned long in advance of the coup. The overthrown regime was also pro-Cuban. Since 1979 the United States had sought to destabilize Grenada by discouraging U.S. tourism and offering little economic assistance. The Reagan administration escalated tensions by urging the World Bank to block funding to Grenada's government. In August 1981, U.S. troops rehearsed a mock invasion of Grenada on the Puerto Rican island of Vieques.

†Reagan is alluding to an old Irish custom of tossing a cap through a doorway before entering, to see if the visitor is welcome. It was later adapted in the American West as the habit of throwing a hat through a doorway to see if it would draw gunfire.

led by former Soviet spymaster Yuri Andropov, is at its highest point in twenty years. U.S. nuclear missiles in West Germany are pointed at Moscow, even as Soviet mobile rockets in East Germany are aimed at America's allies in Europe, among them Great Britain. To combat this threat, Thatcher is currently lobbying for American Tomahawk cruise missiles to be based on her island nation. But public opinion in Britain is heavily against such a deployment. Now, at a time when the Reagan-Thatcher relationship needs to be stronger than ever to confront the new Soviet regime, the British are being treated like powerless American vassals.

"We very much regret the embarrassment caused you," says Reagan, his voice soothing, a trait learned from his radio years. "We were greatly concerned, because of a problem here—and not at your end at all—but here. We have had a nagging problem of a loose source, a leak here. At the same time we also had immediate surveillance problem [*sic*]—without their knowing it—of what was happening on Cuba to make sure that we could get ahead of them if they were moving—and indeed, they were making some tentative moves. They sent some kind of command personnel into Grenada."

"I know about sensitivity," Thatcher responds, alluding to her experience during the Falklands crisis. "The action is under way now, and we hope it will be successful."

"We're sure it is. It's going beautifully."

"Well, let's hope it's soon over, Ron, and you manage to get a democracy restored," she replies in a cold tone.

"We think the military part is going to end very shortly."

"That will be very, very good news. And if we return to democracy that will be marvelous."

"As I say, I'm very sorry for any embarrassment that we caused you."

"It was very kind of you to have rung, Ron."

"Well, my pleasure."

"I appreciate it. How is Nancy?"

"Just fine."

"Good. Give her my love."

President Ronald Reagan and British prime minister Margaret Thatcher
share a private conversation.

"I shall."

"I must return to this debate in the House. It is a bit tricky." The debate, in fact, is a wholesale attack on Thatcher by her Labour Party enemies— all because of Grenada.

"All right. Go get 'em. Eat 'em alive."

"Good-bye."

Ronald Reagan may have succeeded in calming Margaret Thatcher, but new problems continue to emerge all over the world. Even as U.S. forces wrest Grenada from the Marxists, the United States has fallen victim to a new form of warfare: terrorism.

It is 6:22 a.m. on October 23, 1983. This Sunday morning in Beirut, Lebanon, is quiet as the sun rises to the east of the Mediterranean Sea and the nearby Chouf Mountains. American soldiers are just waking up in their four-story barracks at the Beirut International Airport. The First Battalion, Eighth Marines, are part of a multinational peacekeeping force sent to this former "Paris of the Middle East"—a once-beautiful, cultured city now reduced to rubble after years of fighting. The antagonists are the Lebanese, Israelis, the Palestine Liberation Organization, and an Iranian-backed group known as Hezbollah. The sectarian struggle for power in Lebanon is chaotic and furious.

The U.S. Marine unit has a glorious past, having distinguished itself in combat on such famous battlefields as Guadalcanal and Saipan. But today they are not the aggressors.

Outside the barracks, a yellow Mercedes truck approaches the structure nicknamed the Beirut Hilton from a nearby access road. The truck turns into the parking lot in front of the building. At first, the vehicle appears harmless, even as it proceeds to make a single counterclockwise lap around the lot. A five-foot-high wall of concertina wire separates the truck from the marine compound. Beyond that, a six-foot wrought-iron fence also provides a barrier. Just inside that fence is a sentry shack, surrounded by sandbags, where armed marines guard the main barracks entrance.

Six months earlier, in the heart of downtown Beirut, an Iranian suicide bomber rammed a delivery truck loaded with explosives into the U.S. embassy. The blast killed sixty-three people, among them top intelligence agents.

The marine guards watch the Mercedes. They are expecting a supply truck full of fresh water this morning, so they are not on high alert. Their mission in Beirut is to help stabilize the Lebanese government after years of civil war. Several Christian and Muslim militant factions are fighting for control of Lebanon, and all see the United States as a roadblock to their success. Although the marines have engaged in several hellish firefights with armed insurgents, some so bad that the Vietnam veterans among them will claim they have never seen fighting so intense, they must maintain the pretense that firing their weapons is a last resort.

So under the rules of engagement, the sentries' weapons are unloaded this Sunday morning. In fact, they have to ask permission from their superiors if they wish to employ live ammunition.

The circling Mercedes is not, in fact, harmless. Rather, it is packed with the equivalent of twenty-one thousand pounds of dynamite. These are wrapped around butane cylinders to enhance the force of any blast.

Suddenly, without warning, the driver guns the Mercedes directly at the rolls of razor-sharp barbed wire at the compound's perimeter. The wire snaps as he blasts on through, aiming for a gate in the wrought-iron fence that has been kept open to allow vehicles to move freely. The young soldiers on guard duty frantically try to chamber rounds in their M16s— but the truck is coming too fast. Within seconds, the driver runs through the gate opening, past the sentry box, and toward the barracks lobby. One brave marine opens fire, while another throws his body in front of the vehicle—to no avail.

Then the "martyr," as Iran will one day proclaim this murderer, explodes his ordnance. An enormous fireball engulfs the barracks. A crater thirty feet wide and forty feet deep marks the site of the detonation. The entire Beirut Hilton collapses. Bodies fly through the air, some landing more than fifty yards from the building.*

It is an explosion so massive that the FBI will proclaim it to be the biggest nonnuclear bomb in history. The 241 American military killed is the worst single-day toll since the first day of the Tet Offensive, fifteen years ago. When rescue workers attempt to evacuate these wounded peacekeepers, terrorist snipers fire at them.

The violence in Beirut marks the first full-scale use of terror by Muslim factions against the United States. But it is hardly the last. Two months later, the U.S. embassy in Kuwait will be the target of a suicide-bomber

---

*A second suicide bomber strikes the nearby French military compound, killing fifty-eight French paratroopers and six civilians.

attack. And six months from now, CIA Beirut station chief William Buckley will become the fourth of thirty key Americans kidnapped by Muslim extremists in Lebanon.

▬ ▬ ▬

On March 16, 1984, the fifty-five-year-old Buckley rides the elevator from his tenth-floor Beirut apartment down to the parking garage of the Al-Manara building. It is minutes before 8:00 a.m. The career spy lives alone, and has just finished a breakfast of coffee and cereal, accompanied by a recording of Dean Martin singing "Return to Me." Shackled to his wrist is a locked CIA burn bag containing top secret documents—and sandwiches he has prepared for lunch.

One floor down, a well-dressed man carrying a leather briefcase steps into the elevator, then rides wordlessly to the parking garage with Buckley. All at once, the CIA station chief feels a blow to the back of his skull. The assailant's briefcase is filled with rocks, and the American official crumples to the ground. A white Renault containing two men immediately pulls up to the elevator. Buckley is dragged into the backseat of the car, his captors sitting on top of him. The car speeds away in such a hurry that the back door is still open.

Within hours, the CIA is aware that the station chief is missing. Soon after, his captors round up his network of spies and informers within Lebanon and murder them one by one. This confirms to the CIA that Buckley was tortured, and has broken.

But it is not until May 7, almost seven weeks later, that American agents see the real horror. An anonymous videotape is delivered to the U.S. embassy in Athens, showing a naked Buckley being tortured. Ligature marks on his wrists and neck indicate that he has been tied to a rope or chain. Analysts studying the tape note that his body is covered in puncture marks, showing that Buckley has been drugged repeatedly. CIA director William Casey will later remember of his viewing of the video. "I was close to tears. It was the most obscene thing I had ever witnessed. Bill was barely recognizable as the man I had known for years. They had done more than ruin his body. His eyes made it clear his mind had been played with. It was horrific, medieval and barbarous."

Three weeks later, another gruesome video arrives. This one is far more graphic than the last. Finally, after five more months of torture, a third and final video finds its way to the CIA. Buckley is clearly on the verge of insanity, a drooling mess uttering gibberish and rolling his eyes like a crazy man.

But his ordeal is not over. Bill Buckley must still endure almost another year of captivity before he is executed by Hezbollah. Although his Islamic jihadist captors announce the spy's death in 1985, his corpse will not be located until 1991.*

Ronald Reagan was powerless to help Buckley. But he exercised his power by bringing Grenada to its knees.† And while the tiny island nation may have been an easy target, Muslim extremists are not.

However, CIA station chief William Buckley does not die without consequence. Reagan will be tormented by his kidnapping and death. The result will be National Security Decision Directive 138, a bold, top secret decision to counter state-sponsored terrorism "by all legal means." Reagan affixes his signature to the directive on April 3, 1984.

But "legal means" will soon be set aside. Iran is currently engaged in a fierce war with its Middle East neighbor, Iraq, and has run out of military weapons. President Ronald Reagan will secretly authorize the sales of weapons to Iran, a sworn U.S. enemy and the nation responsible for killing hundreds of Americans. Reagan knows this, but he decides that liberating the American hostages is worth breaking the law. Under a plan

---

*Buckley was buried in Arlington National Cemetery with full military honors, Section 59, Lot 346.

†The United States captured Grenada at a cost of 19 American killed and 116 wounded in the seven-week war. Its primary opposition on the island came from a joint Grenadian and Cuban force, which suffered casualties of 70 dead and 417 wounded. They were aided by an additional contingent of Soviet, East German, Bulgarian, North Korean, and Libyan troops, which suffered no casualties.

masterminded by Marine Corps lieutenant colonel Oliver North, American funds will also be secretly funneled to the rebel Contras fighting communism in Nicaragua whom Reagan admires so much.*

So it is that after three years in office, the president of the United States has had many successes: he has turned around the economy, bringing an end to the recession and reducing the level of unemployment; he has countered the Soviet threat in Europe by placing attack cruise missiles in Germany and England; and, simultaneously, he has begun urging the Soviets to join him in efforts to reduce the possibility of nuclear war through voluntary arms control.

But Ronald Reagan still faces problems all over the world. Despite his best efforts, there is growing tension with the Soviet Union. Reagan has invaded the Caribbean island of Grenada with U.S. troops. He has offended his greatest ally, Margaret Thatcher. And just a few days before that, America absorbed a horrific Muslim terrorist attack in Lebanon.

And if all that isn't enough, Ronald Reagan must now begin another exhausting undertaking: getting reelected.

---

*The scandal became known as Iran-Contra. The administration's actions were illegal for three reasons: the Boland Amendment of 1982 prohibited funding of the Contras beyond congressionally approved limits; the sale of arms to Iran was prohibited; and it is against U.S. national policy to pay ransom for hostages. Some thirty million dollars were transferred from Iran to the Contras. Eleven administration officials were ultimately indicted for their role in selling arms to Iran and funneling the money to the Contras, including Secretary of Defense Caspar Weinberger and CIA chief William Casey. Nobody went to prison, and George H. W. Bush pardoned many of the perpetrators in the final days of his presidency. Although two key members of the conspiracy, U.S. Marine lieutenant colonel Oliver North and Secretary of Defense Weinberger, made it clear that Reagan knew what was happening, no charges were ever filed against the president. During the 1985–1987 investigations, Reagan's personal approval rating dropped from 67 to 46 percent but later rebounded.

24

※

Rancho del Cielo
Santa Barbara, California
August 1, 1984
Noon

Ronald and Nancy Reagan stand before their round leather patio table under a blue California sky, gazing out at the oak-covered hills. Nancy is dressed in a cream plaid sweater vest over white denim pants. The president is even less formal in his blue jeans, boots, and open-necked cowboy shirt. The media form a tight scrum behind a rope line on the gravel parking lot in front of them, separated from the president and First Lady by less than ten feet.

This is a photo opportunity where the press isn't supposed to ask questions. Nevertheless, the president often indulges them with a response should they break protocol, though it is something Nancy and his advisers rarely allow. There is too big a risk he might slip up. Normally, the president's every public movement is stage-managed. He is given a daily set of scripted cards telling him what to say and where to stand for any formal occasion.

But today there are no cards. No notes. Just the president and the media throwing one-liners back and forth. The time for questions is limited to just five minutes. There is very little that can go wrong in such a short period of time—or so it seems.

As distasteful as it might be, Ronald Reagan knows he must talk to the media. This is an election year, and the Republican National Convention in Dallas is just three weeks away. After eight months pursuing a Rose Garden strategy, in which Nancy made sure that Reagan barely campaigned, talking to the media will be a nice little warm-up for the months of hard battle that lie ahead in his quest for reelection. The media have been exceptionally generous to him during his first term, leading editor Ben Bradlee of the *Washington Post*, the newspaper that brought down Richard Nixon during the Watergate scandal, to state, "We've been kinder to President Reagan than any president I can remember since I've been at the *Post*."

This comment is made all the more significant by the fact that not only has Bradlee been at the *Post* off and on since 1948, but he was also drinking buddies with President John F. Kennedy.

So Ronald Reagan is not worried about this impromptu news conference. The president is never more relaxed than when here at the ranch. Congress is not in session right now, and he and Nancy are taking advantage of the hiatus by spending two full weeks on this six-hundred-acre mountaintop property. Their ranch house is a one-hundred-year-old white Spanish adobe with faux-brick linoleum floors that Reagan laid himself. There is nothing lavish about this private retreat. It has the air of a summer camp bunkhouse, yet it restores Reagan's soul unlike any place else on earth. During his time in office, he will spend the equivalent of one full year on this mountaintop looking out over the Pacific.*

Ronald Reagan works at the ranch, too, but guards his privacy very

---

*Rancho del Cielo ("Ranch in the Sky") was originally developed in 1841 by Mexican landowner José Jésus Pico. He built the house in 1871. It remained in his family until 1941. Ronald Reagan bought the 688-acre ranch in 1974 for $527,000 from the family of Roy and Rosalie Cornelius. Their daughter, Glenda, had been Patti Reagan's roommate at boarding school. Glenda Cornelius was an accomplished rodeo rider, and her parents had intended for the home to be her inheritance. However, they sold the land after she was killed in a New Year's Eve head-on automobile collision.

closely. He spends much of his time in the small living room, a private sanctuary to which not even his closest advisers are allowed regular access. Ever loyal, Reagan has filled the kitchen with GE appliances. The master bedroom is barely big enough to fit the two small twin frames pushed together to form one bed. The president is too tall for these mattresses, so a padded stool has been positioned at the end. He sleeps with his feet sticking out from under the covers, resting atop the stool.

Nevertheless, Ronald Reagan loves the place—Nancy, not so much. One popular legend is making the rounds among the press. Apparently, one day, while driving up the long, winding road from the main highway to the ranch, Nancy Reagan was whining nonstop about having to endure another vacation at the remote outpost. She would much rather be back in Los Angeles with her friends.

At first Reagan put up with his wife's complaining, preferring to keep the peace. But this time, he snapped. He ordered his Secret Service driver to stop the limo. Turning to Nancy, he thundered, "Get out of this car."

Shocked, she did.

The president then commanded the driver to continue up the seven-mile road. In the rearview mirror, the Secret Service driver could see Nancy standing in the middle of nowhere, looking panicked. Finally, the president relented, ordering the driver to turn around to pick her up.

But on this afternoon, things are calm. Nancy's dominant protective streak is nowhere to be seen. The president is ready for the eight questions the press will be permitted this morning.

The first queries are softballs. Reagan fields them with ease.

Then ABC newsman Sam Donaldson strikes, posing a question about the Russians.

"Is there anything you can do to get them there?" Donaldson asks about a proposed nuclear arms meeting in Vienna, referring to the leaders of the Soviet Union.

"What?" Reagan asks, suddenly befuddled.

Donaldson smells blood.

He has been on the White House beat throughout the Reagan

presidency and is no fan of the administration. He was an eyewitness to the assassination attempt, standing just five feet from John Hinckley when he pulled the trigger. Still, Donaldson feels little warmth for the president, and many members of the media share his disdain.

Donaldson doesn't even bother to speak to Reagan with a tone of civility. He is outwardly antagonistic, often shouting questions. He has publicly insulted Nancy Reagan by comparing her to a venomous snake, calling her a "smiling mamba."

Sam Donaldson is now in full confrontational mode.

"Is there anything you can do to get them to Vienna?" he bellows again.

The man who has spent his life speaking on cue, the entertainer who likes to tell a good joke, the politician who has dazzled millions with his rhetoric, has no answer.

Ronald Reagan is lost.

As journalists and television cameras record the moment, the president seems incapable of rendering an answer to Sam Donaldson.

Finally, Nancy Reagan leans over and whispers into her husband's ear: "We're doing everything we can."

"We're doing everything we can," the president says to Sam Donaldson.*

■ ■ ■

With Nancy carefully controlling his every appearance, Ronald Reagan hits the campaign trail for real in September. The nation is riveted by his "Morning in America" commercials, which paint a patriotic picture of a country rising from the shambles Reagan inherited from Jimmy Carter. The president now enjoys a nineteen-point lead in the polls over Democratic challenger Walter Mondale, the fifty-six-year-old Minnesota native

---

*Nancy's words are picked up by microphones from the various network television cameras. Ten days later, while still at the ranch, Reagan himself will mistakenly speak into a live microphone, joking that he has outlawed Russia and that "we begin bombing in five minutes." As a result, Soviet military forces will go on war alert in preparation for an attack.

who served as Carter's vice president. At this point, Americans seem comfortable with Ronald Reagan as president. Many admire him—as a man and a patriot. They like his rock-solid belief in traditional values, and some voters see him as a father figure, putting their complete trust in his perceived paternal benevolence.

Yet there is also some unease. Relations between the United States and the Soviet Union are still very tense, and Reagan has exacerbated the situation by publicly calling the Soviet Union an "Evil Empire." Many Americans long for reassurance that their president will avoid nuclear war. They also crave relief from high unemployment and a skyrocketing national deficit that gives their dollar less buying power. Just as important, voters want to believe that their seventy-three-year-old leader is still vibrant.

But that reassurance does not come on September 19, when Reagan visits Hammonton, New Jersey. He wears a dark gray suit and crimson necktie. The small town, famous for its blueberries, has turned out in force to see the president. Thirty thousand people fill the town square. A large American flag looms over his left shoulder, accompanied by a sign reading, "America: Prouder, Stronger & Better."

Reagan's unlikely speech for today is based on the recent writings of two very prominent conservative voices. The first voice is that of columnist George Will, who behaves decades older than his forty-three years.

Surprisingly, Will has become a Bruce Springsteen fan. Wearing a bow tie, ears packed in cotton, he watched an entire four-hour show at the Capital Centre in Landover, Maryland, as a guest of Springsteen's drummer. Will comes away inspired by the artist's connection to Reagan. In the Boss, as Springsteen is known, Will sees a powerful believer in the American dream.

"An evening with Springsteen," Will writes admiringly in the *Washington Post* on September 13, "is vivid proof that the work ethic is alive and well."

Another guest at that concert is political correspondent Bernard Goldberg of CBS News, who reports that Springsteen's shows "are like old-time revivals with the same old-time message: If they work long enough and hard enough, like Springsteen himself, they can also make it to the promised land."

It is hard to imagine other 1980s pop icons with whom the aging president could identify. The toe-tapping boogie-woogie of his Hollywood days has been replaced by music that makes listeners swing their hips and shake their heads. Young voters listen to musical sensation Michael Jackson, not Frank Sinatra. They like movies such as *Ghostbusters* and *Footloose* instead of Reagan's beloved Westerns, which hardly get made anymore. So it is only natural that Reagan's campaign staff attempts to make their boss look culturally relevant by cashing in on Springsteen's popularity during this visit to the singer's home state. At George Will's urging, deputy White House chief of staff Michael Deaver has invited Springsteen himself to the campaign event. But the rocker, while having an open date between performances in Philadelphia and Pittsburgh, declines.

Ronald Reagan invokes Springsteen's name anyway, his speechwriters mistakenly believing that the song "Born in the U.S.A." is a patriotic anthem. In reality, the opposite is true. "America's future rests in a thousand dreams inside your hearts," Reagan says to the crowd. "It rests in the message of hope in the words of songs so many young Americans admire: New Jersey's own Bruce Springsteen. And helping you make those dreams come true is what this job of mine is all about."

Chants of "U.S.A." sweep through the crowd, along with a number of incredulous gasps. Reagan's policies have been savaged on Springsteen's latest album, *Born in the U.S.A.* Many of its songs vividly depict the loss of homes and jobs for the working poor. The title track, jingoistic in name only, attacks Reagan's economic policies through the eyes of a down-on-his-luck Vietnam vet. At a time when Ronald Reagan wants to appear as if he is in touch, his staff has succeeded in making him look completely clueless by misinterpreting Springsteen's lyrics.

Later, the singer himself responds directly: "You see the Reagan reelection ads on TV—you know: 'It's Morning in America,'" Springsteen tells *Rolling Stone* magazine. "And you say, well, it's not morning in Pittsburgh.

It's not morning above 125th Street in New York. It's midnight, and, like, there's, a bad moon risin'."*

Ronald Reagan's aides will later claim that his favorite Bruce Springsteen song is "Born to Run," but it is hard for even the most ardent Reagan supporter to imagine this might be true.

"If you believe that," Johnny Carson tells America during his *Tonight Show* monologue one evening, "I've got some tickets to the Mondale-Ferraro inaugural ball I'd like to sell you."[†]

Three weeks later, Ronald Reagan is confused when about to deliver his closing remarks in the first presidential debate with Walter Mondale. The location is the Kentucky Center for the Performing Arts, in Louisville, and television journalist Barbara Walters is the moderator. Walters has a history with the Reagans. In 1981 she paid a visit to the Reagan ranch for an interview, gripping her seat in Reagan's four-wheel-drive jeep as he fearlessly drove it up and down the rugged dirt trails. But the fifty-five-year-old Walters is in her element now, pressing the president to begin his closing remarks. However, Reagan believes he is entitled to one more rebuttal to Walter Mondale's statements. Walters is having none of it and firmly tells the president to wrap it up.

The night has been a catastrophe for Reagan. Walter Mondale was the aggressor throughout the debate, commanding a quick grasp of domestic

---

*Springsteen had been politically ambivalent until this incident, aligning himself with veterans' groups and local food banks but refusing to back political candidates from either party. However, as a result of the "Born in the U.S.A." incident, he will make it a point to openly endorse liberal causes. In 2004 he will endorse Sen. John Kerry for president, and in 2008 and 2012 Springsteen will make campaign appearances on behalf of Barack Obama. However, the misunderstood legacy of "Born in the U.S.A." lives on. Attendees at the 2014 Connecticut Republican Convention were asked to name their favorite Springsteen song. "Born in the U.S.A." was the clear favorite. One delegate even compared it patriotically to "The Star-Spangled Banner."

[†]Geraldine Ferraro is Walter Mondale's running mate. The forty-nine-year-old congresswoman from Queens, New York, is the first female vice presidential candidate from a major party.

policy facts and appearing to be more physically robust than Reagan, despite being two inches shorter.

"I wanted to show presidential stature," Mondale will later remember. "I wanted to show mastery of the issues. I wanted to show that progressive dimension again, I wanted to show I was more alert than the president, without being negative. And I wanted the debate to build around that, that theme."

Mondale senses a mental weakness in Reagan, afterward telling an aide, "That guy is gone." Despite that, Mondale has refrained from attacking the president in a way that would make Reagan look foolish.

As Ronald Reagan begins his closing remarks, his rambling, disjointed speech does what Walter Mondale refuses to do. At a time when voters want reassurance of his vitality, the president looks visibly adrift on this very public national stage.

Looking into the camera, Reagan begins his soliloquy. "Four years ago, in similar circumstances to this, I asked you, the American people, a question. I asked, 'Are you better off than you were four years before?'"

Already, Reagan has lost his place. His eyes do not focus on the front row of the audience, as they should. Instead, they roll slowly from side to side as he struggles to recite the closing remarks that his speechwriters have prepared so carefully for this very moment.

Reagan continues: "The answer to that obviously was no, and as the result, I was elected to this office and promised a new beginning. Now, maybe I'm expected to ask that same question again."

To the discomfort of some, Reagan stutters. He appears a far cry from the man who improvised a brilliant speech within minutes of being called to the podium at the 1976 Republican National Convention.

He continues: "I'm not going to, because I think that all of you, or not everyone—those people that are in those pockets of poverty and haven't caught up, they couldn't answer the way I would want them to—but I think that most of the people in this country would say, yes, they are better off than they were four years ago.

"The question, I think," says Reagan, again stammering, "should be enlarged. Is America better off than it was four years ago? And I believe the answer to that has to also be yes."

There is little authority in Reagan's closing remarks. Walter Mondale beams.

"He seemed to lose his place," Lesley Stahl of CBS News will report. "He'd lose his thoughts. There were a couple of places where the words he was searching for wouldn't come to mind . . . [H]is closing statement didn't come together."

"I flopped," Reagan says to campaign adviser Stu Spencer immediately upon leaving the stage.

The president is correct. Polls show Walter Mondale winning the debate in a landslide. Two mornings later, the *Wall Street Journal* will publish a story stating that 10 percent of all people over the age of seventy-five are senile. Reagan is seventy-three years old.

Even worse, years later medical studies will link invasive surgeries like the one Reagan endured after the assassination attempt to the eventual onset of memory loss.*

"I didn't feel good about myself," Reagan will confide in his diary during a weekend at Camp David to recover from the debate. "The press has been calling him the winner for two days now."

But Ronald Reagan is not finished. He will have one last chance to convince Americans that he is still fit to be their leader.

That chance will come on October 21, in Kansas City.

---

*A 2001 Duke University medical study showed that 50 percent of individuals who underwent open heart surgery suffered immediate memory problems that were often still evident five years later.

25

—◦◦◦—

The man who was nearly murdered three years ago is out for blood.

Ronald Reagan bounds onto the stage and takes his spot at the lectern, where he stands confident and poised. Despite it being evening, a time of day at which he often fades, the president looks crisp and attentive. As the contest gets under way, Walter Mondale stands on the opposite side of the stage, watching as Reagan fields a series of questions. The president does not like Mondale, thinking him a liar who has unfairly attacked his credibility. For Reagan, this second and last debate is personal. His answers now come easily. There is no sign of the stuttering or stammering from the first debate.

There is one question, however, that everyone in the audience knows is coming. Finally, after twenty minutes of debate, Henry Trewhitt of the *Baltimore Sun* gets to the heart of the matter: Is Ronald Reagan too old to be president?

Reagan stands ready to answer.

After the first debate, Nancy Reagan was livid—eager to apply blame on anyone but her Ronnie. "What have you done to my husband?" she screamed at Deputy Chief of Staff Michael Deaver. They were standing in the Presidential Suite at the Hyatt Regency in Louisville. "Whatever it was, don't do it again."

The problem, Nancy quickly decided, is that the president is being bullied in the pre-debate prep sessions. His advisers, notably budget director David Stockman, often interrupt Reagan when he makes a mistake. It is well known in the White House that the troika of Ed Meese, James Baker, and Michael Deaver have a method of slowing down Oval Office meetings if the president does not understand a complex issue. Without insulting him, they diplomatically reframe the discussion until Reagan comprehends.

But there is no time for niceties while preparing for a presidential debate. Stockman is only doing his job, feeding the president facts so that he can easily rebut anything Walter Mondale might throw at him.

On October 17, during the initial debate prep for the final confrontation with Mondale, a newcomer observes the scene. From 2:06 to 4:36 in the afternoon, Reagan stands at a mock lectern in the Old Executive Office Building, fielding questions and arguing with Stockman, who stands at an opposite lectern playing the part of Walter Mondale. At one point, the normally polite Reagan barks "Shut up" at Stockman, filling the room with an embarrassing silence.

Tensions are high.

Clearly, something must change.

Afterward, Reagan returns to the White House, where he meets with the new observer. Roger Ailes is a stocky man with long sideburns. He is part of the so-called Tuesday Team, which has prepared the successful "Morning in America" commercials for Reagan. Ailes also worked for the Nixon administration and is known for his ability to stop chaos cold.

Michael Deaver makes the introduction. "Roger's here to help you with the debates."

"What kind of help do I need?" Reagan responds. Though it is almost evening, Reagan shows no sign of fatigue, other than a slight hand and head tremor.

"You sort of wandered off the highway in the last debate. I'm gonna try and help you focus a little bit," Ailes answers.

"That's a pretty good idea," the president replies.

Roger Ailes agreed with Nancy Reagan that the president's debate problem had nothing to do with age or mental health. Instead, Reagan had been poorly prepared.

"You're giving him too many facts, too much bullshit that he can't use, you're interrupting him," Ailes tells Deaver. "Remember, he's a guy who's used to working with one director, who kind of lays out what the purpose of the thing is, and then he does it. Right now, you got five or six or eight guys interrupting him, all trying to prove they're smarter than he is."

So it is that Reagan's debate preparation is altered. Now it is just Ailes and Reagan, one on one. The president endures long bouts of "pepper sessions," in which he has to answer question after question without reaching for obscure facts or numbers. Instead, he simply speaks from the heart.

Now, with just four days left to the second debate, the strategy seems to be working. The president is upbeat and optimistic. He works hard, rarely seeming to tire.

"When guys brief people for debates," Ailes will later remember, "they want them to memorize what they say 'cause they're the expert. . . . I shifted him back to staying in territory he knew and not trying to memorize a bunch of crap that nobody would remember."

Ailes's strategy has revitalized Reagan. "I can sum up the day in one sentence," he writes in his diary on Saturday, October 20, the night before facing Mondale. "I've been working my tail off to master the four minute closing statement I want to make in the debate tomorrow night."

On the same evening, the president and Ailes have a last-minute discussion about the debate.

"What are you gonna say if they ask you if you're too old for this job?" Ailes asks Reagan. The two men are standing in a White House hallway, walking to the elevator that will take Reagan back up to the second-floor residence.

Michael Deaver, Nancy Reagan, and all of the president's advisers have forbidden any talk about the age issue. But Reagan and Ailes are sure the question will be asked tomorrow night.

Reagan stops in his tracks. He blinks and looks hard at Ailes. "I have some ideas," the president begins.

Reagan tells Ailes what he intends to say. The words are rough and need a rhythm if they are to be effective, but Ailes likes the tone. Once upon a time, Ronald Reagan would have written the line for himself. Even now, he still makes elaborate changes in the margins of the scripts his speechwriters give him. But with his mind filled with debate minutiae, Ailes offers to write the entire response for Reagan.

"Whatever they bring up about age," he tells the president, "you go to this answer. You have to hit it specifically. Deliver it the way Bob Hope would. Don't move on the laugh line. If you want to get a drink of water or something and just stare at him, fine. But here's the line."

"I got it, coach," Reagan responds after hearing Ailes's retort.

As the final debate edges closer to a conclusion, the inevitable age question finally arrives.

Ronald Reagan is ready.

"Mr. President," the balding, bespectacled Henry Trewhitt says, "I want to raise an issue that I think has been lurking out there for two or three weeks and cast it specifically in national security terms. You already are the oldest president in history. And some of your staff say you were tired after your most recent encounter with Mr. Mondale."

Reagan is smiling.

Trewhitt continues: "I recall that President Kennedy had to go for days on end with very little sleep during the Cuban missile crisis. Is there any doubt in your mind that you would be able to function in such circumstances?"

The president waits a beat, surveying the room. He appears to be fully in command of the situation.

"I want you to know that also I will not make age an issue of this campaign," Reagan says casually, allowing the moment to build, taking great care not to rush the punch line. "I am not going to exploit, for political purposes, my opponent's youth and inexperience."

The crowd erupts in laughter. Even Walter Mondale is laughing. Reagan looks down modestly. He knows that even though there are still forty-five minutes in the debate, he has already won.

Two weeks later, on November 6, in a historic landslide, Ronald Reagan is reelected president of the United States.*

The next morning, Reagan celebrates the best way he knows how: with a four-day vacation at the ranch, Nancy in tow.

---

*Reagan wins forty-nine states. Mondale captures just his home state of Minnesota and the District of Columbia. The final Electoral College tally is 525 to 13.

26

Washington, DC
Christmas Day, 1986
6:00 A.M.

The would-be assassin will soon be a free man.

But only for today.

Escorted by the Secret Service, John Hinckley will spend the holiday at his parents' new home in Northern Virginia. Doctors here at St. Elizabeth's Hospital feel that Hinckley is making significant progress in dealing with his mental illness. They also believe that a day with his family will further the healing process. Jack and Jo Ann Hinckley have thrown themselves into their son's recovery, selling their Colorado home in order to move east. Each Tuesday afternoon, they attend therapy sessions with their son and a hospital psychiatrist. The Hinckleys are inspired by the advances John seems to be making. It appears that John Hinckley is "finding his voice," as his father describes it, even getting elected ward president by his fellow patients.

The Hinckleys and the hospital staff, however, are unaware that their son still secretly conceals pictures of Jodie Foster in his room, which is forbidden. Even more disturbing is that John Hinckley is cultivating friend-ships through the mail with murderers. He has secretly become pen pals with convicted serial killer Ted Bundy, now awaiting electrocution in Florida for murdering two Florida State University sorority sisters and a twelve-year-old girl.

Hinckley is also corresponding with Lynette "Squeaky" Fromme, imprisoned in California for attempting to assassinate Gerald Ford in 1975. Unbeknownst to his doctors or his parents, Hinckley asked Fromme to send him the address for the notorious murderer Charles Manson.*

▬ ▬ ▬

Shortly after daybreak, John Hinckley is walked down from his fourth-floor hospital ward by an attendant. He then passes through the locked front doors of St. Elizabeth's and is rendered to his parents. Two Secret Service agents are in charge of supervising the visit.

But it is not his parents with whom Hinckley is eager to spend time. No, it is his girlfriend, forty-year-old Washington socialite Leslie deVeau. Today will be the first time they have the chance to be alone since they met four years ago.

Like John Hinckley, Leslie is a cold-blooded criminal. She was sen-tenced to St. Elizabeth's after murdering her ten-year-old daughter, Erin, in 1982. In an unconscionable act, deVeau placed a shotgun against the sleeping child's back and pulled the trigger. She then turned the gun on herself, but it misfired. Instead of killing her, the blast tore off deVeau's left arm. Like Hinckley, she was declared not guilty by reason of insanity and placed in the mental hospital.

At a hospital Halloween party in 1982, Hinckley sidled up to the petite brunette and began flirting. "I'd ask you to dance if I danced," he said. The two spent the rest of the party in deep conversation, sharing their life

---

*Fromme was a member of the Manson Family, members of which brutally murdered seven people on a two-day killing spree in 1969. On the second night, pregnant actress Sharon Tate was stabbed sixteen times, even as she pleaded to live long enough to give birth. Tate was married to director Roman Polanski, who was not present when the hid-eous crime took place.

stories. Leslie deVeau, who comes from an old Washington, DC, family, did most of the talking. In vivid detail, she told Hinckley about how she'd murdered her daughter. When it came time for Hinckley to talk about his crime, he showed no remorse. Instead, he led deVeau to a hospital bulletin board where a newspaper clipping about his evil deed was posted.

"He was still operating under the delusion it made sense what he did," deVeau would later remember. "That he was supposed to do this to prove his love for Jodie Foster."

Although deVeau knew that Hinckley was still infatuated with the actress, her unlikely relationship with him blossomed. "I was lost until I met Leslie," Hinckley will later write. "Leslie made me want to live again, and she is the sunshine of my life."

Hinckley and deVeau resided on the same floor, but contact between them was restricted. Still, they found ways around the rules in order to communicate. They ate in the cafeteria at different times, but each furtively taped love letters underneath the dining table for the other to find. On the occasions that they actually saw each other in person, they used sign language to message "I love you."

In time, deVeau was granted the special privilege of being let outside to wander the hospital grounds. Hinckley, who had no such privilege, would shout to her from a window, and she'd answer back. In this way they conversed, not at all concerned that the whole hospital could hear them.

A year before, in mid-1985, deVeau was granted an even greater privilege: doctors decided she should be released from St. Elizabeth's and be treated on an outpatient basis. Thus, she no longer sees John Hinckley on a daily basis but returns to the hospital to visit him on weekends, where they can talk face-to-face. They sit across from each other at a glass table on visiting day, holding hands and kissing, ignoring the other patients and their guests all around them. During these visits, deVeau confides that she is still haunted by the night that she shotgunned her daughter to death.

In turn, Hinckley confessed that despite his outward bravado and trademark smirk, he had nightmares about the day he shot Reagan. He went on to tell Leslie that he sometimes dreamed that he was in a wheelchair, like James Brady.

In all the hours spent sitting sharing their feelings, deVeau and Hinckley have always been supervised. All that will change this morning.

As two Secret Service agents stand guard outside, John Hinckley eats Christmas breakfast with his parents and Leslie deVeau. They then spend two more hours in the living room, watching Hinckley home movies.

But as the clock strikes noon, the couple steals away.

Finding a secluded room, deVeau takes the initiative, pressing her body against Hinckley's and kissing him passionately. Normally demure, she is surprised and invigorated by her forward behavior.

Hinckley is flustered, unsure what to do. He has never had a girlfriend, and his few long-ago sexual experiences were limited to prostitutes. "I think he was startled," deVeau will later recall. "What is this woman doing to me?"

Suddenly, a voice calls out from the kitchen. Jack Hinckley, suspecting what is going on, interrupts the couple, calling them back to the living room for Bible study.

By nightfall, a frustrated Hinckley is back in his hospital room alone. It has been an eventful Christmas.

If only Jodie Foster had been there to spend it with him.

27

Ronald Reagan is being watched very closely.

The president sits in his high-backed chair at the center of the mahogany table. His son Ron Jr. is a guest at today's Cabinet meeting, which has put Reagan in a jovial mood. Since their father's being reelected three years ago, the president's children have been cashing in on his fame. Ron Jr. has written articles for *Playboy* and even appeared in his underwear on *Saturday Night Live*, but he has always been loyal to his father. This is not the case with Reagan's other children. Daughter Patti has written a book savaging her father and the entire Reagan household. And soon, son Michael's painful tell-all is due in stores. Meanwhile, the national press has begun a scathing series of broadsides against Nancy Reagan, blaming her for masterminding the recent firing of White House chief of staff Don Regan.

It was a battle so vicious and so public that *Saturday Night Live* lampooned the schism between the First Lady and Regan. All of this has led to growing criticism that the White House is out of control.*

That is why, in addition to Ron Jr., there are four other special guests at the morning's Cabinet meeting.

The new chief of staff, former Tennessee senator Howard Baker (no relation to James), is one of those in attendance. He has asked the White House counsel, A. B. Culvahouse, and director of communications Thomas Griscom to observe the president. The final member of the group, sixty-nine-year-old Washington insider Jim Cannon, is the author of a recent report detailing the inner workings of the White House. Commissioned at Howard Baker's request, Cannon conducted formal interviews with employees throughout the West Wing.

He was shocked by what he learned.

The battle between Nancy Reagan and Don Regan is just the beginning. Cannon has uncovered evidence that the White House is in chaos at all levels. Ronald Reagan's aides are forging his initials to documents, Cabinet members are ignoring presidential policy to push their own agendas, and down in the White House basement, Marine lieutenant colonel Oliver North has spent years illegally selling arms to Iran and then diverting the cash to Contra fighters in Nicaragua. North knew he was breaking the law.

But Ronald Reagan is not engaged in many day-to-day White House activities. He delegates much power to Nancy. Occasionally, he avoids the Oval Office altogether, spending hours during the day watching television reruns in the upstairs residence. Even more troubling, it is no longer a given that the president will take the time to read important policy papers.

---

*Regan was secretary of the treasury during Ronald Reagan's first term in office. In an unusual move, he and James Baker switched jobs in early 1985 because Baker was exhausted from trying to keep the White House running independently of Nancy. The switch was orchestrated almost completely without the president's knowledge. He merely gave final approval to the plan when it was presented to him. The president did not seem to think it a big deal.

After reporting that information to Baker yesterday, Cannon went on to suggest that Ronald Reagan may no longer be fit to serve as president of the United States.

This bold statement is more than mere rhetoric.

The Twenty-Fifth Amendment to the Constitution states that if "the president is unable to discharge the powers and duties of his office, the vice president shall immediately assume the powers and duties of the office as acting president."

But Vice President Bush doesn't know anything about what's going on.

Only if the four observers decide that Ronald Reagan is impaired will Bush be told.

As radical as this might sound, the Twenty-Fifth Amendment has already been invoked during Reagan's presidency. On July 13, 1985, the president underwent a colonoscopy to remove a precancerous lesion. At 10:32 that morning, he signed a document handing the presidency over to George H. W. Bush. For eight hours, the vice president ran the country but ceded power back to Reagan as soon as the president emerged from the anesthesia.

But now Reagan seems to be in permanent decline. In addition to the colon surgery and his hearing aids, Reagan recently underwent surgery for an enlarged prostate, which forces him to use the restroom frequently. He will soon undergo another procedure to have a cancerous melanoma removed from his nose. The president is now visibly frail, no longer the robust older gentleman who entered the White House six years ago. His energy level is lower. He naps frequently. His eyes often have a dull look, and he sometimes has trouble recognizing people that he has known for years.

Little does the president know it, but even loyal and uncritical Ron Jr. believes his father is suffering from Alzheimer's disease.

So it is that Howard Baker, Jim Cannon, A. B. Culvahouse, and Thomas Griscom sit along one wall scrutinizing the president's every action. Reagan does not know about Cannon's report, and the Cabinet meeting does not seem unusual to him.

But it is unusual. If the president shows signs of incoherence, he might not be president much longer.

━━   ━━   ━━

Ronald Reagan's mental and physical woes, however, are not the greatest crisis of his presidency. The real test of his leadership began four months earlier, on November 3, 1986. An Iranian cleric leaked news that the United States was selling arms to Iran in exchange for the release of American hostages throughout the Middle East. Faced with the embarrassing report, Ronald Reagan appeared live on national television and explained that his administration has sold "small amounts of defensive weapons and spare parts" to Iran. But the president denied any knowledge of trading arms for hostages.

"Those charges are utterly false," he told the massive TV audience.

"We did not—repeat—did not trade weapons or anything else for hostages—nor will we."

But the people do not believe him. In a poll taken shortly after the appearance, 62 percent of Americans believe the president is lying.

One week later, Attorney General Edwin Meese confronted Reagan in the Oval Office. Meese knows that Lt. Col. Oliver North and his secretary, Fawn Hall, have destroyed hundreds of documents connected to the so-called Iran-Contra scandal. In fact, North and Hall shredded so many files that the machine jammed, forcing Hall to smuggle documents out of the office in her boots and panties.

But North and Hall were sloppy, overlooking one key memorandum linking the Reagan administration to the illegal arms sale.* In hushed tones, Meese informs Reagan of the smoking gun.

Edwin Meese is a Reagan loyalist. Along with Michael Deaver and James Baker, he has advised Reagan on almost every important issue confronting his presidency. Now serving as attorney general, Meese warned

---

*Hall was later given immunity from prosecution in return for her testimony against Oliver North.

Reagan that he faced impeachment if he did not publicly acknowledge that America sold arms to Iran.

Reagan was stunned but admitted nothing. Instead, he convened a presidential commission to investigate Iran-Contra.*

Nancy Reagan was livid. She did not blame her husband for the illegal scheme that took place with his permission.

She blamed Donald Regan.

The sixty-eight-year-old former marine is a tough Boston Irishman who rose to head the Merrill Lynch investment firm. From there, he became secretary of the treasury and eventually White House chief of staff. He likened his job to that of "a shovel brigade following a parade down Main Street." He said this because he was constantly fighting Nancy Reagan and the messes she created. Nancy's determination to control the president's schedule and her reliance on an astrologer to chart her husband's every move struck him as madness. But she had the president's full backing, so Regan was powerless to stop her.

Early in his White House tenure Don Regan discovered just how strong an adversary Nancy Reagan could be when she insisted that he fire Margaret Heckler, the secretary of health and human services. Heckler was one of only two women holding high positions in the Reagan administration. She was a timid person, but Nancy despised her, feeling she was an embarrassment to her husband.[†] Yet neither the First Lady nor the chief of staff has the power to fire a Cabinet member, especially one who is sitting in a hospital undergoing a hysterectomy.

"I want her fired," Nancy told Regan in a call to his home one night.

---

*Known as the Tower Commission, it was named after its chairman, former Republican senator John Tower of Texas. The commission completed its three-month investigation in late February 1987. Its three-hundred-page report laid the blame for Iran-Contra on Ronald Reagan, demanding that he "take responsibility" for the illegality. The report also blamed his staff for shielding him from a number of key issues involving the sale of arms to Iran. "Yes, the president made mistakes," Tower told the press. "I think that's very plain English."

[†]Heckler's very public divorce was played out in the Washington newspapers. That drama, combined with what some considered her ineffective management skills, were factors in her ouster.

The president was completing his regular evening workout. This was her favorite time to call Regan, who got three times as many calls from Nancy as from her husband. Very often, Regan could hear the sound of the president's rowing machine in the background when he picked up the phone.

"But she's recuperating from a hysterectomy," Regan replied.

"I don't care. Fire her."

"I can't do it while she's in the hospital."

"I don't care. Fire the goddamned woman," Nancy Reagan said, seething.

Regan gave in, and Margaret Heckler suddenly became the ambassador to Ireland—far away from Nancy Reagan.

The same fate befell Secretary of Labor Ray Donovan, White House communications director Pat Buchanan, and CIA director William Casey. Nancy insisted that Casey be fired even as he lay in a hospital bed dying of a brain tumor. "He can't do his job," she argued with Regan, who once again questioned the humanity of the decision. "He's an embarrassment to Ronnie."

By January 1987, as the Iran-Contra scandal continued to erode Reagan's credibility, Nancy had taken complete control of the White House.

"The President's schedule is the single most potent tool in the White House," Regan will write, "because it determines what the most powerful man in the world is going to do and when he is going to do it. By humoring Mrs. Reagan we gave her this tool, or, more accurately, gave it to an unknown woman in San Francisco who believed that the zodiac controls events and human behavior and that she could read the secrets of the future in the movement of the planets."

Regan was referring to the astrologist Joan Quigley. Thanks to Nancy's intervention, Ronald Reagan now goes nowhere and does nothing without approval from Miss Quigley. Nancy is also receiving advice from a second stargazer, Jeane Dixon, but it is Quigley who has Nancy's ear and who is telling her the president should not appear in public until May because of "the malevolent movements of Uranus and Saturn."

Donald Regan was appalled. He insisted that the president needed to be seen in public. Hunkering down in the White House at the height of the Iran-Contra fiasco made it look as if he were hiding something. But other than his State of the Union address on January 27, 1987, and some other official business, Ronald Reagan does as Nancy tells him.

The president and Regan actually got along famously, often spending time alone together in the Oval Office, telling jokes. This only made Nancy Reagan more determined to edge out the chief of staff. The sniping between her and Don Regan soon seeped out into the public domain. Twice, Regan hung up on Nancy when she called to hector him. Her power continued to grow, and there was growing speculation that the president was dependent and weak.

"What is happening at the White House?" New Mexico Democrat William Richardson asked on the floor of the House of Representatives. "Who is in charge? A constituent of mine asked, 'How can the president deal with the Soviets if he cannot settle a dispute between his wife and his chief of staff?'"

As tensions rose, Nancy becomes so insistent on firing Don Regan that the president ordered her "to get off my goddam back."

This, too, seeped into the headlines. "Mrs. Reagan," ABC newsman Sam Donaldson asked Nancy on camera, "did the President ask you to get off his back about Donald Regan?"

"No," she replied curtly.

Donaldson immediately followed up with a different angle: "Have you been fighting over this?"

"No," she insisted.

Finally, as Nancy knew he would, Ronald Reagan gave in.

"Something has to be done," Ronald Reagan admitted to Nancy, who had already lined up former Tennessee senator Howard Baker to be Regan's replacement. The president did not deliver the news to his chief of staff in person. On February 27, Regan discovered he was out of a job when Nancy issued a statement to cable news outlet CNN.

Four days later, Nancy Reagan gave an address to the American Camp Association in which she viciously mocked Regan. "I don't think most people associate me with leeches," she told the audience of eighteen hundred, "but I know how to get them off. I'm an expert at it."

Soon the storm passes. As the president's staff likes to say, "He has his good days and he has his bad days." Today, March 2, 1987, is a good day for Ronald Reagan. Even though his chief of staff has been fired, and the Tower Commission has leveled blame for the Iran-Contra scandal on him, he is in a jovial mood and jokes his way through the Cabinet meeting that his son watches. To the four men observing Reagan, he possesses an easy command of facts while telling his usual anecdotes about his Hollywood days. At lunch, the president is even looser, swapping jokes with new chief of staff Howard Baker and looking every bit the most powerful man in the world.*

Without knowing that he has done so, Ronald Reagan has passed a test.

There will be no invoking the Twenty-Fifth Amendment.

But another stern trial is just two days away.

---

*Reagan loyalists insist that Reagan was firmly in control of the executive branch at all times. They reject any reportage to the contrary. It should be noted that Ronald Reagan retained his acting skills and rarely showed physical or mental distress to anyone but Nancy, whom he trusted implicitly.

28

⊱⟨ɷ⟩⊰

Ronald Reagan is in trouble.

Wearing a dark blue suit and speckled blue tie, the president prepares to speak to the nation. His face is drawn and lined, with a red flush. His eyes look just to the left of the camera as he reads off a teleprompter.

"My fellow Americans:

"I've spoken to you from this historic office on many occasions and about many things. The power of the Presidency is often thought to reside within this Oval Office. Yet it doesn't rest here; it rests in you, the American people, and in your trust. Your trust is what gives a President his powers of leadership and his personal strength, and it's what I want to talk to you about this evening."

Since January, the president has testified before the Tower Commission twice. Both times he looked confused. During his second appearance Reagan was so lost that he made the blunder of reading from a top secret memo when asked what he knew about Iran-Contra.* The media, sensing that Reagan could soon be facing the same fate as Richard Nixon, are now on the attack. Ben Bradlee of the *Washington Post* openly compares Iran-Contra with Watergate.

"For the past three months, I've been silent on the revelations about Iran," the president continues. "And you must have been thinking: 'Well, why doesn't he tell us what's happening?'" He continues: "Others of you, I guess, were thinking: 'What's he doing hiding out in the White House?' Well, the reason I haven't spoken to you before now is this: You deserve the truth. And as frustrating as the waiting has been, I felt it was improper to come to you with sketchy reports, or possibly even erroneous statements, which would then have to be corrected, creating even more doubt and confusion."

Many watching the Reagan broadcast know the president has denied committing any illegal acts, but now he seems to be admitting his denial was false.

"A few months ago I told the American people I did not trade arms for hostages. My heart and my best intentions still tell me that's true, but the facts and the evidence tell me it is not."

These devastating words do not seem to affect Reagan very much. In fact, a paternal grin now crosses his face. For the first time in his presidency, he is about to admit some level of memory loss. This passage of the speech has been written very carefully—the message coming across is that the problem does not lie with him but with the people who work for him.

"One thing still upsetting me, however, is that no one kept proper records of meetings or decisions." He speaks into the camera. "This led to my failure to recollect whether I approved an arms shipment before or after the fact. I did approve it; I just can't say specifically when."

The speech is Reagan at his paternal best, letting the nation know that he is still in charge and is managing merely a clerical situation.

"You know, by the time you reach my age, you've made plenty of mis-

---

*The memo concerned efforts to coach Reagan through the Iran-Contra affair.

takes. And if you've lived your life properly—so, you learn. You put things in perspective. You pull your energies together. You change. You go forward."

With that simple statement, Reagan is putting Iran-Contra behind him once and for all. He will move forward.

"Good night, and God bless you."*

Three weeks later, Ronald Reagan's political soul mate is trying to save her own skin. Margaret Thatcher is in Moscow for meetings with Soviet leader Mikhail Gorbachev. Thatcher, who is in the midst of a bitter reelection campaign, now sits with Gorbachev in the Kremlin, speaking to him about his recent capitulation to America in reducing his arsenal of nuclear missiles. It is the first time a British prime minister has come to Moscow in more than a decade.

Gorbachev has been in power two years. He is different from former Soviet leaders, more open to closer relations with America and Britain, simply because he has to be. The Soviet economy has been destroyed by years of military buildup and failed Communist economic policies. The Soviet Union is on its knees financially. Only by aligning himself with the West can Gorbachev ensure the viability of his country.

Mikhail Gorbachev is a bureaucrat. He worked his way up through the Politburo by holding positions such as secretary of agriculture and chairman of the Standing Commission on Youth Affairs. But his rise through the Soviet system has been an unlikely one, for he was born the son of peasants and once seemed destined to live out his life as a farmer. It was his father who encouraged him to attend Moscow State University,

---

*Ronald Reagan was never held accountable for Iran-Contra. In 1990 he testified behind closed doors to Iran-Contra prosecutor Dan Webb, in the federal trial of former national security adviser John Poindexter. Reagan's defense was that he could not remember any details of illegalities. Poindexter and Oliver North were among the thirteen members of the Reagan administration indicted for Iran-Contra. Both men were found guilty of several felony charges, but their convictions were overturned. Not a single person went to jail for the Iran-Contra conspiracy.

from which Gorbachev graduated cum laude with a law degree in 1955. As he went on to a career in politics, Gorbachev displayed a skill for organization and diplomacy that helped him move from unknown to general secretary within thirty years. Unlike his predecessors, the fifty-six-year-old Gorbachev is not a ruthless killer, nor is he a heavy drinker or womanizer. A balding man with a wine stain birthmark high on his forehead, he has enjoyed the favor of the Soviet people, who have rallied behind his youth and warmth. Even Ronald Reagan trusts him, believing "there is a moral dimension in Gorbachev" that was lacking in previous Soviet leaders.

Gorbachev is trying to find solutions to the problems his country faces. He has not given up on socialism, but he is introducing market reforms and individual freedoms through "glasnost" and "perestroika"—"openness" and "restructuring." But even openness has its limits. Gorbachev knows he cannot appear weak before Margaret Thatcher or Ronald Reagan. So the Soviet leader scolds Margaret Thatcher. He is angry that she has referred to his nation as evil, a phrase that Ronald Reagan has also used. Gorbachev thinks this makes him look weak.

"No, you can't have thought that!" Thatcher answers through her interpreter. Gorbachev and Thatcher each has a small number of advisers witnessing the conversation. "Nobody thinks that the Soviet Union is weak. The Soviet Union has enormous power. You have superior intermediate-range weapons and strategic offensive weapons, if we count warheads, as well as chemical and conventional arms. You are very powerful, not weak."

Gorbachev likes her tone. Just like Ronald Reagan, he has tremendous respect for Margaret Thatcher. Despite their ideological differences, he enjoys their verbal jousting.

"Once again I want to emphasize that the most important thing is to remain grounded in reality, otherwise we will all be in grave danger," he warns the prime minister.

She replies: "It is very important for us that you give up the doctrine of communist world domination."

"We never proclaimed such a doctrine," Gorbachev says. "There is the Truman Doctrine, the Eisenhower Doctrine, the neo-globalist Reagan Doctrine. All of these doctrines were publicly proclaimed by presidents. But you will not find our statements about 'planting the domination of communism' because they do not exist."

Six thousand miles away, Ronald Reagan pays little attention to the verbal duel. He has spent forty years battling communism, and doesn't much care what Mikhail Gorbachev has to say. That's because Ronald Reagan is already forming the words that will stun the world.

≡ ≡ ≡

Two months after Margaret Thatcher and Mikhail Gorbachev meet in Moscow, she is reelected prime minister for the third time. On June 8, Thatcher spends time with President Reagan while both are attending a high-level economic summit in Venice. Both are in agreement that the time is right to strike a blow for freedom, and perhaps end communism throughout Europe forever.

So it is that Ronald Reagan stands before the Berlin Wall giving the speech that will define his presidency—if not his entire life. The date is June 12, 1987. Reagan is fully recovered from the Iran-Contra affair, and is standing in almost the exact same spot where the American general George S. Patton stood forty-two years ago. Back then, Patton warned that World War II would never truly be over until the United States defeated the Soviet Union militarily. The world did not listen to Patton. Not only did the Soviets remain in Eastern Europe, but they built a concrete barrier around West Berlin. The so-called Berlin Wall is a symbol of the Cold War. It divides the democratic West Berlin portion of the city from the Soviet-occupied area known as East Berlin.*

In 1963, President John F. Kennedy traveled to Berlin and told the

---

*The wall was actually two walls, separated by 160 meters of open ground. This space was mined, contained trip-wired machine guns, and was patrolled by guard dogs. Watch towers overlooked this no-man's-land, and East German soldiers shot on sight all who tried to escape into West Berlin.

world that the Soviet Union was enslaving people. Now Ronald Reagan wants to build on Kennedy's historic speech.*

Flying from Venice to Berlin, Reagan arrived just before noon and traveled by motorcade through the heart of the city to the historic Brandenburg Gate, where a crowd numbering tens of thousands now awaits his words—"people stretching as far as I could see," he will write in his diary.

Reagan is theatrical, positioning the Berlin Wall behind him as he stands on an elevated platform. The weather is gray and overcast, with a light wind blowing. Reagan begins his speech at 2:00 p.m.

"Behind me stands a wall that encircles the free sectors of this city, part of a vast system of barriers that divides the entire continent of Europe," Reagan says. "From the Baltic, south, those barriers cut across Germany in a gash of barbed wire, concrete, dog runs, and guard towers. Farther south, there may be no visible, no obvious wall. But there remain armed guards and checkpoints all the same—still a restriction on the right to travel, still an instrument to impose upon ordinary men and women the will of a totalitarian state."

At least eighty people have died trying to escape from East Berlin into West Berlin. Communist authorities are ruthless and claim the wall exists to protect people by keeping out subversive capitalist influences.

The president continues: "Yet it is here in Berlin where the wall emerges most clearly; here, cutting across your city, where the news photo and the television screen have imprinted this brutal division of a continent upon the mind of the world. Standing before the Brandenburg Gate, every man is a German, separated from his fellow men. Every man is a Berliner, forced to look upon a scar."

The president, like Margaret Thatcher, has enjoyed better relations with Soviet leader Gorbachev in the past year. But Reagan has taken a hard line in arms reduction talks, going so far as to walk out of one summit

---

*John F. Kennedy spoke to the people of West Berlin on June 26, 1963. He expressed solidarity for their freedoms and disgust about the newly built Berlin Wall, telling the crowd, "Ich bin ein Berliner" ("I am a Berliner").

meeting when Gorbachev's terms of negotiation were not to his liking. The Russians respect toughness, not appeasement, and Reagan knows that backing down will be seen as a sign of weakness. He is not afraid of verbally scorching the Communist ideology.

"In the 1950s, Khrushchev predicted, 'We will bury you,'" Reagan says emphatically. "But in the West today, we see a free world that has achieved a level of prosperity and well-being unprecedented in all human history. In the Communist world, we see failure, technological backwardness, declining standards of health, even want of the most basic kind—too little food. Even today, the Soviet Union still cannot feed itself. After these four decades, then, there stands before the entire world one great and inescapable conclusion: Freedom leads to prosperity. Freedom replaces the ancient hatreds among the nations with comity and peace. Freedom is the victor."

Ronald Reagan standing before the Brandenburg Gate and Berlin Wall, June 12, 1987. With him are Chancellor Helmut Kohl (right) and President of the Bundestag Philipp Jenninger (left).

Ronald Reagan is in complete control. There is no sign of weakness. His voice rises as he drives home his point. He was warned before the speech that by using the wall as a backdrop, his speech would automatically be "provocative."

But Ronald Reagan *wants* to be provocative. His message today is so powerful that he will be interrupted twenty-eight times by cheers and applause.

"Are these the beginnings of profound changes in the Soviet state? Or are they token gestures, intended to raise false hopes in the West, or to strengthen the Soviet system without changing it? We welcome change and openness; for we believe that freedom and security go together, that the advance of human liberty can only strengthen the cause of world peace.

"There is one sign the Soviets can make that would be unmistakable, that would advance dramatically the cause of freedom and peace." Reagan pauses, knowing the world is hanging on his words.

"General Secretary Gorbachev, if you seek peace, if you seek prosperity for the Soviet Union and Eastern Europe, if you seek liberalization:

"Come here to this gate! Mr. Gorbachev, open this gate!

"Mr. Gorbachev, tear down this wall!"*

---

*Reagan noted in May 1975 that "Communism is neither an economic or a political system—it is a form of insanity—a temporary aberration which will one day disappear from the earth because it is contrary to human nature. I wonder how much more misery it will cause before it disappears." By the time Reagan entered office it was clear that the Soviet Union was struggling economically and that its people were becoming unhappy with the ever-increasing hardships. Reagan's presidential foreign policy of "peace through strength" was a master plan to bankrupt the Soviet economy by building up America's military, forcing the Russians to keep pace—knowing all the while that they could not.

29

———∞∞∞———

Two years after Ronald Reagan demanded the Berlin Wall be dismantled, it is still standing, and time has run out for Ronald Reagan. It is the last day of his presidency. He and Nancy have just said their final good-byes to the household staff at an emotional gathering in the State Room. Now Ronald Reagan takes a final walk along the Colonnade to the West Wing and his cherished office. Workers have already cleaned out his files, removing every vestige of the Reagan presidency from the Oval Office, right down to the jar of jellybeans he always keeps within arm's reach. At noon, new president George H. W. Bush will be sworn in at the Capitol.

President Reagan rose early, eating a final White House breakfast in the residence with Nancy before getting dressed. At age seventy-eight, he is leaving political office for good. But Reagan is not retiring. Concerned about income, he is already planning to supplement his annual presidential pension of $99,500 by making paid speeches around the world.*

Reagan's last correspondence as president was a parting letter to Margaret Thatcher, reaffirming their deep friendship. She and her husband, Denis, visited Washington last month, fittingly making Thatcher the last foreign dignitary to meet with Reagan in the White House. "Our partnership has strengthened the ability and the resolve of the Western alliance to defend itself and the cause of freedom everywhere," Reagan would later write. "You have been an invaluable ally, but more than that, you are a great friend. It has been an honor to work with you."

Thanks to the efforts of Reagan and Thatcher, global communism has been severely weakened. Before Reagan's election, it was almost unthinkable that the Soviet Union and its satellite countries in Eastern Europe would embrace democracy, but that process has already begun. Poland is just five months away from its first partially free elections since 1928. Emboldened, the people of East Germany will soon rise up and do as Ronald Reagan demanded of Mikhail Gorbachev: ten months from now, on November 9, 1989, the Berlin Wall will collapse.

None of this would have happened without Ronald Reagan's unswerving lifelong belief in freedom and America's exceptionalism. England's Iron Lady understands that: "Your beliefs, your convictions, your faith shone through everything you did," Thatcher responded to Reagan's letter. "You have been an example and inspiration to us all."

Ronald Reagan opens the top drawer of the empty *Resolute* desk and checks to make sure the workers did not remove a note he placed there yesterday. It is tradition for the outgoing president to leave a simple message for his successor in the Oval Office. Reagan's handwritten letter wishes Bush good luck and reminds the new president that he will be in his prayers.

---

*As an orator, Reagan is managed by the Washington Speakers Bureau and earns fifty thousand dollars per speech, minus a 20 percent agent commission. In addition to speaking with corporate groups in America, Reagan made $2 million on a ten-day speaking tour of Japan shortly after leaving office.

Despite the warm tone, there is tension between Reagan and Bush, stemming from the campaign. Ronald Reagan endorsed the candidacy of his former vice president but did very little campaigning on his behalf. Some believe Reagan was snubbing Bush, but the truth is the Bush campaign wanted the candidate to be his own man. A barnstorming Ronald Reagan could easily have overshadowed the less charismatic Bush.

The residence has become a beloved home to Ronald and Nancy. Reagan is a sentimental man and very much moved by the sense of history filling that space. The president is convinced that the ghost of Abraham Lincoln haunts the residence. He has stated that he can sometimes hear the creak of Franklin Roosevelt's wheelchair gliding from one room to another, and he once told a friend he could easily imagine the ghost of Teddy Roosevelt mumbling his trademark cheer of "Bully."

"We were familiar with every room and hallway," Reagan will later write, "and had the warmest memories of our life in that beautiful historic mansion."

But now it is time to go.

National Security Adviser Colin Powell steps into the Oval Office to give Reagan his last-ever daily briefing. "The world is quiet today, Mr. President," the former army general says succinctly.

Reagan reaches into the jacket pocket of his crisp blue suit. He pulls out the plastic card he has carried with him every day since taking office. It authenticates that he is president of the United States. In the event of a nuclear war he will present this to the military attaché who remains near him at all times, whereupon the special briefcase known as the "football" will be opened and the nuclear launch codes revealed.

"What do I do with this?" he asks Powell.

"Hang on to it," Powell replies. "You're still president."

Ronald Reagan's last official act as president of the United States takes place just before 11:00 a.m., as he hands the plastic authentication card to his air force military aide. Now, at 12:40 on a bitter cold Washington day, with George Bush already sworn in as the forty-first president of the United

States, Ron and Nancy Reagan step aboard a government helicopter to begin the journey back to California. As he is no longer president, the call name Marine One no longer applies to the official aircraft. It is Nighthawk One that lifts off from the Capitol, taking the couple to Andrews Air Force Base.

The moment, in Nancy's words, is "wrenching." They have participated in a long list of "final" scenes in the past few weeks: final visit to Camp David, final dinner in the White House, and final moment with the press. This morning, at their good-bye reception, is when it hit Nancy the hardest that it was over. "We were supposed to have coffee, but I don't remember drinking any. Then it was time to leave for the inauguration," she will later write.

As she and Barbara Bush share a limousine to the swearing-in, Nancy gazes out the window at the White House Lawn, wondering if the magnolia trees she planted will survive long enough for her grandchildren to see them. "My heart ached as I looked at those beautiful grounds I was unlikely to see again."

Time and events have changed Nancy Reagan. Shortly after her return from Berlin in 1987, the First Lady was diagnosed with breast cancer and underwent a mastectomy to remove one breast. The procedure was a success, and Nancy's very public ordeal softened her in the eyes of many. With the end of her husband's presidency, whatever animosity may have existed between the Reagans and the media has now been replaced by nostalgic warmth. Walter Cronkite brought the Reagans onstage for a round of applause at the recent Kennedy Center Honors, leading the orchestra in a chorus of "Auld Lang Syne." And even Sam Donaldson, the ABC newsman who has been baiting the Reagans for eight years, approached Nancy recently to say that he would miss them.

As the helicopter lifts off, the Reagans take one last look at the White House. They push their faces against the windows, straining to see the glory of their former home. Below them sprawl the vast lawns, fountains, and famous columns they have come to know so well. Even as they look down, movers are hauling their furniture into trucks for transport back to their new home in Beverly Hills. The Bush family furniture, meanwhile, is being installed in its place.

"Look honey," says Reagan, not taking his eyes off the White House. "There's our little shack."

The pilot finally banks away, steering the VH-60N helicopter to Andrews—the Reagans vanishing into the clouds.

30

⎯⎯∽◈∽⎯⎯

MAYO CLINIC
ROCHESTER, MINNESOTA
SEPTEMBER 8, 1989
11:00 A.M.

Eight months later, the White House is the last thing on Ronald Reagan's mind.

A surgical drill hums as the former president lies flat on his back in an operating room. Fifty-nine-year-old brain surgeon Dr. Thoralf Sundt presses the bit against the right side of Reagan's skull and carefully opens a hole the size of a nickel in his cranium. Two months ago, Reagan was thrown from a horse while riding at a friend's ranch in Mexico, just south of the Arizona border.

The horses used during the ride were unshod and left to run wild when not saddled, leading Secret Service agent John Barletta to warn Reagan against the ride. Nancy took the advice, but the former president did not. On the second day at the ranch, Reagan's horse was spooked by a wild bull. It began bucking wildly. At first, Reagan was able to hang on. But the frightened horse continued kicking its hind legs straight up into the air, and on the third buck, Reagan was hurled from the saddle. He flew so high that his entire body rose above the heads of those riding alongside him.

Reagan landed hard, slamming his head into the rocky soil, just missing a patch of cactus. "Rawhide down," Agent Barletta yelled into his radio, marking the first time those words had been uttered since the assassination attempt of eight years earlier.

Reagan lay unconscious, but he soon revived. At first he appeared uninjured. Nevertheless, he was flown by military helicopter to an army hospital in Arizona, where he was treated for scrapes and bruises, then brought back to the ranch to continue the vacation—albeit without any further horseback rides.

But unbeknownst to Reagan and his doctors, a blood vessel in his head ruptured during the fall. For two months fluid has been leaking into his skull, causing a clot that is slowly putting pressure on Reagan's brain. This condition, known as a subdural hematoma, alters mood and vision and elevates levels of dementia. Patients often complain of headaches or simply fall into a stupor before seeking treatment. But Reagan's hematoma is a silent killer, with no outward symptoms other than his usual forgetfulness. Were it not for his annual physical here at the Mayo Clinic, the former president's condition might never have been discovered. But a precautionary CAT scan located the clot, and Reagan was rushed into surgery.

Dr. Sundt removes the drill, then looks through the opening at Reagan's brain. In the course of his job, the esteemed surgeon glimpses the human brain on an almost daily basis. But this is the brain of a living president. Dr. Sundt has the unique opportunity to save Reagan's life.

Clinically, the procedure Reagan is undergoing is known as a burr. In many cases, it is necessary to drill a second and even third hole to ease the pressure, but the brain surgeon is satisfied that one burr is enough for Reagan.

And that, seemingly, is that. Less than an hour after being sedated, Ronald Reagan is wheeled into the recovery room. His doctors are satisfied that Reagan shows no signs of the stroke, nerve damage, or paralysis so common in elderly patients suffering from head trauma. But the truth is that despite the operation, the fall has accelerated Reagan's debilitating condition.

Nancy Reagan will one day sum it up best: "I've always had the feeling that the severe blow to his head in 1989 hastened the onset of Ronnie's Alzheimer's."

▰ ▰ ▰

Four years later, Ronald Reagan is still functioning. The date is February 6, 1993, and the occasion is Reagan's eighty-second birthday. Reagan and Margaret Thatcher chat amiably about their lives since leaving office. Unlike Reagan, Thatcher did not go of her own accord. She was forced out by her own Conservative Party in 1990 and cried as she left 10 Downing Street for the last time.* Now, at age sixty-seven, she makes her living giving speeches at fifty thousand dollars per appearance and works on her memoirs. The state of dementia in which she will spend her twilight years is still almost a decade away, and she is sharp as she stands next to Reagan in the "Oval Office."

The birthday fund-raiser is not at the White House but in Simi Valley, California. Tonight Reagan and Thatcher are standing in the exact replica of the Oval Office now on display here at the Ronald Reagan Presidential Library. Thatcher and a host of celebrities have gathered for this five-hundred-dollar-per-plate dinner to raise money for the library. Old Hollywood friends Jimmy Stewart and Merv Griffin and media mogul Rupert Murdoch are among the five hundred guests at the black-tie affair. The festive night sold out immediately.

Reagan and Thatcher move into the great white tent pitched on the library lawn, where dinner will be served. The menu is crab-stuffed fillet of sole, prime rib, and baby potatoes, all washed down with the California wines Ronald Reagan has long enjoyed. Dessert will be another longtime Reagan favorite, Häagen-Dazs ice cream topped with fudge sauce.

The night belongs to Ronald Reagan, and it is Margaret Thatcher who rises first to pay homage. She praises him for bringing "the Evil Empire crashing down."

---

*Thatcher's popularity was in such decline by the late 1980s that her reelection appeared all but impossible. A poll tax she advocated led to widespread rioting, and she was deeply mistrustful of Britain's participation in the European Union, thinking it eroded its power. Opinion polls showed her approval ratings to be below 40 percent at the time her party pushed her aside. Voters said that she had grown out of touch with the people.

"If Ronald Reagan's birthday is celebrated warmly in California," continues Thatcher, "it is celebrated even more warmly in Prague, Warsaw, Budapest and Moscow itself."

Then it's Reagan's turn to toast Thatcher. "Thank you, Margaret, for those very kind words," he begins. Reagan's toast continues at length. He wrote and memorized it beforehand. On paper, the speech fills four type-written pages. "I don't think I really deserve such a fuss for my birthday. But as George Burns once said, 'I have arthritis and I don't deserve that, either,'" he says with a smile.

Reagan continues. "Margaret, you have always been a staunch ally and a very dear friend. For all of us, I say thank you for the immense role you have played in shaping a better world. And I personally thank you for the honor of your presence tonight."

As he finishes, the entire tent thunders with roars of "hear, hear" and the clinking of glasses.

Moments later, Reagan stands to deliver a second toast.

Anticipation grows as the former president stands erect, his blue eyes shining, his tuxedo perfectly fitted to his body, which looks a decade younger than his actual age of eighty-two. To the casual observer, Ronald Reagan appears to be fit and healthy.

Slowly, he turns to Margaret Thatcher and raises his glass once again. Mrs. Thatcher is beaming, and the audience eagerly awaits Reagan's next memorable line. Smiling, he begins to speak.

"Thank you, Margaret, for those very kind words," he says, raising his glass. "I don't think I really deserve such a fuss for my birthday. But as George Burns once said, 'I have arthritis and I don't deserve that, either,'" Reagan says with a chuckle.

Immediately, shock envelops the room as Ronald Reagan, word for word, delivers the same exact four-page toast to Margaret Thatcher that he uttered just a few moments ago.

Reagan continues for two excruciating minutes.

"And I personally thank you for the honor of your presence here tonight," the former president tells Margaret Thatcher, raising his glass once again.

Reagan's friends sit in stunned silence.

31

———⟡⟡⟡———

LOS ANGELES, CALIFORNIA
JUNE 1994
MORNING

The man with ten years to live has been dealt a stunning blow.

His daughter, forty-one-year-old Patti Davis, is now fully exposed for the entire country to see. *Playboy* magazine is on newsstands everywhere, its cover promising a father's ultimate humiliation. Patti wears nothing but a smile as the hands of a muscular unseen man cup her bare breasts. The magazine's lurid headline promises that "Ronald Reagan's Renegade Daughter" will tell all.

As Patti Davis has intended, her father is deeply wounded by his estranged daughter's latest attempt to embarrass him. For years, Reagan has struggled to deal with his rebellious children. But Patti has always been the biggest problem. From her defiant liberal politics to her open use of marijuana, she has striven to be the polar opposite of Ronald and Nancy Reagan in every way.

Just two years ago, Patti published a tell-all memoir about life in the "dysfunctional" Reagan family. The book revealed Nancy's dependence on tranquilizers and diuretics, along with the fact that Patti was so afraid of becoming pregnant and parenting as her mother had that she had herself rendered infertile with a tubal ligation at the age of twenty-four. In addition, Patti openly led a lifestyle that flaunted a libertine attitude on social issues. One writer described her as "an angry daughter with scores still to settle."

Now, grinning on the cover of *Playboy*, she has humiliated her mother and father—and the whole world knows it.

Patti Davis publicly states that her rebellion is Nancy's fault, saying that her mother was physically and emotionally abusive, a chronic prescription drug user who slapped her daughter when she ate too much and even slapped her when she began menstruating at a very young age. When she told her father about the abuse, Davis alleged, Ronald Reagan called her a liar.

"Patti you are hurting us—your parents—but you are hurting yourself even more," Reagan wrote to his daughter in 1991, when word leaked that she was writing her tell-all memoir.

"We are not a dysfunctional family," Reagan's letter continues. "Patti, in our meeting at the office you said your mother didn't like you. That's not true. Yes, she's unhappy about the way things are but again I can show you photos in which the love between you is unmistakable. And these pictures are at almost every stage of your life. Pictures don't lie."

Reagan concludes: "Please Patti, don't take away our memories of a daughter we truly love and who we miss.

"With Love, Dad."

But Patti Davis did not listen, and her defiance is clear in each and every photo in *Playboy*. She looks straight into the camera, knowing that every click of the photographer's shutter publicly will humiliate the man whom she considers a failure as a father.

It is a stunning betrayal.

Two months earlier, Ronald Reagan experienced another episode of public embarrassment.

The date is April 27, 1994. Ronald and Nancy Reagan are attending the funeral of Richard Nixon. Twenty years after the Watergate scandal brought him down, and less than a year after his beloved wife, Pat, succumbed to lung cancer, the thirty-seventh president of the United States is dead of a stroke at the age of eighty-one. Nixon is being laid to rest on the grounds of his birthplace and presidential library in Yorba Linda, California. Despite hitting afternoon traffic on the drive south from Beverly Hills, it takes the Reagans just a little over an hour to arrive for the 4:00 p.m. ceremony.*

There are four former presidents and the current chief executive, Bill Clinton, at the funeral. In addition, a crowd of four thousand sits in folding chairs, awaiting the start of the ceremony. Among the last to be seated are the former presidents and their wives. There is no formal introduction, but as a Marine Corps band plays light triumphal music, each couple walks to their seats, to polite applause.

Gerald and Betty Ford, Jimmy and Rosalynn Carter, George and Barbara Bush, and President Clinton and wife Hillary all take their seats.

But it is the arrival of Ronald and Nancy Reagan that steals the show. As the television audience and those in attendance look on, Reagan's confusion is apparent. Making their way down the steps after Ford and before Carter, the former president holds tight to Nancy's hand. She leads him like a child, walking in front and pulling him along. Reagan looks bewildered and frequently swivels his head. He wears a fascinated smile, as if not sure what all the hoopla is about. As the audience breaks into applause, Nancy whispers to her husband, telling him to wave to the crowd.

He dutifully obliges.

As the Reagans take their seats between the Carters and Bushes, Ronald Reagan's physical decline is clear as well. Compared to Gerald Ford, who at age eighty is just two and a half years younger, Reagan looks frail

---

*Nixon's last residence was not in California, but in Park Ridge, New Jersey. His stroke occurred as he was sitting down to dinner on April 18. After his death four days later, his body was flown to California aboard the same Boeing VC-137C that transported the casket of John F. Kennedy back to Washington, DC, after his assassination in 1963. As with his departure from the nation's capital following his resignation in 1974, Nixon's plane landed at El Toro Marine Corps Base. Nixon's body was then transported by motorcade to his final resting place twenty miles north.

Ronald and Nancy Reagan at President Richard Nixon's funeral

and wrinkled. Ford thinks he looks "hollowed out," and Bush is telling friends that he is deeply worried about Reagan. Carter, for his part, thinks that Reagan's responses to everyday questions are "not right."

But even as these former presidents are well aware of Reagan's decline, there is a general consensus among the media that the matter must be kept hushed until the Reagan family chooses to make it public.

Nixon's funeral is Ronald Reagan's last major appearance. After a lifetime of performing, the actor has now left the stage.

Four months after the Nixon funeral, Ronald Reagan is back at the Mayo Clinic for his annual physical. It is August 1994. Southern Minnesota is humid and hot this time of year, but it is cool and comfortable in the small examination room in which Ronald Reagan now sits. His hair is turning silver in a show of his advanced age. As he does every year, the former president is having his blood pressure checked as a doctor listens to his heart.

But at Nancy Reagan's behest, the esteemed physicians of the Mayo Clinic are also conducting a different sort of test today.

"What did you have for breakfast?" Ronald Reagan is asked.

It is a simple question, something anyone with a memory could answer immediately.

Reagan stammers. He smiles as he racks his brain. He does not know what he had for breakfast. In fact, it is not clear if he knows what breakfast is.

The doctors take notes. The truth is the former president is now totally dependent on Nancy. Reagan has begun asking Nancy questions such as "What do I do next?" and observing aloud, "I'm not sure where I am." He no longer recognizes old friends. Nancy Reagan listens in on his phone calls to prompt him when he experiences memory failure. When asked by *Time* magazine journalist Hugh Sidey about Watergate shortly after Richard Nixon's death, Reagan cannot even recall the scandal.

"Forgive me," Reagan finally admitted to Sidey, "but at my age, my memory is just not as good as it used to be."

Now, at the Mayo Clinic, Reagan fails to answer the breakfast question. He also cannot recite a short three-item list after it is presented to him. The situation is clear.

"Over the past twelve months we began to notice from President Reagan's test results symptoms indicating the possibility of early stage Alzheimer's Disease," reads the diagnosis. "Additional testing and an extensive observation over the past few weeks have led us to conclude that President Reagan is entering the early stages of this disease.

"Although his health is otherwise good, it is expected that as the years go on it will begin to deteriorate. Unfortunately, at this time there is no cure for Alzheimer's Disease and no effective treatment exists that arrests its progression."

Three months after his Mayo Clinic physical, Ronald Reagan joins past presidents and First Ladies who have made public their health woes. It was Franklin Roosevelt whose frank admission about polio in 1938 launched the charity known as the March of Dimes. Betty Ford's honesty about her breast cancer, and later her battle with alcoholism, helped make those two emotional topics open for public discussion.

Now, despite his growing confusion and forgetfulness, Ronald Reagan is still alert enough to be aware of the fate that has befallen him. On good days, he understands he is helpless to stop the advance of Alzheimer's. The disease is fatal, killing its victims in four to twelve years. The only drug currently on the market, Tacrine, is not a cure but a stopgap to improve memory temporarily.

The world is still learning about Alzheimer's. They lump it together with terms such as *senility* and *dementia*. The date is November 5, 1994, as Ronald Reagan takes pen to paper to tell the world.

My Fellow Americans,

I have recently been told that I am one of the millions of Americans who will be afflicted with Alzheimer's Disease. Upon learning this news, Nancy & I had to decide whether as private citizens we keep this a private matter or whether we would make this news known in a public way. In the past Nancy suffered from breast cancer and I had my cancer surgeries. We found through our open disclosures we were able to raise public awareness. We were happy that as a result many more people underwent testing. They were treated in early stages and able to return to normal, healthy lives.

So now, we feel it is important to share it with you. In opening our hearts, we hope this might promote greater awareness of this condition. Perhaps it will encourage a clearer understanding of the individuals and families who are affected by it.

At the moment I feel just fine. I intend to live the remainder of the years God gives me on this earth doing the things I have always done. I will continue to share life's journey with my beloved Nancy and my family. I plan to enjoy the great outdoors and stay in touch with my friends and supporters.

Unfortunately, as Alzheimer's Disease progresses, the family often bears a heavy burden. I only wish there was some way I could spare Nancy from this painful experience. When the time comes I am confident that with your help she will face it with faith and courage.

In closing let me thank you, the American people, for giving me the great honor of allowing me to serve as your President. When the Lord calls me home, whenever that may be, I will leave with the greatest love for this country of ours and eternal optimism for its future.

I now begin the journey that will lead me into the sunset of my life. I know that for America there will always be a bright dawn ahead.

Thank you, my friends. May God always bless you.

Sincerely,

Ronald Reagan

With his fate sealed, Ronald Reagan sits in a pew at the Bel Air Presbyterian Church. A tall wooden cross rises from behind the pulpit as senior pastor Michael Wenning leads the congregation in the Lord's Prayer. "Our Father," says Reagan, in words he memorized as a child. He fixes his eyes on the cross. "Who art in Heaven, hallowed be thy name . . ."

Next to Reagan sits Nancy, who also prays aloud.

And next to Nancy is Patti Davis. After years of bitter isolation and estrangement, Ronald Reagan's Alzheimer's diagnosis has finally brought his daughter back. Incredibly, she is about to move home, mending a lifetime of wounds to be near her father in his last days. Patti Davis's turnaround is amazing.

Like her siblings, she has set aside the past. Gone are the days of angrily mocking her father's politics. Her aim is now reconciliation instead of rebellion.

"Amen."

It is a February afternoon in 1996, a day of cool sunshine and clear skies in Southern California. George Shultz sips tea with Ronald and Nancy Reagan at their Bel-Air home. The azaleas along the driveway are just beginning to bloom. The former secretary of state has come to say hello to his former boss, a man whom he served for six and a half years. Together, they spent countless hours crafting the foreign policy that would come to define the Reagan administration, ending the Cold War and bringing an end to Communist influence around the world. They traveled together aboard Air Force One and sat together at the bargaining table as Reagan coolly negotiated a new arms treaty with Soviet leader Mikhail Gorbachev.

But Ronald Reagan remembers none of that. He has even begun to forget that he was once president of the United States. And although he keeps regular hours at his nearby office in Century City, his time is spent mostly reading the comics and sitting in the nearby Armand Hammer Park, watching children at play.

On the outside, Reagan still looks healthy. On the inside, he is dying. Sometimes Reagan wakes up in the middle of the night thinking it is time for breakfast. He can still dress himself, sometimes tying a neat Windsor knot. His handshake is still firm. And when he ventures out to the Los Angeles Country Club to play golf, he is very much like other golfers on the course, exulting in good shots and swearing angrily when his drives go astray. But Reagan's round is limited to one or two holes instead of eighteen.

Perhaps the most telling sign that the end is near is that Reagan's beloved Rancho del Cielo is for sale. No longer able to ride a horse or clear brush, Reagan never goes to the ranch. It is now up for sale to the highest bidder.

Of this, Ronald Reagan has no idea.

As George Shultz and Nancy Reagan continue to visit on this warm winter afternoon, Reagan finally stands and leaves the room, followed by a nurse.

"Who is that man sitting on the couch with Nancy?" the former president asks the nurse. "I know him. He is a very famous man."

32

━━◦◦◦◦━━

St. John's Health Center
Santa Monica, California
January 20, 2001
9:05 a.m.

Nancy Reagan sits in a chair next to her husband's hospital bed, watching a new president being sworn in.

"I, George Walker Bush, do solemnly swear . . ."

Ronald Reagan also watches the ceremony, completely unaware that he took that same oath twenty years ago today. There is a faraway look in his eyes as he gazes at the television. It is now seven years since the Alzheimer's diagnosis. Reagan will turn ninety in two weeks. Eight days ago, he broke his hip in a fall at home, and upon his release from the hospital he will be bedridden for the rest of his life. The former president's rugged physique has grown frail, his daily workouts a thing of the past. His once-broad shoulders are shrunken; the bones in his back are clearly visible, pressing through his thin flesh.

But Ronald Reagan is unaware of his physical condition. He also does not even recognize his own wife. "My mother speaks of the loneliness of her life now," daughter Patti writes in her journal. "He's here, but in so many ways he's not. She feels the loneliness in small ways—he used to put lotion on her back. Now he doesn't. And in the huge, overwhelming ways—a future that will be spent missing him."

Nancy knows that her unswerving devotion to her husband made her a target of scorn in their White House days, and for that she makes no apologies. "I'm the one who knows him best, and I was the only person in the White House who had absolutely no agenda of her own—except helping him," she stated in her autobiography.

The Reagans' good friend Jimmy Stewart once noted that if "Nancy had been Ron's first wife instead of his second, he would have been a real star in Hollywood, with a couple Oscars to show for it."

Instead, Nancy guided him to the presidency. "As much as I love Ronnie," she writes, "I'll admit he does have at least one fault: He can be naive about the people around him. Ronnie only tends to think well of people. While that's a fine quality in a friend, it can get you into trouble in politics."

In this way, Nancy Reagan had a hand in changing the world. Now, as she and her Ronnie watch the presidential inauguration just hours before Reagan will be released from the hospital, her commitment to him continues. Since the fall, he never leaves the house anymore, other than on those occasions when he is placed in a wheelchair and rolled outside to the patio.

"My father is the only man in the house these days, except for members of his Secret Service detail who occasionally come in," Patti Davis will write. "It's a house of women now—the nurses, my mother, the housekeepers."*

It is a tedious life for Nancy. She remains at her husband's side night and day, leaving only occasionally to have a Cobb salad and chocolate chip cookies with friends at the nearby Hotel Bel-Air. The relief is needed because Ronald Reagan can no longer do anything for himself. His home

---

*Ronald Reagan's home is watched over by a Secret Service detail. There is also a day nurse and night nurse, along with a full cooking and housekeeping staff. There are bedrooms for two servants, a wine cellar, an exercise room, and a hothouse for growing flowers outside near the pool.

office has been turned into a bedroom. There, next to the desk on which he once wrote so many letters and speeches, he spends his days on a hospital bed, tended to by his staff and Nancy. He cannot feed himself or even speak.

He is simply waiting to die.

■ ■ ■

"I christen thee United States Ship *Ronald Reagan*, and God bless all those who sail on her," says Nancy Reagan on March 4, 2001, standing before a crowd of thousands in Newport News, Virginia. She swings the traditional bottle of champagne, shattering it against the ship's steel hull. Nancy smiles as the audience of naval personnel and dockyard employees breaks into applause. Her husband would love knowing that a nuclear-powered aircraft carrier is being commissioned in his honor.

On this day, she and Ronald have been married forty-nine years. But Ronald Reagan does not know this as he lies almost still, day after day, in California.

"It's lonely," Nancy will tell Mike Wallace in a rare televised interview for *60 Minutes*. "When you come right down to it, you're in it alone. And there's nothing that anybody can do for you."

■ ■ ■

So it is that one year after the USS *Ronald Reagan* is launched, the Reagans' landmark fiftieth wedding anniversary comes and goes without fanfare. "There were times I had to catch myself," Nancy will recall of March 4, 2002. "Because I'd reach out and start to say, 'Honey, remember when . . .'"

■ ■ ■

Two years later, it is clear that Nancy Reagan's lonely vigil will soon come to an end.

Ronald Reagan, asleep, is struggling to breathe, unaware that his daughter Patti sits atop his old desk, watching him slip away. Ron Jr. has cut short a Hawaiian vacation and is on his way to California. "We are witnesses to the end of a life," Patti will write, "and even though we have known this is coming for years, it feels as if we have never considered it as a reality."

But Nancy Reagan will not say good-bye to her husband. Throughout his decade of decline, she has tended to him as if he were still sound of body and mind. Nancy still sleeps in their bed, keeping as many traditions alive as possible.

From the day they met in 1949, she made it her mission to marry Ronald Reagan and then mold him into the man she thought he could be. She has endured years of scathing attacks, all because of her loyalty to her husband.

Even now, in the midst of what doctors are calling "continual neurological degradation," Nancy protects the former president. No outsiders are allowed to see him, other than family. Right to the end, she is managing the legacy of Ronald Reagan, even as she struggles to imagine life without him.

"He's there," she once told an interviewer, explaining why she could not say good-bye to this man with whom she'd shared a wondrous lifelong journey. "He's there."

Two days later, on June 5, 2004, a sobbing Nancy finally acknowledges the reality.

Ronald Reagan is gone.

33

NATIONAL CATHEDRAL
WASHINGTON, DC
JUNE 11, 2004
NOON

The whole world is watching.

"We have lost a great president, a great American, and a great man, and I have lost a dear friend," says Margaret Thatcher, her face appearing on the big-screen monitors arrayed throughout the cathedral. "In his lifetime, Ronald Reagan was such a cheerful and invigorating presence that it was easy to forget what daunting historic tasks he set himself."

Nearly four thousand mourners fill this century-old Episcopal church, watching as Thatcher praises her dear friend on videotape. Among the crowd are the Reagan family, President George W. Bush, and former presidents Ford, Carter, Bush, and Clinton. Thatcher herself is in attendance, dressed all in black with an enormous hat, seated up front next to Mikhail Gorbachev. She is frail and hunched, her doctors having ordered her not to travel. Thatcher has ignored them out of respect for her longtime friend. However, fearing that she might embarrass herself by speaking live at the service, Baroness Thatcher videotaped her anticipated eulogy for Reagan months ago in London.

=== === ===

But not everyone is giving tribute. In Communist Cuba, the government greets Reagan's death with a proclamation attacking his conservative policies, stating, "He should never have been born."

And in America, the far left's opinion of Reagan's passing is summarized in *Slate* magazine: "He was as dumb as a stump," writes Christopher Hitchens. "I could not believe that such a man had even been a poor governor of California in a bad year, let alone that such a smart country would put up with such an obvious phony and loon."

=== === ===

Reagan's funeral is the largest in America since that of President John F. Kennedy more than forty years ago. Security is extremely tight, as this is the first major national event since the September 11, 2001, terrorist attacks on New York City and Washington, DC. But once Reagan's body rests inside the Capitol Rotunda and the doors are opened to the public on the evening of June 9, a wave of humanity arrives to pay their respects. Many have been waiting two days for this opportunity. All through the night and the next day, five thousand visitors per hour walk past the casket of Ronald Reagan.

On the morning of June 11, which President George W. Bush has declared a national day of mourning, the body of Ronald Reagan is delivered to the National Cathedral for the first state funeral since that of Lyndon Johnson in 1973.

With a global television audience looking on, and 3,700 mourners in the pews, Margaret Thatcher's taped eulogy concludes.

"Ronald Reagan's life was rich not only in public achievement, but also in private happiness. Indeed, his public achievements were rooted in his private happiness.

"The great turning point of his life was his meeting and marriage with

Nancy Reagan kisses her husband's coffin.

Nancy. On that, we have the plain testimony of a loving and grateful husband. 'Nancy came along and saved my soul.'"

Television cameras and all within view turn to Nancy. Despite the ten long years of Reagan's decline, and the ample time she has had to prepare for this moment, she is consumed by grief.

"We share her grief today," Thatcher continues. "For the final years of his life, Ronnie's mind was clouded by illness.

"That cloud has now lifted. He is himself again, more himself than at any time on this Earth, for we may be sure that the Big Fellow upstairs never forgets those who remember him. And as the last journey of this faithful pilgrim took him beyond the sunset, and as heaven's morning broke, I like to think, in the words of John Bunyan, that 'all the trumpets sounded on the other side.'"

A subtle smile creases Thatcher's lips on the screen as she ends her eulogy. As she does so, it is possible to see the slight facial paralysis from her recent series of strokes, and yet her voice is clear and deliberate.

"We here still move in twilight, but we have one beacon to guide us that Ronald Reagan never had.

"We have his example."

= = =

That evening, the body of Ronald Reagan is buried in California. Margaret Thatcher is there. So is Jane Wyman. Nancy Reagan kisses the coffin and whispers, "I love you," before stepping away for good. Nancy, clutching the American flag that once draped her husband's coffin, dissolves in tears. She looks pale, fragile, and frightened.

Four F-18 fighter jets thunder overhead while a military band plays "America the Beautiful." Symbolically, one of the jets suddenly peels away, leaving the other three to fly on in the "missing man" formation.

"I know in my heart that man is good," the inscription on Reagan's tombstone reads, "that what is right will always eventually triumph, and there is purpose and worth to each and every life."

Afterword

In January 2015, the *Journal of Alzheimer's Disease* published a study examining the press conferences of Ronald Reagan's presidency. Researchers were looking for changes in his vocabulary that might have signaled an early onset of dementia. They found three specific symptoms: Reagan's use of repetitive words increased, as did his habit of substituting "it" or "thing" for specific nouns. Meanwhile, use of unique words declined. The study's authors also noted that trauma and the use of anesthesia can hasten dementia. They specifically mentioned that the 1981 assassination attempt could also have played a pivotal role in Ronald Reagan's decline.

The man who shot Reagan, **John Hinckley Jr.**, remains at St. Elizabeth's Hospital in Washington, DC, to this day. More than thirty years after being found not guilty of attempting to assassinate the president by reason of insanity, Hinckley may not remain in custody much longer. In December 2013 a federal judge declared he was "not a danger" and authorized unsupervised visits of up to seventeen days at his mother's home in Williamsburg, Virginia. Hinckley is allowed to drive a car but not to talk to the media. The judge requires that he carry a GPS-enabled cell phone in order that they can track his movements. In time, he may become a completely free man, following in the footsteps of attempted presidential assassins Squeaky Fromme and Sara Jane Moore, who were released in 2009 and 2007, respectively. Both women served more than three decades in prison for attempting to kill President Gerald Ford.

In January 2015, prosecutors declined to press additional murder charges in the August 2014 death of Reagan press secretary **James Brady**—despite the fact that Hinckley's bullets were directly responsible for the wounds that ultimately killed Brady at age seventy-three. Brady never fully recovered from the ordeal, spending the second half of his life dealing with constant pain, slurred speech, paralysis, and short-term memory loss. As a result, his wife, Sarah, who sat with Nancy Reagan in the hospital chapel on the day of the assassination attempt, became a ferocious advocate for gun control. **Sarah Brady** died of pneumonia at the age of seventy-three in April 2015, less than a year after her husband passed away.

Tim McCarthy, the only man in Secret Service history to take a bullet for a president, currently serves as the chief of police in the Chicago suburb of Orland Park. "I'm glad I got to do it," he told the *Chicago Tribune* in 2011. "I'm glad to do what I was trained to do."

District of Columbia policeman **Thomas K. Delahanty**, Hinckley's final victim, sued the gun manufacturer whose bullet ended his police career. He also sued John Hinckley, though the courts ruled against him in both cases. Delahanty made cameo appearances in two movies about the assassination attempt but never returned to police work.

As of this writing in August 2015, **Nancy Reagan** still lives in the Bel-Air, California, home she once shared with Ronald Reagan. The former First Lady, who in the words of one reporter "rescued the Reagan presidency," laid a wreath on his tomb in 2011 to celebrate the hundredth anniversary of his birth. She has endured her own health problems, including a fractured pelvis in 2008 and broken ribs sustained in a fall four years later. Yet while often confined to a wheelchair and in declining health, Nancy Reagan continues to be an advocate for Alzheimer's research.

The Reagan children remain in the public eye. **Patti Davis** once again posed nude, this time for *More* magazine in 2011, at the age of fifty-eight, and continues to make a living as a freelance writer.

Ron Reagan Jr. lives in Seattle, where he currently works as an advocate for atheism and for stem cell research. In March 2014, he lost his wife of thirty-three years, Doria Palmieri Reagan, to a progressive neuromuscular disease. Ron Reagan continues to be a liberal advocate, often appearing on cable news programs.

Michael Reagan is a longtime conservative radio talk show host. He called his adoptive half brother, Ron, an "embarrassment" for suggesting in a book that their father suffered from Alzheimer's disease while serving as president. Michael Reagan's life has not been easy, as he has been involved in a variety of civil lawsuits.

The only child of Ronald Reagan to attempt a political career, **Maureen**, died of melanoma in 2001 at the age of sixty. She is buried at Calvary Catholic Cemetery in Sacramento.

Jodie Foster not only survived the media scrutiny that came with the Reagan assassination attempt but has thrived. After graduating from Yale in 1985, she went on to a distinguished Hollywood career as an actor, director, and producer. Foster has won two Academy Awards for Best Actress, the first in 1989 for her role in *The Accused* and the second in 1992 for her signature lead role in *The Silence of the Lambs*. John Hinckley was reportedly outraged when Jodie Foster came out as a lesbian in 2013.

Two thousand thirteen was also the year **Margaret Thatcher** died, at age eighty-seven. The former British prime minister was elevated to baroness in 1992 and made a member of the House of Lords after a lifetime as a commoner. Her memory began to fail her in 2000, but it was a series of small strokes in 2002 that led her to withdraw from public life. Her taping of Ronald Reagan's eulogy was the last public speech she ever gave. The ashes of Margaret Hilda Thatcher are interred on the grounds of the Royal Hospital Chelsea in London, next to those of her husband, Denis, who died in 2003.

James Baker III, Ronald Reagan's chief of staff during his first term in office, is still active as a political adviser at the age of eighty-five, as is his fellow member of the Reagan troika, **Edwin Meese**. At age eighty-three, Meese lives in Virginia, where he serves on a number of educational boards and public policy think tanks.

Reagan's third adviser, **Michael Deaver**, fell prey to pancreatic cancer on August 18, 2007. Deaver left the Reagan White House after the first term, opening a successful Washington lobbying agency. On March 18, 1987, he was convicted of five counts of perjury during an investigation into his use of insider influence and power with his new firm. His crime was perjuring himself to Congress and a federal grand jury. For that, Deaver was sentenced to three years' probation and fined one hundred thousand dollars. Despite Deaver's request, Ronald Reagan did not extend the offer of a pardon before leaving office. Nancy Reagan did not attend Deaver's funeral, but she issued a statement saying that Deaver was "like a son." Michael Deaver was sixty-nine years old when he passed away.

Nancy's feelings were obviously not as warm toward **Don Regan**. After the White House chief was fired because of her, Regan turned to landscape painting as a way to pass his days. He was content in his artistic endeavors, often spending as much as ten hours a day painting. Don Regan died of cancer on June 10, 2003. He is buried in Arlington National Cemetery.

Ronald Reagan's first wife, **Jane Wyman**, lived to be ninety years old. After divorcing Reagan, Wyman went on to have one more husband, bandleader Fred Karger, whom she married and divorced twice. By the time of her death in 2007, she had become such a devout Catholic that she was laid to rest in the habit of the Dominican Sisters religious order. Jane Wyman is buried in Forest Lawn Cemetery in Los Angeles, California.

Ronald Reagan's mother, **Nelle Reagan**, died on July 25, 1962. She was seventy-nine years old. Her husband, the hard-drinking Jack Reagan, died in 1941 at age fifty-seven. Both are buried at the Calvary Cemetery in East Los Angeles. Ronald Reagan's lone sibling, his older brother Neil, died in 1996 of heart failure. His body was cremated.

Ronald Reagan's beloved **Rancho del Cielo** was sold in 1998. But the property has not been developed or subdivided, nor has the white adobe ranch house been torn down. Rather, the property remains exactly as it was during the time Ronald and Nancy Reagan owned it. A conservative group known as the Young America's Foundation purchased the land from Nancy Reagan, who lowered her asking price significantly to make the sale possible. A museum in Santa Barbara, California, recounts the history of the ranch, while also displaying a number of items of Reagan memorabilia. There are a limited number of tours of the property, allowing visitors to comprehend firsthand exactly why Ronald Reagan knew such contentment at this mountaintop retreat.

To this day, there are those who contend that the ghost of Ronald Reagan is present on the property.

Last Word

In researching and writing this book, Martin Dugard and I were extremely careful to use only material we could confirm through at least two sources, and even then we tried to be very fair in presenting facts that might put certain individuals in a bad light.

In the last year of his presidency, Ronald Reagan was aware that some close to him were questioning the way he was running his administration. Critical books by daughter Patti, Donald Regan, former spokesman Larry Speakes, and others apparently wounded Reagan, who valued loyalty. The president, however, kept his own counsel, rarely saying anything in public.

On May 16, 1988, he finally let loose in a private letter to his friend and adviser John Koehler. That letter is now owned by me and so it is fitting to publish it in this book, thereby giving Ronald Wilson Reagan the last word.

He deserves it.

BILL O'REILLY
Long Island
New York

May 16, 1988

Dear John:

Thank you very much for your May 10 letter.
You were more than kind, and Nancy and I
thank you from the bottom of our hearts.
You know, John, one of the hardest things to
bear in all of this are the outright falsehoods.
Nancy never opened her mouth about Casey,
Donovan or Heckler, and she certainly didn't
fire Don. Truth is, he'd told me several months
earlier he wanted to get back to private life,
and I left it to him to name the day. And,
of course, we haven't been charting our course
by the stars.

Nancy sends her thanks, and from both of us to
Dorothy; and again we deeply appreciate your
words and your prayers.

Sincerely,

Ronald Reagan

Mr. John O. Koehler
One Strawberry Hill Avenue
Stamford, Connecticut 06902

Sources

Ronald Reagan lived his entire adult life in the public eye. This media scrutiny could be burdensome to him at times, but it worked very well for our purposes, greatly assisting our research process. One particular advantage is the enormous supply of video documenting his acting and political careers. The reader is encouraged to look at the many press conferences, inaugurations, speeches, presidential debates, and myriad other public appearances, and even *Saturday Night Live* sketches, available online.

And while this book is about Ronald Reagan, the powerful historical moments that defined the careers of Richard Nixon, Gerald Ford, Jimmy Carter, Alexander Haig, Margaret Thatcher, and so many other towering figures are also available for all to see. Video does not go as deep as letters and diaries, but it does allow the researcher to see the anguish or joy on an individual's face (Margaret Thatcher's eulogy of Reagan is heartbreaking in this regard), to hear the rhythm of spoken words, and to know the context in which those words were delivered. Reagan's "Tear Down This

Wall" speech is all the more powerful when watching him deliver those words.

As with the other books in the *Killing* series, we consulted a wide variety of sources to tell Ronald Reagan's story in vivid detail. In addition to video, sources included books, magazine articles, archives, newspapers, FBI and CIA files, online databases, presidential libraries, and transcripts of interviews with people who worked with him in a personal and professional capacity. The Zillow website, for instance, allowed us a tour of the Reagan home in Pacific Palisades, which was recently on the market. It was also very helpful that the Margaret Thatcher Foundation (margaretthatcher .org) and the Ronald Reagan Presidential Library (reaganlibrary.gov and reaganfoundation.org) have catalogued not only the letters of these great leaders but also the transcripts and even audiotapes of their discussions, allowing us to listen in.

The Miller Center at the University of Virginia (millercenter.org) is a treasure trove of information about all things presidential. Reagan's diary entries and daily White House schedule can be found online at reaganfoundation.org. On a different note, the White House Museum (whitehousemuseum.org) takes readers throughout the entire building, with behind-the-scenes photos of the West Wing and the residence through the years.

Travel, as always, was vital to adding great descriptive detail, sending us to locations in the United States and around the world that were pivotal to Reagan's personal and political life. Most pivotal was the day spent at Rancho del Cielo, just north of Santa Barbara. Thanks to Andrew Coffin of the Young America's Foundation for the lengthy and engaging private tour.

What follows is a brief list of the many books, magazines, and newspapers that we used in the writing of this book. Much thanks to the world of Google Books, which allows writers to research a library's worth of great reference works without leaving the home office. These meanderings drew in a number of other historical figures and unchronicled events. Hundreds of books, magazine articles, and newspaper stories were bookmarked and cross-referenced as we wrote. We have chosen to list the ones most crucial to this research. The books include: All the works of Kiron K. Skinner, Annelise Andersen, and Martin Anderson, particularly *Reagan: A Life in Letters* and *Reagan, In His Own Hand: The Writings of Ronald Reagan that Reveal His Revolutionary Vision for America*; Edmund Morris, *Dutch: A Memoir of Ronald Reagan*; Kitty Kelley, *Nancy Reagan: The Unauthorized Biography*; Jane Mayer and Doyle McManus, *Landslide: The Unmaking of the President, 1984–1988*; Nancy Reagan, *My Turn: The Memoirs of Nancy Reagan*; John R. Barletta, *Riding with Reagan: From the White House to the Ranch*; Del Quentin Wilber, *Rawhide Down: The Near Assassination of Ronald Reagan*; James W. Clarke, *Defining Danger: American Assassins and the New Domestic Terrorists*; Peter Schweizer, *Reagan's War: The Epic Story of His Forty-Year Struggle and Final Triumph over Communism*; Stephen Vaughn, *Ronald Reagan in Hollywood: Movies and Politics*; Jimmy Carter, *White House Diary*; Lou Cannon, *President Reagan: The Role of a Lifetime*; Michelangelo Capua, *William Holden: A Biography*; Marc Eliot, *Reagan: The Hollywood Years*; David Gergen, *Eyewitness to Power: The Essence of Leadership*; Jonathan Aitken, *Margaret Thatcher: Power and Personality*; Patti Davis, *The Long Goodbye: Memories of My Father*; and the very emotional *Breaking Points*, by Jack and Jo Ann Hinckley.

We also consulted a broad number of magazines and newspapers marking the passage of Reagan's life and career through the many stories published in their pages. Listing each of the hundreds of articles would have been unwieldy; instead we've given the publications upon which we relied most: the *Los Angeles Times*, the *New York Times*, *Vanity Fair*, *Time*, the *National Review*, the *Washington Post*, the *Daily Mail* (London), the *Daily Telegraph* (London), the *Philadelphia Inquirer*, the *Boston Globe*, the *Atlantic*, *Billboard*, *Variety*, *Forbes*, and the *Pittsburgh Press*.

The authors would also like to thank Roger Ailes, Pat Caddell, Lou Cannon, and Lesley Stahl for their personal insights. In addition, Dr. Jimmy Byron at the Richard Nixon Foundation was particularly helpful.

Acknowledgments

The usual suspects helped me get it all down on paper: my assistant for more than twenty years Makeda Wubneh, literary agent to the stars Eric Simonoff, perspicacious publisher Steve Rubin, wise editor Gillian Blake, and my TV boss Roger Ailes. Thank you, guys!

—BILL O'REILLY

Thanks to Eric Simonoff, the world's greatest agent and the man who made the O'Reilly/Dugard team a reality. To the calm and very organized Makeda Wubneh. To Steve Rubin and Gillian Blake at Holt, for their wit, insight, and quick reads. To Al and Rosemary Dugard. To my boys: Devin, Connor, and Liam. And as always to Calene, who makes me a better man.

—MARTIN DUGARD

Illustration Credits

———oOo———

Index

Page numbers in *italics* refer to illustrations.

About the Authors

BILL O'REILLY is the anchor of *The O'Reilly Factor*, the highest-rated cable news show in the country. He is the author of many number-one bestselling books, including *Killing Lincoln, Killing Kennedy, Killing Jesus,* and *Killing Patton.*

MARTIN DUGARD is the *New York Times* bestselling author of several books of history. He and his wife live in Southern California with their three sons.